ArtScroll® Series

Rabbi Nosson Scherman / Rabbi Meir Zlotowitz

General Editors

Published by
Mesorah Publications, ltd

CHINUCH
IN TURBULENT TIMES

PRACTICAL STRATEGIES
FOR PARENTS AND EDUCATORS

RABBI DOV BREZAK

FIRST EDITION
First Impression ... September 2002
Second Impression ... July 2003
Third Impression ... November 2005
Fourth Impression ... June 2007
Fifth Impression ... February 2008
Sixth Impression ... July 2009
Seventh Impression ... March 2014
Eighth Impression ... November 2019

Published and Distributed by
MESORAH PUBLICATIONS, LTD.
4401 Second Avenue / Brooklyn, N.Y 11232

Distributed in Europe by
LEHMANNS
Unit E, Viking Business Park
Rolling Mill Road
Jarow, Tyne & Wear, NE32 3DP
England

Distributed in Australia and New Zealand
by **GOLDS WORLDS OF JUDAICA**
3-13 William Street
Balaclava, Melbourne 3183
Victoria, Australia

Distributed in Israel by
SIFRIATI / A. GITLER — BOOKS
POB 2351
Bnei Brak 51122

Distributed in South Africa by
KOLLEL BOOKSHOP
Northfield Centre, 17 Northfield Avenue
Glenhazel 2192, Johannesburg, South Africa

ARTSCROLL® SERIES
CHINUCH IN TURBULENT TIMES
© *Copyright 2002, by* MESORAH PUBLICATIONS, Ltd.
4401 Second Avenue / Brooklyn, N.Y. 11232 / (718) 921-9000 / www.artscroll.com

ISBN 10: 1-57819-755-4 / ISBN 13: 978-1-57819-755-2 (hard cover)

Typography by CompuScribe at ArtScroll Studios, Ltd.

Printed in the United States of America
Bound by Sefercraft, Quality Bookbinders, Ltd., Brooklyn N.Y. 11232

סֵפֶר זֶה מוּקְדָּשׁ

לזכרון עולם ולעילוי נשמת
מורי חמי
איש ירא ד' נהנה מיגיע כפיו
אדם ישר וענין
נעים לבריות אהב את התורה בכל לבו

ר' אברהם יהודה בן ר' מרדכי גרינפעלד ע"ה

הלך לעולמו י' מרחשון תש"נ

ת.נ.צ.ב.ה.

יהי זכרו ברוך

ישיבת גבעת שאול

ירושלים תובב״א

רח׳ אהלי יוסף 17 ת.ד. 34280, ירושלים, טל׳ 02-5001943. פקס. 5001954

הרב ר׳ דוב בריזק שליט״א כתב ספר נפלא על החינוך בדורנו. הספר מקיף כל הבעיות השייכות עם חינוך הילדים ומבאר בכל הבעיות המתעוררות מהו הדרך האמיתית המביאה את הילדים לבריאות נפשית בהתפתחותם. מהלכים נפלאים בטיפול עם כל המצבים של ילדים מתגלים בספר זה, ובלי שום ספק יראו כל ההורים וגם המורים תועלת אם יתנהגו דווקא בהצעות שהספר הזה מציע. מאושרים יהיו ההורים הלומדים ספר זה ומתנהגים כפי הדרכתה.

הכרת הטוב מגיע לכבוד המחבר הרב בריזק שליט״א. ספרו הוא ספר הצלה בדורנו שבו צריך להתנהג בדרך מיוחדת בחינוך, ודרך זאת מבוארת בסייעתא דשמיא בספר הזה.

תודה חמה מגיעה להמחבר שליט״א, ויברכו השי״ת בברכה גדולה.

ברוב הוקרה להמחבר שליט״א

י״ב תשרי תשס״ג

בס״ד

שמואל קמנצקי
Rabbi S. Kamenetsky

2018 Upland Way
Philadelphia, Pa 19131

Home: 215-473-2798
Study: 215-473-1212

Rabbi Shmuel Auerbach
Jerusalem

שמואל אוירבאך
פעיה"ק ירושלים תובב"א

ערב חג סוכות תשס"ג

הנני בזה להכיר ולהוקיר את יקרת ערכו הרם של האי גברא יקירה איש אשר רוח בו המחנך הגדול הרב ר' דוב בריזק שליט"א.

ומכיר אני אותו משכבר הימים, וביחוד נוכחתי וראיתי אשר הרבה ברכה בו בשטח החינוך, כי הוא יורד לנפש התלמידים ומתמצה וחודר לנבכי הבעיות, ויש בו גם כושר וגישה מיוחדת בזה, וגם צבר בזה הרבה נסיון, ולמעשה הוא תל"ה מומחה מיוחד, והרבה מצליח בזה, כאשר ראיתי ונוכחתי בעיני. ואשר על כן בודאי יהיה הרבה תועלת, במה שימסור וינהוג עין יפה לציבור, וילמדו ממנו עתה הרבה תושיה ודעת להציל ולחנך ילדי ישראל, להוציא אותם מקטנותם ולהביא כל אחד לכוחות הנפש הצפונים בו, ויתן ד' ויקוים בנו בקרוב ממש ומלאה הארץ דעה את ד' כמים לים מכסים.

הכותב וחותם לכבוד ולמען החינוך הטהור אשר זה יסוד קיומנו ולכבוד של מע"כ המחנך הדגול הנ"ל שליט"א.

RABBI YAAKOV HILLEL
ROSH YESHIVAT HEVRAT AHAVAT SHALOM
45/33 ARZEI HABIRA JERUSALEM
ISRAEL

יעקב משה הלל
ראש ישיבת ״חברת אהבת שלום״
ארזי הבירה 45/33
פעיה״ק ירושלים תובב״א

בס״ד, ערב סוכות התשס״ח

דברי המלצה וברכה

בא לפני ידידי היקר **כהר״ר דוב בריזק שליט״א**, והראני קובץ מאמרים שכתב בענייני חינוך, ופרסמם כמאמרים בודדים, ועתה הוא חפץ להעלותם על מזבח הדפוס כספר כלול בהודו והדרו, ובקש ממני הסכמה.

ואכן רואה אני את כוונתו ואת מעשיו רצויים מאד, כי הרי נושא החינוך הוא סוגייא עמוקה וקשה שנוגעת לכל הורה מישראל. והגם שהעולם חושבים שעניינה לחנך את הילדים, האמת ניתן להאמר שתחילה צריכים לחנך את ההורים כדי שידעו איך לחנך את הילדים. ולמעשה לא מעט ואולי רוב הפעולות שעושים והדיבורים שאומרים הורים בכוונה טובה לחנך, בעצם הם מקלקלים והורסים, יותר ממה שהם מתקנים ומטיבים ויותר ממה שיצליחו לחנך על ידי תוכחות ומוסרים, יעלה בידם בהצלחה על ידי שמשתמשים כדוגמא אישית. וראיתי לפרש מ״ש: ״ושננתם לבניך ודברת בם,״ דאם רוצים שהבנים ילמדו בהתמדה, ולקיים ״ושננתם לבניך,״ הדרך להצליך הוא על ידי ״ודברת בם,״ שהאב בעצמו ילמד תמיד בזמנו הפנוי, ובכך ילמד ממנו בנו על חשיבת הלימוד. וכן הוא בענין המידות הטובות, ושאר הנהגות ישרות. ולעולם יסוד החינוך הוא בחיוב ולא בשלילה, היינו בעידוד ובאהבה חום ורגש, ולא בכעס וקפידות ותרעומות.

באופן שהסוגייא היא עמוקה מאד, וצריכים ההורים להבין לנפש הילד, ולמצביו ונסיונותיו וכו׳. והרי שהמשך הצלחת דורותיו תלויים בדבר. ולכן בואו ונחזיק טובה להאי גברא ויקיירא, שהוא ידוע ירא וחרד לדבר ה׳, ומפורסם ומוחזק כמחנך דגול עם נסיון רב, וזכה לשמש לשמש גדולי ישראל בנושאים אלו, ופעל ועשה להלכה ולמעשה בנושאים אלו. וכן עיין וחקר והעמיק ודרש כתרי אותיות של הסוגייא הזאת, וכתב מאמרים בה, ופרסמם, והיו לעיני רבים, ומצאו חן בעיני חכמים ומומחים, וכבר אישרהו וקיימוהו רבנן, וכפי שראיתי בהמלצות שכתבו לו גדולי הדור שהם נודעים כמרביצי תורה ומוסר ומחנכי תלמידים לאלפים ולרבבות וברכו על חבורו ברכת הנהנין.

ולכן הסכמתי לבוא במכתב המלצה זו והגם שלא היה לי הפנאי כאת לעיין בדבריו, וחזקה על חבר שלא יוציא תקלה מתחת ידו. ואולם אני מכירו מכבר, כבעל מדות טובות ושכל ישר וצנוע ומעלי, ובנושאים אלו אתמחי גברא.

ולכן אברכו שיזכה להפיץ מעיינותיו חוצה, ורבים ילכו לאור ספרו, ויהנו מעצמותיו והדרכותיו, ותרבה הדעת, ותרבה בהתעסקות רבים בסוגייא נפלאה ונחוצה זו, ובכך יזכו לדורות ישרים ומבורכים ממשיכי מסורת התורה מדור דור עד לביאת גואל צדק במהרה דידן אכי״ר.

החותם ומצרף ברכה העולה ומצרף לברכת התורה ומביאה לקיים

יעקב משה
הלל

פה

Table of Contents

A Note to the Reader

The methods in this book are recommended by *gedolei Yisrael* and are tried and proven. Nevertheless, one should take note of the following points.

(1) This book is about our responsibility as parents and educators. It discusses certain techniques and methods best suited to fulfill this responsibility. Ultimately it is only the Master of the World Who will decide our destiny. Only He will determine the success of our efforts. Still, this does not absolve us from our responsibility to use those methods proven to be the most helpful and successful for our generation.

(2) *Chinuch* is a natural process of growth. Any methods or techniques mentioned here must be used with patience and perseverance. Just as one who plants a seed cannot rush its growth by applying more heat or using more water, neither can one expect these techniques to work overnight. They must be applied consistently with patience and perseverance, and for a lengthy span of time.

(3) Certain methods mentioned here may be utilized and nevertheless there will be no noticeable improvement. Be aware that the techniques may not have been properly applied, although the parent/educator may think that they have been. How many times have I heard parents say how much love and understanding they show their children, only to hear the children say that the parents do not love them or understand them at all. In cases such as

these, involving a spouse or third party can provide an accurate and unbiased assessment of the situation.

(4) It is not perfection that we seek; it is improvement. Every bit of improvement is success. If you see improvement you have achieved success. Continue and you will see more improvement with the help of Hashem.

Since this book was first published,

I was plunged into mourning by the loss of my mother,

רחל בת מנחם מנדל ברוך ע"ה

My mother gave all her heart to help others,
but above all, she was dedicated to her family.

The way my mother treated me
is what has given me any abilty I may have to help others.

She taught me unconditional love and acceptance.

She taught me devotion and understanding.

She gave me a love for life, people and the Ribbono Shel Olam.

I learned not by what she preached,
but by how she treated me.

A copy of Chinuch in Turbulent Times was placed in her grave.

It was her merit and her chinuch.

It was her book.

תנצב"ה

Acknowledgments

When expressing thanks, one bears the risk of sounding redundant. Nevertheless, this is only true with regard to the reader. As for the recipient of the kindnesses, each expression of gratitude points to a different and unique benefit received. In this case the more the thanks, the more onerous is the debt of gratitude incumbent upon the beneficiary. The humbling awareness of my inability to repay is all that I have to offer in return.

This book had its beginnings almost three years ago in the form of articles appearing in *Yated Ne'eman*. That very first phone conversation with Rabbi Pinchos Lipschutz remains etched in my mind. The belief he demonstrated was instrumental in starting me along a path that has resulted in guidance and encouragement for parents and teachers worldwide.

My thanks to you Rabbi Lipschutz, for giving me a chance. May you have continued success and true *nachas* from those dear to you, always.

I wish to express gratitude to Moshe Shapiro of Jerusalemcom for his suggestion to write articles on *chinuch*.

My appreciation to Mrs. Sara Chava Mizrahi for her editing cannot be adequately expressed in the small space allotted here. Her style and expertise greatly enhanced these articles and helped their success. Still, it is for her unwavering dedication that I wish to express special appreciation. For all those instances when things did not work out as planned, for the many difficult hours, for the copious technical complications, and for doing it all *b'sever panim yafos*. May you have continued success, as editor of the *Hamodia*, and may you and your husband have true *nachas* from your children, always

I wish to equally express my gratitude to Mrs. Aviva Rappaport. Alongside her keen understanding and editing expertise is a unique ability to preserve the author's original style. Her editing has given the articles a new dimension and has enhanced their quality as well. I have found her keen understanding and sensitivity to be of great benefit. Thank you for everything. May you and your husband have continued success and *nachas*, always.

A special thanks to Rabbi Meir Zlotowitz and Rabbi Nosson Scherman, for the privilege of joining that enormous mechanism of *Kiddush Hashem* referred to as ArtScroll.

Transforming these articles into book form was no easy task. My thanks to Rabbi Avrohom Biderman and the entire ArtScroll staff for helping me see this goal to fruition. A special thanks to Mrs. Judi Dick for expert editing, together with the many hours of discussion and review, and wise suggestions. And special thanks to Mrs. Mindy Stern whose meticulous proofreading enhanced the final product. I would also like to thank Hershy Feuerwerker for his cover design; Mrs. Leah Weiner, Tzini Hanover and Menucha Mitnick, who paginated the book; and Libby Zweig, who entered the editorial corrections.

I find in this book an opportunity for expressing thanks to those who have accompanied me along the way. Entire volumes would not suffice to express the gratitude owed the many that I have benefited from throughout the years. Still I wish to single out a few of those special individuals.

I thank my many teachers, rebbeim, and the many wonderful friends and neighbors I have been privileged to know. Special thanks to R' Noach Orlowek for the hours he invested in me when I first became a teacher. A note of thanks to R' Yochanan Lombard for everything.

A special thanks to the staff of Talmud Torah Ezrat Torah, Jerusalem, including my dear friends R' Menachem Orenstein and R' Ben Zion Litenazky.

I express thanks to my extended family, for their constant support and encouragement throughout the years. My brothers- and sisters-in-law, Rabbi Mordechai and Esther Greenfield, Moshe and Reana Greenfield, Dovid and Yahudis Hershkowitz, Hillel and Shany Moerman.

Special mention goes to my venerated brother-in-law, R' Yehuda Cahan, rav of Congregation Zera Avrohom in Denver, Colorado, and to my sister, Rebbitzen Faygie Cahan. Thank you for everything.

Special thanks to my esteemed mother-in-law, Mrs. Esther Greenfield, for being the special person that she is. May she enjoy many more years of *nachas* and may she merit to see the coming of Mashiach, speedily and in our days.

Of my parents, Dr. Joseph and Mrs. Rikki Brezak, I can only say that they are two of the most unselfish people on earth. It is through their love and total dedication that I came to understand what *chinuch* truly is. My only regret is that they left me with too difficult an act to follow. I don't even begin to thank you as it is totally beyond me. I can only pray that Hashem grant you both long life to see true *nachas* and the rebuilding of the *Beis HaMikdash,* speedily and in our days.

I wish to express thanks to my children: Shaya, Menachem, Tova, Sara, Yanky, Nossy, Elisheva and Miri. I thank Hashem for giving me such wonderful children. I am very proud of each and every one of them. Their devotion and loyalty is a constant source of *nachas* for me.

I wish to thank my *eishes chayil,* Lieba. Her devotion and loyalty to me are unsurpassed. In all honesty it is only through her *mesiras nefesh* that I have achieved anything.

To quote R' Akiva, "*Sheli veshelachem shelah* — Mine and yours, it all belongs to her."

I write these acknowledgments the day after Yom Kippur.

At such a time when we are purer of the spirit, our clarity and perception of Hashem's lovingkindness becomes sharpened. It is at this point in time and on this occasion of the publishing of this book that I humbly ask:

How can I repay You, Hashem, for all Your kindness to me?

Aharon Dov Brezak

11 Tishrei, 5763
Yerushalayim

Introduction: Chinuch

"If You Don't Know Where You Are Going, How Will You Know When You Get There?"

Modern day Hebrew contains many rather interesting words. Take the word *ksilophone;* the English translation for this word is xylophone. How about the word *tempayroment.* The English translation for this word is temperament. Let us not overlook other words such as *leftenent komander,* which is Hebrew for lieutenant commander, or *moksimum* which is the Hebrew version of maximum. These words are obviously simple to translate. There are still other words, which although they do not have their roots in English are readily understandable, such as *kadur* (ball), *yeled* (boy), and *tabaas* (ring).

With regard to the word *chinuch* something is lost in the translation. The Hebrew dictionary translates *chinuch* to mean education or upbringing. The Oxford American Dictionary defines *upbringing* as "training and education during childhood." The definition of *education* is "systematic training and instruction designed to impart knowledge and develop skill."

Is *chinuch* only a way to teach knowledge and to develop skill? There is so much more to *chinuch* than that. In Deuteronomy, we find that a person who has just purchased a new house and has not yet done *chinuch* on it is commanded to leave the battlefront. How does one educate a house?

Chanukah finds its roots in the word *chinuch*. Was any particular skill taught during the Chanukah miracle?

Is *chinuch* only training or instruction? Isn't showing love to one's children and forging a close bond with them also *chinuch*? Does not encouraging a student and building him up involve *chinuch*?

Rashi, in his commentary on verse 14:14 in Genesis, explains *chinuch* as the beginning of the entry of a person or implement into the craft or task in which he/it is destined to stay, i.e. along the particular path that it will continue on.

Chovas HaTalmidim, in the introduction to his classic work, expounds on this definition of Rashi. He explains *chinuch* to mean developing the potential contained in a being or object and bringing it to fruition.

In the case of an object it means using the object in a way that will bring out the particular feature or service which the object was designed to provide. In the case of people it means to begin to develop in them those potential talents or abilities which lie dormant within them.

Hence, living in a new house can be called *chinuch,* and the rededication of the Temple can be called Chanukah.

With regard to a Jewish child, *chinuch* means for the parents, teachers, or anyone else concerned, to involve themselves in those behaviors and actions that will bring out the endless talents and abilities contained in the G-dly spirit lying dormant within the child, eventually causing his soul to flame with a love for G-d and His Holy Torah.

That is the purpose of this book: to be of assistance to those interested in the successful *chinuch* of their children, a task which may be especially challenging in these turbulent times.

With sincere wishes for your success and with a brief prayer that you see true *nachas* from your children/students, always.

1

Criticism— Is It Constructive?

Failure Warrants No Effort

Forgive me for beginning our discussion with a rather offensive question, but it is one which I consider to be most instructive:

If someone wishes to excel in developing negative character traits — what should he do? What path should he follow in order to become superb at conceit, or fabulous at becoming angry?

The answer is, *"Absolutely nothing!"* He should do nothing at all.

The Chazon Ish (*Emunah U'Bitachon*, Ch. 4) explains that where positive effort is not expended, "nature" takes its course. Without any effort whatsoever, a person will be pulled down by the spiritual "force of gravity." It is guaranteed that he will excel in developing negative character traits unless he *does something!*

After twenty years of active involvement in *chinuch*, as parent, teacher and principal, I still dare not consider myself an expert on this very sensitive topic. Yet I choose to share my insights for, as the holy Rabbeinu Bachya wrote, "If all who wished to accomplish something great would hold back from even that which they are capable of doing, for lack of ability [to achieve their goal in its entirety], then no one would benefit, and the paths of good would remain desolate" (*Chovos HaLevavos*, Introduction).

Thus, I approach this endeavor not as a master offering infallible instruction, but rather as a friend in conversation with his fellow, so that together we may strengthen one another in a matter of vital importance to all of us — the successful *chinuch* of our children. I pray that the thoughts expressed here will serve as a vehicle that will enable you to draw upon *your own* wellsprings of talent and will bring forth the Divine assistance necessary to make your efforts successful.

Our Sages have taught us that Hashem tests only those who have the potential to succeed. If today we are faced with unusually difficult trials in educating our children in the proper path, it follows that Hashem has already given us the strengths and the ingenuity we require to succeed in this challenge. We are all blessed with the two crucial ingredients of success: ability and help from Above. Let us never underestimate the power of either of these magnificent resources.

It Is No Longer Just a Matter of Character Traits

In our turbulent times, far more than "just" good character is at stake. R' Yaakov Kanievsky, (better known as the Steipler Gaon) wrote (*Chayei Olam*, Vol. I, Ch. 31) that nowadays, "when atheists and apostates among us hold their heads high and act like non-Jews, when children are exposed to a barrage of evils at every turn, anyone who does not give his children a proper Torah education is *almost certain* to see them drawn away entirely from the Holy Torah."

In previous generations, said the Steipler, the "street" — the sheltered Jewish society in which the child was reared — took care of 50 percent of a child's *chinuch*. Today, a child lacking adequate parental guidance will be drawn far beyond negative character traits, to an attitude that is altogether anti-Torah.

We might claim, "These concerns do not apply to me, because I *do* invest a great deal to give my children a proper religious education." A valid claim, but only partially correct. The fact is, we are witness to literally thousands of yeshivah-educated children (boys *and* girls) who have left the path of the Torah. (This conservative estimate is by no means exaggerated; it has been verified by a number of experts in the field.) Those who wish to enable their children to find the strength to resist the ubiquitous pull *away* from Torah that pervades our society must redouble their efforts. We can no longer rely on the fact that we have registered our children in the finest religious schools available. School alone cannot ensure a child's spiritual success.

Thus, the first principle of *chinuch* is *effort*. The parents must be willing to *do something*; *chinuch* does not happen by itself. Without hard work on the parents' part, nothing can guarantee the direction a child will take. (As with any rule, there are exceptions, but no one wants to place his faith in the remote possibility that his child will be the exception.)

Our great rabbis understood this principle and incorporated it in their lives, giving freely of themselves for their children's *chinuch*. The Brisker Rav stated that in the time he devoted to the *chinuch* of his children, he could have learned through the entire Babylonian Talmud another five times. The Chasam Sofer (whose descendants became foremost scholars) would sit for hours on end after the Passover Seder was over, relating inspirational stories to his daughters. When he was asked the secret of his consistent success in guiding his children along the proper path, he removed his large hat and turned it upside-down, saying, "I filled this hat with the tears of my prayers for my children's success!" Praying is one type of effort in which every one of us can quickly become expert, for it is a prime facet of our very identity as Jews.

A large investment of time and effort is required of every parent, but the returns are great indeed, for an abundance of Divine assistance accompanies our efforts.

In this book we will present practical suggestions, many of them quite simple, which, experience has shown, can create a complete turnabout in children's attitudes and behaviors. Nowadays more than ever before, parents' calculated involvement in their children's emotional and spiritual development is absolutely necessary.

Criticism — It Just Won't Work

Many people have come to believe that criticism is *chinuch*; this is a widespread misconception. At best, criticism — administered carefully and only on rare occasions — has its place, but it bears no relation to *chinuch*.

Chinuch can be defined as placing your children on the correct path, so that eventually they will choose to follow it of their *own free will*. R' Shlomo Wolbe, one of the foremost educators of our generation, describes the process of child-rearing as "holding a match to a candle, until the candle's flame burns on its own." Thus, our goal is to bring our children to the point at which *they themselves want* to do all that we know is right.

Having clarified our goal, we can examine which approach will be more effective to help us reach that goal. It is universally acknowledged that the more confidence someone has in his own abilities and potential, the more he will accomplish. (Note that confidence is not arrogance. Someone who is *arrogant* thinks that he is more deserving of advantages, admiration and accolades than others are, while someone who is *confident*, in the Torah sense, realizes that Hashem has given him abilities, and he is ready to use them in the way that Hashem desires of him. This type of confidence leads one not to conceit, but to humility, to responsibility, and to feeling good about oneself.)

Encouragement — the Surest Way

The surest way to cultivate confidence within our children is to encourage them. One father wanted his young son to excel at the sport of bowling. After the pins at the end of the bowling lane had been set up automatically, this father placed several additional pins in the gutters, so that the child's ball could not miss hitting bowling pins, and the father could point out to him his "success." This father "taught" his son that he could succeed. When the child grew up, he bowled professionally. Following one extraordinarily successful tour, an interviewer asked him to reveal the key to his outstanding success. "I had a very unusual father" was his enthusiastic response.

We can see from this real-life example what powerful effects encouragement can have. Encouragement focuses on abilities; criticism, on the other hand, points to faults. When we concentrate on a child's faults, invariably we *lower* his self-confidence. In fact, criticism that is administered often and with a concerted effort can effectively destroy a child's self-confidence altogether.

Criticism Does Not Motivate

There are parents who do not know how to end the self-perpetuating cycle of criticism they have created. "How will he learn if I don't teach him?" they may ask. "How can he fix things if I don't show him he's wrong?" However, a far more pointed question is, "How can a child fix anything if he's always being knocked down?"

A person — whether child or adult — will fix only that which he is *motivated* to fix. Knocking a child down through constant criticism will never motivate him to do better; on the contrary, it will turn him into a "shattered vessel," lacking the emotional tools necessary to accomplish much in life, because all along he has been absorbing the message that he is incapable of accomplishing much.

The importance of this point cannot be underestimated. A child's intellect is not developed to the point that he can recognize his own strengths and talents. He is totally dependent on the adults around him to develop for him his picture of himself. If we constantly criticize and point out a child's faults and the things he does wrong, in effect we are painting for him a picture of incompetence, and that is the way he will perceive himself, *even when he grows up.* As an adult, it will take much effort on his part to change this image of himself, and all his efforts may not even lead to success.

We Are Unaware of How Often We Criticize

Many people are unaware of how often they criticize their children. A very telling cartoon, recently published, depicts a parent describing his theories on how he encourages his son, as opposed to what he actually says to his child:

> *Since Johnny was young, the father says, we've always ...*
> - *been honest with him {"You're a hopeless clod!"}*
> - *encouraged him {"Get off your seat and do some work already!"}*

- *helped him set goals {"If you fail that exam I'll break your neck!"}*
- *given him responsibility {"I blame you ..."} and of course,*
- *given him direction! {"Why can't you be more like your older brother?!"}*

One renowned Torah educator of our times requested of one set of parents that they tape all that is said in their home for several days, and then, listening to the tapes, count how many times they criticized their children in one day. The results of this simple experiment shocked the parents. They never dreamed to what extent they had been bombarding their children with criticism.

Criticism and Praying

Our children's actions often frustrate us, and we are quickly "fed up" with their behavior. This is perfectly natural. However, showing our children this frustration accomplishes nothing in the way of curtailing their undesirable behaviors. One of our contemporary great rabbis related that he observed a father and son sitting together in the synagogue. Every few minutes, the father turned to his son and made some harsh sound — "Nu?!" "Um!!" Apparently, his son was not concentrating enough for him. When the prayers were over, this rabbi approached the father for a private word with him.

"If you continue in this way," the rabbi told the father, "one of two things will result: Either your son will stop being religious, or he will stop being normal!"

"So what should I do when he daydreams in synagogue instead of praying?" asked the father.

"Leave him alone."

Imperfection in a child's behavior does not always call for parental response. In the area of praying in particular, criticism can be especially damaging. Over the years, in our school, we have often encountered children daydreaming during prayers. When we consulted R' Elyashiv (one of the leading rabbis of our generation), he advised us strongly *not* to reprimand them. Instead, we have worked on *positive* ways of motivating them to tune in to their praying, with much success.

A Matter of "Principal"

As a principal, it is expected that I be critical of the students in our school. In fact, a member of the staff once criticized *me* for being overly friendly with the students. A more stern demeanor on my part, it seems, would have been more satisfactory to this teacher. I discussed this with R' Wolbe, who responded with enthusiasm, "Yours is the *only* way! Do not change your approach."

R' Wolbe then related a conversation he had had with the Chazon Ish many years earlier. Today's yeshivah students are different from those of previous generations, R' Wolbe told him. Perhaps in the past students were able to accept harsh rebuke, but nowadays this leads only to discouragement, and has no positive effect whatsoever. Students today need encouragement. The Chazon Ish indicated his emphatic approval of R' Wolbe's thesis.

"When I walk from my office to the bookcase for a book," continued R' Wolbe, "I always pass five or six students along the way, and I make it a point to give them a good word, or a stroke on the cheek, to otherwise encourage them." (R' Wolbe was speaking of students ages 18 through 22!)

Criticism may be useful when meted out in very small doses, very seldom and only in a carefully thought-out, constructive way. But more often than not criticism is a painful, destructive force. It is certainly not the main tool for building a child.

Catch Them Doing Things Right

Encouragement is that tool! It is crucial that we find things the child does right, and praise him for those things — even if what he has done is less than "perfect." The more "right things" you can point out to your child, the more he will improve.

If, for example, your child has put a great deal of effort into studying for a test, but did not do well because he first began studying the night before the test, it will not help him at all if you say, "I told you not to wait till the last minute!" Instead, say something like, "I see you're really interested in doing well in school; I saw how hard you studied, and I *appreciate* that!" Having praised him for his efforts, it may be appropriate to add, "A responsible boy like you might do better on the test if you would start earlier in the week, to give yourself a few extra days to study."

There is nothing "fake" about encouraging children; when we do so, we are merely adjusting our focus to recognize what they are doing right; and the more we focus on what they are doing right, *the more our children will do things right!* If we train ourselves to approach our children in this way, undoubtedly we will have more success directing them in the path we wish them to follow. And isn't *succeeding in the chinuch of our children* what we all want?

Reuven (not his real name), a student in our school, has no father. A very quiet boy, he would not participate in class *at all.* For months he had done nothing in class but sit quietly. One of our supervisors took action. Reuven's class was scheduled to take an oral exam on Thursday. Calling Reuven aside before the exam, the supervisor discussed the material with him, preparing a few questions and the correct answers with him. He then told the examiner to ask Reuven only those questions. Naturally, Reuven received a grade of 100 percent on the test.

From that moment on, Reuven began to open up, steadily participating more in his classes. Reuven continues to do well. The supervisor contrived an opportunity for success, and it has turned Reuven's life around. Catching a child doing something right can start a change for the better in your home, too!

I can guarantee that the more you encourage your children as part of your everyday routine, the more changes you will see in your family — dramatic changes for the better.

Love—
a Source of Light

2

Food or Warmth?

What does the Torah ask of us in all our interpersonal relationships?

Every commandment between man and his fellow-man is based on a single premise, says R' Wolbe in his classic *Alei Shur* (Part I, p. 190). That foundation is "To bring light to the lives of others."

Did you ever notice how a baby reacts when you smile to him? He "lights up," basking in the radiance of your smile. For him that smile is pure pleasure.

Uninhibited by fears, shyness or other social and emotional factors, often a baby will readily show you his pleasure. An older child may not be so quick to show pleasure, but a smile is no less meaningful to him. On the contrary, such demonstrations of warmth and affection to children are vital in many ways. The *Alei Shur* (ibid.) stresses:

> Who knows which is more beneficial for a child's health and development — the food he eats or the warmth he is shown? [Warmth and affection mean so much more to children than just pleasure; these factors are absolutely necessary for their healthy emotional development.] And it is known that it is impossible for a child who has been raised without any warmth to be healthy emotionally.

Dr. Rothschild, the director of Maayanei Hayeshuah Hospital in Bnei Brak (also the doctor of R' Yaakov Kanievsky, the Steipler Rav) is quoted as having said that even in the first days of a child's life, there is a noticeable difference between those infants who have been hugged and touched by their mothers and those who have not.

Love — Its Hidden Message

When we show warmth or express our love to others, we are in effect sending them a message telling them that they are important, and even more significant, that they are *accepted*.

David (not his real name), a young rabbinical student, once received a wedding invitation accompanied by a handwritten note from the bridegroom expressing his strong wish and sincere hope that David attend his wedding. While he recognized the name, David did not remember having had any special relationship with the groom. At the wedding, when an opportune moment presented itself, David approached him and asked how he had come to merit receiving a personalized, handwritten note with his invitation.

"Because of you I remained in yeshivah!" The bridegroom explained. "When I first entered the yeshivah I had no friends at all and I was very lonely. After I had spent a few weeks there, I decided to return home. On the last Shabbos before I was to leave, as we were waiting in line to greet the head of the yeshivah with the traditional Shabbos greeting, I felt someone touching my jacket. I turned around and saw you — smiling at me in a friendly way — adjusting my collar, which had not been lying flat as it should. It was at that moment that I began to feel I belonged, and I made up my mind there and then to stay in yeshivah — because of you!"

It Must Be Expressed

In speaking of giving love and warmth to others, two points must be emphasized: (1) that these feelings must be *expressed*, not just felt inside; and (2) that the love and acceptance one shows must be unconditional.

One must express love and warmth to one's children *consistently*, both through words and through actions. Such consistent expressions of our feelings are a positive thing, and must not be confused with spoiling children. "Spoiling" a child implies giving in to his every demand, without considering whether it will ultimately benefit the child.

We must smile to our children often. Likewise we must tell them in clear, direct language how much we love them and how much we enjoy having them around. It is also imperative that at times we joke and laugh with our children. All this is part of creating a genuine relationship with them.

In addition to expressing our love to our children with words, we must do so with *actions*. I consulted with a prominent rabbi regarding a particularly rebellious student. The rabbi recommended that from time to time the boy's father should buy a very small gift — worth only a dollar or two — to bring to his son. When he presents it, he should tell him that he bought it because he was thinking about him. Eventually, after the father has done this a number of times, the message will get through to the child that his father truly cares about him, and a change for the better in the child's behavior will follow.

Along the same lines, it is important simply to talk with your child — just to make casual conversation, as you would with a friend. Of course we speak with our children a great deal, but it is instructive to note the topics of the typical conversations we have with our children. Often they concern things that we must know, such as how they are doing in school, and whether they have taken care of their responsibilities. Recognize the importance of other types of conversation as well, conversation on more general topics. Such conversations demonstrate to our children how important they are to us, and work wonders in showing our children that we love them and that we simply enjoy their company.

One world-famous educator would meet with his son once a week — not so that they could learn together, or to discuss matters with his son that needed to be addressed, but just to go out together for a pizza. This father's sole purpose in their weekly afternoons out was to spend time with his son, talking with him about "nothing special." Spending such time with our children is one of the greatest acts of kindness we can do for them.

Set aside time to get to know your child: What are his interests? What makes him happy? What gets him upset? Fostering close, loving relationships with our children is the essence of "bringing light to the lives of others," which the *Alei Shur* cites as the foundation of all commandments between man and man, for our obligation "between man and man" to our children is no less than that which we owe to others. These acts we do to show our love to our children make them feel important; but more than that, they make them feel *accepted*. They make them feel that they belong.

Unconditional Love

The second point, which we mentioned earlier, cannot be emphasized enough: our demonstration of love and acceptance for our children must be one of unconditional love; it must be a constant factor in the relationship, and *cannot ever* be dependent upon circumstances. A child must always be made to feel loved and accepted, *regardless of his actions*.

This point is so crucial because, as stated above, a child's receiving unconditional love is necessary for his basic emotional health. Just as we cannot refuse to offer a child food to eat, even if we are not pleased with his actions, neither can we refrain from *expressing* our love for and acceptance of him, even if we are not pleased with his actions. As R' Wolbe told me, it is the parents' emotional support that gives children the strength to overcome all obstacles and difficulties, whether in a school setting, with friends, or in any other situation they encounter. If we as parents withdraw our support from our children when they are experiencing difficulties, from where will they draw the strength they so desperately need to help them cope?!

(Of course, there are times when it is necessary to punish children, and in this way to define for them the parameters of acceptable behavior. During the time when we are punishing them it may not be appropriate to *demonstrate* our love. Even so, before and shortly after we punish our children, we should definitely *show* them our love [as the Vilna Gaon comments on the passage in *Proverbs* 3:12, *Hashem admonishes the one He loves, and like a father He mollifies the child*]. Even when we must punish our children, we should do so only out of love, with the feeling that, "I am punishing my child because I love him and I want to help him.")

A Strange Pair of Glasses

Showing constant and unconditional love to children can be especially difficult for some parents, particularly if they have high expectations for their children. If this is the case, an attitude of "seeing things through the *child's* eyes — not through my own eyes" — is a very valuable tool for providing us with perspective regarding our children. This means truly understanding the child, his needs, and the difficulties he may be experiencing.

A well-known author employed a novel method to bring this point home to an audience. In order to show how one person cannot influence another unless he is looking at the situation through the "eyes" of the other, he borrowed a pair of glasses from someone in his audience, and gave them to "Dan," another audience participant. Immediately when he put on the glasses, Dan recoiled, as the prescription was quite strong.

The author attempted to influence Dan to accept the new situation and to be happy with it, but Dan was not in the least happy with the glasses. The more the author attempted to make him accept the glasses, the more uncomfortable Dan seemed to be with them.

Then the author tried to motivate Dan: "You can really do it if you only try. Try harder! It's your attitude! If you would only think positive, everything would work out."

But Dan was no happier with the situation. The author then played the role of Dan's parents: "You know how your mother and I have sacrificed for you. Don't you realize how much we've done for you? And this is how you respond? I want you to be happy with these glasses!!"

None of the approaches helped. Dan was still unhappy. How could he be happy wearing someone else's prescription glasses, when he had 20/20 vision? But someone would realize that only if he were seeing things through Dan's eyes, or at least attempting to understand the situation according to Dan's perception.

The same author relates the story of the little boy whose father had warned him not to go around the corner. The boy did not heed the warning, and numerous times he was punished for going around the corner, yet still he continued to repeat this undesirable behavior. Once, after being punished yet again for the same infraction, the boy approached his father with tears in his eyes and asked "Daddy, what's a 'corner'?"

When our children do things of which we do not approve, or when they do not live up to our expectations, it is imperative that we first try to understand their perception of the situation. How do they view matters and why do they feel this way? Perhaps they are experiencing difficulties, not because of lack of cooperation or motivation on their part, but because they are unable to overcome certain challenges on their own, and they need our help. If we will ask our children — with love — about what happened from their point of view, and if we will carefully examine the situation with a true will to understand without accusing and without blaming, we may be surprised to find that *our* entire perception will change.

More important, this type of approach may help us to be better able to show our child our love and acceptance, which he deserves, consistently and unconditionally. Knowing that he has our constant support, our child can find the wellsprings of strength he needs in order to overcome all obstacles, so that he will be successful and fulfilled, and he will bring us true satisfaction.

3

Anger: the Solution or the Problem

Off-track Most of the Time

Are you aware of the following amazing fact? Although no commercial airplane travels without a specific flight plan, throughout most of the flight the airplane *does not travel on course!* Many factors, such as atmospheric conditions and air currents, move the plane slightly off course.

How then can the plane arrive at its destination? The answer, of course, is through the pilots' ongoing navigation. They guide the plane according to the planned path, never straying too far from it, always keeping it in mind and in view, until eventually they reach their destination.

A well-known author aptly described our responsibilities in guiding our children in terms of an airplane pilot's flight plans. We cannot hope to stay perfectly on course at all times, for too many factors we encounter affect our ability to respond as we would hope to under all circumstances.

It is imperative that we view all the guidelines set forth in this book as "flight plans." The thoughts expressed and the courses of action recommended in these pages are considerations to be borne in mind; we should not lose track of them, for they serve to guide us toward our destination. Yet to remain on track all the time cannot be expected of us. So many elements work against us, pushing us off course; everyone has his or her own pressures in life, which must not be underestimated, and coping with the endless and varied needs of a large family can absorb us completely and throw us off course. What we must do is to keep the proper path in mind constantly, so that we can navigate toward it, make sure that we do not stray too far from it, and eventually reach our "destination."

Focus on Improvement, Not on Perfection

In addition to all the other elements in our lives that prevent us from pursuing single-mindedly our goals for our children, our path is complicated by a most severe handicap that we possess. I myself have suffered from it for many years. This chronic condition is called "being human." Since we are all human, it follows that we are all imperfect. A very revealing comic strip portrays an older fish coaching a younger fish, as they swim deep in the sea. The older fish, trying to help the younger fish cope with his fears, said that he understood the younger one's fear of getting caught — but as to his fear of water, he said, "That's an obstacle you will just have to overcome."

Likewise our frustration with being less than perfect is something to which we all have to adapt ourselves, for we cannot change the situation. Since Hashem has created us as imperfect beings, it follows that He does not demand perfection from us. What He asks is that we strive to improve; He asks for progress. Every step in the right direction therefore is success. As long as we are moving forward as opposed to standing still, we are succeeding. To quote a famous poet, "The only failure is — not falling down — it's staying down."

R' Avraham Grodzinsky states that the joy we experience over even the smallest measure of growth and improvement in our lives should equal the happiness and excitement of one who has found a buried treasure (*Toras Avraham,* p. 22). (Imagine how you would feel if you just found out that you won a $100 million lottery.)

Chinuch: Our Calling

Granted, educating our children and students properly is no easy assignment; but in this generation, it is our calling. The Slonimer Rebbe writes that each generation has a specific mission wherein lies its improvement. The call of our generation, he says, is *chinuch*. This is our principal task in life, and we must make it our absolute priority (*Nesivos Shalom,* Introduction to *Nesivos HaChinuch*).

The Highest Form of Kindness

Parents and educators need to realize how exceptionally unselfish they really are when they relate to their children and students. Kindness that is extended to others without any intention of being compensated is certainly the highest form of kindness, and it is what parents and teachers do constantly, investing in their children and students far more than anything they can ever hope to receive in return. They give of themselves without seeking recognition, and with full awareness that the recipients of their many acts of kindness will never really know or appreciate how much they have given them. Recognize the profound degree of your own selflessness! This is not conceit, by any means. On the contrary, it will give you the strength you need to continue in your efforts, to achieve and to overcome the many obstacles in your path, and to progress toward ultimate success in the education of our children and students.

Quality vs. Quantity

In this book we have discussed fostering warm loving relationships with our children. It is important to note two crucial points regarding this issue: (1) that the *quality* of the time we give to our children is far more effective than the amount of time we give them, and (2) that anger is one of the most destructive forces we can employ in relating to children.

The dean of the Kol Torah Yeshivah in Jerusalem told me this true story:

> *Two famous rabbis attended an affair; one stayed for only five minutes, while the other stayed for several hours. When the first rabbi left, everyone was happy and expressed appreciation to him for having come. Much later, when the other was about to leave, someone asked him, "Why are you leaving already? You just came!"*

The rabbi who had stayed longer at the affair asked his colleague, "What is your secret? How is it that you come for only a short time and everyone is happy, yet although I stay for a long time, no one is satisfied?"

"It's really very simple," said the other. "I spend only five minutes, but during those five minutes my heart is totally involved in the occasion. You may stay longer, but from the moment you walk in, you can't wait to leave. It's clear that your heart isn't in it. No wonder people say you've just come — they never really felt you were present!"

When spending time with your children, concentrate on injecting *quality* into that time. If you are with your children with all your heart, then even if you spend less time with them, they will feel it more. (This point can be very important for teachers who must divide their time and attention between many students, or for parents blessed with large families.)

Seize the Opportunity

The time when a child is in bed ready to go to sleep provides an excellent opportunity to spend quality time with your child. You might want to sit and talk with him, even for just a few minutes. Expressions of love shown at bedtime can actually be therapeutic, and can even divert crises.

A psychologist whom R' Wolbe recommends highly told me that a number of cases of severe emotional problems he has treated were eliminated by one simple act: the mother would give the child a small kiss on his forehead when he was in his bed, before he went to sleep. (This "therapy" has proven effective in many cases, even for boys past bar-mitzvah age.)

There are many other opportunities throughout the day for giving quality individual attention. If you are going shopping or running errands, consider taking a child with you; a task that you cannot avoid can thus turn into a very special time for a child. If you are waiting for an appointment together with your child, you can utilize that wait — even if it is only 10 minutes — to get to know him. If your heart is totally in it, it is true quality time!

When a child is on his way out of the house to go to school, it is a good chance for "quality time." These hectic moments may not be time to talk, but it is an excellent time to deposit some warmth in the child's emotional bank account. As he is leaving the house, if you only smile to him and wish him a great day, it can have a potent effect on the child's whole day and is well worth the effort.

Anger Alienates

On the opposite end of the continuum, anger and its various manifestations (screaming, for example) alienate children and can fill them with fear. In his classic *Alei Shur* (Vol. I, p. 261), R' Wolbe addresses this topic:

> Nothing can ruin the warm relationship between parents and children so effectively as the parents' causing their children to fear them excessively. In addition to destroying family relationships, parents who cause their children to fear them can lead their children to rebel totally, Heaven forbid, when the children are older.

Many years ago I was present when someone approached R' Yaakov Kamenetsky to discuss the teaching of our Sages that states, "*Le'olam al yatil adam eimah yeseirah besoch beiso* — A person should never bring excessive fear into his house." The person had inferred from these words that "a lot of fear is not good — but a little fear is good." Upon hearing this Reb Yaakov replied, "I don't know if any fear is good. What is necessary is for the parents to relate to the family in a way that automatically inspires their respect. Clearly, acting out of impulsive anger does not inspire anyone's (not even your own children's or students') respect. The *Orchos Tzaddikim* states, "One who gets angry often does not find favor in the eyes of others; in fact he arouses their hatred."

Worse than any of these adverse results, though, constant anger (and its manifestations) can be emotionally damaging to a child. (Being that we are human, we get angry occasionally. It is when a child is exposed to angry outbursts consistently that anger can be damaging.)

R' Yehudah Greenwald, in the book *Lada'as BaAretz Darkecha* (p. 275), presents a common scenario:

> It could happen the moment I enter the house: The children are jumping all over, with no inclination to go to sleep. My wife, exhausted after a long day, genuinely needs my help.
>
> How will I react? My first thought is that a few screams and a slap or two will do the trick; my gut feeling is that showing anger will bring the quickest results. Nevertheless, I must stop to think clearly, to consider whether this is really the correct approach. "One who becomes angry constantly is hated by others" (Orchos Tzaddikim, as above). Moreover, constant anger could damage the children emotionally.
>
> In general, the time has come for me to clarify whether anger is the most effective response. Couldn't I achieve the desired result if I were to take my child firmly by the hand and put him to bed with a warm, loving smile? Perhaps I could begin to sing a song and then suddenly pick my child up and start dancing with him — I could then dance him straight to bed — and put him in. One of two things would happen: the child will be either shocked or ecstatic, but in either case he probably won't even realize that he was put to bed. (I once heard R' Wolbe describe this very scenario.)

Overcoming Anger

R' Greenwald in the aforementioned book suggests two methods of overcoming one's anger: (1) to speak softly (as mentioned in the letter of Nachmanides), especially during a tense period, and (2) to show love to your child at the moment of intense anger. He describes a friend who, when he felt himself giving way to his angry feelings, would give his child a strong hug. His anger would dissipate immediately.

Many of our grandmothers had their own methods of dealing with anger: when a child would annoy them, they would give the child a few sincere blessings ("*Oy*, you should be *gezunt* (healthy)

... May you live a long life, etc."). This is a very effective way for us to put things into perspective for ourselves when our anger seems about to overcome us.

The most important thing we can do for our children, however, is to realize that our anger, consistently expressed, can drive our children away from us in the long run, while the love and closeness that exist between ourselves and our children will lead us to success in our children's *chinuch*, particularly in our turbulent times.

A Word for Teachers

The principles mentioned above apply as well to the positive influence teachers can have on their students. Although in practice the details must necessarily be carried out somewhat differently, the general rules are the same. Schools often cannot avoid assigning large classes, which greatly limits many of the teachers' activities, but I stress again that the *quality* of every encounter is the teacher's most powerful tool.

When I first began my teaching career, I sought R' Wolbe's advice, asking what was most important for me to know. He answered that a teacher must love his students. The Klausenburger Rebbe made the same point, explaining that every craftsman has his own special trait through which he succeeds in his trade. The trait that enables a teacher to succeed at his "trade" is his love for his students.

However, if a teacher becomes angry, he will not be able to keep his students' best interests in mind, and so will not be able to educate them properly. R' Shlomo Zalman Auerbach related this personal experience which occurred when he was a young child in yeshivah: In the midst of a lesson, when the rebbi was deeply involved in his presentation, the young Shlomo Zalman climbed under the table. Rather than reacting, the rebbi walked out of the room. Ten minutes later, the rebbi came back, only to turn around immediately and walk out of the room again.

Years later, R' Shlomo Zalman questioned this rebbi about the incident. The rebbi replied that at that moment he had been at the high point of his lesson. When R' Shlomo Zalman climbed under the table the rebbi became enraged, and was about to react.

Realizing that he would have been acting out of anger, not out of desire for his students' benefit, he removed himself from the situation and waited 10 minutes. When he returned, however, he found that he was still angry, so he walked out again.

A teacher who is so careful to do only what is beneficial for his students can succeed in raising a Torah giant like R' Auerbach. A teacher's leaving the classroom for an extended period of time is not recommended, but the need to avoid anger is no less urgent.

Even though our Sages have recommended that we *show* our students anger on occasion, they are not giving us license to *be* angry. Rather, they are suggesting that we sometimes (but certainly not very often) portray anger in cases where it might prove beneficial. Nevertheless, the teacher's intention must always be how to best benefit his students.

It is clear that in the long run, especially nowadays, it is our warm and caring relationship with our students that will bring them to success.

4

Praying, Learning, and the Shabbos Table: a Pleasure or a Pressure

The Most Important Thing in the World

The following incident (related by the renowned educator, R' Y.Y. Yaakovson) actually took place.

A teacher in one of the higher grades of a yeshivah elementary school was discussing with his class the importance of Torah learning. To emphasize his point, he asked his students what he assumed was a rhetorical question: "What's the most important thing in the world?" The answer was not long in coming, as one of the students called out, "CHULENT!"

Understandably, the rabbi was extremely annoyed, and he made his way over to the desk of the culprit, intending to inform him in no uncertain terms that this kind of silliness was in bad taste, and certainly was not in the student's best interest. However, as he approached the student's desk, the rabbi noticed the expression on his face, an expression that reflected anger and bitterness. The rabbi realized immediately that his student was not trying to be silly at all; understanding that the matter was quite serious, the rabbi decided to drop it for the moment, leaving it to be handled by others who were more equipped to deal with this child's problems.

When the principal questioned him, the boy explained that it was his father who had taught him the importance of chulent. "Did your father actually tell you that chulent is the most important thing in the world — even more important than learning Torah?" asked the principal kindly.

"No," said the child, "but it's obvious! When I say words of Torah at the Shabbos table, my father doesn't pay any attention to me. He just sits there eating his chulent, saying 'yes, yes' — pretending that he's listening. And he doesn't care if anyone else at the table is listening to my Torah, either."

The Child's Perception Determines the Success of Our Influence

This dialogue illustrates that a child will be influenced only in accordance with *his perception* of a situation, even if this perception has nothing to do with the reality. (In fact Torah learning was a very high priority for this boy's father, who spent half of each day studying Torah.) Moreover, if this perception is based on something the child has actually experienced, as opposed to his merely having observed it, it will have a far stronger influence on him.

Thus if we hope to influence a child, especially in matters relating to Torah and mitzvos, it is imperative that we take his feelings into account. How will *he perceive* our actions? What is he *experiencing* when we attempt to teach him, to help him, to reprimand him, to inspire him? For it is only our child's perception that will determine whether our attempts to influence him will succeed.

Pressure in Religious Matters Can Be Harmful

This point cannot be understated. Many well-intentioned parents put forth great effort to pressure their children in areas of religion, yet all their effort may be wasted, and may even be damaging their children's delicate process of spiritual development, if they are not taking their children's feelings into account. Such parents might feel that the fact that they have their child's best interests at heart is sufficient, and that it is unnecessary for them to relate to the child's feelings. This attitude may be compared to the attitude of a doctor who makes a diagnosis and recommends treatment without knowledge of the patient's symptoms. Even if the doctor's intentions are sincere, most likely his diagnosis will be inaccurate and his recommendations harmful.

> One set of parents sought the advice of R' Y.Y. Yaakovson. "We would like to move our son to a different school," they said. "This other school has a longer day of learning, and begins teaching Talmud to children at an earlier age. Why shouldn't we push our son to be great in Torah? True, he's happy where he is now, but that should not be the deciding factor. We want our son to become great, and the new school with the additional pressure will do the trick."
>
> R' Yaakovson answered the parents, "When someone is pressured to learn more than he is able to, not only will he gain nothing, he will develop the habit of daydreaming and will eventually become indolent. When a child experiences strong pressure to advance in Torah and mitzvos, it can cause severe adverse reactions that could prevent the child from becoming a proper Torah Jew altogether, G-d forbid."
>
> R' Yaakovson then pointed out to the parents numerous side effects their child was displaying as a result of the pressure they had been placing on him: the child had begun to stutter, bite his nails, wet his bed, act out in school, and most notably, he had begun to act violently.
>
> On R' Yaakovson's advice, the parents eased their high-pressure approach, and there was a marked improvement in their child's condition and behavior.

These parents had not been taking their child and his feelings into account, and they were not even *aware* of the harm they themselves had been causing their child. Taking a child's perceptions and emotions into account is crucial. It is impossible to influence anyone by force and applied pressure — it simply will not work, and will more likely have an effect that is opposite of that which we hope to accomplish.

"I Put So Much Effort
Into My Son's Praying"

R' Yaakovson described another instance involving a boy who had totally rejected his parents' lifestyle and was no longer religious. When told that his son does not even pray, this boy's father expressed his amazement. "I put so much into my son's praying. How do you explain the fact that, in spite of all my efforts, I did not succeed?" The father then proceeded to describe how he had "taught" his son to pray. "I was always careful that he should come with me to minyan and sit next to me. During the prayers I didn't even allow myself the luxury of concentrating on my own prayers, for I kept my eye constantly on my son. I made sure that he was following the place in his siddur, and if he would start daydreaming I would immediately step in to make sure that he would get right back to praying."

This very question was presented to the boy himself. His bitter response was, "There's nothing that I hate so much as praying. I've waited years for the day when I would be old enough to be able to stop praying. Just walking into the shul building gives me a bad feeling. I think it's because my father was so hard on me about praying that it became such an unbearable burden. I have no patience to sit through praying, or even to think about Hashem and Gehinnom."

This boy's experience of *davening* brought him to identify Judaism with Gehinnom.

The Goal: a Pleasant Experience

What then is the correct way to influence our children? *How can we successfully instill in them a love for Hashem and His Torah?* How can we guide them toward greatness?

The most essential ingredient for success in influencing our children — without it, no influence will succeed — is for us to make sure that their experiences in religious matters are *positive* experiences. They must be experiences that the *children them-*

selves view as positive and pleasurable. It is *only* such experiences that will instill in children — or in anyone — a love for Torah and mitzvos, and that will keep them strong and growing in the *long* run.

This goal must be our guide in every interaction on a spiritual level that we have with our children. If we will focus on this goal, we may well find that so many other concerns and goals fade into insignificance. This applies constantly in the everyday flow of life with our children.

Learning With Your Child

Learning Torah with a child, for example, should be a pleasant experience. The child will not benefit from such learning if the atmosphere is charged with tension. This is not the time for the parent to act out the role of examiner; it is a time for both parent and child to enjoy learning with one another. The father would do well to focus on that portion of the material that his son knows well, and to encourage his child by expressing his satisfaction at the child's efforts. Putting his arm around his child while they are learning together will make the session even more effective.

As we have stated, our main concern is that *the child* must see the experience as a positive one, for it is this that will truly influence him. Even if the child is finding his learning to be very difficult, when we review with him we can express to him how much we enjoy learning with him, and how we love to help him. In this way we give him the opportunity to take pleasure in the joy he gives us, making the *learning itself* more pleasurable. It is these and similar actions that will make learning with our children an altogether positive experience.

A parent might argue that he is obligated to address other goals. He must be able to monitor his son's progress; he must know how his son is doing in school. Indeed this is an important goal, but it pales in significance when set against the goal of helping our children grow with a love of Torah (rather than with resentment for it). Yet the fact is that if you learn with your child in this manner, creating a pleasant, loving atmosphere, you will be able to assess how much he knows — but at the same time you will have given him a desire, even an eagerness, to learn more.

This is not an untested theory by any means. Where these recommendations have been implemented in countless real-life situations, they have led to major, successful changes in the lives of parents and children.

In generations past our great teachers knew these principles. It is related that one sage had a very wild nephew who was not willing to learn in the conventional system. This rabbi advised the parents to hire a special teacher who would teach the child while the child was sitting up in a tree, the teacher standing at the foot of the tree. The parents followed his advice, and this child grew up to be one of the leading sages of the generation.

The Gaon of Vilna certainly was aware of this. In his famous letter entitled *Iggeres HaGra* he wrote regarding his *own* children: "Do not pressure them unnecessarily; guide them only with gentleness, for Torah learning is instilled within a person only through an approach of serenity and gentleness."

It is obvious the Gaon of Vilna knew that the only way for children to succeed in their learning is through an approach of "serenity and gentleness."

Praying

Praying too should be viewed as a positive experience by our children. We must make this goal our highest priority when we take our children to shul. We can insist that our child come to shul and sit near us — but *we should not try to force him to pray*. In an earlier chapter, we cited the halachic ruling of R' Elyashiv that if a child daydreams during praying we should leave him alone, allowing him to dream, as is normal for most children (and even for some adults).

There are many things related to the shul experience that a child will enjoy naturally, such as the singing, the goings on, the presence of his friends, and the general atmosphere that pervades the prayers. We can make the time he spends in shul an even more pleasurable experience for our child by smiling at him now and then during the course of the prayers. This will demonstrate to him how much we love him, how much we like being with him and how much we appreciate his praying; it will certainly contribute to making our child view praying in shul as a positive experience.

Another factor that can play a major role in inspiring our children to pray well is the role model we represent. R' Y. Hutner described two fathers. One of them made it a habit to scold and reprimand his children constantly during prayers. It is obvious, R' Hutner explained, that the father himself could not manage to pray properly, however he consoled himself with the notion that he was educating his children to pray properly. The result of his educational approach was that when his children grew up and became fathers themselves, they acted in the same way toward their own children, constantly scolding and reprimanding, "making sure" that their children would pray properly. This trend continued within this family for generation after generation.

The second father would have his children sit with him in shul, but would make no comments to them whatsoever regarding their praying. Instead, he would concentrate on his own praying, trying his best to pray with great devotion. His sons observed their father's example, and eventually began themselves to pray with great devotion, and when they became fathers, they related to their sons the same way in which their father had related to them. This second father raised generations of fathers who prayed with great devotion and who taught their sons to do likewise, while the first father raised *generations* of fathers who could not bring themselves to pray well — and who would instead try to get their children to pray.

It is crucial, however, to note that the role model a father represents will have a positive effect only if the child views praying on the whole as a positive experience.

The Shabbos Table

At the Shabbos table, too, our main goal is that our children view this as a positive experience. In order to achieve this principal goal, we might have to overlook other concerns we may have at that time, such as disciplining the children. Disciplining our children harshly at the Shabbos table will not make it a positive experience in their eyes. This is not to say that we should allow children to speak with disrespect at the table, or that we should ignore major infractions; we must maintain a basic level of decorum at the Shabbos table. Nevertheless, there are many times when we could act with more patience and understanding if we would constantly bear in mind our most important goal: to give our children *what they consider to be* a positive experience. It is impossible to overstate the importance of this goal.

There are innumerable ways by which to make the Shabbos table a positive experience for our children. Children love attention, and the Shabbos table offers many opportunities to give our children a great quantity of healthy attention. They enjoy immensely repeating the Torah thoughts they learned in school. They also love to have the chance to say their own Torah thoughts that they might have prepared beforehand — with their parent's help. (These Torah thoughts do not have to be lengthy or complex; even brief words of Torah can give a child tremendous satisfaction.)

Children also love to share the events and experiences of their lives with their parents, and when the family is sitting together at the Shabbos table it is an excellent time for such sharing. It would work wonders for our children — and for our relationship with them and our ability to influence them — if we would give them our *full* listening ear when they tell us about the things that happen to them.

Shabbos Guests and the Children

When we invite guests to join us for our Shabbos meals, they might claim most of our attention. However, we must bear in mind that if we ignore our children, directing our attention exclusively toward our guests, then the children will not have viewed this meal as a positive experience. One might argue that children should learn from our example how to act at a Shabbos table, but if they receive no attention whatsoever when the meal is in progress, it is not likely that they will absorb this lesson. As we have stated, the basis of the influence we can have upon our children is that *they view it as a positive experience*, and if they do not view it as such, no example will have the intended effect.

A solution to this dilemma might be to give the children our full attention during the first half-hour of the meal, after which we can allow them to leave the table. Then we can give our guests the attention they deserve. I have noticed that guests are generally very much impressed by parents who devote time to their children at the Shabbos table, and they have a great deal of respect for these parents.

Ways to Enhance the Shabbos Table

Singing with our children is another way to enhance the Shabbos table experience. There are many songs, in addition to the standard *zemiros*, that children enjoy singing. Give your children a chance to sing these songs with you at the table. Singing the Grace After Meals together with the children also gives them much pleasure, and is worthwhile. Giving a treat to a child who participates nicely certainly encourages him, and makes it a positive experience.

One parent I know bought cards with questions from *Tanach* printed on them. At the Shabbos table, he asked each person at the table a question in turn. Anyone who knew an answer got to hold that card until the end of the meal. This generated a very happy atmosphere at the table, but I was most surprised to see the response of the 16-year-old son. This boy was a problematic child who had been expelled from yeshivah, and at that time he was "on the street"; he would not accept any educational or religious structure in his life. Yet he was participating enthusiastically in this family activity at the Shabbos table.

Another parent prepares a quiz on the weekly portion for the Friday evening meal, and another quiz on a topic of halachah for the Shabbos morning meal. (Questions capture a family's interest, such as, "Where do we find the color brown in this week's Torah reading?") Children love questions and enjoy the challenge.

Yet another parent taught his children the names of all the tractates in Talmud and together they put those names to music, singing the tractates at the Shabbos table, to a familiar tune which they all knew.

Of course all these activities require some preparation — but so does the Shabbos food, yet no one refrains from having food at the Shabbos table, just because it requires preparation.

Some families find it worthwhile to shorten the Shabbos meal to prevent their children from becoming bored, as children are not able to sit for very long. Others allow their children to leave the table after a half-hour or so as a matter of course, while the adults continue the meal as long as they like. In this way, the meal remains a positive experience for both children and adults.

Making a positive experience of the Shabbos table is no less significant for grown children and guests.

> A neighbor of mine, a widower named Reb Aryeh, was a very happy, positive person, and was always ready with interesting stories to relate. One Shabbos, his good friend Reb Berel was hosting two non-religious boys who had been considering changing their lifestyle. At that time the boys hardly presented the picture of Jewish youth we hope to see. Their earrings and long hair told a story of their own.
>
> Toward the end of the meal, Reb Aryeh stopped by Reb Berel's house for a visit, as was his custom on Friday nights. He stayed quite late into the night, entertaining Reb Berel's guests with stories, anecdotes, interesting comments and fascinating conversation.
>
> Just a week or so later, one of Reb Berel's children happened to meet those two boys, and found them completely transformed. Among other things, their earrings were gone, and they both had haircuts. In fact, in that short time they had made their decision to become religious and had registered in a yeshivah for ba'alei teshuvah. When the boy asked them what had prompted them to make this decision, they answered, "Our former way of life had nothing to offer us that could compare to the Shabbos evening that we spent at your house."

There are many more tools we can employ to influence our children in areas of religion, such as personal example, stories, discussions, and various forms of encouragement. Yet they are all ineffective if we do not make spirituality a positive experience in our child's eyes.

And if we do, we may be surprised to find that spirituality will become a more positive experience for us as well.

5

Developing in Them a Love for Torah and Mitzvos

Plants Under "Stress"

As I write these words, we in Jerusalem are recovering from a recent snowstorm that effectively paralyzed the city. Snow is rare in this part of the world, so it is always accompanied by much fanfare and excitement, by adults and children alike. People were building snowmen, having snowball fights, or just walking outside, enjoying the scenery and noting how beautiful everything looked all covered in white. Many people presented Torah thoughts and *gematriyos* about the snow. Among all the activity and changes in routine engendered by the snow were a number of fallen trees.

After the storm, I was walking with a friend of mine who is an expert in the field of botany. Before he moved to Israel, he worked in a plant nursery in Los Angeles, where his customers included a number of well-known film celebrities. Pointing out various trees that had fallen in the snowstorm, he told me, "This tree was a weed; no preparation was put into its planting — that's why it fell."

I asked him if some plants did not succeed even if people did invest time and effort into planting them. He explained that careful planting is not enough; the ground needs to be well prepared beforehand. Ground is naturally often hard and compact, and unless it is turned over and softened, roots cannot penetrate and take hold. In his work in the Los Angeles plant nursery, he noticed that this was the source of a common mistake people make. They invest money in seeds and in various materials to help the plants grow, but the plants themselves would die or would be uprooted when they were exposed to even a small measure of "stress." Upon investigation it was discovered that their owners had not prepared the ground before planting them. For plants to take root and last, one must soften the ground first.

Planned Planting

I was struck by the aptness of this metaphor as it applies to influencing our children. We must realize that when we are in a position to influence our children, in everything we are and in everything we do we are planting seeds. What ground is more fertile than the pure soul of a child? Just as we must prepare for the planting of seeds, so too must we carefully plan the ways in which we will influence our children. Positive influence cannot result from our spontaneous reactions if we have not placed thought into them. Someone might feel that he works so hard to influence his children, when in reality he might not have planted any true seeds at all. During daily interaction, he might simply have reacted to his children's actions. "Put that toy away." "Put your plate in the sink." "Did you brush your teeth?" This cannot be considered to be "prepared planting." At best it is like allowing a weed to grow on its own. At the slightest stress, it may fall under, not having the strength to persevere.

Our influence over our children must be planned, and if we plan it right, preparing the *groundwork* and then planting the right seeds under the right conditions, our influence can and will succeed, with the help of Hashem, to take root.

> *A father once took his children to visit a number of tzaddikim on Chol HaMoed, but he was greatly disappointed, for he found no one was home. Walking through the streets with a heavy heart, the father suddenly caught a glimpse of a great tzaddik buying aravos (willow branches, used on Hoshana Rabbah) at a sidewalk stand. In genuine excitement, he ran over to the tzaddik to ask for a blessing for his children. The tzaddik gave some thought to what he would say and gave the children a beautiful blessing; he then proceeded on his way. This particular tzaddik was accustomed to bowing his head*

slightly while speaking to people, as a sign of humility. Months later, the father was discussing the trait of humility with his children. "Abba, remember the humble tzaddik?" they shouted enthusiastically. The influence of what they had witnessed had taken root, although the father had not even pointed out the tzaddik's humility in that instance. The Yom Tov atmosphere, the tzaddik's actions, and the father's enthusiasm had combined to create a lasting impression on the children.

Methods to Avoid

Yet before we discuss how to prepare the ground and how to plant seeds — how to successfully influence our children — it is important first to discuss how *not* to influence. One cannot influence successfully through criticism and negativity.

One teacher was punishing a student most severely. As he was administering his very harsh punishment, he was also reprimanding the child. "Even if I were your father," he told the boy, "I would do this to you." With these words the teacher was confident that he was getting his message across, but the child responded, "If you were my father, I would rather have been an orphan!"

R' Yaakovson, renowned educator and speaker, tells of an educator in Israel who was addressing a group of teenaged boys who had been brought up religious, but had adopted other ways of life. He asked them to tell him what comes to mind when they hear the words "Fear of G-d." The associations they offered him were: punishment; Gehinnom; prohibition; self-inflicted pain; and even depression. The sad fact is that these words identified their experiences of "Fear of G-d."

One of the boys in this group volunteered that he believes that the reason he left religious observance was just so that his parents would appreciate what he *does* do. "Now when I come to shul, or when I do not desecrate the Shabbos, my parents are really glad, and they show it," he said.

> *I dealt with one high-school student who was having difficulty with his desire for learning. Nevertheless, he was putting forth a strong effort, and he even arranged a two-hour daily learning session for himself during the upcoming*

vacation, something I considered to be quite a feat for a boy with little desire. One of his teachers "caught" him during a recess break one day planning a touring trip for the upcoming vacation. The teacher did not approve of the fact that this boy's thoughts were involved in vacation trips, when vacation was still a number of weeks off. Presumably, he was determined to influence the child to desist from such behavior in the future. To this end, he called the boy up in front of two other teachers, and began to scream at him, "You're a good for nothing! You're a good for nothing!"

Unfortunately, the teachers words became a self-fulfilling prophecy. Devastated, the boy lost his desire for learning altogether, and all areas of his observance began to deteriorate. Years later the boy admitted that he had considered a non-Torah lifestyle. Only through a miracle did he remain religious.

A Monologue

R' Yaakovson quoted from the despairing monologue of a teenager who became non-religious. This boy was later killed tragically in a car accident. His words were published with the hope that they would open the eyes of those parents who still feel that criticism is the only way to relate to children who do not meet our expectations. May the influence of his words be a merit to his *neshamah*:

> *Try to understand the feeling of waking up every morning knowing that just another day of depression is waiting for you. If you won't pray, you'll feel bad the whole day. Nothing will help. I haven't been praying for two years now, and I feel bad. I'm afraid of Gehinnom. I try not to think about it, but it doesn't help. So what can I do about it? Pray, maybe? If you pray, Gehinnom is still waiting for you. Why? Because you have no patience; you just sit nervously waiting for the prayers to be over. You go crazy from the boredom.*
>
> *So let's say that you really try to pray — it's impossible to succeed! If you weren't concentrating when you said the name of Hashem, you have a sin. It's as if you said the*

Name of Hashem in vain. If you weren't concentrating in the first pasuk of Shema, you transgressed a positive commandment, a mitzvas asei, and you said the blessings of the Shema in vain. The same goes for the first blessing of the Shemoneh Esrei.

Let's say you've already worked hard and now you are actually concentrating when you pray. You think that maybe you were successful in your prayers — hey! — aren't you ashamed of yourself?! Your tefillah isn't sincere! The only reason you prayed well was to impress the rabbi and the other students, and you did it at a time when Hashem is standing in front of you, watching you. Just you wait, you hypocrite! When you get to Heaven everyone will see who you really are.

What will be with you? You start to wish that you were born irreligious, so whatever you don't do right wouldn't be your fault and you'd get no Gehinnom; you'd be blameless having been brought up in a non-religious family and not knowing any better. You'd have no mitzvos or aveiros.

You go around with these feelings until you feel like you're going to lose your mind, like you'll just explode. And in the end you leave the yeshivah. You try to be a heretic, but it doesn't go ... you know the truth! So now what? There's really no choice; either way Gehinnom is waiting for you, and you have to run away from it. It's easier to run away when you're on the streets!

This unfortunate boy, may he rest in peace, was never allowed to feel that he was a success at religion. He was constantly criticized, and endless demands were placed on him. Much work was invested in trying to help him, but, as he himself said, "Theoretically, it's clear to me that Hashem loves me and wants me to succeed — but I can't overcome these feelings, and all the theoretical proofs don't help me a bit!"

Clearly, criticizing and making unreasonable demands on children are *not* ways to influence them to pursue a life of Torah. In truth, they are powerful tools to influence a child to hate himself, and the negative impressions they will leave will be lasting ones.

Children Learn What They Live

I am reminded of a poem entitled, "A Child Learns What He Lives," which reads, in part:

If a child lives with criticism
He learns to condemn.
If a child lives with hostility
He learns to fight.
If a child lives with fear
He learns to be apprehensive.
If a child lives with ridicule
He learns to be shy.
If a child lives with shame
He learns to feel guilty.
If a child lives with tolerance
He learns to be patient.
If a child lives with encouragement
He learns to be confident.
If a child lives with praise
He learns to appreciate.
If a child lives with approval
He learns to like himself.
If a child lives with acceptance
He learns to find love in the world.
If a child lives with honesty and fairness
He learns what truth and justice are.
If a child lives with sharing
He learns to be generous.
If a child lives with serenity,
He learns to have peace of mind.

The Successful Way

How then does one successfully influence children? Taking a lesson from the botanist, we can learn to follow three steps of planting for successful growth: (1) soften the ground; (2) consider weather conditions; (3) protect the growing plant from strong wind forces.

Soften the ground: The general atmosphere of a child's environment, especially at the time when we are attempting to influence him, must be one full of love — a love that is expressed often, and one in which the child feels secure.

> I once had reason to ask a small group of children if their parents love them (not a recommended practice under normal circumstances). Most of the children looked at me as if I were crazy. "Of course they love me!" came their emphatic response. One child, however (from a very fine family), said, "Well, all parents love their children ... so I guess they love me." This boy had to make "mathematical calculations" to prove to himself that his parents love him.

R' Eizik Sher, head of the Slabodka Yeshivah, said that if you want to influence a student you must first pour on him *bucketsful* of love.

The Chazon Ish told R' Michel Yehudah Lefkovitz of Bnei Brak that in *Ethics of Our Fathers* first is mentioned "*oheiv es habriyos* — he loves other people," and only afterwards, "*mekarvan laTorah* — he brings them close to Torah."

Consider weather conditions: Before attempting to plant, one must always make sure that weather conditions permit it; if the air is very cold, the ground will be hard and impenetrable. The *worst* time to influence a child is when he has done something wrong, especially when he is being punished. At that time the ground will be so hard that no seeds will be able to take root.

R' Yaakovson says that the best time to influence a child is after he has done something very *right* — after he has succeeded in doing a good deed. It is at that point that the "ground" is fertile and ready to accept the seed. The child wants to feel the significance of his actions. He wants his good actions to be considered important and, at this time, he has a vested interest in hearing about what he has done.

Of course there are many "neutral times" when interactions between parent and child can have a very strong positive influence. When the atmosphere is pleasant and non-defensive, such as when the parent is walking with his son, or perhaps when they are out together on a trip, a parent's words and actions can have a profound effect on a child.

Protect from strong wind forces: If the personal example you present sharply contradicts what you are saying, it forms a "strong wind" that will uproot the seeds of influence, even if those seeds were planted properly initially. As one author said, "What you *are* is screaming so loudly that I cannot hear what you *say*."

> A wealthy man once asked a famous rabbi with whom he had a close relationship, "How is it that I told my children constantly about the importance of learning Torah, yet at the first opportunity, they went into business?"
>
> In response, the rabbi reminded him of two incidents that he had witnessed, both during a single Shabbos: One Friday night, the father had just reprimanded his 5-year-old son. The child, angry and anxious to get back at his father, turned the light on, knowing that it was Shabbos. The father reacted quite calmly, telling his son that he was hurting only himself by turning on the light.
>
> "Your controlled reaction surprised me," the rabbi told the father. "When I asked you about it at the time, you answered that he's only a small boy and doesn't really understand anything. Yet on the following morning, when the child was acting wild, he knocked over a very expensive crystal vase, and you became very angry. You grabbed your son — the very child who 'doesn't understand anything' — and gave him a sound beating.
>
> "In these two reactions, you showed your son that material matters are more important than spiritual matters. That is why your words about the importance of Torah learning didn't have any effect on him."

What we show our children is much more powerful than what we say. Of course we cannot expect to be perfect, but we must ensure that our actions do not dramatically contradict the lessons we try to teach our children, for then the seeds of our lessons will be uprooted by the contrast that our actions present.

Fortunate in This World!

In seeking the best ways in which to influence our children, first and foremost our focus should be to plant trees of appreciation for Judaism. We want our children to develop a love for Torah and fine character, not only because it will bring them joy in the World to Come, but also because it brings them joy in this world! R'

Shach has told educators on numerous occasion that nowadays it is imperative that we make our children and students aware of how a Torah-loyal Jew truly enjoys *this world*.

> *A couple from South Africa once was visiting Israel, and came to see R' Shach. They gave the appearance of being quite religious — what we might refer to as ultra-orthodox chareidi. When they were brought in to speak with R' Shach, he began a long discourse on the beauty of Shabbos. He spoke of how the father comes home on Friday afternoon, washes and changes into special clothes; how the family members all sit around the table together, and so on. He spoke about the simple delights and benefits of Shabbos.*
>
> *The person who had brought this couple to see the rabbi was baffled. Why should R' Shach be telling such basic things to chareidi people? However, after they came out, the husband confessed that he was not a Shabbos observer. He said that, after this discussion, he felt he wanted to begin keeping Shabbos.*
>
> *Several months later, the husband wrote a letter explaining that his daughter had been on the verge of marrying a non-Jew, but since the father started keeping Shabbos, she began to enjoy it so much that she broke off with her non-Jewish boyfriend and was on the road to becoming observant.*

Types of Seeds

There are many different types of "seeds" we can use to plant trees of love for Torah and mitzvos. One is sharing our own excitement, enthusiasm and appreciation for religious matters with our children. Such feelings are bound to be contagious.

Everyone has specific aspects of Torah observance that he or she particularly enjoys. Some people especially love weddings, feeling there is no occasion like a Jewish wedding. If you feel this way, verbalize it to your children. They will feel your excitement, and high-quality seeds of influence will be planted. Perhaps you enjoy certain words of Torah. Tell your children brief parts of these Torah thoughts. They will absorb your enthusiasm for Torah. In our school, we ask the teachers to teach a book on ethics that they personally enjoy. Only in this way will they be able to make a strong impression when they teach it to their students.

If a child consistently hears his parents make statements such as, "I really enjoy the Shabbos table," or "I just love the peace and quiet of Shabbos," or "I feel so fortunate to be Jewish," he will grow up with a deep appreciation for genuine Judaism and he will have been "vaccinated" against all the adverse influences that can be found in the streets. Such a child has no need to look for substitute stimuli to give him pleasure in life, because he has "the real thing," and it is part of him.

Another way to plant seeds of appreciation for Torah living is through telling stories that stress the beauty of belonging to our Holy Nation.

> For example, the story of R' Yona Susna has inspired many young people with the genuine sincerity it demonstrates. R' Yona was neither a rabbi nor the head of a yeshivah, but was careful to give charity in a way that would not embarrass the recipient. When a certain wealthy person went bankrupt, R' Yona would have him come secretly to his home at 2 a.m. every Monday morning, when he would give him money. One week R' Yona was sick in bed with fever. Nevertheless, at the appointed time, he tried his best to pull himself out of bed. Using every ounce of energy he could muster, he dragged himself as far as the stairs, but there his strength failed him, and he fell down the stairs. It was discovered later that he had broken several ribs in the fall. His family, awakened by the noise, immediately called an ambulance. As he lay on the floor in agony, R' Yona called over one of his children, and asked him to give the money quickly to the man who stood waiting at the door, so that he would be able to leave before the ambulance arrived, and he would not be embarrassed needlessly. These were the thoughts of a "simple Jew" as he was himself suffering in terrible pain.

It is important to stress to your children how special is the Nation of which they are a part. Let them know that the soul of a Jew is so holy that in a place where ten Jews are assembled, even if they are not praying or learning, the angels, in awe of the holiness, are afraid to enter.

> *Children would do well to hear about the non-Jew whose car was stalled on the roadside. He stood by his car wearing a yarmulke, and an observant Jew soon stopped to help him. They struck up a conversation, and the non-Jew admitted that he was not Jewish. He had noticed, he explained, that if one stuck on the road is wearing a yarmulke, it is almost inevitable that someone will stop to help him. He therefore decided to keep a yarmulke in his glove compartment in case he was ever in need of assistance on the road. Jews are the kindliest people on the face of the earth!*

> *On a recent fundraising trip to America, I experienced an extraordinary act of kindness. The family with whom I was staying hardly knew me. One night I returned to their home well after midnight. Although I had the key to let myself in, I found one of the family members waiting up for me, worried that I had not eaten. She was waiting to warm supper for me so that I could have a hot meal. "Who is like you, O Israel, one nation upon this earth!"*

Stories like these can have an especially potent effect if told to a child after he has performed an unselfish act of kindness. He will then be able to identify with the story even more strongly, and will internalize its lessons in a very meaningful way.

It is also important to illustrate to children, through *simple explanation*, and sometimes in parable form, how religious observance benefits us tremendously in our daily lives. (We do not do the mitzvos for the sake of these benefits, but realizing how much good they do us can strengthen our love for the mitzvos.)

One example of how observing the Torah offers us physical benefits is the Torah's prohibition against constantly becoming angry. This is one of many ways in which Hashem protects us: *The New York Times* published data put together by certain researchers indicating that chronic anger is one of the major causes of early death, possibly *taking more lives than cigarette smoking*, overweight and a harmful diet.

The use of parables is a very powerful way to get our point across. When the story is stated in very down-to-earth terms, its impact can be very great indeed.

The Correct Way to Teach Yiras Shamayim

The educator who spoke with the group of boys mentioned earlier — who found "Fear of G-d" to be so very depressing — addressed the same group with a question: "What would you say about a driver of a car who wants to be free and unrestricted? He doesn't listen to anyone and follows no rules; he changes gears improperly and at the wrong times. He moves the steering wheel in all directions and is always hitting the brakes suddenly."

Of course the boys criticized this driver harshly, saying that the only way to enjoy driving is to follow the rules of driving, controlling yourself and your car.

"That is exactly what Fear of Heaven is," explained the educator. Fear of Heaven helps us to control ourselves and our 'cars,' so that we can drive safely and securely through the highway of life, and enjoy every minute."

His message, expressed through a parable the boys could understand and relate to, hit home. "Isn't it a pity," the boys exclaimed, "that no one ever taught us about Fear of G-d in that way!"

Let us learn to avoid the pitfalls of *chinuch*, so that we can give our children and students a love of and appreciation for Judaism, planting within their hearts and souls the seeds of positive experiences and influences. They will then be able to grow strong trees of Love of Torah and Fear of Heaven, being loyal to Hashem all their days.

6

The Right Way to Fix It

The Quick Fix

On a recent visit to the bank on a particularly busy day, I was pleasantly surprised to find that waiting on a line in the bank need not always be a frustrating experience. I observed the following interaction between one of the bank personnel and a client. The worker was trying unsuccessfully to print out from his computer some important information that the client needed.

"I've been having a hard time with my printer lately," said the clerk, and he began to give the printer a good thrashing (i.e., a few hard bangs), hoping that in this way he would gain his printer's cooperation.

"You can't fix it like that," said the client. "You have to open it up and see what's wrong."

This brief exchange intrigued me, for the client's words rang true, yet I myself have seen an electrical appliance begin to work after I banged on it, when it had not been functioning as it should. Wondering why this should happen, I later called a neighbor of mine, who is an electrician and a whiz with appliances, to ask him about this phenomenon. He explained that when a wire or two are loose, knocking on the appliance can actually move them into place. Nevertheless, this tactic is rarely effective; most of the time, banging will do even more harm, throwing more things out of place. The real way to fix it, he insisted, is to open it up, look inside, and find the root of the problem.

We sometimes tend to react impulsively in an attempt to fix something, even though

(1) it does no good;

(2) it will probably do even more damage;

(3) the real way to fix it is to open it up and find out what's wrong.

How Can We Fix Anything Properly if We Do Not Even Know What Is Wrong With It?

This is the very question we must ask regarding the *chinuch* of our children.

One hyperactive child disturbed his class continually, and we felt the situation warranted further investigation. To this end we invited his mother to the school to discuss her child's problems (the father was ill at the time, and could not have participated).

"How is your relationship with your child?" we asked.

"Fine," came the mother's quick response.

"Does he act up at home?"

"In fact he does," his mother admitted, "quite often."

"How do you deal with it?" we asked.

"Well ... sometimes I throw him out of the house and lock the door. Even though he bangs on the door and screams, we keep him outside for as long as our nerves can withstand the noise. My husband has even had occasion to wrestle him to the floor when he's wild and out of control, just to stop him from breaking something or hurting someone." (The boy was almost 12 years old.)

"Has your son always been wild?"

"I guess it started around second grade."

"Did you ever take him to a professional to assess the situation?" we asked.

"Actually, we did," replied the mother. "He said that my son was born with a dysfunctional nervous system."

"Have you done anything about that problem?"

"No," came her starkly honest reply.

For years, this boy has been going through the motions of functional living, lacking the standard advantage of a normal nervous system. Is it any wonder that he is hyperactive?

> *Another parent was working with his little girl, who was having difficulty with her math at school. He tried every method he could think of to teach her the principles of subtraction, to no avail. Finally he took five apples, removed three, and asked her, "If I take away three apples from five apples, how many am I left with?" to which the girl replied in wonder, "Daddy, I didn't know that subtract meant 'take away'!"*

Children Believe Their Parents

Criticism ranks very high on the list of impulsive reactions parents have in their attempts to "fix up" a situation. But impulsive criticism does not help; in fact it can be most damaging. Criticism highlights faults, and tells a child that he is incompetent.

No matter what parents say, their children tend to believe them. If parents tell a child consistently that he is incapable, the child comes to believe himself to be incapable, and it follows that he *becomes* incapable. One author expressed this thought concisely when he said, "Whether you think you can or whether you think you can't, you're right."

R' Y.Y. Yaakovson cited a number of letters from a girl and her mother. The girl had serious emotional problems. She had absorbed her mother's many criticisms only too well.

> *When the mother was told that her criticism was damaging to her daughter's emotional state, the mother responded, "I'm surprised at your comments regarding my 'criticism' of my daughter. I criticize her to help make her better — not because I've given up hope on her, and certainly not because I wish to cause her to despair. Besides, I don't really criticize. I just sort of laugh at her failures with lighthearted humor. I don't think this can cause damage. She herself smiles when I joke about her failures.*

The daughter, on the other hand, saw her mother's criticism in an altogether different light, and wrote at length one small example to illustrate her feelings:

My mother likes things to be neat and orderly. Two days ago we had guests who stayed late. My mother had to leave for work in a rush, and had no choice but to leave the house a mess. I really felt bad for her — you should have seen the look on her face. I knew how she would feel if she would come home to the house looking like that after a full day's work.

I decided to surprise her, and I began to straighten up the living room. But right away I felt this feeling of despair coming on. The guests' children had made such a mess that I was afraid I would never be able to get the place looking neat again. I decided to go to the kitchen instead, and do the dishes. Maybe doing one thing successfully would give me the momentum to push further. I rinsed a few dishes and felt myself despairing once again. I knew I wouldn't get through them all.

My mother always calls me "The Beginner." She says that I always begin things but don't finish them. This time I really felt she was right. I felt as if I were hearing her voice inside my head saying, "Nu, Miss Beginner; have you managed to do anything yet?" I burst out crying. I ran to my room, fell on my bed, and just cried until my mother came home. I don't want to tell you what my mother said to me "jokingly" when she found me crying in bed.

A parent might counter, "Do you mean that I can't even criticize my own children?" In fact, there are healthy ways of expressing criticism that is necessary for children to hear. It is beyond the scope of these chapters to delineate what one "can" or "cannot" do; our purpose is rather to present some guidelines to make parents aware of what will help and what will hurt. Experience has shown just how harmful impulsive criticism can be. (It is important for us to bear in mind that we are all human and all make mistakes from time to time. Our mistakes do not necessarily destroy our ability to influence our children in beneficial ways. It is the consistent repetition of these mistakes, coupled with our refusal to recognize or to accept that we may have made a mistake that can cause irreparable damage.)

"Labeling"

One very harmful type of criticism is "labeling." One should refrain at all costs from labeling one's child negatively. Under no circumstances should a parent resort to name-calling, such as calling his child a "fool," "liar," "slob," "good-for-nothing," or any of countless other labels a frustrated parent may be tempted to use. One fine scholar I know of had to contend with serious emotional problems as an adult, as a result of something his mother once said to him when he was young. "You're *tamei* (impure)!" she had told him.

We cannot underestimate the damage a label can cause. Precisely because children generally believe their parents, a label can become a self-fulfilling prophecy.

> R' Yaakovson cited the case of a kindergarten teacher who was teaching his class about the evils of lying. He was explaining to them that someone who lies is not accepted by his peers, and he is considered despicable even in the eyes of Hashem. The rabbi noticed that one of the children in his class seemed to be staring at him intensely. Fearing that something was wrong, he moved inconspicuously closer to that child as he was addressing the class. When he was standing near him, he noticed that the child had turned pale and was shuddering.
>
> "Are you feeling okay?" asked the teacher. At this, the child put his head down on the table and began to cry uncontrollably. The teacher immediately sent the other children to the yard for a recess break. He then sat down next to the boy and waited until he calmed down a bit. Then he asked the child, "Why are you crying?"
>
> "I'm a liar! Hashem hates me! I won't be able to greet the Divine Presence!" he blurted out.
>
> "What do you mean, you're 'a liar'?" asked the rebbi. "Do you tell many lies?"
>
> "Y-y-yes," stammered the boy in response.
>
> "You're not so sure you lie a lot, right?" asked the rebbi. The child nodded that this was true. "So how do you know you're a liar? Who told you?"
>
> "My father and mother," said the boy.
>
> "But even if you've been a liar until now, there's still no reason to cry," said the rebbi. "You can just stop lying."

"I can't stop lying," said the boy, trying hard to make his rebbi understand his situation. *"I'm a liar!"*

Let us not make the mistake of thinking that only young children react so strongly to the labels that are placed on them. R' Yaakovson discusses the case of a boy who was involved in serious criminal offenses involving theft and cheating. When he was young, his mother had often told him that he was crooked and dishonest. When he was older, as a delinquent teenager, the boy was asked if there had been opportunities for him to cheat or steal, when he had overcome his inclination and did not transgress.

He answered that there certainly had been such times, but he was quick to add, "That doesn't change anything. I'm a crook and I can't be any different. It's my nature, and that's the way it is!"

Positive Labeling and the Rebbitzen

Consider, on the other hand, the potential effects of positive labels.

R' Yaakovson tells of the well-known rebbitzen who used to offer her services to babysit so that mothers could run their errands unburdened. Once a woman brought her two sons to the rebbitzen to watch. While they were there, the older brother began to fight with the younger one, and threw an object at him. The object hit the glass that fronted the breakfront, shattering it. Of course, the older boy was terrified. The rebbitzen came into the room and, saying nothing, handed the boy a broom and dustpan. Later, when the mother came to pick up her children, the rebbitzen made no mention of the incident, and the boy did not tell his mother about it.

Not long after that, the mother brought her two sons to the rebbitzen's house once again. She did not feel uncomfortable about bringing both boys, nor did she apologize, for she was totally unaware of what had transpired on their previous visit. Upon seeing both boys, the rebbitzen said happily, "I'm so glad you both came!" Then, turning to the older brother, she continued, "You are a responsible boy and have experience. You can help me watch your younger brother. I know I can rely on you!"

After she witnessed the way in which the rebbitzen related to him, the mother began to tell her older son often, "You're a responsible boy; I know I can rely on you." These words worked wonders for the boy, bringing about a major transformation for the better. Much later, the boy told his mother about the incident of the broken glass at the rebbitzen's house, with all the details. When he finished, he said, "Mommy, when I grow up I want to marry only a rebbitzen!"

Finding the Root of the Problem

When something in our children is not "working properly," what we must do is to open the "machine," look inside and find the root of the problem (to quote my friend the electrician).

The key that can open our children up is *understanding*. If we try to understand our children with love, if we try to put ourselves in their place and try to picture what they are going through, we may begin to get a clear picture of the root of their problems.

Our great rabbis certainly understood children and knew how to respect their feelings.

> *Someone came to the Steipler to discuss problems he was having with his child. The Steipler told him to learn ethics with his child daily, using an easy book such as "Orchos Tzaddikim." After a time the father returned to the Steipler and expressed his frustration, for his son was not responsive to his attempts at learning with him. "I told my son that the rabbi said he has to learn ethics," the father lamented.*
>
> *"That's not the way to do it," explained the Steipler. "The way to approach your son is to tell him that you would like to learn ethics — for yourself — and that you need a study partner. Then ask him if he would be willing to learn it with you."*

Rabbi Dr. Abraham J. Twerski recounts an incident that took place in his father's house when he was yet a young

child. As young as he was, he was known to be a chess prodigy. One Rosh Hashanah a guest in the house, who was also a rabbi, cajoled the young boy into playing a game with him, which the boy won. The rabbi had told him that it is permissible to play chess on Rosh Hashanah.

The next evening (the second night of Rosh Hashanah), his father heard about the incident and called his son into his study. "I heard that you played chess on Rosh Hashanah," said the elder Rabbi Twerski, shaking his head back and forth in a show of disapproval and disappointment. The young boy absorbed his father's message fully. His father then turned to him with a twinkle in his eye and said, "At least you checkmated him, didn't you?"

Although his father was disappointed in his son and felt he had to teach him a lesson, he made it clear to his son that he understood him, and loved him in any case.

Listening — a Most Effective Tool

We may well ask how *we* can come to understand our children. What tool will aid *us* to open up our children so that we can come to see what is really going on inside them? In fact there is a most effective tool that we can use: it is the subtle art of *listening*.

Our great rabbis are — and always were — wonderful listeners. Certain incidents that I had the good fortune to witness have left lasting impressions on me.

One erev Pesach, I was in the office of a well-known rabbi who is the leader of his community. Everyone is extremely pressured on erev Pesach, but the pressure that a rabbi experiences at that time can be almost unbearable. Besides his own responsibilities, the burden of the community rests on his shoulders, and he must tend to many last-minute duties, such as selling everyone's chametz and answering questions and inquiries.

As I waited in the rabbi's office that erev Pesach, someone called him on the telephone with a question. After the first five minutes of the call, it became obvious to me that *this caller was a typical "nudnik" — one of those people who call the rabbi with even the most irrelevant questions, just to get his attention.*

The rabbi listened calmly and patiently for some 20 minutes, as the caller asked him one trivial question after another. When the rabbi finally hung up, unable to contain myself, I asked him why he did not simply hang up on this caller. "Who has time for such things on erev Pesach," I asked. The rabbi looked at me and replied, "But he was also created in the image of G-d!"

Another time, at the home of R' Chaim Kanievsky (the Steipler's son), I was discussing an urgent matter with the rebbitzen (who is the daughter of R' Elyashiv). While we were speaking, the rebbetzin received an "important" phone call. Over the phone, the rebbitzen repeated a strange set of phrases again and again: "Yes, nothing will happen to you. Not today and not tomorrow; not here and not anywhere. To others it might have happened, but to you it won't happen. Nothing will happen to you; everything will be fine." This went on and on for over a quarter of an hour, with the rebbitzen listening and then repeating: "... It happened to others, but it won't happen to you; not here and not anywhere; not today and not tomorrow."

When she hung up, I asked her about the strange scene I had just witnessed. She explained that the unfortunate woman with whom she had been speaking is very nervous and is frightened by dreams. The rebbitzen listens to her and tells her that everything will be fine and that she has nothing to fear. The woman is not reassured until the rebbitzen goes through the whole litany of comforting phrases. "When I speak to her," she told me, "it usually helps for a few hours." I understood that this woman calls the rebbitzen often, and each time the rebbetzin goes through the entire ritual of listening and responding, just to make the woman feel good for a few hours! (She does this even on erev Shabbos, when she is involved in cook-

ing for Shabbos and has a house full of people, many of whom are likewise waiting to speak with the rebbitzen.) How fortunate are we to be part of this holy Nation, among such giants!

These acts of listening to people who are not entirely stable, when we are under extreme pressure, require character traits that are almost superhuman, and might be beyond our abilities. Listening to our own children, however, under normal, everyday circumstances, is not beyond our abilities. If you listen to your children with love, trying genuinely to understand them, you will be amazed at how much you will learn about them. Your children will *open up* to you, giving you a very clear picture of what is going on inside. Then you will be able to get to the *root* of things, and to fix the problem, with the help of Hashem.

Make It Safe for Them to Open Up

However, a word of caution is in order: A child may be afraid to open up to his parents for fear of their reaction. He may be afraid of their anger or of some punishment that may follow any revelation he makes to them.

> *In one tragic case that came to my attention, a child had been accosted by a stranger and abused. When she arrived home, her parents greeted her with anger, screaming at her, "Why are you late? ... How many times have we told you to come home early?" and other such critical remarks. At that moment the child, already in a deep state of trauma, could not bring herself to open up to her parents, and simply went to bed. Her parents found out what really happened only much later, when they took the child for professional counseling for complex problems that had resulted from the trauma she had suffered.*

Listen carefully to your children and do not be quick to punish. Even if a word of reprimand is necessary, express the reprimand in a way that will allow the child to realize that you truly understand him. This will keep the lines of communication open, and will enable your children to confide in you and to seek your help — even in matters where they might otherwise keep their feelings to themselves.

A teenager whom I had the opportunity to interview explained to me how children leave religion. (This boy happens to have many friends who have been turned off to religion and who have confided in him, so I consider his opinion to be fairly authoritative.) Children need and want their parents' help and guidance, he remarked, especially when they start to get into trouble. Yet too often, when they try to speak openly with their parents, the parents respond only with anger and punishments. This accomplishes nothing, as the children do not curtail their undesirable behavior as a result of their parents' strict response; on the contrary, they continue their activities, but, having experienced their parents' reactions, they learn to do things behind their parents' backs and without their consent. Eventually, they reach a point of no return.

We are our children's greatest allies. They need us to understand them and guide them. If we truly listen to them, they will turn to us. If we turn them away, to whom will they turn?

It is only this attitude that will keep our children close to us, allowing us to give them the help and guidance they so desperately need, helping them to follow in our ways, and to remain loyal to Hashem all of their days.

7

To Believe or Not to Believe (in Your Children)

Everyone Wants to Be Good

The young boy gripped the bat, and as he prepared to throw his ball into the air he muttered to himself, "I'm the best hitter in the world." He then tossed the ball up, swung and missed. "I'm the best hitter in the world," he said again, and again he tossed the ball up, swung and missed. Several times more he repeated this ritual until finally he exclaimed, "What a great pitcher!"

The child's response may seem irrational, but it is nothing more than human nature in the raw. People will sometimes go to great lengths to justify their actions or their accomplishments, even if their justifications have no basis whatsoever in reality. "Under this coat lies a weary heart," said one man, "yet a kind one; one that would do no one any harm." Do these words evoke warm feelings of pity and empathy? They were spoken by one of the most notorious killers in the history of New York City.

These examples may be extreme and somewhat unsettling, but they demonstrate a very powerful force that is at work deep within the human soul: the innate drive of every human, created in the image of G-d, to *want to be good*. This drive — although it may not prevent them from debasing themselves with crime or other adverse behavior — causes the most depraved of men to see themselves as good people.

No matter how difficult a child may seem, no matter how vehemently he may appear to reject all our efforts to lead him along the proper path, there exists within every child the desire to be good. *Our greatest task as parents and teachers is to discover ways to reach and nurture that drive within each and every child. This is the essence of chinuch.*

Prayer and Effort: the Winning Combination

Chinuch has always been of the utmost importance. R' Wolbe said, "It is a mission of the highest priority; in fact the very continuity of the Jewish people depends upon its success." While R' Wolbe's words have applied to every generation throughout history, in our turbulent times they cannot be overstated. R' Chaim Kanievsky stressed this point on a number of occasions. "Nowadays," he said, "there is no guarantee that *any* child will become a proper *Torah observant Jew*, even if he comes from the best of homes. It is incumbent upon *everyone* to invest much effort and much prayer."

If we hope to bring up our children in the ways of Torah, we have no other option: it is crucial that we put forth the proper effort, and we *must pray for the success of our children*; and with the help of Hashem, we will succeed.

I myself have watched these miracles happen in a number of instances where children had broken away from their parents' influence, after the parents had despaired of their ever returning. Yet these parents never stopped praying; the many tears they shed for their children were sincere and powerful, and their prayers were answered: eventually their children came back to a life focused on Torah.

There is no reason for any parent to wait for a frighteningly serious situation to develop. It is certainly worthwhile to pray frequently for *each* of your children, and this need not necessarily involve sitting for hours over a book of *Tehillim* (Psalms). Short prayers, preferably in your native language, may be said often — while waiting in your car, waiting for the train, or standing on line (be discreet, however; do not allow others to see you "talking to yourself" — they may think that you are not quite normal) — thus transforming time that might otherwise be wasted into opportunity. I recommend that you pray for each of your children at least twice a week.

Ever since the first day I began teaching, I have not entered a classroom, whether to teach or to speak to the students, without praying. Countless times I have found myself in the most difficult situations, knowing that it was only the short prayers that I said before and during an incident that rescued me, my students and my career.

> *A friend of mine had been going through a most difficult stage with his mother; they had not been getting along well, and frequently she became upset with him. On erev Rosh Hashanah during that period, he inadvertently left the light on in his mother's room. His mother knew that she would not be able to fall asleep in the light and that her entire Yom Tov would be ruined, and she was livid. My unfortunate friend went outside to look for a non-Jew who would turn off the light, but all his waiting and searching proved fruitless. Finally, despondent and with nowhere to turn, he uttered a brief, despairing prayer to Hashem: "Hashem, please save me!" and just a few minutes later the light bulb in his mother's room burned out and the room went dark. Prayer can be effective in ways we may never have imagined. It is our refuge, our salvation and our obligation.*

Yet our obligation to put forth as much *effort* as possible to guide our children along the proper path is equally strong. So much depends upon our efforts; we must never allow ourselves to be lax when it comes to our children's *chinuch*. It is most helpful to bear in mind that the child with whom you are dealing was created in the image of G-d. He wants to be good, for this desire is inherent in the nature of every human being, and it is even more active in the holy soul of a Jewish child. A *tzaddik* of a previous generation, in order to infuse himself with holiness, would go to a yeshivah and ask the little children to learn or to recite *Tehillim* with great fervor. He would then walk back and forth among them saying that he was *immersing* himself in the holy words emanating from their pure souls.

How different is this Torah attitude from an attitude that is devoid of Torah! In a recently published book, one non-Jewish author said that parents must view themselves as *wild animal trainers*. He cited recent research indicating that there are only *three* children in all of America who respond properly to words and reasoning. (This can certainly inspire us to have devotion when we recite the blessing each day, "… *shelo asani goi.*")

The Slonimer Rebbe (in *Nesivos Shalom — Nesiv HaChinuch*) explains that the foundation of Jewish *chinuch* is that we must view our children as *diamonds*. It is our *belief in our children* that will carry them (and us as well) through the most difficult of times, for one need not despair if a diamond becomes dirty, or if its shine has been dulled. On the contrary, simply cleaning and polishing it will restore its natural luster.

Lasting Impressions

And because the *neshamah* is so holy it is highly sensitive. The influences that touch it leave a lasting impression. Even if it *seems* that our methods of reaching our children are not meeting with success, the effect they have on our children is actually very powerful, albeit imperceptible.

A group of religious mothers of children with severe brain damage visits the institution where their children dwell, several times a week. Each time they come they place yarmulkes and *tzitzis* on their children, and recite the prayers with them. When a worker questioned them, asking what purpose such actions could possibly serve, one of the mothers answered, "Besides the body that you see, there is a soul here that you do not see. It is that soul that I am helping!" We must never underestimate the capacity of the soul to absorb our positive influences.

> *I have a friend who has been highly successful in his efforts to rescue young people from cults and other deviant lifestyles. One set of parents hired him to save their son, who was studying to become a priest. My friend traveled out of town for this purpose, and spent a great deal of time with the boy. He approached the matter from every angle he could possibly think of, but after two weeks, he had made no headway at all. He returned home deeply disappointed over his failure.*
>
> *Several months later, answering a knock at his door, he found a young man wearing a yarmulke, his tzitzis dangling from his belt. "How can I help you?" asked my*

friend, scanning the unfamiliar face. "Don't you recognize me? I'm the priest you visited a few months ago," came the shocking response. Soon they were sitting together amicably, discussing 'old times.'

"None of your arguments impressed me," the boy explained. "But after all the time we spent together, one thought gave me no rest: I felt that you were truly closer to G-d than I was. This thought played on my mind continually, until eventually it brought me to see the truth."

Recognizing the powerful potential of our own influence, coupled with knowing that an abundance of Divine assistance accompanies all our efforts, greatly increases our chances for success. In fact, in all my years of meeting with parents, I cannot cite *even one instance* when I did not witness an obvious manifestation of Divine assistance as a result of parents taking a more active interest in their child(ren).

Realize How Unselfish You Are

Another point that can give parents a tremendous advantage in bringing up their children is cultivating an awareness of just how unselfish the parents really are. Do you ever ponder how much and how selflessly you have given to your children for so many years?

On numerous occasions over the years we have worked with groups of children to raise their awareness of their obligation of honoring their parents. Through many different exercises we try to help the children learn to appreciate their parents' efforts. We have often asked children, for example, to list all the acts of kindness their parents have done for them all through their lives, from the moment they were born. "Your parents brought you home from the hospital," we begin, in order to give them an idea of how activities can be broken down into details. "They feed you; they clothe you; they get up at night for you; they take you to the doctor. They give you emotional support; they give you a house and a room; they take you on trips; they pay your expenses; they do the laundry for you ...." The lists have eventually included hundreds of items.

We then go into still more detail, viewing a given action from various angles. We discuss how many times each act was done for the child: "How many hours has your mother spent in making you meals since you were born?" We try to calculate how much time it takes to prepare one meal. How much time does it take to go to the store to buy the necessary ingredients? How much time does it take to wash the dishes from one dinner? How much time does it take to prepare each vegetable — to peel and wash each carrot and potato, for example? Then we calculate how many meals a child eats in a week, and how much time is involved in preparing all the meals of an average week. Of course preparation for the Shabbos meals is in a separate category.

Sometimes I try to calculate with a group how much money the parents have spent on them during this year alone, and then we go on to calculate previous years, from the year they were born. Other times we try to figure out how much a full-time maid costs per day ... per week ... per month ... per year. We discuss the fact that Mommy does all the work of a live-in maid, but of course she does not get paid; she does not even get proper recognition for all her labors.

Whenever I lead a group in these or similar exercises, the figures we arrive at are *astounding*, and never fail to arouse in the children a deep feeling of appreciation for their parents.

You would do well to engage in these and similar exercises yourself, whether you write lists on paper or only think about them. It will awaken within you a well-deserved appreciation *for yourself.* Anyone who experiences all that the average parent goes through — the work and the aggravation, the pressure and the pain — surely can recognize how unselfish he really is! Parents must realize how very much they do for their children. Of course, there is always room for improvement, room for becoming even better parents, but no one can play down what he has already done for his children, nor should he.

Thinking thoughts such as these is *a great mitzvah*, and I consider it an obligation *for every parent* to do so.

When I was a teacher, the renowned educator, R' Noach Orlowek, advised me that every teacher must learn to pat himself on the back (that is, he must recognize his own accomplishments). This will give him the encouragement and the incentive he needs to continue putting forth his best efforts on behalf of his students, and to ensure his continued success. "If you don't do it for yourself, no one else will," R' Orlowek concluded. If this advice is important for teachers, who spend only part of the day with their students, how much more necessary is it for parents, who must tend to their "profession" 24 hours a day, and receive no salary in return!

To those who fear becoming haughty through this practice of patting themselves on the back, we say, "Recognizing what you've done brings to humility, not to conceit." I heard R' Wolbe explain that conceit results from *not* being happy with oneself. Often, someone who does not recognize his own strengths and the good things he does, and who does not feel good about himself, must construct artificial means by which to think highly of himself; that is haughtiness.

Encouragement Is the Answer

Giving yourself encouragement works wonders to make you a more effective parent. You could work wonders for your children as well by giving them large doses of encouragement, consistently.

R' Y.Y. Yaakovson made an amazing statement: "We have *never* come across a case in which encouragement did not improve the situation. Even if a child does not seem to react positively to encouragement, one should not conclude that encouragement is not the answer, but rather that it was not given properly." *Encouragement* (properly administered) *is the answer.*

We cannot underestimate the power of encouragement. Recently, a friend brought this story, told by a non-Jew, to my attention:

> *One day, when I was a freshman in high school, I saw Kyle, a kid from my class, walking home from school, carrying all of his books. I thought to myself, "Why would anyone bring home all his books on a Friday?" I had quite a weekend planned, so I shrugged my shoulders and went on. As I was walking, I saw a bunch of kids running toward him. They purposely knocked all his books out of his arms and tripped him so he landed in the dirt. His glasses went flying, and I saw them land in the grass about ten feet from him. He looked up and I saw this terrible sadness in his eyes.*
>
> *My heart went out to him, so I jogged over to him and as he crawled around looking for his glasses, I saw a tear in his eye. I handed him his glasses and said, "Those guys are*

wild animals. They really shouldn't be let loose on the streets." He looked at me and said, "Hey, thanks!" There was a big smile on his face, one of those smiles that showed real gratitude. I helped him pick up his books. As it turned out, he lived near me. I had never seen him before, because he used to attend a private school. I would never have hung out with a private school kid before. We talked all the way home, and I carried half his books. He turned out to be a pretty nice kid. I invited him to play football with me and my friends. We spent all weekend together and the more I got to know Kyle, the more I liked him; my friends liked him, too.

On Monday morning, there was Kyle with that huge stack of books again. I stopped him and said, "Boy, you are really gonna build some serious muscles with this pile of books everyday!" He just laughed and handed me half his books.

Over the next four years, Kyle and I became best friends. When graduation came around, Kyle was valedictorian of our class. He had to prepare a speech.

On graduation day, Kyle looked great. He was one of those guys who really found himself during high school. But at that moment I could see that he was nervous about his speech. So I smacked him on the back and said, "Hey, big guy, you'll be great!" He looked at me with one of those looks (the really grateful one) and smiled. "Thanks," he said, and walked up to the podium to speak.

"Graduation is a time to thank those who helped you make it through those tough years," he said. "I am here to tell all of you that being a friend to someone is the best gift you can give. I am going to tell you a story." Then I just looked at my friend with disbelief as he told the story of the first day we met. He had planned to kill himself over the weekend. He described how he had cleaned out his locker so his Mom would not have to do it later, and he was carrying all his stuff home. He looked hard at me and gave me a little smile. "Thankfully, I was saved. My friend saved me from doing the unspeakable."

I heard the gasp go through the crowd as this popular boy told us all about his weakest moment. Not until that moment did I realize its depth."

The friend then confided in me that he was in a situation that was nearly identical to Kyle's early high-school experience.

It happened around the time that I was in the Givat Shaul section of Jerusalem on the way to fix my cell phone. I noticed this friend waiting at the bus stop and I greeted him with a smile. "How are you doing," I asked. "Not so good," he replied. I politely acknowledged and continued on my way. I then stopped myself and an inner struggle ensued. One inner voice said, "Perhaps I should go back and show interest." A conflicting voice said, "You don't always have to be 'Mr. Nice guy.'" Thank G-d, my good inclination got the best of me and I went back. "Is there anything I can do?" I asked. "No, but thanks for asking," he replied. About a week later he brought me the letter containing the story of Kyle and confessed that at that particular time, while he was waiting for the bus in Givat Shaul, things looked so bleak that he was contemplating suicide. It was only the fact that I came back and took an interest, that caused him to change his mind. A small amount of genuine concern and encouragement saved his life!

It Works Even With Difficult Children

Encouragement proved a lifesaver in another way for one extremely difficult boy in our school (we'll call him Shimshon). His audacity would sometimes be beyond control as can be seen in an incident that occurred one year on Israel's Memorial Day. On that day, an air-raid siren is set off at precisely 11 a.m., and for a period of two minutes all traffic stops. Many drivers get out of their cars and stand at attention. Our students are inside the building at that time, but Shimshon wanted to see all the traffic come to a standstill. He ran out to the Shmuel HaNavi / Bar Ilan Street intersection. Much to our consternation, he caught the attention of some television reporters, who began to interview him.

"Don't you stand at attention?" they asked.

"No," the boy answered.

"Don't you care about the soldiers who were killed?"

"No."

"Is this what they teach you in your charedi (ultra orthodox) schools?"

"Yes," he responded, unruffled.

"You mean that your teachers don't care at all about the soldiers who were killed?"

"That's right," he answered proudly. (This is certainly not what we ever taught Shimshon or any other student who has ever studied in our school.) That night, this "newsworthy" interview was broadcast nationwide (although it is illegal for the media to interview a child under 18 without parental consent).

Anyone would consider Shimshon to be quite a difficult case. We worked with him patiently, using encouragement as our main approach. When Shimshon graduated from our yeshivah elementary school, he continued his studies in a fine yeshivah high school. Several months later, I came across him one night after a fast. He was still in shul 20 minutes after he should have broken his fast. I asked him what he was doing there, and he was loathe to tell me, but after I asked him several times, he finally admitted that he was waiting until 72 minutes after sunset to break his fast (following the opinion of the more stringent halachic authorities). More recently, Shimshon called me to say that he wanted to send money to the school to cover the costs of the minor damages he had made to the building when he had attended our school years earlier, before his turnabout!

The Results Can Be Amazing

In his book, "Kindness: Changing People's Lives for the Better" (Artscroll/Mesorah), R' Zelig Pliskin relates the following story, but he does not reveal whom the story is about:

I used to view myself as being uncreative. I remember the day a prominent neighbor told me that I was creative. "Yes, I did a couple of things that might seem creative, I argued against my own best interests. But I'm not really creative. And what I did wasn't totally original."

"Look at it objectively," I was told. "You have to admit that there were elements of creativity in what you did." He was correct. There were creative aspects in what I had done. And from then on I have viewed myself as creative. This has made a major impact on my entire life. I now feel an obligation to help other people discover their strengths the same way someone helped me find mine.

R' Pliskin is my friend and I consult with him often. He informed me (and gave me permission to repeat) that in this story he was describing himself and the change that was wrought in his life as a result of the encouragement he received. Before this brief conversation took place, he had published two books. Afterwards, he went on to write eleven more books, which have benefited the lives of thousands of people. I myself never cease to be amazed at his creativity. And it still amazes me that a few short sentences of encouragement can reap benefits for thousands of people.

Quite a few years ago, a student entered my class at the beginning of the school year with a 60 percent grade average. We encouraged him, and by the end of the year he had brought his average up into the high 90's. Just recently he presented me with a gift of a book on Jewish law that he himself authored. I keep it on my desk to encourage me to encourage others.

Twice in my teaching career, I made a major "mistake" in judging a student. Since as a matter of policy I do not look over students' records from previous years, I must draw my own conclusions about each student's abilities. On each of these two occasions, I had the mistaken impression that a certain boy was one of the best in the class. In fact, both boys had been major troublemakers the year before. Nevertheless, each of them rose to the head of the class, undoubtedly riding on my "mistake."

Actually, these two children had been outstanding all along, yet no one ever treated them as such, so they had not been living up to their potential. *Every* Jewish child — including yours — is outstanding. In fact, he's a diamond! With belief in yourself and in them, with sincere encouragement for yourself and for them, and with consistent, sincere prayers, you *will* have true *nachas* from them.

8

Lessons From a Palm Pilot

Peace of Mind?

"Improve your performance and peace of mind," said the ad. "You'll discover products to help you manage your life and pursue your dreams. Our mission is to help you experience happiness and peace of mind greater than you've ever imagined."

This advertisement promotes one of modern technology's latest innovations. Known as the "Palm Pilot," it is a compact electronic diary that can fit into the palm of your hand. It can hold more than 12,000 telephone numbers, five years of appointments, and a huge amount of additional data.

Just a few months ago I purchased a palm pilot, anticipating that it would fill my need for a compact device that could hold the vast quantities of information I need to have always available at my fingertips. Besides, I am certainly interested in pursuing my dreams!

True to its reputation, my new Palm Pilot was extremely helpful, allowing me to store telephone numbers, appointments, task lists and a host of other information in one small gadget, which I could keep in my pocket. It simplified my life in other ways, too; once, for example, when I had to give a phone number to a friend who also has a Palm Pilot, I just held my Palm Pilot opposite his and *beamed the number into his machine.*

I might have thought that I was on my way to plenty of happiness and peace of mind, until last night.

After Shabbos I opened my Palm Pilot to locate a phone number, and was shocked to find that all of the information I had recorded there over the course of months — everything — was gone. An error inside the mechanism had caused my Palm Pilot to reset itself, automatically deleting all that its memory contained.

Luckily, I recently made backup computer files of the information stored in my Palm Pilot, so I was able to recover it. Nevertheless, at that moment it became perfectly clear to me that this device was not going to bring me more happiness and peace of mind than I had ever imagined. I learned the hard way that we should not believe every advertisement that comes our way.

Focus on the Results of Your Writing #1

Yet the most important lesson we can glean from the Palm Pilot is one we can learn when it *does* function as it should.

A special feature of this device is that one can have it store information by actually handwriting into it. Unlike other digital diaries that require one to type, the "Palm" has an option to write. One writes the letters in a small space on the bottom, and they appear on the larger screen above, as if they had been typed.

This feature is a boon to those who are accustomed to writing with pen on paper, although it is not exactly the same. In order to write into it, one must learn to use the Palm Pilot's special "graffiti alphabet," for that is the only alphabet its computer recognizes. It is not difficult, and in a short time anyone can master the Palm Pilot, and be able to write to his heart's content, just as he would with pen and paper.

But a word of caution is in order here: simply writing into the Palm Pilot is not sufficient. The person who is writing must make sure that the Palm Pilot is entering his characters correctly. While writing, he must keep checking to see that the letters he is marking down are the same letters that are being recorded on the screen. Many times, in my haste to get data into the machine, I thought I was writing the letters "j ... k ... p," for example, only to find that the machine read my letters differently, and on the screen the letters "s ... h ... o" appeared in their place. Obviously, I had deviated slightly from the correct way to write the special alphabet characters. The Palm Pilot is a very precise instrument, picking up my incorrect writing and reading it as something other than what I intended.

This is the main lesson we can learn from our friend the Palm Pilot: looking at what we are writing is not enough. We must focus on the *results* of our writing: what is being produced on the screen as we write?

Focus on the Results of Your Writing #2

Those of us who are blessed with children or students are writing all the time; we write on our children's hearts. And as we write, it is crucial that we focus on the results that are coming up on the screen. When we say harsh words, or when we withhold our encouragement, we are in fact writing. We are recording on our children's hearts that they are faulty; that they are not good; that they cannot succeed. Although we may think that we are helping them through our harsh criticism, for that is certainly our intent, that is not the message that comes up on their hearts.

I once had occasion to work with a boy who was suspended from high school. When he called his father with the "good tidings," the father reacted with patience and hope. "Don't worry," his father told him, "we love you. Come home, and we'll see how to work things out."

The boy, who had been anticipating a harsh reaction, confided in me that at that point he had been in the midst of a major emotional and spiritual crisis. He had already decided that, had his father reacted harshly, he would then and there have left religion altogether.

In his later years, R' Eliyahu Lopian said that he was sorry for *all* the times he had dealt harshly with his children. "*Mit kinder darf men gein mit guttens* — With children one must deal kindly," he said.

To fully appreciate R' Lopian's commitment to kindness, we must realize that all his life he worked intensively on the trait of anger. Even in his younger years, he never punished his children when he suspected that his own anger — rather that the true benefit of his children — might be motivating him. On one occasion, he waited two weeks before punishing his son, as only then was he sure that no trace of anger remained within him. Yet this spiritual giant expressed regret over all the times he had dealt harshly, and felt that his children would have benefited more had he responded to them only with warmth.

The Sewing Course

The following story that was told by the woman to whom it actually happened, gives us a glimpse of the permanent damage that harshness and insensitivity can cause.

"Sara, tomorrow we will buy you a new dress for Yom Tov," said the mother.

"Mommy, why don't you sew me a dress?" Sara asked her, trying to be helpful. "It's much cheaper."

The mother did not answer, for her mind was drifting back to her childhood years ... She was 10 years old and her parents had registered her in a sewing course. Little Rachel did not do very well. Precision and order simply were not her strengths. Of course her teacher noticed this. What proved a cinch for others would take her hours, and even then she could not match up the pattern exactly, but little Rachel was not one to give up. She worked hours upon hours, cutting and sewing again and again late into the night. Even though her dresses were not coming out right, Rachel knew that she was improving. She took her sewing very seriously and never missed a class.

As the course was drawing to a close, the instructor informed the girls that there would be a "final exam." Each girl was to make the nicest dress she could, and the teacher would grade the final result. Everyone took to the task; some students even created original patterns to impress the teacher. Rachel, however, chose an easy pattern, hoping to finish it successfully. She wanted to prove to herself and to the teacher that she could do it. Night after night, she stayed up late sewing, cutting and pinning. She pricked herself numerous times in the process, but she felt that the pain was a small price to pay for success on this project.

When the dress was almost finished, she realized that she had made a mistake in the measurements. Instead of despairing, she redid the entire dress, taking it apart and putting it back together again. Finally, at 4 a.m., the dress was finished. It certainly was not a masterpiece; it was obvious that it had been redone. Still, it was better than any dress little Rachel had ever made before.

When class began, all the girls lined up beside the teacher's desk, holding their creations. Some girls told the teacher how it had taken them only an hour to complete their patterns, but little Rachel was not fazed.

When her turn came, Rachel placed her dress on the teacher's desk. Noticing the dress' many flaws and the seams that had been ripped and restitched, the teacher commented, "Rachel! You're not a 'total' failure!"

At that moment Rachel felt as if a needle had pricked her heart. Never again did she attempt to sew.

"Mommy, why don't you learn to sew me a dress?" repeated Rachel's daughter Sara.

Pulled back to the present, Rachel answered her, "I can't sew; I just can't. You see, I was once hurt by something very sharp."

We Are Talking — What Are They Hearing?

Few things are sharper than words of criticism, which can leave their mark for a lifetime — to which Rachel can attest. Everything we say to our children is written in some form on their hearts. If we constantly criticize them and point out their faults, the writing that comes up on their "screen" is that they are failures, that they are incapable of success. Even if we intend to help them with our criticism, it is like writing the letter "s," while on the screen the letter "g" is coming up.

One boy I know of had gained a reputation as the class troublemaker. One year, however, he decided that he would turn over a new leaf. His Bar Mitzvah was not far off, and he wanted to try his very best to be a true tzaddik.

When the new school year began, he was enthusiastic in his pursuit of his goal. On one of the first days of school, as he was reviewing the Gemara diligently, giving it his all, his new teacher walked over to him and shouted at him in front of the class, "You're not going to make trouble for me like you did for your previous teachers. I'm going to see to that!"

That moment marked the beginning of a pattern of increasing alienation for this boy, and before long he left Torah life altogether.

It is critical for every parent and teacher to keep in mind that it is not enough to look at what *we* are doing. We might think that we are writing the letter "a," when in reality we are causing the letter "r" to show up on the screen. We must always monitor the "screen" of the child's heart to determine what we are actually writing on it.

A fine couple I know once approached me for advice on how to motivate their son. He was lazy, they said. All he liked to do was to lie around and read. When I spoke with the child, however, he claimed that his parents hated him, and that they constantly scream at him.

Of course this child's parents love him very much, but through their screaming and constant criticism, the result that came up on the screen of the child's heart was that they hated him.

If we want the screen of our child's heart to read, "I can do it ... I can succeed ... I'm important ... I feel happy with myself and with my life," then *we* must write these words on their hearts, through our words and actions.

Encouragement — What It Is Not

The words and actions that inscribe such feelings of confidence and security on children's hearts are those of encouragement and love.

It is important to understand what constitutes encouragement, but first let us explain what encouragement is *not*. Certain phrases that we may intend as encouragement can be just the opposite. "You could if you only wanted to" is not encouragement; it is rather a rebuke, for with words such as these we are reprimanding the child for *not wanting* to do what we expect of him.

"You did well this time — why don't you do well other times?" is not pure encouragement; it is encouragement accompanied by a complaint, and it can do much damage to a child.

"This is so easy, anyone can do it," is certainly not encouragement; in fact it is a criticism, for it points to the child's failure and highlights it, by showing how anyone *else* is able to perform this task so easily.

Encouragement —What It Is

What then is encouragement? In general, encouragement is anything — whether it takes the form of words or actions — that will empower the recipient to achieve more. It will give him the courage to strive and to push forward, and to overcome any obstacles he might encounter. Specifically, encouragement points out to someone the success that he is *already having*.

If we want our children to succeed, and to be happy and motivated in life, we must point out what they are *already doing right!* Especially in areas where children are experiencing difficulty, we must search for even the smallest measure of their success. By calling it to their attention and showing that we appreciate it, we are writing a powerful message on their hearts. We are writing, "I can do it!"

Writing such messages can result in truly amazing changes. R' Yaakovson cites two fascinating cases.

Encouragement and the Difficult Child

Pinchas almost never listened to his parents. After they would scream at him a number of times, he would occasionally do some portion of what they asked. The situation deteriorated to the point where his parents avoided asking anything of him unless it was absolutely necessary. They would then immediately resort to screaming; they knew that speaking with him was fruitless, so they did not even try.

Realizing that this situation could not continue, they sought advice. They were told to encourage Pinchas. This was no easy task, considering that they were dealing with a child who gave them nothing on which to base their encouragement. Yet they were determined. They looked for even the smallest indication of success in order to encourage him.

Normally, the hour when Pinchas' father came home from work was a time of reckoning. The mother would tell him all the antics Pinchas had pulled throughout the day. When they began their campaign of encouragement, however, they changed this routine. When the father came home, making sure Pinchas could hear her, Pinchas' mother said, "Pinchas behaved better than usual today. Normally I have to yell at him six times before he gets out of bed. This morning, he got up after I yelled only two times. I know it was hard for him and I'm pleased with the improvement. His father approached Pinchas, held out his hand to him and said with pride, "I appreciate your efforts."

Do not be deluded into thinking that from that moment on everyone lived happily ever after. On the following morning it took more than two screams to get Pinchas out of bed. But his parents continued to encourage him — that is, to look for what he was doing right and to praise him for it. "Yesterday you might have been more successful," they told him, "but today you also tried hard, and that's what's important."

These parents informed the rebbi of their plan, and he joined in their efforts. One day when the rebbi needed a monitor in class, he turned to Pinchas, saying, "Your parents are very happy with you. They say that you are really making an effort to change. You must be quite mature then. You're the man for the job!"

Two and a half years later, the parents could hardly even remember that they had ever had a problem with Pinchas!

Fear of the Dark

In another case, Yossi, an excellent student in the fifth grade, was afraid to leave his house at night. His father, describing his problem to the principal, said, "My son is a coward, and nothing can be done about it. I've tried countless times to help him, to no avail." When the principal asked what methods he had used to help his son, the father replied, "I've reprimanded him, embarrassed him, and made him feel very uncomfortable, in the hope that he would control his fearfulness. I've even called him a coward, so that he would prove me wrong. Sometimes I physically forced him out of the house at night."

The principal then spoke with Yossi. "Why are you afraid at night?"

"Because I'm a coward," came the quick response.

"What are you afraid of?"

"Arabs, terrorists … things like that," answered Yossi.

"Why aren't you afraid of these same things during the day? Is it because at night it gets dark?"

"Yes. At night you can't see what's going on around you," said the boy.

"That's very natural," said the principal. "Hashem gave everyone this fear as a gift, to make us more cautious at night. Our test is for us to overcome the pure fear, and to transform that fear into caution. You can do that by practicing."

"But I can't," Yossi insisted. "I'm a coward!"

"Do you ride a bicycle?" asked the principal.

"Yes," came the answer.

"But aren't you afraid of falling? Don't forget, you're a coward." Yossi smiled uneasily. "Think about it," said the principal. "You were afraid, but you practiced, until the fear turned into caution. That's exactly the way you can handle your fear of night. Do you keep the lights on in your room when you go to sleep?"

"No."

"Are you afraid?"

"A little."

"Excellent!" said the principal. "This means that you are a little afraid and a little not afraid. You've already overcome your fear a little. You've already trained yourself not to be afraid, a little. With patience, you can do even more. Every night when you go to sleep, repeat to yourself, 'I've already succeeded in sleeping in the room with the light off.' Keep telling yourself that, until you feel your success."

The principal then instructed the parents to turn off the light in the living room when Yossi went to bed, gradually increasing the time it remained off. At first they were to close it for a period of five minutes, eventually working up to 15 minutes at a time, leaving on only the small bathroom light. After a month, they were to leave the living room light off for the entire evening. He also instructed them to take Yossi out at night for a few minutes at a time, and to stand nearby. Gradually, they were to move farther away from him while he was outside.

Seven months later, there was no longer any trace of the problem.

The Entire Hospital Moved

Encouragement — pointing out what the child is *already* doing right, and praising him for it — can truly work wonders.

> *Rebecca suffered from a debilitating disease. By the time she was 12 years old she had lost the use of her legs. Although the doctors had little hope that she would ever walk again, Rebecca remained optimistic. Eventually she was transferred to a special hospital in San Francisco, where she underwent intensive therapy. It was there that she learned the art of imagery: as part of her therapy she was to imagine herself being already the way she wanted to be. She would sit in her hospital bed for hours picturing herself moving her legs.*
>
> *One day, as Rebecca lay imaging, her bed started to move, and she began to scream with excitement, "I did it — I'm moving!" What she did not know was that the entire hospital was moving; an earthquake was in progress! Yet after the event, no one was able to convince her of that fact. As far as she was concerned, it was she alone who had moved her bed, with her own legs.*
>
> *Eventually Rebecca regained the use of her legs and walked without any assistance.*

Messages of encouragement certainly write letters on the screens of children's hearts. These letters say: "I can do it; I will do it; and I will succeed!"

And who would not want this message to appear on their children's hearts?

A Heartfelt Plea

I turn to all parents and teachers with a heartfelt plea: Of course one must discipline! Of course one must be firm, but not all the time; not even most of the time! Most of the time we must literally shower our children (and students) with love and encouragement, especially considering what our children are up against nowadays!

> *I have a friend who lives in the U.S. who saves children; he literally picks them off the streets to work with them*

and bring them back to a Torah life. On a recent visit to Israel, he spoke to me about his work with 10- and 11-year-olds who grew up in religious homes, but who have been drawn into drug addiction.

He took me on a tour of one of the areas where Jerusalem's youth "hang out." He pointed out one spot to me where, a few days earlier, he had come across a former yeshivah student, drunk on the street. He engaged the young man in conversation, and eventually the boy opened up to him and told him how he had decided to leave his yeshivah values behind.

The student had been very close with a particular teacher. One Purim both the student and his teacher had become drunk, and the student opened his heart to the teacher, speaking to him about personal issues that were very meaningful to him. The teacher, however, lost patience with him and pushed him away. (One might say that it was only Purim; but is it ever only Purim?)

Devastated, this boy became disillusioned with all that his teacher represented, and he immediately began to distance himself from a yeshivah mentality. In the depth of his pain, the student told my friend that he did not believe that he or anyone else would put up with him — everyone would leave him, he said. My friend stayed with him through the night, listening and talking. "You'll leave me like everybody else did," the boy kept telling him. Again and again, my friend told the young man, "I won't leave you. I'll help you." At 4:30 a.m. he took the boy back to his room. When they arrived, the boy, overcome with emotion, hugged and kissed my friend.

Never turn your children away; never turn your students away. Keep them close to you always. Shower them constantly with love, and give them mounds of encouragement. Then they will remain close to you and close to Hashem, throughout their lives.

9

Keeping Your Children "Tied" to the Torah

Mashiach and the Egged Bus Company

Surely you must have heard that Mashiach will be here very soon! One person I know cited a recent turn of events as a clear sign that right now we are actually on the verge of welcoming Mashiach. Such an upheaval, he said, could indicate nothing less than that.

Some background information might help you to understand this comment. Here in Israel, the atmosphere is very casual as compared to other countries, where people relate to one another in a more formal manner. Even government representatives might be seen at public gatherings in shirtsleeves and jeans. In fact, I saw a picture of one of Israel's former prime ministers sitting in his study wearing shorts!

Of course there are advantages to this lifestyle. Someone traveling on a bus here can automatically feel at home. Entering the bus, he will come across tens of people carrying on lively conversations, interacting in a most friendly, if not necessarily quiet, way (unlike in other countries, where people tend to sit quietly and keep to themselves on buses). You might say that Israelis infuse the country with a generally warm feeling.

This system has its disadvantages as well. Years ago, when I was traveling on a city bus in Haifa, the bus became increasingly crowded as it proceeded on its route. Before long, the passengers were packed together most uncomfortably. One of the passengers shouted out at the driver, "How long will you leave us packed in here like sardines?!"

The bus driver did not particularly appreciate this "friendly remark." He countered with some inferences about the passenger. "You are a _____," he said, "and your father is also a ." There ensued a screaming match between the two, which escalated until the passenger promised to teach the driver an important "lesson" after the bus reached the end of the route. At that point the bus driver, altogether disgusted, turned off the main road, taking a detour to some destination, as yet unknown to us. The confused, helpless passengers were in a state of turmoil, until finally the driver brought the bus to an Egged bus depot and got out. "I'm not driving this bus," he said, and left us all to our fate.

Fortunately, a solution was found within a short time and, as I remember, another driver was dispatched to resume the route. Nevertheless, it was obvious to me that informality is not always advantageous.

As for Mashiach ... recently, the Egged Bus Company required of all its drivers to wear a uniform consisting of a solid-color shirt, matching pants and, yes, even a necktie (the necktie is not compulsory). No longer will you see Egged bus drivers in jeans, shorts or polo shirts. And, said my friend, if Egged bus drivers are wearing ties, Mashiach can't be far off.

Chanoch LaDor Al Pi Darko

In truth, we really cannot know how close Mashiach is. Yet we do know for certain that we are living in the times directly preceding the coming of Mashiach. Thus, we are witness to radical changes taking place at a very rapid pace, such as the great advances in technology, and, far more significant, the breakdown of values in secular society. A U.S. congressional study pointed out some of the shocking differences in the preservation of values in America between fifty years ago and today:

In the 1940's, the leading disciplinary problems in the public schools were: talking out of turn, chewing gum, making noise, running in the halls and littering.

In the 1990's, the leading disciplinary problems in the public schools were: substance abuse, suicide, robbery, assault and some other indecencies that are not appropriate for these pages.

In view of the dramatic changes that have taken place over the last half-century, we must realize that *extra effort* and *special techniques* are necessary to educate children nowadays. In the past, if these vital ingredients were lacking, it might not have made such a major difference in children's lives. Nowadays, however, they can be crucial, for in today's world situation true spiritual values are in peril. A secular author wrote, "I am convinced that if we as a society work diligently in every other area of life and neglect the family, it would be analogous to straightening deck chairs on the Titanic."

The Slonimer Rebbe writes in *Nesivos HaChinuch* that just as the verse tells us "*Chanoch lana'ar al pi darko* — Raise the child according to *his* own path," meaning that each child must be dealt with in a way that is suitable to his (or her) particular needs (*Proverbs* 22:6) — so too must we take care to "*chanoch lador al pi darko* — deal with each generation in accordance with its particular circumstances and needs."

The Mask

In addition to recognizing the tremendous trials our children are faced with, we must take into account the differences in individual personalities. People today are no longer strong and confident; many of them are soft and fragile, and they have a desperate need to be understood. Even those people who appear tough on the outside — especially children — are usually only wearing a mask.

The following composition was published anonymously:

> *Don't be fooled by me. Don't be fooled by the mask I wear. For I wear a mask, I wear a thousand masks, masks that I'm afraid to take off, and none of them is me. Pretending is an art that is second nature with me, but don't be fooled.*
>
> *I give the impression that I'm secure, that all is sunny and unruffled with me, within as well as without; that confidence is my name and coolness is my game; that the waters are calm, that I'm in command and I need no one. But don't believe it; please don't.*

I idly chatter with you in suave tones. I tell you every-thing, but really nothing, nothing of what's crying within me. So when I'm going through my routine, don't be fooled by what I'm saying. Please listen carefully and try to hear what I'm not saying; what I'd like to be able to say; what for survival I need to say, but I can't say. I dislike the hiding. Honestly I do. I dislike the superficial, phony games I'm playing.

I'd really like to be genuine, to be me; but you have to help me. You have to help me by holding out your hand even when that's the last thing I seem to want or need. Each time you are kind and gentle and encouraging, each time you try to understand because you really care, my heart begins to grow wings. Very small wings. Very feeble wings. But wings. With your sensitivity and sympathy and your power of understanding, I can make it. You can breathe life into me. It will not be easy for you. A long conviction of worthlessness builds strong walls. But love is stronger than strong walls, and therein lies my hope. Please try to beat down those walls with firm hands, but with gentle hands. For a child is very sensitive, and I am a child.

The Purim season is an appropriate time to apply this under-standing. One Purim I witnessed a phenomenal shedding of a mask.

I have known Chaim for years. He is considered a wayward boy, who has been bounced from yeshivah to yeshivah. Ostensibly, he seems exceptionally tough, and apathetic where religious matters are concerned. On Purim, though, when he became very drunk, I caught a glimpse of his real self, the self he keeps carefully hidden behind a mask.

That Purim, Chaim was pleading desperately for love of Torah. "Ani lo shaveh klum — I'm not worth anything," he cried. "I want only love of the Torah; that's all there is. I want Hashem to give me desire for learning Torah. That's what's important." And so he went, crying and screaming through the streets.

It seems that he is not as wayward as people think. If only his teachers could recognize who he really is. Chaim has always been a daydreamer and has a difficult time organizing himself and his things.

Keeping Your Children "Tied" to the Torah / 97

In school he was constantly berated for his daydreaming and his lack of orderliness. Eventually all the criticism took its toll. Yet on Purim (when so many others put *on* masks), Chaim's mask came off.

Tied to the Above

Bearing in mind the differences in people's personalities nowadays, and the fragility of human nature, we must accept that conventional methods of rearing and educating children are no longer enough. Nowadays, we must take strong, positive steps to see that our children remain TIED very strongly to Torah and mizvos.

> *I have a friend who visited Tzefas together with his father-in-law, who is not religious. While there, they paid a visit to the famous cemetery, where many great tzaddikim are buried, including, among others, the Arizal and the Beis Yosef. As they passed the Arizal's grave, my friend's father-in-law tripped and fell. The matter disturbed the father-in-law greatly, giving him no rest. He and my friend consulted one of the holy rabbis in Tzefas, who told them, "I can't tell you why you fell, but I can tell you that 'mi shekashur lema'alah, eino nofel lematah — someone who is tied to the Above does not falter here below.'"*

How can we "tie" our children to the One Above? *It is not necessarily our spiritual interactions with them that will accomplish this.* It is rather by showing them and expressing to them how important they are to us. There are many ways by which we can accomplish this. One way is by expressing our love to them. As simple as this may sound, it may often be neglected.

I asked one father who consulted with me if he expresses love to his son. "I'm not the emotional type," he said.

"It Won't Happen in Your House!"

R' Yaakovson describes a discussion one of the educators in Israel had with a group of boys who had left their Torah life behind.

> *The boys described the difficulties they had experienced in coping with the strong pull of the negative influences*

they had encountered. The educator asked them a very poignant question: "What can a parent do to help his child fight these influences? What can I do to ensure that it won't happen in my house?"

"It won't happen to you," one boy reassured him.

"What makes you so sure?" asked the educator.

"Because I know you well," said the boy, "and I know how you act with your children. You love your children very much, and you show them how much you love them. You hug them, you kiss them, and you aren't embarrassed to play with them. I'm very jealous of your children. To be in such a house is the greatest pleasure in the world. One who lives in such a house doesn't need all the garbage that the streets have to offer. We are in the streets, looking for a substitute, but the substitute is never as good as the real thing."

One of the other boys in the group remarked, "I'll tell you the truth. Even today, when I see a father hugging his son, my eyes fill with tears. I think that says it all."

The Power of Unconditional Love

A fellow named Lee is an expert at showing unconditional love, even to strangers. He created what he calls a "hugger kit," a package that contains thirty small red embroidered hearts with adhesive on the back of each one. He goes around to people offering them a little red heart and a hug. Through these simple acts he has become so well known that he is often invited to keynote conferences and conventions, where he shares his message of unconditional love.

At a conference in San Francisco, a local newsman tried to discredit Lee's success. "This may work here," he said, "in the conference room, with individuals who came to be here of their own free will, but it will never work in the real world. Try to give away some hugs on the streets of San Francisco."

A television anchorman threw him a great challenge. "Look, here comes a bus. San Francisco bus drivers are the toughest, meanest people around." Lee accepted the challenge. As the bus pulled up to the curb, he approached the bus driver saying, "Hi. I'm the 'hugging judge.' Yours has got to be one of the most stressful jobs in the whole world. I 'judge' that you need a hug and I'm offering hugs to people today to lighten the load a little. Would you be interested in one?" The 6'2", 230-pound bus driver got up from his seat, stepped down and said, "Why not?" The judge hugged him, gave him a heart, and waved good-bye. The television crew was speechless.

One day, Lee visited a home for the disabled. Together with several staff members, he went from ward to ward, and in the last ward, he found thirty-four of the worst cases he had seen in his life. The last person he saw was a severely disabled man named Leonard.

Leonard was wearing a big white bib, on which he was drooling profusely. Lee took a deep breath, leaned down and gave Leonard a hug. All of a sudden, Leonard began to squeal, "Eeeeehh, eeeeehh!"

The judge turned to the staff for some sort of explanation, only to find that every doctor, nurse and orderly was crying. "What's going on?" he asked the head nurse.

"This is the first time in twenty-three years that we've seen Leonard smile."

"You Make a Difference To Me"

The tremendous power of expressing and showing love cannot be underestimated.

One public school teacher in New York decided to give a tribute to all her students. She called them to the front of the class, one at a time, and told each of them how he or she had made a difference to her and to the class. Then she presented each of them with a blue ribbon imprinted with gold letters that read, "Who I am makes a difference."

Then, as a class project, she gave each student three more of the blue ribbons, and instructed the class to use the ribbons to show similar recognition to others. Students were to report back to the class on their experiences a week later.

One of the boys in the class went to a junior executive he knew and thanked him for his help in planning his career. The boy attached a blue ribbon to the executive's shirt, and then gave him the two ribbons that were left. "We're doing a class project on recognition," he explained, "and we'd like you to find someone to honor. Present that person with a blue ribbon, and ask him or her to use the other blue ribbon to honor someone else as you honored him."

Later that day, the junior executive went in to his boss, who was known as a grouchy fellow. He asked his boss to sit down, and he told him that he admired him deeply. He asked if he could place the blue ribbon on his jacket. Surprised, his boss said, "Well, sure!" Then the junior executive gave his boss the extra ribbon. "Would you take this ribbon and honor someone else with it?" And he explained about his young friend's class project.

That night, the boss came home and sat with his 14-year-old son. "The most incredible thing happened to me today," he told his son. "One of my junior executives came in, told me he admired me, and pinned this blue ribbon that says, 'Who I am makes a difference,' on my jacket. He gave me an extra ribbon, and told me to find someone else to honor.

"I want to honor you. My days are really hectic, and when I come home, I don't pay a lot of attention to you. Sometimes I scream at you for not getting good enough grades in school, or for the mess in your bedroom. But somehow tonight I just wanted to sit here and tell you that you make a difference to me. Besides your mother, you are the most important person in my life. You're a great kid, and I love you."

The startled boy cried and cried, his whole body shaking. Finally he looked up at his father, and through his tears he said, "I was planning on committing suicide tomorrow, Dad, because I didn't think you loved me. Now I don't need to."

Children need to be shown love, today more than ever before, with actions and with words. Showing our children how important they are to us will certainly tie them to the One Above in a very powerful way.

Treating Children as People, Not as Objects

Yet showing love is not enough. We must also cultivate a *caring attitude* toward them.

> *A college athlete was in a major slump. He had been one of the greatest high school players in the country, "real pro material," everyone said. During his first college season, however, he was benched and moving down a road toward disaster. His coach was baffled. "This boy is the finest athlete I've seen in twenty-five years," he said. "Not only that, he's also by far the smartest kid on the team. He has it all, yet he's not functioning." The coach went on to say he had tried everything. Experts were called in to speak to the athlete.*
>
> *When he was questioned, the boy revealed his true feelings. "The coach treats me like an object, not like a person. He doesn't care about me; he isn't interested in understanding me. He just knows that 'we've got to get this boy playing ball.'"*
>
> *The therapists who spoke with this athlete began to understand what was really bothering him. This, combined with a little guidance, saw the athlete out of his slump, and by the following day he was already performing well.*

We must look at *everyone* not as objects, but as people. We must likewise see our children as people, not just as objects. There is no interaction with an object. Relative to an object, our only considerations are our own desires and goals, and how to fit the object into the scheme of achieving our goals. In dealing with people, however, we must also take their feelings into consideration.

Strengthening the Parents' Position

This does not imply that children are to be considered equal to adults. Nor does this approach weaken in any way a parent's authority. On the contrary, when a parent treats a child in a respectful (as opposed to a condescending) manner, the child will have more respect for his parent. When a parent takes his child's feelings into consideration, the child will automatically be more considerate of his parent's feelings.

Do not make the mistake of thinking that taking feelings into consideration means giving in to a child's feelings. It means only that we must care about our child's feelings and consider them before making our own decisions. At times, just listening to and understanding a child is enough to make him feel that you care, even if you do not do anything more than that. Knowing that someone cares is itself therapeutic.

> *Once when a mother was suffering from laryngitis, her young son came crying to her after his friend had hurt him. All she could do was hug him, since she could not speak. She was filled with frustration over the fact that she could not talk to him and give him guidance. After a minute or two, however, her son, feeling completely better, said, "Thanks, Mom!" and ran off.*

The Key to Success

Our Rabbis certainly understood this concept of treating children like people. In his younger years, R' Yaakovson was apprehensive at the thought of embarking on a teaching career. As the saying goes, "A shoemaker steps on leather, a cobbler steps on nails, and a teacher steps on souls." He was hesitant to undertake such an awesome responsibility. He went to the late R' Yechezkel Abramsky to seek his advice. R' Yechezkel told him, "If you will fulfill these words of our sages, you will never have anything to fear: 'Yehi chevod talmid'cha chaviv alecha keshelach — The honor of your students should be as dear to you as your own.'"

Hashem Wipes Away the Tears From Every Face

Our sages were always careful to treat children with respect, seeing them not as objects, but as people.

> *R' Yechezkel Abramsky was an extremely busy man (as the leaders of the generation generally are). For health reasons, he would take daily walks through the Bayit Vegan neighborhood in Jerusalem, where he lived.*

During these walks, many distinguished rabbis would accompany him to discuss various matters of great urgency. On one of these walks, in the midst of an important discussion, R' Yechezkel and another rabbi passed a little girl who was crying.

R' Yechezkel interrupted his conversation with the rabbi, bent down to the girl and asked, "What's your name, little girl, and why are you crying?"

The hysterical girl answered him, "My name is Shoshana, and Miriam said that my dress is ugly."

"Well, Shoshana," said the sage, "you go tell Miriam that your name is 'beautiful,' and so is your dress."

The girl, beaming with happiness, ran to her friend. The other rabbi then asked R' Yechezkel what it was that he saw in this little girl's emotional issue that was more important than the urgent communal matters they had been discussing.

R' Yechezkel answered, "In the book of Isaiah it says: 'Umacha Hashem Elokim dim'ah me'al kol panim — Hashem wipes away the tears from every face.' It is therefore incumbent upon us to follow in His ways and to do the same."

The Prohibition of "Ona'as Devarim" — Hurting Others With Words

The incident that follows has been published in a slightly different version, however I heard it directly from a rabbi who knew the Chazon Ish personally:

The Chazon Ish was walking with a student in Bnei Brak when some children started throwing sand at the Chazon Ish. The student asked them to stop, and when they ignored him, he warned them in no uncertain terms that they would be punished severely. The Chazon Ish called his student aside and told him that he was transgressing the prohibition of ona'as devarim — hurting someone else's feelings with words.

"But I have to teach them," insisted the student.

"You are not the one who is responsible for teaching them," said the Chazon Ish. "Since you are neither their parent nor their teacher, for you it is pure ona'as devarim."

Although the student may have had a right to prevent the children from throwing sand, the Chazon Ish felt he had no right to frighten them and hurt their feelings in the process.

Our present-day rabbis also know this secret. R' Pam took this concept a step further. While speaking recently on the subject of *ona'as devarim*, he said that many children can be turned off from religion as a result of being mistreated verbally, either by parents or teachers, who use sarcasm or insult them in public. This is included in the Torah prohibition of *ona'as devarim*. Our only license to rebuke our children and students is that we have the mitzvah of *chinuch*. If what we say will not contribute to our child's *chinuch*, and will have only negative repercussions, then it is not the mitzvah of *chinuch*; it is the prohibition of *ona'as devarim*.

Indeed, the Torah itself teaches us to relate to our children as people, not as mere objects.

How different is this attitude from the attitude of those who are far from the Torah. One mother felt that she must treat all her children equally, so that there would be no jealousy among them. One of her daughters had very pretty, curly hair, while her other daughter had plain straight hair. In keeping with her philosophy, the mother took the first to the hairdresser, and had all her curls shorn off. The girl spent the entire day crying bitterly, and would speak to no one. Even today, as an adult, she has not gotten over the pain her mother inflicted on her. Such acts of cruelty are possible only if someone views a child as an object rather than as a person.

Some Practical Applications

Many behaviors are natural outgrowths of the attitude of treating children as people. When we make a policy of relating to our children in this way, we can surely tie our children to the One Above in a very strong way:

(1) Talk to your children in a respectful manner, using words such as "thank you," "please," "excuse me," "I greatly appreciate it," "would you do this," "it's my pleasure to give you ..." and so

on. Respectful words such as these will certainly cause your children to respect you even more.

(2) Do small kindnesses for your children.

(3) Do something for your child that your *child* considers important. Every child has certain things that mean a lot to him, whether it is a small treat, a prize, a new cassette, or even helping him with something that he wishes to accomplish. One mother was aware that her daughter was overwhelmed with schoolwork and extra-curricular activities, and had no time to clean her room; the mess had begun to accumulate. One day when the girl was not at home, her mother cleaned her room for her and left her a note: "From Anonymous, with love." When the girl discovered what her mother had done, she was tremendously appreciative, and could not stop thanking her.

Find out what your children like and what is important to them, and then try in various small ways to help them do it or obtain it.

A great fringe benefit will result from such actions. Your child will begin to feel that you are *on his side*. He will then begin to come through for *you* and listen to you much more willingly. When a parent asked me how to get children to cooperate willingly in doing household chores, I told him he must understand that everyone is a bit lazy. Nevertheless, I said, if he can show the children that he is *on their side*, and that he is out only for them, then the children's attitudes will change dramatically, and they will be out for what is important to their parents.

In our school we have successfully changed many students' lives and brought about major turnarounds, using this secret.

(4) Understand your child and his needs with true concern. Listen to your children. Find out what their needs are. While we do not necessarily have to give in to their needs, our sincere understanding of them and their needs is a great thing. It makes the child feel accepted. It makes him feel that you care.

This understanding can prevent many conflicts at home. For instance, if your child wants to do something or buy something that is not in accordance with your set of values, instead of just saying "no" and leaving it at that, say something like, "I really understand your feelings. You really want to look stylish." If such words are said with genuine sincerity, they can have a soothing effect on your child. Soon afterwards, you may add, "I really understand how you feel, but we are not allowed to wear such clothing."

I feel it is necessary to stress that this will work only if it is said *sincerely*. Your child must see that you understand him and genuinely care for his feelings. How vital are these attitudes in our turbulent times. "*Chanoch lador al pi darko* — deal with each generation in accordance with its particular circumstances and needs."

Encouragement for Parents

I would like to repeat a few words of encouragement: In a previous chapter we pointed out that an airplane is off course throughout most of its flight. It is only because the pilot keeps the flight plan constantly in view that the airplane reaches its destination safely. The ideas in these chapters are flight plans. Of course, one may not be able to keep to them all the time, but always keep them in view, and never sway too far from them.

Let us take a lesson from the Chinese bamboo tree. One well-known author described the growth pattern of this tree in order to give us hope. After the seed of the Chinese bamboo tree is planted, one sees nothing — absolutely nothing — for four years, except for a tiny shoot coming out of a bulb. During these four years, all the growth takes place underground, in a massive root structure that spreads deep and wide. Then in the fifth year, the Chinese bamboo tree grows to a height of 80 feet.

Follow the flight plan! Persevere! Pray! And you *will* see true *nachas* from your children and students.

10

The Power of Understanding

The "Shtiblach"

The modern world has filled our lives with an abundance of conveniences, easing the way for us in spiritual matters no less than in material matters, and leaving us much for which to be thankful. Many innovations have allowed us to function in ways that would have been inconceivable just a few years ago. Although this applies to all areas of our lives, the specific example that comes to my mind is the "*minyan* factory," or, as we call it in Israel, the "*shtiblach*." In many of these "*shtiblach*" one can find nonstop *minyanim* (quorum of ten men necessary for communal prayer) throughout the day. This is of tremendous advantage to people such as myself, whose schedules are unpredictable. As long as I can locate one of the *shtiblach*, I always know that I have not missed *davening* with a *minyan*.

> Nowadays, we are blessed with one or two of these "*shtiblach*" in just about every neighborhood in Jerusalem, and in many other cities as well. Not long ago, after a late morning minyan in one of the "*shtiblach*," I overheard an interesting dialogue. One of those who had attended expressed his dissatisfaction with the one who led the minyan. This chazzan had apparently prayed a bit too quickly for his tastes. "Those who pray in this minyan are not in any hurry to get to work," he said. "Anyone

who is in a hurry gets up earlier. This minyan is for taking your time to daven."

"On the contrary," another man countered. "The fact that it's late just puts me under more pressure. I must finish praying quickly so that I can get to my appointments on time, even though I overslept."

Who is right? A difficult question to answer, but I can understand both of their viewpoints.

The Drunken Man on the Subway

Understanding is a powerful tool, and can accomplish things that other, more forceful methods often cannot.

At a subway station in Tokyo a rather large, drunken man entered one of the subway cars. He was clearly in a rage, and most of the passengers were terrified. One young American, however, was not afraid, for he had spent the past three years in Tokyo studying martial arts. He jumped to his feet and seized this opportunity to save innocent people, while testing his new skills. He stood directly opposite the drunk, ready for action.

A fraction of a second before he could act, there was a shout, "Hey!" There stood a small Japanese man, well into his '70's. "C'mere and talk with me," he said, beckoning to the drunk.

The big man followed. "Why should I talk to you?"

"What have you been drinking?" asked the old man.

"I've been drinking sake [a Japanese alcoholic beverage made from fermented rice]... and anyway, it's none of your business!"

"Really?" responded the old man disarmingly. "Sake was it? Every night I warm up a little bottle's worth of sake and take it out into my garden. There I sit with my wife on an old wooden bench and gaze at the old persimmon tree. My great grandfather planted it, and as I look at it I wonder if it will recover completely from those ice storms we had last winter. I really love that persimmon tree."

"I also love persimmons ...," said the drunk, his fists slowly unclenching.

"Yes," said the old man, smiling, *"and I'm sure you have a wonderful wife, too."*

"No," said the drunk. *"My wife died."* He then began to cry uncontrollably. *"I have no wife. I have no home. I have no job ... I'm so ashamed of myself."*

The old man shook his head and said, *"Oh, my ... this is truly a difficult predicament. You must sit here and tell me about it."*

As the young American got off at his stop, he saw the drunk sitting with his head on the old man's lap, the old man softly stroking his filthy, matted hair.

Understanding can transform even a violent drunk into a civilized human being.

The Number One Challenge of Our Generation

Recently, I discussed this book with a well-known rabbi, and I explained that my main theme is showing love and understanding to one's children. He responded that this is the Number One challenge of our generation: to show love and true understanding effectively, not only to our children, but to our spouses and acquaintances as well. In fact, he stressed, this is the essence of the mitzvah of *ve'ahavta lere'acha kamocha* — love your friend as yourself.

I was surprised at first to hear this sage include one's children within the parameters of the mitzvah of *ve'ahavta lere'acha kamocha*, but it should not have surprised me at all. This thought was expressed long ago:

> There are people who are careful not to hurt anyone's feelings; in fact they treat everyone with love. Yet these same people hurt their own children's feelings, claiming that "this behavior is not sinful, since Hashem placed these children in my hands, and He compelled them to accept my discipline, as it says: 'Honor your father' .... And my intention, after all, is to discipline them in the

ways of the Torah." In truth, however, their words are not at all logical, nor are they in accordance with the Torah — for why shouldn't their children be included in the commandment of *ve'ahavta lere'acha kamocha*?

The truth is that hurting a relative warrants a more severe punishment, and therefore one who unjustly causes pain to his own child will certainly be punished more harshly.

(*Sefer HaBris* II 13:16)

Discipline Is Like Medicine

Indeed R' Shimon Schwab said that the Torah requires parents to be their children's best friends, to be their children's closest and most intimate confidants.

Let us not misconstrue this statement; a parent should not feel that he must never discipline his children. Quite the opposite is true: precisely because he is his child's closest friend, he is trying constantly to benefit his children in any way possible. His goal is to guide them in the correct path.

Children need boundaries and limits in order to ensure their emotional security and stability. They need to be *taught* self-control, so that they can grow up to be "Noble Jews." Under no circumstances should a parent give his children free reign, allowing them to do everything their hearts desire.

However, establishing and maintaining our children's boundaries must be done in a way that will *benefit* the child. It is the child's benefit, not our own, that we must keep in mind always.

An alarming percentage of parents are almost never at home. One set of parents I know of are constantly involved in their business, and attending social events, taking classes and doing acts of kindness. In the little time they actually spend with their children, most of their interactions are of a disciplinary sort. They sent their son to a therapist, as he was not listening to them. These parents obviously do not have their child's benefit in mind. It seems that their child is an obstacle to their lives, standing in the way of their many endeavors. To accommodate the parents' needs, their child must simply stay calm and cooperate, so that they can carry on their flurry of activities that keep them away from home so often, without having to pay the price. These parents are certainly not fulfilling their responsibility of being their child's best friend. It is no wonder that the child requires therapy.

Discipline is like medicine. Parents whose entire relationship with their children consists of disciplining them can be compared to parents who feed their children nothing but medicine. Would we expect a child who is nourished in this way to grow up problem-free?

Taking Their Feelings Into Account

If our sincere desire is to help our children, we must spend time with them. We must get to know them and get to know what they are feeling. Our acquaintanceship with them and with their emotional needs is imperative for their well-being.

In our turbulent times, spending time with our children can be critical; it may have a life-and-death effect on their spiritual development. A child who enjoys a close, open relationship with his parents is far less likely to be attracted by what the streets have to offer. As we mentioned earlier, one boy who had succumbed to the influences of the streets said, "Someone who has the real thing does not need to search for substitutes."

Of course there are pressured times, when children get out of hand, or times when they will deliberately test the limits their parents set for them. At such times a strong dose of discipline may do the trick. Nevertheless, we must realize that this is nothing more than first aid, and should be administered only as an exception to the rule.

As a rule, every parent must take his child's feelings into account before he disciplines, bearing in mind that discipline is a strong medicine. Has any doctor ever prescribed medicine or administered treatment before checking thoroughly to determine what is wrong with his patient?

As our children's best friends, we want only to benefit them with our discipline. This being the case, we must first know what they are feeling; only then can we properly assess the situation.

> I know of one father who wanted to teach his daughters to excel in self-restraint. He would allow them to read mystery novels, and would note when they had read a good portion of the book. Then, when they were deep into the plot, he would take the book away from them for a short while. This is only one example of the systematic methods

he would employ to frustrate his children for the purpose of teaching them to overcome their desires. This parent was clearly not taking his child's feelings into account at all. In fact, he was administering a "medicine" that is far too strong for many adults to take. The adverse results in his children were not long in coming. The anxiety and insecurity that had been imposed upon them led them to develop bizarre habits, and they became unmanageable in many ways.

The practice of always taking our child's feelings into account, or, more accurately stated, understanding our children, begs the question: If I have no idea what my child is feeling, how can I take his feelings into account? If I have no idea *why* he is doing something wrong, how can I react accordingly?

The answer is that we are obligated to *develop* a strong connection with our children. By spending time with them on a regular basis, and by showing them understanding, rather than anger or frustration, the lines of communication will start to open up, and we will come to understand more about our children than we ever thought possible.

Once we begin to understand our children, we will be able to help them in many effective ways. When a parent truly understands his child, relating to his child with love and care, he may be surprised to find that discipline or force may be totally out of place. One who does not understand his child, on the other hand, will likely make serious mistakes.

Recently a teacher who is a friend of mine showed me a note that a boy had brought him to class. The note, apologizing for the fact that the boy had come late to school, was "signed" by the boy's mother. It was perfectly obvious that the note was forged. The handwriting showed a childlike lack of coordination, the letters were inconsistent and there were basic spelling mistakes that an adult would never make.

The teacher was about to react harshly, but a moment's reconsideration made him decide to investigate first. He called the boy's mother, who verified that indeed she had written the note herself. Coming from France, she had moved to Israel only recently, and bare-

ly knew Hebrew, which was clearly reflected in her handwriting and spelling.

Early in my career I made a major blunder that I will never forget, the consequences of which left an indelible impression on me. Once during my first year as principal, when a teacher was absent, I stepped in to teach his class. I remember thinking how terribly important it was that I make a strong impression on the students. As the saying goes, one never has a second chance to make a first impression.

> *As I was teaching, I noticed one of the students whispering to his neighbor. I decided on the spot that this was a most serious matter which I must not overlook. If the students do not have proper respect for their principal in the beginning, things will just get worse as time goes on. Determined to lay down the law, I called the boy up to my desk and chastised him severely for his disrespect. There is no doubt that, in my overly conscientious zeal to set things right, I overdid it. (I no longer resort to such tactics, but to my regret, and his misfortune, I had to learn the hard way.) Terrified, the boy ran out of school. I sent some boys to look for him, but to no avail; he was long gone.*
>
> *It was then that some of the students approached me to explain, with as much respect as they could muster, that this boy had only recently moved to Israel from Australia, and could neither speak nor understand Hebrew. He had been seated next to a boy who speaks English, and was asking him to translate what I was saying.*
>
> *Naturally, the boy's mother was livid when she heard about the incident, and her totally justified fury added to my own remorse.*

Can we ever discipline properly without knowing the whole story? Can we punish if we are not aware of what our child is feeling inside?

If we are our children's best friends — and of course we are — then we must think in terms of how we can help them, and we cannot *truly* help them unless we understand them. For how can we fix anything if we do not know *why* it is not working properly?

Many years ago, every night at 10 p.m., a public notice would be broadcast over the media saying, "It's 10 o'clock. Do you know where your children are?" This public notice may be revised for our turbulent times: "Mashiach is coming. Do you know *who* your children are?"

Stealing

A father approached me to discuss his son, who had been stealing from him on a regular basis. Naturally the father was upset about the fact that his son was stealing, but he was far more upset about the fact that his son was lying about it to him. This father is a paragon of truth, and he tried his best to instill this trait in his children. He would constantly tell his children stories stressing the value of speaking the truth, but the message did not seem to be getting through.

I told the father that in order to help his son, he must understand his son's feelings. Why is he stealing? Only once you understand why things are wrong do you have a chance of fixing them. A quick discipline "fix" is not the answer. I know of children who stole because their parents were neglecting them — the children themselves told me this, years later when they were young adults. I advised this father that he must develop a close, open relationship with his son, a relationship in which his son feels close and wishes to confide in his father, one in which the son is not afraid to open up to his father.

A short time later, the father told me that he had taken his son out for the evening, and had spoken to him about all sorts of "unimportant" matters. The son had a grand time, and so did his father. Again and again throughout the evening, the son asked his father in disbelief, "Dad, what did I do? Why did you take me out?" And his father would answer him, "I wanted to spend time with a very close friend of mine."

This report moved me almost to tears. If this father will continue to spend time with his son on a consistent basis, they will develop a very close relationship, and I can guarantee, *b'ezras Hashem*, that the boy will no longer steal from his parents, and he will never lie to them.

Forge a Bond With Your Children

The way to cultivate a close relationship is to spend time with your children. Take walks with them; talk to them; but more important, *listen* to them. Get to know them — their likes and dislikes, their feelings and opinions. R' Noach Orlowek cites *Rashi* in *Bereishis* (18:19), which states that if a person cares for someone, he draws him near and makes the effort to get to know him intimately.

Getting to know our children does not require any extreme measures. Spending even 15 minutes with each child individually can be enough, but one must spend this time with each child on a *consistent* basis, at least once in two weeks.

One father I know learns with each of his children for only five minutes a day, but they spend those five minutes learning something the child enjoys, and when the five minutes are up, they continue to sit together, simply chatting. In this way he maintains a close connection with each one.

Yet this connection need not necessarily be forged through learning, as we saw in the case of the renowned educator who took each of his children individually out for pizza regularly. One of his sons was a wayward boy. I knew the boy personally, and I was seriously concerned about his future. His father's close connection with him paid off, however, for today this boy is a fine student, excelling in a top yeshivah.

You Are Your Child's Only Parents

Unfortunately, not all parents are aware of the importance of developing close relationships with their children. One father, whose son was experiencing serious emotional problems, was advised by experts to spend some time exclusively with his son. "Take him to the zoo," they said. The father took his son to the zoo twice, but no improvement was forthcoming. When he was asked what he does during those trips to the zoo, the father replied that he learns from a Gemara he takes along, so that the trip not involve wasting time from Torah learning.

This father did not realize that maintaining a relationship with his child is a mitzvah that no one else can fulfill. This boy has no other father or mother to take him places. He has no other parent with whom he can develop a close relationship. And if the boy's own parent does not provide this connection, the boy will grow up never having had it at all.

In our turbulent times, such a connection between parent and child is "like a barrier to ward off disaster." Parents who develop such a connection with their children are protecting them against countless negative influences. They are saving their children from seeking substitutes for the warmth they need so desperately; their children will not need any substitutes, because they will have the *real thing*. Their parents are their true *closest friends*.

Yom Tov Preparations

Yom Tov — what a perfect time to begin building a stronger relationship with our children. Spend time with your children, and enjoy their company. Enjoy their company when the family is together, and enjoy their company when you are alone with them. If you do not find a holiday to be such a pleasant time, then *plan* it, so that it *will* be a pleasant and enjoyable time for you and your family. Plan it so that the outings you go on will be enjoyable for all of you. Plan it so that the meals will be enjoyable for you *and* for your children.

Take the Yom Tov of Pesach for example. We plan so many things relating to Pesach — the cleaning, the shopping, the matzah baking, the Seder arrangements — shouldn't we also plan the holiday so that it will be an enjoyable time for us and for our children? Shouldn't we plan it so that it will be a time during which we can develop a truly close connection with those who are most precious to us? If *we* do not do it for our children, no one else will.

In our turbulent times, this is imperative. It is certainly our obligation — to be our child's best friend.

11

Effective Discipline for Our Times

The Spoiled Brat

"The information in this book has been researched carefully, and all efforts have been made to ensure accuracy. The author and publisher assume no responsibility for any injuries suffered, or for damages or losses incurred during or as a result of following this information. All information should be carefully studied and clearly understood before taking any action based on the information in this book."

This disclaimer was printed on the inside cover of a recently published book. Its subject: how to avoid overindulging one's child. In modern society, where overindulgence is often considered acceptable, and may even be encouraged, and where effective discipline is a rare commodity, we encounter a phenomenon known as "the spoiled brat."

The author of the above mentioned book describes one of his siblings who has been so lavishly indulged that today, at the age of 40, he cannot tolerate any external noises or any discomfort when he is trying to sleep. He sleeps under a deluxe electric blanket accompanied by a sound machine that cost hundreds of dollars, which simulates Victoria Falls during the rainy season. The author, in a tongue-in-cheek attempt to empathize with the "poor soul," suggests that perhaps someone should invent a tubular device connecting his bed to the refrigerator, so that this 40-year-old "baby" would be able to enjoy "overnight feedings," giving him a feeling of total security.

On the topic of indulging one's whims, R' Eliyahu Lopian asked what it is that differentiates human beings from animals. Is it that aspect of free will that gives one the freedom to choose to do what one wants? Surely that cannot be the difference, explains R' Lopian, for an animal can certainly do what it wants; if an animal wants to eat, it will eat. What then is the difference? R' Lopian insists that what distinguishes a human being is his ability to choose *not* to eat what he wants, for an animal is not capable of abstaining from pursuing its desires. An animal *must* do what it wants; it has no choice in the matter!

How vital is it then that we learn the fine art of self-discipline, for this is the very quality that distinguishes man from animal. And how vital is it that we communicate the principles of discipline and structure to our children, so that they can grow up to be "mentchen" — decent human beings.

Nevertheless, it is not uncommon to find parents who do not discipline their children at all. Not long ago, a friend told me about a problem he was having with his neighbor, who lived directly upstairs from him. This neighbor's 9-year-old girl had taken to entertaining herself by throwing garbage onto my friend's porch. The problem involved more than my friend's aesthetic sensitivities, for his children were getting hit by the garbage that was thrown. When he complained, his neighbor listened sympathetically, but was powerless to help him; he simply was unable to prevent his own child from throwing garbage at his neighbors. At that point my friend turned to me for advice.

An acquaintance of mine related how he had observed children in one family hitting, biting and scratching their parents. When this would happen, the parents would sometimes ask their children to stop, a gentle request that was often ignored. "What can I do?" the beleaguered parents would say with a sigh, "that's the way the children are nowadays."

In the secular world, things are totally out of control.

> *A millionaire and his wife who live in Tel Aviv allowed their 11-year-old child to invite some friends over for a small party. The parents agreed to give the child the run of the house while they took their youngest along with them to visit some relatives, telling the children that they would return around 11 p.m.*

They came home a bit earlier than they had expected. It was about 10:45 when they knocked on the door of their home, and heard their child's voice asking, "Who is it?"

The parents, who were feeling the strain after a long day (and night), identified themselves and asked to be let in. In a fit of anger, the child shouted at them through the locked door, "You lied! You said you would be back at 11 o'clock. You better not come in — I'm calling the police if you don't leave now!"

Exhausted, the helpless parents returned to their car with their infant son, and there they waited until 11 o'clock, when they were permitted to enter.

The following morning, the father had a business meeting with a religious man in Bnei Brak, who happened to have brought his son along. The millionaire was astounded at the extreme respect this boy showed his father. "How did you manage to teach your son such beautiful behavior?" he asked the father.

"Our Torah teaches 'Kabed es avicha — Honor your father.' This is what our children are taught in their schools, and this is the way we live." From that moment on, the millionaire took an intense interest in his faith.

It is imperative that we not allow ourselves to succumb to the influence of an overly permissive society. We must teach our children limits. We must give our children structure. We *must* discipline our children!

Yet I am reminded of the book's disclaimer. We must be ever so cautious to avoid the countless injuries or damages that are liable to be incurred through administering discipline improperly.

Prerequisites for Effective Discipline

"*Chanoch lador al pi darko* — Deal with each generation in accordance with its particular circumstances and needs." In our generation, where so many children are leaving the path of Torah, we must carefully reevaluate our approach to discipline. Methods that may have worked in previous generations are ineffective for our generation. In fact, methods that worked for our parents or grandparents might have the exact opposite effect if we attempt to use them with our children. However, certain principles apply universally to *chinuch*.

The first prerequisite for all discipline is that one maintain a warm, loving relationship with one's children, a relationship in which parent and child share a feeling of *mutual trust*. With such a relationship, a child will be willing to accept his parents' discipline, and will be unlikely to rebel.

Another universal principle is that criticism is not discipline.

R' Yaakovson cites a shocking incident that illustrates this point clearly:

> *A teacher asked his students to explain the verse from Ecclesiastes (2:17), "Vesaneisi es hachayim, ki ra alai hama'aseh — I hated life, for the action was bad for me."*
> *One of the students composed this original commentary:*
>
> *Everything I do is bad. Every day I clean my room, yet not once have I been told thank you. I am only criticized: Why did you leave the closet door open? Why is the bedspread creased? I say it's not easy for me … I worked hard at it. My parents answer that for lazy people everything is hard. Why don't you hold your fork properly? Why don't you do something constructive instead of reading all the time? How many times have we told you that you can pick things up from the floor even without being told. Someone your age is allowed to help even without being told. What will become of you? Why … why … why … why … in short, why are you alive at all?*
>
> *That is the meaning of the verse — because the action is for me, because I have to do it, that makes it bad … because everything I do is bad. That's why "Vesaneisi es hachayim — I hate life."*
>
> *I can't do anything without being criticized. They ask how was school today. I answer, "Okay." They say, "Can't you answer like a mentch? We're taking an interest in you, trying to build a relationship with you, and you just push us away." This life is disgusting — more distasteful than anything in the world. I'm afraid to make a move, afraid to open up my mouth.*

"I want to speak to you," says my father. "The teacher says you lack self-confidence. You have to overcome this, you know." I say okay — and run to my room crying. Then they come in and say, "Why are you crying? What happened, anyway? We can't even tell you anything — you're so sensitive!"

Criticism is a terribly destructive force. Far from serving as a tool for discipline, it leaves tremendous damage in its wake. Criticism points to faults, painting for the child a picture of himself as incompetent. If we criticize a child often we are teaching him that he is incapable of accomplishing much; we are instilling in him self-doubt, as opposed to self-confidence.

Someone I met recently told me that his mother was never happy with him. In fact she would tell him that she was sorry he was her child. After he grew up, married, and was living in his own home, he decided that he must verify for himself that it was not as bad as he remembered, that at least some of the constant pain and self-doubt with which he had grown up was imagined. Mustering all his courage, he asked his mother, "Ma — didn't I ever do anything right?" His mother's curt reply was, "NO!"

Criticism is certainly not discipline, nor is it any form of *chinuch*.

In another instance R' Yaakovson describes, parents sought advice regarding their son who was discouraged and bitter, and was not succeeding in any area of his life, be it scholastic, social, or at home. The child would not face up to any challenge or bear any responsibility.

These parents were extremely upset with their son. "Are you angry at him?" asked the counselor.

"Certainly!" said the angry father.

"Why?"

"What do you mean, 'why'? Isn't the way our son acts enough to drive anyone crazy? Tens of times every day, day after day, we rebuke him for acting that way, but he continues with his bitter attitude; he's depressed and he has no motivation for anything."

"But have you helped him in any way?" asked the counselor. "Have you encouraged him? Have you guided

him to help him recognize how he can become better? Or have you only told him how bad he is?"

"Do you think that this child is a fool?" the father replied. "Do you actually think that he doesn't know the right way to behave?"

"That's not the point," said the advisor. "He may know the right way to behave, but he obviously doesn't feel he can do it. He's convinced that he is incapable of changing. So what good can it possibly do to criticize him? Your criticism is only making matters worse, convincing him that he really is bad."

"So what do you suggest?" the parents asked.

"First, stop all criticism," said the advisor.

The father answered in no uncertain terms, "Nothing doing. We came to ask advice on how to better educate our children. We are not looking for advice on how to stop educating them altogether."

These unfortunate parents harbored the grave misconception that criticism is *chinuch*, and they could not change this attitude even when they were shown how their criticism was damaging their child's ability to function.

One young boy I know was criticized severely and often by his parents. The boy left yeshivah and today he is no longer following in his father's path.

Step #1: Express Your Wishes

How then are we to discipline in this generation?

First, we must aim for *communication, not condemnation.*

Rather than accusing and complaining to the child, blaming him for the way he is acting, we should simply tell him specifically what we want him to do or what we want him to stop doing. We should express our desires clearly and explicitly, without any vagueness and leaving no room for confusion.

Thus, it is not helpful for a parent to say, "Shmuel, I want you to be a good boy and behave." Rather, we should tell Shmuel precisely what it is that we want of him: "Shmuel, please stop ripping the plastic tablecloth with your fork," or, "Shmuel, I want you to put your spaghetti back on your plate."

Two Vital Points

In discussing discipline, two points are vital: (1) a parent's word is valuable; do not overuse it, and (2) as a child grows older, it is necessary to command less and communicate more.

A parent's word is valuable. It is neither wise nor necessary to overburden our children with too many rules and regulations.

R' Shach said that a major rule in *chinuch* is to ignore much of what we see; to "look the other way." One need not notice and discipline a child's every minor infraction. Surprisingly, by ignoring things our children do, and by disciplining less often, our *chinuch* will be more successful.

Equally important is to limit the number of rules one establishes in the home. It is impossible to properly enforce one's rules if there are too many of them, and this circumstance makes the rules meaningless.

I know a mother who was a stickler for rules; she imposed endless rules to keep her household running smoothly. Although all her mountains of rules proved to be too much for her children, they observed them in her presence, since they were afraid of her. When she was not there, however, her children ignored her rules. This mother effectively taught her children to transgress rules. Is it any wonder that two of her children left religion?

As a child grows older, parents should command less and communicate more. Of course a parent's decision must always be the final word, but as the child begins to mature (beyond the age of 11), it should become unnecessary for parents to resort constantly to commands. Parents should develop an open relationship with their children, one in which they can communicate with the children on an adult level, and can discuss with the children how they would like them to behave and why.

> *One incident that occurred at my school taught me a crucial lesson about communicating with children. One of the older students in the school committed a serious infraction by bringing tear gas to school. Of course, I asked him to hand the tear gas vial over to me, and I put it away in my office. Shortly thereafter the boy was caught once again with tear gas — he had gone out and bought another vial — and I felt that his behavior warranted strong discipli-*

nary measures. The boy had brazenly challenged both my authority and the school rules.

Before taking action I decided to consult with one of the great tzaddikim of today. In discussing my considerations I said that on the one hand, if I were to talk with the boy about the gravity of what he did, I felt I could get through to him, since my relationship with the boy was strong and positive. I was sure that through communicating with him, I could prevent him from repeating his behavior. On the other hand, I felt that his actions called for chinuch. Since the boy had the audacity to repeat his behavior even after he was caught at it once, we are obliged to educate him.

The rabbi told me: your goal is to get him to behave. If he will behave as a result of your explaining and communicating with him, then you have accomplished your goal. If he will have learned his lesson (albeit as a result of your communicating with him as opposed to punishing him), then you have successfully educated him. This is chinuch.

As we have mentioned, at the time when a child is doing something wrong, a parent should *not* try to reason with the child; he should only state, in a clear and direct manner, precisely what he wants the child to do or to stop doing. Some other time, when the child is not misbehaving, the parent should make it a point to explain to him why certain behaviors are unacceptable. The older a child is (from about the age of 11 and up), the more necessary it is to explain the reasons for *certain* rules. Understanding why the rules exist makes it easier for a child to accept and follow these rules.

"Say Little"

When a child is misbehaving, however, parents should observe the principle of *"Emor me'at* — Say little!" It is not the time for explanations, for every child must know that his parent is the authority in the home, and that his parent's word is final.

Parents should state explicitly which behavior they wish the child to change. If necessary parents can repeat themselves once or twice (but no more than that). A parent should always stand calmly and firmly by his word. He should not go into any explanations or apologies, nor should he become emotional about the child's behavior. This may be difficult at first, but as the parent sees his disciplinary measures succeeding more and more, it will become easier.

Sentences like "You're not listening to me," "I'm so upset with you," "Why are you doing that," and "You drive me crazy," are unnecessary. In fact, the parents' demonstration of anger or frustration might actually provide reinforcement for the child's misbehavior, "encouraging" him to persist in his undesirable behavior. Children sometimes have a vested interest in making their parents upset. They may enjoy the feeling of power they gain from doing so. When a parent is telling a child what he must do or stop doing, it is not the time for a discussion with the child about whether the parent's demand is correct or fair. The message the child must receive is that the parents have the last word.

So just swallow those huge feelings of frustration and anger, and say softly but firmly, "Shmuel, I would like you to put your spaghetti back on your plate." If necessary, repeat your request once or twice more. If your child protests or complains, you should respond calmly but firmly, "I know; but even so, Shmuel, I would like you to pick up your spaghetti and put it back on your plate."

Consequences — When and What

If the parent has said something for the third time and the child has not listened, a consequence is necessary. Although we may have a tendency to overexaggerate in the consequences we give our children, effective consequences need not necessarily be severe, if they are enforced in a consistent manner.

Following are some suggestions for types of consequences that can be very effective: (1) sending the child to his room for 10 or 15 minutes; (2) taking a certain daily privilege away from the child, such as withholding a treat after supper, taking away 10 minutes of his playing time before he goes to bed, keeping him in the house, and so on; (3) insisting that the child do what you want before he can do what he wants, for example, not allowing him to go outside to play before he cleans up the mess he made at the table. The sooner the giving of the consequence follows the misbehavior, the more effective it will be. If a child misbehaves today and receives a consequence tomorrow, the consequence loses its effect.

Another important element of administering consequences is consistency. Although these consequences may seem small, if they are followed through firmly, consistently and without exception, then the child will begin to behave properly. The order this will bring to the home and the peace of mind that will follow is certainly worth all the emotional effort parents must invest in order to be firm and consistent in their discipline.

Positive Discipline

There is yet another type of discipline that I call positive discipline. Instead of a being given a negative consequence for misbehavior, the child can be offered a positive consequence for behaving properly. There are various ways of doing this. (Note: I am not in favor of children being given prizes for fulfilling their basic responsibilities and completing their chores. Children should not have to be rewarded for listening to their parents, taking out the garbage, or helping in the Shabbos preparations. However, where the child is having particular difficulty with fulfilling parents' wishes in some specific area, and he must work to overcome a "handicap," positive discipline can give him the motivation he needs to succeed.)

One method of positive discipline is the "jellybean method." The parent prepares an empty cup with a bag of jellybeans nearby, and puts one jellybean into the cup each time the child behaves in accordance with his parents' wishes. This can also be done in a collective system involving the whole family. For every hour that the children do not fight, for example, a jellybean is put into the cup. When the cup is full, the child/children have earned a prize.

A variation of this method is to let the children earn certain privileges according to their actions (as specifically agreed upon in advance).

In one juvenile correctional facility where the youths were out of control, a new system was instituted with amazing results. Each delinquent child had basic privileges, but he could improve the quality of these privileges based on points he earned for good behavior. For example, the standard prison breakfast consisted of porridge and milk. Yet with points an inmate earned, he could enjoy quite a fancy breakfast. In fact, with enough points, he could have steak at meals. It was not long before the juvenile prisoners were displaying exemplary behavior.

Positive Discipline and Laundry

A home is certainly not a prison, and one need not earn his breakfast (or any other necessities); nevertheless, this method can be used with slight variations and can lead to tremendous improvements, even with older children and teenagers.

One mother, for example, wanted her teenaged children to fold and put away their laundry. This seemed very hard for the children, and always led to a hassle.

Finally, the mother sat down with her children and drew up terms for an agreement with them. Since the children often wanted to buy new clothing beyond the necessities of their basic wardrobes, the mother agreed to give them a clothing allowance each week. They would save this up and use it to buy the clothes they wanted. In return, they were to fold and put away their laundry. Each child was to write down how many times he had folded and put away laundry.

Once a week, they would sit together for an accounting session, and an allowance would be handed out in accordance with the work each child had done. An additional feature of this system was a box that was placed in the hall, and any clothing found on the floor would be placed in the box. In order to retrieve their clothing, each child would have to pay 25 cents per item.

In the beginning everyone was excited and the system ran smoothly. They folded and put away their laundry, and received their allowance accordingly. After a few weeks, however, the kids found themselves extremely busy, and they began to neglect their responsibilities. The mother kept to her part of the agreement. Allowances were given according to the amount of clothing folded and put away, and she deposited many items of clothing in the box in the hall.

All this time, the mother made no comment; she let her agreement work for her. When the children came to her several weeks later with their requests of, "Ma, I want to buy a new shirt," and "Ma, I want a new pair of pants," she replied, "No problem. I can take you to the shopping mall right now. Do you have money?" The children hemmed and hawed, but the message was perfectly clear. They had all agreed, after all.

It was not long before the children were putting their clothes away regularly without being reminded. The mother's *discipline* paid off. Positive discipline is an extremely helpful method, especially in providing children with the incentive they need to do things that may be hard for them. If we strengthen their incentive, they will *want* to do what we want them to do, and isn't that all *we* really *want?*

12

Ensuring the Eternity of Klal Yisrael — a Tribute

Hashem Is a Teacher

After I had been teaching for a several years, I resolved to return to kollel (full-time graduate studies) so that I would be able to resume a full-time regimen of learning. Although I had experienced many successes in my teaching, I decided that they had been gained at too high a price; I felt I was not growing sufficiently in my own Torah learning.

Before making my final decision, I consulted with R' Shlomo Zalman Auerbach. Much to my surprise, he told me that I must continue teaching. To console me, he cited the teaching of our Sages that compares teachers to stars. Although stars look small, he explained, that is only because they are so distant from us. If we could get a close-up view of them, we would be amazed at just how big they really are. In the same way, here in this world, teachers may not seem to be very special, but when we get to the World to Come, we will see how truly great they are.

(The Chozeh of Lublin insisted that if people would know what a lofty place teachers hold in heaven, they would be running to become teachers.)

Still feeling a bit depressed, I asked R' Auerbach, "But Rebbi, am I stuck in this role just because I'm doing it already? Wouldn't it have been better had I never entered this field to begin with?"

"Hashem is a teacher!" came his enthusiastic reply. "Hashem is a teacher!"

The Shout

It is a wonderful privilege to develop a close relationship with any of the great *tzaddikim* of our generation. I have enjoyed the privilege and the opportunity to meet with R' Shlomo Wolbe on many occasions to discuss significant issues in the field of *chinuch* with him. R' Wolbe is one of the foremost ethical personalities alive today and an educator par excellence. I believe it is not an exaggeration to say that he does not move a muscle without carefully calculating and planning its purpose. I am convinced that if R' Wolbe shouts at someone, we can be absolutely sure that he thought it through fully before shouting, and concluded that it was the most beneficial thing to do. I was privileged to have R' Wolbe shout at me on two separate occasions, one that I wish to share.

After I became principal, I found myself once again beset by regrets. When I was working as a rebbi, at least I had been able to set aside regular hours for learning Torah. As a principal, however, I was (and am) busy with children throughout the day and night, leaving precious little time for learning. I asked R' Wolbe whether I had done the right thing in becoming a principal. For a moment R' Wolbe looked at me in silence, then suddenly he shouted out, "Who knows what kind of Gehinnom would have been waiting for you had you not agreed to become a principal!"

R' Wolbe's respect for teachers is boundless. When I was still a classroom teacher, he told me that he envied me. He was once a teacher, he explained, and he so wished that he could go back to doing just that. I expressed my surprise at his sentiments, and told him I thought he must be joking. He assured me that he was quite serious. In no other calling can one gain the rewards of teaching.

Have you ever heard the angels sing "Song" to Hashem? In the year 2000 I was at the Torah Umesorah convention for Shabbos, and its message was so effective and touched me so deeply that I am moved to describe it, and to submit this tribute to the unsung heroes of our nation.

I consider it a great honor to have been able to attend the Torah Umesorah convention. I cannot contain my amazement at the great sanctification of Hashem's Name that I witnessed at that gathering. It is hard to say which specific incident made the greatest impression on me.

Selfless Devotion

Was it seeing the principal who, when given credit for his efforts that were vital to the convention's success, discounted the recognition he was accorded, stating that all that mattered was the honor of Hashem? Was it the numerous rebbis and teachers who expressed to me how much love they feel for their students, and how much they care for their success? I even overheard one rebbi telling another how careful he is never to hurt a child's feelings. Many teachers approached me for advice in working out practical applications of methods that would help them in the classroom. The love and concern these teachers feel for their students was clearly evident.

There was a "networking breakfast" at the convention, where educators were seated at tables together with other educators in similar positions, or with those who taught parallel grade levels. I was seated at a table together with other principals, and every discussion was purposeful and beneficial, everyone seeking ways and means by which to improve our schools for the sake of our students. Our conversations at the "principals' table" were not unlike others taking place throughout the room. There were dozens if not hundreds of such discussions going on at every table throughout the dining room.

In his speech R' Pesach Krohn related that a child in Pre 1-A woke up at 5 a.m., and when his parents asked him what had roused him so early, he explained, "Today we're learning 'tzeire' in class, and I can't wait to go to school!" When his parents asked him what it was about learning tzeire that had excited him so, the child described how, on the previous day, the rebbi had danced with the class, singing, "Tzeire-dalet: 'day.' Have a nice day! Tomorrow we're learning tzeire!" The impression his rebbi's enthusiasm made on this boy left him so excited that he simply could not wait to go to learn.

Feelings of responsibility and sincerity surrounded the event, and above all, the feeling of unity was tangible. We perceived the common course along which we all move, that of ensuring the eternity of our people. In our hands lies the task of giving over the tradition of Torah and mitzvos to the next generation, the tradition that we received from our teachers, and they from their teachers, all the way back to Mt. Sinai.

The Novominsker Rebbe referred to the educators of today as the guardians of our people. He stressed that they are truly angels (read: messengers), entrusted with the Divine mission to raise the nation of Hashem; to raise loyal servants of G-d in turbulent times the likes of which our nation has never seen in its entire history.

It is from these angels that I heard the Song emanate, not only from their beautiful songs during the various prayers, but from all of their heroic actions, clearly testifying to their selfless devotion for the sake of our children's future.

Express Your Appreciation

Naturally we want the best for our children, but there is a point that I feel must be stressed. Of course teachers and educators are not perfect; nor, for that matter, is any other human being, and certainly there are matters that should be brought to a teacher's attention. Nevertheless, there are so many things that educators and teachers do correctly. It is imperative that we catch those who teach our children doing things right. Are we aware of how much these teachers sacrifice for the success of our children? Your child's teacher may have been speaking with me, or with many other teachers and principals at that convention, seeking ways to help your son or daughter!

Try to encourage your children's teachers when they do things for your children that *you* enjoy and appreciate. Perhaps a teacher spent hours making a beautiful *Megillas Esther* for your child before Purim or an exquisite crown before Shavuos. Perhaps a rebbi took your son aside to speak with him, giving him an extra dose of inspiration and encouragement. Perhaps your son is having unusual success in this rebbi's class, or you see that one teacher is having a strong positive influence on your child. Do not miss the opportunity to express it to the teacher: give a call; write a note; tell him personally. Parents have no idea how many teachers care deeply about their children, and how hard these teachers work for their students. Spending so much time with so many teachers and principals at the convention, I saw firsthand their devotion to our children.

Our educators are the unsung heroes of our nation; without even the hope of recognition, they invest all their energies for the sake of our children. It is to them I wish to pay tribute.

I want to pay tribute to this holy Nation: to you the teachers; to you the parents, who so selflessly give of yourselves for your children without any hope of remuneration or recognition; and to all those who together make up a People so unique that they are unequaled anywhere on the face of the earth.

13

Putting
Discipline in Its Place

The Misplaced Key

During the past several months I have had occasion to be at the airport numerous times, and have found it to be a source of many interesting experiences.

Recently, after I dropped off some family members at their terminal in Kennedy Airport for their return trip to Israel, I went to park my rented car in the airport parking lot. The parking lot was quite full, and finding a spot was no simple task. When I finally had the car parked, I was anxious to join my family in the terminal, and in my haste I got out of the car and slammed the door without giving much thought to what I was doing.

As I was rushing toward the terminal, someone pointed out to me that I had left the car running. Feeling none too proud I returned to the car only to discover, much to my dismay, that the door was locked and the key was, of course, inside.

At that point I was thankful to learn that the airport employs a driver with a tow truck to help people out of precisely such predicaments. (The service is free of charge, although the driver is quick to remind you that a tip is in order.) Using only a flat metal bar not unlike a simple 12-inch ruler, it took only moments for this experienced "break-in artist" to open the most up-to-date of cars.

Embarrassed, I asked the driver if I was the only one to whom this has happened, and he told me, "This is just about the only thing I do all day — open car doors in the parking lot for people who left their keys inside."

It can be tremendously frustrating when things are not in their proper places. No matter if it was the car key, or if it was me, who was outside of the car rather than inside with the key, where I belonged, something was very much out of place.

Sometimes when things are not in their proper places it can be far more than just frustrating; it can also be detrimental, and we are not always so fortunate as to have others available — as the tow-truck driver in the airport parking lot — to bail us out.

Discipline is one such example. Discipline definitely has its place, and as we have often mentioned, it can be most detrimental for children if their parents refrain from disciplining them properly. Yet at the same time it can be at least as detrimental if parents apply discipline where it is out of place.

Discipline and Praying

Not long ago in shul on a Friday night, I saw a father praying with his young son, who appeared to have been about 8 years old. The room was hot, the hour was late, and the boy was tired. Taking a short break from his prayers, the boy rested his head on his father's shoulder. The scene aroused my compassion for this child, who surely must have been tired after such a long hot day. I was therefore shocked to the core to see the father first jab the boy and then smack him. He was angry that his son had dared to take a break from his praying, and he intended to make sure that he would not slack off again. He held his son's finger on the place, forcing him to return directly to the prayers.

This scene repeated itself a number of times — the boy would rest his head on his father's shoulder, and the father, who would not stand for any nonsense, would jab him in the stomach. The boy shrugged his shoulders in silent protest, but he really had no choice in the matter, and so he continued to pray, denied the luxury of being able to rest, and lacking even the solace of his father's support.

This misguided father did not understand that when it comes to praying, discipline is totally out of place. Our goal is to instill in our children a *love* for praying. To accomplish this, we must somehow awaken their desire to pray so that they, *of their own accord*, will want to pray properly. To do so we must "educate" them to pray, and as R' Wolbe states, the process of *chinuch* is parallel to the lighting of the Menorah in the Holy Temple: the Kohen holds the fire to the wick, "... until the flame rises of its own accord." In our efforts to educate our children, our task is to kindle the child's will until he himself prays properly.

Discipline will do nothing to develop within a child a love for praying. In fact it will accomplish precisely the opposite; it will make praying altogether distasteful to a child, and so will discourage him from *wanting* to pray.

Help Your Child Develop a Love for Davening

The way to help a child develop a love for praying is to impress upon him how significant his prayers really are. One child who entered our school at the beginning of this past school year had been labeled as hyperactive, and had a most difficult time in the school he was attending previously, for his teachers simply were not equipped to deal with him. Our main approach in working with him was to give him as much encouragement as we could. When he had been in our school for only a short time, his father exclaimed to me, "My son has started to eat again!" It seems this boy had lost his appetite as a result of all the pressure and aggravation he was experiencing. Encouragement gave him renewed hope.

Before Yom Kippur, when I spoke to all the students in our school, I discussed the parable of the Dubner Maggid:

A father and son who were traveling together came to a stream. Turning to his father the son complained, "Abba, it's too deep for me. I can't cross this stream." The father answered him, *"Don't worry, my son. I will take care of you."* Immediately he lifted his son and carried him across the stream, and they continued on their way.

Suddenly they were attacked by a band of robbers. The father said, "My son, stand behind me and you will be safe." The child obeyed, and with the stick he was holding, the father fought the robbers and warded them off. (When I was about 8 years old, my father did the same for me. We lived in a mixed neighborhood, and once when I was playing with a friend, an Italian boy approached me, called me a derogatory name and shoved me. I was no pushover, and so I shoved him back. He left, but a quarter of an hour later he was back with quite a number of his friends, apparently intending to teach us a lesson. My father came running out of the house with a baseball bat, screaming at the top of his lungs, and the gang ran away terrified.)

The father and his son continued on their way, but soon came upon a tall fence. "Abba, I can't possibly climb up this straight fence," said the boy. But his father said, "Don't worry, my son," and, taking the boy on his shoulders, he climbed the fence together with him.

When finally they reached their destination, they found the gates to the city locked. They searched everywhere for an opening. Suddenly, the father cried, "My son! Look! Here is a small opening. I would never be able to get through it, but you can." He then spoke gently to his son, "My child, I've carried you and taken care of you during this entire journey. Through all our trials and tribulations I have helped you. Now it is your turn to help me. This opening is too small for me to fit in, but if you get through it, you can open the gate for me!"

In the same way, said the Dubner Maggid, at times the gates of *tefillah* are closed to adults. We are too big and have to many sins. It is now the time for you — the children — to enter through the small opening that remains. Go in, children, and open the gates for us; pray for us. If you will pray for the adults, your prayers will be accepted.

I then explained to the children that many of them make a mistake in assuming that the primary *tefillos* are those of the adults, and that their *tefillos* are of secondary importance. In fact, just the opposite is true! The prayers of the children are the main ones, and their prayers help and support us, the adults. I then urged them to pray for their parents, for their siblings, for other family members, and even for their neighborhoods and for other people and causes.

After Yom Kippur, the hyperactive student in our school brought me a note from his father describing how he stood for *hours* davening with great devotion on Yom Kippur. "He literally came to life!" his father exclaimed. Realizing how important his *tefillos* actually were brought him to love the *tefillos* and to pray with all his heart, something that no disciplinary measures could have achieved.

Discipline and Torah Learning

Teaching children to love Torah and appreciate Torah learning is no different. Recently I had occasion to spend many hours with a group of children-at-risk. In order that parents could learn how to relate to their own children more effectively, giving their children a desire to follow in their path, I asked the boys to share with me their reasons for having abandoned their Torah lives.

One of the boys related that when he would come home from school not knowing the Gemara he had been taught in class, his father would take away every privilege he could possibly think of. Unfortunately, his father's methods accomplished the very opposite of what he had hoped, driving his son away from Torah. Even though this father's intentions may have been sincere, his methods were altogether unsuccessful.

> R' Yaakovson describes another father who learned with his son for an hour each day. His son hated these daily learning sessions, and the father was at a loss to understand his son's strong negative emotions. The father was asked how he approached these learning sessions, and he described how he would sit opposite his son, listen to him review what he had learned, and correct his errors. Not only were this father's methods upsetting his child, they were completely unsuccessful, for despite all the time the

father invested, his son was not succeeding in school. "Imagine being in your son's place, sitting opposite an impatient person," the rebbi told the father. If you are afraid of this person to begin with, and you know that his only intention during this hour is to examine every single word you are saying to see if you are up to par, would you enjoy such a session?"

The father was advised to change his approach to their hour of study. He was told to sit next to his son with his arm around him; to look for what his son would know correctly and to encourage him based on that; to tell him how much he enjoyed learning with him; in short, to do whatever he could to make that hour of learning something his son would enjoy and look forward to.

Two months later, the father was called to report on his son's progress. "Not only are we both enjoying the learning," said the father, "but my son has been showing great improvement in his learning at school. His rebbi is very pleased with him. It's practically a miracle!"

Fortunately, the positive change in this boy's attitude and progress in school was not a "miracle"; it was rather a simple, natural process. When a father makes learning pleasant for his child, then the child will grow in his love for learning; and if the child can see that he is succeeding (this boy's father made sure to encourage him, pointing out to him when he was correct), he will be motivated to strive for more and more success.

Discipline — in Its Proper Place

Discipline is a tool that can help children develop self-control. It helps them to define what are the proper boundaries. At times when our children are out of control, or when they need to be shown boundaries, discipline has a place. Children must be taught self-control and boundaries, since they cannot understand life's experiences on their own.

It follows, therefore, that when our children are acting up, or are *intentionally* failing to listen to us, discipline is in order. (Note that discipline need not consist of punishment. Stating clearly what we want from a child in a calm, firm voice, perhaps repeating ourselves once or twice, may suffice to teach our child the lesson he needs to learn. Only if such efforts have not succeeded should we resort to various consequences, as described in the previous chapter.)

Nevertheless, discipline is not a means by which to increase our children's desire and love for the Torah and mitzvos; nor is it a method of instilling in our children the Torah values that we hold in such high regard, such as modesty, honesty, and so many others. And even when we find discipline in these areas necessary in order to define the boundaries for our children, let us not think that discipline alone is sufficient. It may serve to maintain a certain degree of external order, however when it comes to influencing our children to *want to do what we want them to do*, discipline cannot suffice.

Hashem Believes in You!

To make them want to do what we want them to do, truly believing in our children is vitally important. It is amazing how much our believing in our children can change their image of themselves and the world.

Before Shavuos, one teacher was speaking to a class of children from more "liberal" homes about the importance of the giving of the Torah. One child called out, "My father says that religion is outdated!" While the class was absorbing this statement, the same child declared, "I don't believe in Hashem!" The teacher responded calmly, "You may not believe in Hashem, but Hashem believes in you." Apparently these few words were all the child needed to hear; after that, for the duration of the class he listened quietly and attentively to what the teacher had to say, and did not interrupt again.

During the hours I spent with the group of children-at-risk, I saw a clear picture of how important it is to understand them, and how desperately they need someone to believe in them. As we walked together into the wee hours of the morning, they expressed sincere feelings of love of Hashem and fear of Heaven, in their own unique way. At one point, when I took a drink and made a blessing out loud, one of the boys answered "Amen," then turned to me with tears in his eyes and exclaimed proudly, "Rebbi, I'm still counting *sefirah* with a blessing!" Many of the boys told me how they wished Mashiach would come soon, and their parting words to me were, "You promised to tell us some Torah thoughts!"

This glimpse of how much they care is truly hard to believe. The incongruous combination of the inner and outer lives of these boys touched me profoundly. My heart goes out to them, for they have such a strong desire to be good, and they are groping for a genuine connection with Torah and mitzvos. Yet they need help in overcoming the many obstacles they have encountered in their lives. I quote from a letter written by one such child:

> What nobody realized was my pain — my hurt. I am confident that each and every child that heads to the fringe has a tremendous hole in their life that they are endeavoring to fill. Have you ever paused to consider the towering unhappiness and deep pain that it must take to drive a child — to alienate him/herself from their family and engender the disdain of the community?

How important it is for us to realize that our children really want to be good. They really want to excel in Torah and mitzvos, although this desire may be hidden deep inside of them. We must nurture that desire and help bring it to the fore until it becomes a driving force within them. We must give them the emotional strength and courage they need to overcome the many obstacles that beset their lives; by believing in them, by showing them that we know they can do it, we can bolster their inner resources and help them find their way.

Helping a Child Develop Pleasure in Learning Gemara

I am often asked how to help a child who has no desire for learning Gemara. Such a situation offers an excellent opportunity to apply on a practical level the principles presented here:

(1) To encourage a child to *want* to learn, discipline is totally out of place. A boy's lack of desire has nothing to do with the need to educate him in the proper boundaries, or to teach him self-control.

(2) What will encourage his desire to learn is understanding him and believing in him.

Quite often, a child who has no desire for Gemara is a child who finds Gemara learning difficult. (This can be due to a number of reasons, which we will not address at present.) It is helpful, then, to attempt to make it *easier* for him to succeed. One rebbi I know asked one of our leading sages what to do about a certain boy who did not pass his test and to whom he would have to give a failing mark. The rabbi told him that no one in his class should be failing a test. He explained that if a child gets a failing mark he should be allowed to take the test again, with the rebbi's help and encouragement, until he succeeds. (Obviously, employment of this method would depend on each individual rebbi's classroom situation.)

Many educators make it their practice, through any of a variety of methods, to make the tests easier for those children who find them especially difficult. They may require those students to answer fewer questions; allow them to take the test with their tutor; they may sit with a student who is taking the test in order to explain the questions to them, making sure they understand all the questions clearly; or they may explain the questions in such a way as to bring a student closer to the answers, without actually giving away the answers.

Whatever method is employed, the objective is to make success easier for the child. In our school we ask our teachers to follow these principles wherever it is appropriate, and we recommend that parents whose children have difficulty with Gemara hire a private tutor. However, when hiring a tutor, one must ascertain that the tutor has proven, through previous successful experience, to be properly qualified. Moreover, in order for this plan to succeed, parents must keep in touch with both the rebbi and the tutor (they should speak to the rebbi at least once every two weeks, and to the tutor every few days).

While working with both teacher and tutor to make it easier for the child to succeed, it is worthwhile for parents to design their own program to strengthen their child's incentive. One might draw up a plan or a contract with the child, making every test that he passes with a grade of 80 percent or higher worth a specified number of points. The tutor can participate in this arrangement as well, giving the child points for his progress. When the child earns enough points he receives a big prize. In situations such as these, incentives can do much to boost a child's desire to learn, provided the child does his share and earns the incentive.

Putting Discipline in Its Place / 143

Once the child begins to improve even a little, parents should be quick to point out to him his success and to let him know how pleased they are. This will give the child further incentive to continue along the road to success.

Discipline and Mischievous Behavior

One mother approached me to discuss her 8-year-old son Chaim, who often becomes silly and difficult. When he is told to put on his pajamas, he might come out with his pajamas on his head, dancing as he chants, "Okay, I put on my pajamas!" If her baby is playing with his spaghetti and making it into a hat, Chaim will run over and add to the pile of spaghetti on the baby's head, "not caring to realize that while these antics may be amusing when a baby performs them, they are not funny when an 8-year-old tries them," as his mother told me.

At the Shabbos table Chaim is particularly difficult. During *Shalom Aleichem* he may rip the plastic tablecloth with his fork. During *Kiddush* he makes silly faces, and when it is time to wash he will hold his finger to the faucet, splashing water all over the kitchen. The mother often finds herself yelling at him in order to snap him out of his silliness and gain his cooperation.

In this case, discipline *must* be used as a means to teach Chaim self-control and proper boundaries. A method of firm yet consistent discipline with consequences, as we have mentioned in previous chapters, might be very helpful. When disciplining there is no need to scream or reprimand harshly, as it does not benefit the situation in the least, and it may in fact detract from the effectiveness of the discipline. Parents should state explicitly which behavior they wish the child to change. If necessary, they can repeat themselves once or twice. Without going into explanations or apologies, the parents should stand calmly yet firmly by their word. (Sentences like, "You're not listening to me," "I'm so upset with you," "Why are you doing that," or "You drive me crazy," are unnecessary.) If a parent has said something for the third time and the child has not listened, a consequence becomes necessary. (See Chapter 11 where we explain how small consequences, given on a consistent basis, can be extremely effective in bringing order to your home.)

Discipline Alone Is Not Enough

Discipline alone, however, cannot correct the source of the problem. It is obvious that the child is acting up for a reason or reasons, and discipline does not address these reasons.

The reasons for a child acting up in such situations may vary. Perhaps he is jealous of his baby brother and wants attention. If he acts up and becomes the family clown, he is assured of getting the attention he wants so badly; after all, he reasons, if his baby brother can do it, why can't he? On the other hand, he may be at odds with his mother and may gain a certain feeling of power when he gets on her nerves and makes her angry.

It is possible that his parents are putting the child under too much pressure, demanding that he act more mature than should be expected of a child his age. I once dealt with a girl named Naomi, who often acted up, especially at the Shabbos table. She would behave in ridiculous ways, doing such annoying things as putting her hands into a bowl full of soup. After careful investigation it was discovered that her father was an overly strict disciplinarian who required that his children act in ways that could not be expected of someone their age. Naomi could not handle her father's demands and simply rebelled against his unbearable pressure.

Chaim's mother would do well to make time for him, time when she would be there for only him. Perhaps at bedtime she could spend 10 minutes sitting by his bed talking with him (or listening to him). If she would plant a kiss on his forehead and tell him how much she loves him before he goes to sleep it would certainly enhance Chaim's pleasure in the time she spends with him. She could spend daytime hours with him as well; she could take only him along with her on an errand, or set aside a special time *just* for him at least once or twice a week. The point is for him to receive special attention from her *on a consistent basis*, so that he will feel less of a need to search for it in other ways.

Spending time with a child strengthens the connection between parent and child, and the closer the connection between the two, the less the child will be inclined to cause his parents anguish. Chaim's case is a clear example of how discipline alone can help to create order, but will not truly rectify the situation. The symptoms of the problem can be controlled through discipline, but unless the root of the problem is dealt with, the problem will come out in other ways.

Parents — the Most Unselfish People on Earth

Chinuch is not easy, and it is often difficult to see the fruits of the tremendous efforts we put into our children's *chinuch*. Parents are the most unselfish people on earth; they sacrifice everything for their children, not receiving any remuneration in return, not even recognition. They are on duty 24 hours a day, with no vacation. Parents should never allow themselves to become discouraged, for they must realize that their efforts themselves represent success.

> *One teacher in the public school system would regularly teach her class inspirational phrases that she felt would one day benefit them. The students did not take these phrases seriously but, given no choice in the matter, they memorized them. One of her students, who was particularly difficult, was eventually expelled from the school and sent to a juvenile prison.*
>
> *Sitting in prison in a state of despair, the boy saw himself as a total failure and decided to commit suicide. He slit his wrists, and as he was lying there waiting to bleed to death, a phrase he had learned from this teacher crossed his mind: "The only failure is not trying." He realized then that if he would allow himself to die, it would be a prime instance of the "only failure." At that moment he decided to save his own life, and he called for help.*

The very fact that you are reading this means you are willing to try; it means that you are already a success. May Hashem help you to have *continued* success, and true *nachas* from all your children.

14

The "Power Struggle"

"Travel — the Perfect Freedom!"

This phrase accompanied a logo I saw on an aerogramme. I remember questioning its validity the first time I saw it; if I had ever entertained a thought that there might be a grain of truth to this catch phrase, my recent travels back and forth between Israel and the U.S. banished any doubts from my mind.

I certainly would not describe my recent experience of a four-hour delay in the airport on the night before a holiday as the perfect freedom. Nor would I apply this phrase to the extreme heat I encountered after we were finally allowed to board the plane. At that point, we had to remain in our seats on the plane during a further delay, while the cabin air conditioning unit was not functioning. While the passengers sweated profusely, the flight crew walked up and down the cabin distributing bottles of water to help people cope with the heat.

If, through all this, I still thought even for a moment that travel could somehow be the perfect freedom, the incident that followed set me straight.

Sitting as patiently as I could in my seat on the plane, I heard a sudden outburst of screaming and fighting. I looked up to see one uniformed U.S. soldier and two plain-clothes policemen escorting a man onto the plane. They *wrestled him into a seat as he, in his reluctance to leave the U.S., was fighting them tooth and nail, screaming all the while, "No go China! No go China!" It appeared that the U.S. was deporting this illegal alien back to China via Israel. Obviously, he had no interest in this travel adventure. Matters became violent as the poor man made a last, desperate attempt to break free, but his efforts failed. The U.S. agents forced him into his place and handcuffed his feet to the legs of the seat. Then they used belts to strap him securely to the chair so that he could not move at all.*

This little demonstration convinced me beyond any doubt that travel is not necessarily the perfect freedom. It certainly was not the perfect freedom for this unfortunate man, nor was it for me; I was sitting directly in front of the hapless individual and was not feeling the least bit comfortable with the thought of sitting out the long flight in such close proximity to a potentially dangerous man. In fact, it was not the perfect freedom for any of the passengers on that flight who, feeling the draining effects of the unreasonably long delay, the intense heat, and this incident to complete the ambiance, were clearly tense and impatient. In an appropriate contribution to the atmosphere, one woman began to scream uncontrollably.

No — travel is not the perfect freedom. I cannot help but think of the holy words of the Ibn Ezra, "*Eved Hashem hu levado chofshi* — Only a servant of Hashem is truly free."

A Successful Power Struggle

Once the plane took off, however, my attention was drawn to a fascinating development. The man who had been fighting desperately and screaming nonstop as long as the plane was on the ground, changed his behavior dramatically after the plane was airborne and we had begun our journey.

He calmed down totally; so much so in fact that the crew felt it safe to untie him so that he could eat his meals in comfort. He even enjoyed watching the airline's audio-visual programs appearing on the screen in front of him.

He seemed altogether relaxed, in complete contrast to his earlier state, just minutes before.

I saw this as an excellent illustration of what we call a "power struggle." That the soldier and police, who had every advantage in numbers and in strength, succeeded in their efforts to force him into the position where they wanted him to be was only to be expected. The surprise was how quickly his demeanor changed the moment he realized there was no longer anything he could do to alter the situation. He immediately resigned himself to his lot and even accepted it in good spirits. It was truly amazing to see one person change so drastically in so short a time. I learned that a power struggle can be a rather successful method to achieve a desired outcome — at times.

The Winner Is the Loser

When it comes to our children, however, this is not necessarily the case.

One of the main modes of conflict between parents and children is the power struggle, in which both parent and child attempt to get their way by force.

A power struggle usually results in one of three outcomes: If the parent is stronger, then eventually the child gives in, resigning himself to the situation and accepting his parent's will; if the child is stronger or has the advantage in this situation then the parent, lacking the time, the patience and/or the stamina to keep up the fight, gives in and lets the child do what he wants; or both parties, unwilling to give in, may remain at a stalemate, horns locked and neither able to move the other from his steadfast position.

It is inevitable that numerous opportunities for conflict between parents and children will arise in almost every household. In situations where a child has a hidden agenda, such as if he is looking to test his parents or to "get back at them" for something, these conflicts will certainly escalate. It is important to note that as a child grows older, his desire for independence grows with him, becoming stronger as he grows. A power struggle with an older child becomes far more complex and difficult, and a parent's chances of gaining from it what he wants become progressively less.

We might think that power struggles have their place when we are attempting to guide our children in the proper path, and can perhaps be of some benefit — at least in situations where the parents emerge victorious. On closer consideration, however, one should come to realize that a power struggle yields no benefit whatsoever, even if the parent wins that particular battle. The reason is that the *struggle* itself diminishes the strength of the parent's position. Simply being a parent gives one a certain strength of authority, and the parent should not become caught up in a struggle to prove that strength, since in allowing himself to be pulled into the struggle for power, the parent actually weakens his own authority.

> *Many years ago a young, inexperienced rebbi I know invited his students to visit his home on Purim. At one point during the day, when the rebbi opened the door he was greeted with a barrage of shaving cream, which hit him directly in his face. "Happy Purim!" his student cried. As the rebbi had never been one to endure humiliating experiences quietly, and as he was already by then a little "in the spirit of the day," a wrestling match between rebbi and student ensued. The boy proved a formidable opponent, but the rebbi won the contest.*
>
> *I was there at the time, and it is obvious to me that the rebbi, although he won the match, turned out to be the real loser. Allowing himself to be dragged into the struggle diminished his authority in the eyes of his students, and lowered the respect they had for him.*

Since then this rebbi has learned to avoid such conflicts. In fact the *chinuch* techniques he has since developed have earned him love and respect. The respect he has won was due not to any struggle for power, but rather to his policy of sidestepping such struggles.

Three Possible Options

On a practical level, when a child tries to force a parent into a struggle, the parent has a number of options open:

(1) If it is a minor issue, the parent can give in to the child's whims. By avoiding a fight, the parent actually turns out to be the stronger one.

R' Yitzchak Zilberstein of Bnei Brak describes a scene in which a mother and her young daughter were walking down the street. The daughter began to whine and scream that she was tired and wanted to sleep. All the mother's attempts to placate her, telling her that they would be home soon, accomplished nothing.

The smart mother then stopped near a bench. "Do you want to sleep?" she asked her daughter. "Climb up on the bench and sleep, and I will wait for you until you wake up." The daughter climbed up and lay down on the bench, and after just a few seconds she jumped off her "bed" and continued happily on her way. This mother did not allow herself to be pulled into a struggle with her daughter, and she emerged the stronger of the two.

Parents need not be physically stronger or more powerful than their children; they need to be *smarter*.

(2) If a parent finds it necessary to punish a child (not out of frustration or anger, but with the conviction that this is truly the best thing for the child), he need not necessarily relate to his child's threats. When a child responds to punishments by threatening his parents, it is a clear sign that he is engaging in a power struggle because he does not want to accept his punishment; he is trying to gain power through frightening his parents with his threats. But like the man on the airplane, if the boundaries within which he is able to function are made solid and unalterable, the child will eventually accept and adjust to the needs of the situation. When a parent remains firm and calm, he can retain his position without becoming involved in the child's struggle for power.

Not long ago, a mother approached me to discuss her 9-year-old child. Whenever she punishes him, her child responds with all sorts of threats, saying things such as: that he will run away from home, or that he will stop working to do well in school.

In the case at hand, the mother had planned out her disciplinary measures well in advance and it was clear that her child knew that the punishment was fair. This child was also well aware of how much his parents loved him. It was obvious therefore that his threats were a form of protest and were made only to contest the parents' authority. I was confident that he would not actually carry out his threats.

I advised the mother to ignore these threats. If parents can remain calm and unimpressed by their child's threats when these threats are clearly bluffs, then their authority will be strengthened.

(This recommendation cannot be applied to every similar case. Situations vary depending on the age of the child, on the relationship that prevails between parent and child, and on the situation at home. Not every home is free of strife, and the child is not always strongly aware of how much his parents love him. Every individual situation warrants careful consideration; it is often appropriate to seek advice in such cases.)

(3) One can sit down in an informal "conference" with a child to work out a solution with which both the parent and the child can feel comfortable. Parents are often surprised to find that after they and their children reach an agreement in this manner, their children cooperate more than they ever imagined they would. However, in order to achieve this level of cooperation, one must first listen closely to the child and ascertain his needs. Parents can then state their wishes, and together they can work out a solution that is amenable to everyone involved. If the relationship between parents and children is generally a healthy one, these conferences can work wonders.

In his book, "Reward and Punishment in *Chinuch*," R' Meir Munk (principal of Toras Emes Yeshivah in Bnei Brak) cites the verse: "The wounds inflicted by one who loves are faithful, while the kisses of one who hates are burdensome" (*Proverbs* 27:6).

A child will accept discipline and internalize it only if he is convinced that the person who is disciplining him truly loves him, is on his side, and cares only for his benefit. In an earlier chapter we cited the incident of a rebbi who was punishing a student very harshly, telling the student all the while, "Even if I were your father I would do this to you." The student's reply was, "If you were my father, I would rather be an orphan!" The child could never have been fooled into believing that this harsh punishment was based on any deep love his rebbi had for him; such love simply did not exist in that situation.

Recently I came across a beautiful poem entitled, "If I Had to Raise My Child All Over Again":

> If I had to raise my child all over again,
> I would finger-paint more
>   and point the finger less;
> I would do less correcting
>   and more connecting;
> I would care to know less
>   and know to care more;

I would stop playing serious
  and seriously play;
I would be firm less often
  and affirm much more;
I would build self-esteem first
  and the house later;
I would teach less about the love of power
  and more about the power of love.

The Power of Love

The power of love is our strongest response to power struggles. Although power struggles present themselves often enough and can be almost impossible to avoid (at least on the child's part), the main feeling in the house, on a consistent basis, must be one of love and warmth.

A well-known author wrote in a recently published book, "The consensus of almost all experts in the field of child development is that creating a warm, caring, supportive, encouraging environment is probably the most important thing you can do for your family."

The power of love, warmth and encouragement cannot be underestimated, and this must be the dominant atmosphere in the home. When these feelings suffuse the home, then even when it is necessary to discipline, it will not lead to a power struggle; rather the child will realize that the parent is truly concerned with his welfare.

The Chafetz Chaim's children wrote that he treated them always with respect, as if they were his brothers and friends (the only exceptions being if they were excessively wild or if they caused harm to others). They all attested to the fact that the Chafetz Chaim never caused his children to fear him. As opposed to teaching by force, all his efforts constantly were to make the Torah and mitzvos beloved to them.

Chinuch vs. Crime Control

While I was writing this chapter, I received a fax from someone who maintains that acting with *harshness* to our children is necessary: The path of *chinuch*, said the author of the fax, is to train the child through habit and to make him know it must be done;

"this, of course, through harshness and fear." He proceeds to state that it is wonderful to inspire our children, but that is not sufficient. We must rebuke, scream and cause fear in children, until they know that they *must* keep the Torah and mitzvos. Then when they grow older and they will be exposed to allurements that may be more appealing to them than the beautiful inspirational words of the Torah, they will not succumb, because they will know well that it is forbidden.

The author of this fax discusses two mayors of New York City to prove his point. Mayor Dinkins tried to be understanding, he says; Mayor Guliani, on the other hand, is tough when it comes to law and order. When Dinkins was mayor, there was a significant increase in crime, whereas under Guliani, "our city has been brought back to shape."

On one point I am in agreement with the person who composed this fax. Children must be taught that they must keep the Torah and mitzvos, however this cannot be accomplished through force. The author is mistaken in equating *chinuch* with the prevention of crime. When it comes to crime prevention, law and order are necessary, and must at times be applied harshly. However, in this area we are concerned only with the results in maintaining an orderly society. Of course fear and rules enforced by the government are necessary to create law and order. As our Sages say, "Were it not for fear of the government, man would swallow his fellow man alive."

In the *chinuch* of our children, however, we must cultivate within them the proper attitude, so that they will choose to follow in the right paths *of their own accord* — and when they are *not with us*. When we try to force *chinuch* of Torah and mitzvos on our children it cultivates rebellion.

Recently, I met two problematic teenagers. One told me explicitly that he was taught only that *you must* keep Torah and mitzvos; about the *beauty* of Torah and mitzvos he was taught not at all. The other was reared with harshness. On numerous occasions I have had the opportunity to come to know problematic teenagers and to discuss with them what it was that caused them to abandon the ways of their parents, and I have heard similar stories from all of them. In the overwhelming majority of cases, their exposure to Torah and mitzvos was only through force — in attempts to teach them that they *must* keep Torah and mitzvos. Unfortunately, *experience shows* the grave mistake of teaching by force.

Love of Fear of Heaven

Certainly we must discipline our children, but we must not discipline in a harsh way; rather we must take a firm and consistent approach. Yes, we must teach fear of Heaven in addition to love of Hashem; but we must also teach our children how to *love* fear of Heaven. We must make sure our children are not made to feel like the group of problem children who were asked to give synonyms for fear of Heaven and came up with words such as Gehinnom, self-inflicted torture, punishment, hypocrisy, prohibitions, and depression. The great rabbis have taught us how careful we must be with our children's precious souls. The Chafetz Chaim, the Chazon Ish, R' Elyah Lopian, R' Eliyahu Dessler, R' Yaakov Kamenetsky, and the leading sages of our generation, including R' Shach, R' Elyashiv, R' Pam, R' Wolbe, and R' S. Z. Auerbach all teach us to be *mechanech* our children with love and not with harshness.

Any parent who is shouting at his children, rebuking them harshly and instilling fear in their hearts, must accept the full responsibility to ensure that his methods will not cause any adverse side effects that will show up only years later. Experience in the field has proven, time and time again, that harshness is *not* the key to raising children who will continue in the ways of their parents.

The great rabbis, who in their wisdom can see and understand where our generation is headed, have been guiding us to adjust our methods to meet the emotional and spiritual needs of this generation, when people are less tough and have less stamina than in previous generations. (This applies to physical as well as to emotional stamina. A friend of mine told me that his grandmother claimed that she would not feel any physical effects of a fast at all until she had been fasting for two days straight.)

R' Shlomo Zalman and the Shoes

R' Y.Y. Yaakovson brings the following story about a young child who once came to R' Shlomo Zalman Auerbach with a question: "It says that Hashem wanted to bring merit to the Jewish people, therefore He gave them much Torah and many mitzvos. But I haven't been able to feel that Hashem is doing me any favor with all this Torah and all these mitzvos. The more mitzvos there are, the harder it is for me to keep them, and so I end up doing even more aveiros."

R' Shlomo Zalman replied with a smile, "Certainly you know the halachah about how a person is supposed to put on his shoes. He should first put on the right shoe, then the left, and then he should tie the left shoe before the right shoe. Let us think about this halachah together: Do you know any child who puts on both shoes at one time?"

The child smiled as he answered that he did not. "And so," replied R' Shlomo Zalman, "look at what a beautiful kindness the benevolent Hashem has done for us. He tells us, 'My dear children, in any case you put on one shoe before the other, and in any case you tie one shoe before the other; so come, and I will teach you which to do first, so that you can turn what you are doing already into a mitzvah.' Here I am already an old man, and I've trained myself always to put on my shoes according to the halachah. I've already accumulated thousands of mitzvos just by doing this small activity that I would have done anyway. Can there be a bigger act of kindness than that?"

When this boy challenged the kindness of Hashem, R' Shlomo Zalman did not shout at him or rebuke him in any way, for the great rabbis knew — and know — how to raise children successfully.

After this child grew up, he himself describes how this chinuch affected him in later years:

It would be no exaggeration to say that this answer changed my life significantly. A short time after my discussion with R' Shlomo Zalman, I learned that there is also a halachah to give preference to the right side over the left side in putting on clothing. I remember well how happy I was when I learned this halachah. It was the first time in my life that learning a new halachah gave me pleasure, and I rejoiced at the opportunity to keep it.

As I grew older and entered high school, I thought about the fact that everyone gets up at some point in the morning, for without getting up in the morning, a person cannot function. Hashem did a great kindness for us, I thought, when He said, "In any case you have to get used to getting up on time, so you might as well get up for praying, and get a mitzvah out of it." With this thought I became the one who rose earliest in my yeshivah.

A great many mitzvos between man and man were transformed for me into serving Hashem happily, because any civilized person acts in a refined way. But for me, the good manners I employed in all my social interactions that I had to carry out in any case, I transformed into mitzvos. Even in areas of pure Divine service — which I could not clearly define in terms of the same line of reasoning, for I could not find the "anyway I would have done it" aspect — I started to enjoy doing mitzvos more. Apparently, once I started enjoying the service of Hashem, I became more able to enjoy doing mitzvos more even when they were done totally for the sake of Heaven.

With his simple yet profound formula, and with his keen understanding into the nature of chinuch, R' Shlomo Zalman effected a significant change in me that was to play a major role in my life.

May we merit to educate our children
with wisdom, not with fear;
with firm discipline, not with harshness;
with influence and understanding, not with force,
so that they will become true servants of G-d,
loyal to Hashem *all their days.*

15

Praying
for What You Want
— a Powerful Tool

Lost on Route 17

One of my more jolting travel experiences occurred during a trip I took with my parents on our way to the Catskills for a brief vacation. I had not bothered to find out exactly where in the Catskills we were going; my only interest was that we were headed for the mountains.

We started out toward evening, driving through the dark. We were anticipating a drive of several hours and it was raining. The squeaking windshield wipers were working overtime, and the accompanying noise of the defroster made it difficult for us to hear one another speak, so I settled myself comfortably in the back seat and, through most of the trip, remained silent. I considered it hardly worth the effort to make myself heard; there would be plenty of time to talk once we reached our destination.

Sometime close to 11:30 p.m., when we pulled over at the side of the road for a short break, I got out of the car to stretch, then I opened the back door to get some water. From the back seat I took the jug of water and a cup and, standing next to the car, I closed the car door. Hearing the door slam shut, my parents assumed I was inside and began to drive away. As the car picked up speed I ran after it, banging on the trunk to make my parents stop. My efforts proved fruitless. The combined noise of the windshield wipers and defroster muffled the sound most effectively. They drove off, leaving me stranded on Route 17.

This was a tough dilemma. I considered staying where I was, hoping my parents would realize I was missing and come back for me soon, but with a rainy midnight approaching and the road deserted, this option simply did not seem feasible. Nor did the "beware of animals crossing" signs help my positive visualization efforts. To be honest, I was scared stiff. On the other hand, were I to begin walking, where would I go? I had no idea where my parents were going. I considered hitchhiking, but the thought made me shudder — who knows what kind of person would stop for me? And if I would hitchhike, it would only make the search more difficult for my parents; if they would come back for me, they wouldn't find me where they had left me.

Turning my eyes heavenward, I hoped that Hashem would help me out of this mess. Then I decided to begin walking, although I had no idea where I was headed. Yet with every step I became more uncomfortable. At that moment, walking on a deserted Route 17 late at night seemed just too dangerous, so when a few cars passed I attempted to hitch a ride, but no one stopped. Apparently a 19-year-old walking alone on Route 17 holding only a jug and a cup was not a sight to inspire confidence among passing motorists.

Before long I reached an exit — #103 — and again I grappled with my options. Should I turn off or should I continue walking along Route 17? For some reason I decided to continue my trek along the highway. Soon, however, feeling no more secure, I again tried my luck at hitchhiking.

Surprisingly, someone stopped, although I was not as pleased with my stroke of good fortune as I thought I would be. In fact, I was afraid to get into the car. After all, I told myself, anyone who would stop for me at that hour couldn't be altogether normal. Besides, I knew very well how dangerous hitchhiking can be, even under the best of circumstances; I certainly never imagined that I would avail myself of this means of transportation. But at that moment I was convinced that walking alone on this deserted highway was even more dangerous, and I felt I had no choice. I approached the car hesitantly, and as I did so I looked the driver over thoroughly. The driver seemed normal enough. We talked as we drove, and I learned that he was a student on his way back to school in upstate New York. In his turn he asked me where I was going.

"I don't know," I answered. Then, assuming he must have thought me insane, I told him the whole story of how my parents had left me on the road alone, assuming I was in the car with them. He advised me to get off at the next exit, someplace where I could find a phone to call the state police. It is most likely that my parents were already in touch with them, he assured me, and we would be able to reconnect. And so we turned off at the next exit — #102.

The first place we passed was a bar. I had no interest in being left there, so I asked my host to drive a little farther. He complied cheerfully, and we continued on a bit until we reach a roadside motel. A car in the motel parking lot struck me as strangely familiar.

"That's my parents' car!" I cried out ecstatically, and he drove up next to it. Thanking him profusely, I wished him well and let myself out of his car. Sure enough, there stood my father, and as I walked towards him, he gave me a puzzled look and asked, "Who was that?"

Under the circumstances, I found my father's nonchalance unsettling. "Abba, what do you mean?" I asked. "That's the fellow who brought me back!"

His response was no less unsettling. "What do you mean, 'brought you back'?"

"Don't you know that I've been lost for the past 45 minutes?"

My father's puzzled look turned to one of shock as he replied, "No! You went into the motel with your mother to get us rooms for the night. Here she comes now — let's ask her." Walking toward my mother as she was returning *from the motel's front desk, my father asked her, "Where has Dov been for the last little while?"*

"What?!" she asked, even more puzzled than my father had been. "He was sleeping in the back seat!" said my mother.

I must interject that I don't know anyone more unselfish, or more interested in their children's welfare, than my parents. That they had not been aware that I was gone is not surprising, considering the late hour, the inclement weather and the background noise in the car. For all those reasons, little communication had passed between us throughout the trip, and they were not expecting me to speak to them. There was a blanket in the back seat, so it even looked like I was in the car, sleeping under the blanket, and it seems they had assumed that is where I was.

The Master of the world had answered my tefillos even beyond my expectations. Not only did He reunite me with my parents, He did it without causing them any distress whatsoever, such that they did not even know that I was missing in the first place.

A Means of Teaching Divine Providence

There are many lessons that we can derive from this story. One very basic lesson is that we need never despair. Even in what appears to be the most hopeless of situations, the A-mighty can bring so complete a salvation that the pain and danger were never even felt. We must pray in all situations, with absolute confidence that Hashem is capable of fulfilling all our needs and bringing complete salvation, in every place and at all times.

Another lesson we can glean from the story of the reluctant hitchhiker is the amazing providence with which Hashem directs our lives. This is true relative to the world at large, and it is even more applicable to us, His beloved children, the children of Israel.

Even were it only for purely pragmatic reasons, it is very worthwhile for us to teach our children to develop an awareness of Hashem's presence and Divine Providence. Children who have been reared with such awareness will undoubtedly find greater success in their lives. To quote the book *Shomer Emunim:* "One who conditions himself to be aware of Divine Providence will not become angry, nor will he harbor resentment toward others, nor will he become discouraged by the obstacles he encounters in his path."

Undoubtedly, the benefits our children will gain from our inculcating in them this attitude can be endless. Among these benefits are: self-confidence; optimism; awareness of G-d; peace of mind; success in their endeavors; and courage.

R' Wolbe has been quoted as saying that the reason there are so many rebellious children nowadays is that they were not taught to have a sensory awareness of Hashem and His deeds. We can help to ensure that, throughout their lives, our children will treasure the same values that are important to us, by instilling in our children awareness of these lofty ideals.

How can we teach these basic values? What can we do to impart this awareness to our children? There is a powerful tool that we have seen work wonders with the children in our school. In fact, it has worked wonders in my own life:

I asked one of our generation's great rabbis for guidance on how I should work on becoming more aware of Hashem. His simple advice was that I should pray for anything that I want — even for mundane things, things that may be of no spiritual significance. If I am waiting for a bus and want it to come sooner, for instance, or if I want a certain person to be my friend, I should ask Hashem to make it happen. (Anyone who begins to pay attention to all the many things he wishes and hopes for, will find that there is no end to his wants.)

In my own words, I began to say short *tefillos* throughout the day — not necessarily during *Shemoneh Esrei* or any of the standardized *tefillos*. I would say these *tefillos* at any moment, even (and especially) before or during an important event.

Another important ingredient of this discipline, the *tzaddik* told me, is that I should thank Hashem after my *tefillos* have been answered. This, he explained, makes a person aware of Hashem in every facet of his life.

I can honestly report that this behavior has changed my life dramatically. It has certainly changed my approach to teaching. To this day I never enter a class without praying beforehand. In the most challenging circumstances imaginable, I have resorted to *short*, English-language *tefillos*, and I have experienced amazing results,with the kind grace of Hashem. I am convinced that I could not have succeeded as a rebbi, principal, school director, or at any other endeavor in my life, had Hashem not answered my *tefillos* in the most critical moments.

It is this behavior that we teach the students in our school. Before major occasions, such as Chanukah or Purim parties, or before any event that is very important to them, we *daven* with them. School trips in Israel can be extremely exciting events. Each year we take the students on a major trip, known as the "*tiyul shenati*." Every class is taken somewhere that is appropriate for that age level.

Before they leave the school grounds, we board the buses briefly to join them in praying that the trip should be a success, that all should go safely and smoothly, and that the children should have the most fun possible. While the students are praying in their own words, I watch to see whether they are taking their praying seriously. After they pray, I inform them that I can always tell in advance whether the trip will be a successful one: if the boys are laughing when they should be praying, or if they are not taking their *tefillah* seriously, I know that the trip won't go altogether smoothly. Generally I tell them about other trips when the students did not take the *tefillah* beforehand seriously, and at some point during the course of the trip they got stuck; then the students first started to become serious about praying, and wanted to say another prayer, but by then it was too late to change what had gone wrong in the trip. (At that point I notify the boys that it would be worthwhile for them to pray again.)

Our students have learned that it is always worthwhile to pray — even if only for the practical benefits that will result. They know that the way to merit things in this world is to pray for them. On numerous ocasions I have asked students in various classes to compose lists of things that they want very much (making sure that they do not list anything that would be detrimental to them), and have encouraged them to pray for those things. What is unique about this exercise is that we are teaching children to turn to Hashem not only for spiritual matters, but for anything and everything that they want in life.

This Is the Accepted Custom

I would like to stress several important points regarding this *chinuch* approach:

(1) I have had reason to debate this issue several times in the past with those who have insisted that we are not allowed to pray for every little thing we want. They say that this practice should not be recommended at all, and certainly should not be taught in a yeshivah.

To bolster my response to these naysayers, I approached R' Chaim Kanievsky of Bnei Brak (the son of the Steipler Rav), who told me that praying for the countless little things that one wants *is* the accepted custom.

(2) Praying for the purpose of getting what you want in life may appear to be the paradigm of *shelo lishmah* — serving Hashem for ulterior motives. It seems that we are teaching children to pray for what they want purely as a means by which to obtain their desires.

In actuality, however, by having children pray for *what they want* we are teaching the children a very basic, important lesson regarding their relationship with Hashem: the *only* place for anyone to turn to receive what they want is to Hashem. There simply is no other way to attain one's needs and desires, except through Hashem!

(3) There is a marvelous fringe benefit in teaching children to daven for what they want: R' Wolbe, in his book *Zeriah U'Binyan BeChinuch*, explains that there are two facets of *chinuch*: (a) *binyan* — building, and (b) *tzemichah* — development. When we accustom a child to act in certain ways, we develop within him proper habits. This is the essence of building, and it is crucial to a child's *chinuch*, but alone it is insufficient, for even if we succeed in training a child to acquire the proper behaviors, we must work to develop his *attitudes* as well. If we train him only in the proper way to act, then he will lack the *desire* for Torah and mitzvos. To quote R' Wolbe, "He will be a mere robot, a lifeless automaton." In our day and age, with all the trials and challenges that society presents, it is unlikely that this child will be able to overcome them. If, on the other hand, we work to develop his desire for Torah and cultivate his attitudes so that he will *want* to do the mitzvos, then he will find the strength to stand up to all the challenges of our generation.

Judaism Without Flavor —
but an Empty Shell

So many times, wayward boys have told me that they were never given any "flavor" in Torah observance. There was no beauty there; all they recall being taught was, "Don't do this; don't do that." Thus their observance, being but an empty shell, was not strong enough to protect them from the temptations of a decadent society.

The way to cultivate a desire for Torah is not through force or pressure, but rather through enjoyment and a feeling of satisfaction. The more enjoyment a child finds in Torah and mitzvos, the more he will *want* to keep them. It follows then that we should invest a great deal into making the Torah and mitzvos more enjoyable for our children.

When R' Eliyahu Dessler was already a world-renowned educator, he recalled his youth. From the time he was 9 years old, he would wake up with the rest of his family at midnight on Friday nights, to learn Torah until the morning *tefillah*. What is so significant about R' Dessler's recollection after so many years had passed, is that he remembered the wonderful taste of the cakes that his mother would serve in the middle of the night. R' Dessler writes, "When my mother got up it was like a Yom Tov for me. She served us royally, with hot coffee and home-baked pastries that tasted marvelous." He attested to the fact that this enjoyable treat played a strong role in his eagerness to get out of his bed on those Shabbos nights.

Indeed it was a feeling of the "enjoyment" of Torah and mitzvos (as opposed to the pressure and force that is sometimes associated with them) that helped R' Dessler become one of the foremost *tzaddikim* of his day.

Children who learn to pray for what they want have an automatic sense of enjoyment, a built-in incentive to want to do this mitzvah and come even closer to Hashem. The children in our school have grown considerably through this behavior. Moreover, I have seen a number of adults whose lives have been changed when they learned to say short *tefillos* in their own words for anything they need or want.

Two sages of our generation had a fascinating conversation. One related the conversation to his entire yeshivah during one of his ethical discourses: He had asked the other, "What is the secret of your success? Which method did you use to reach such great heights?"

The other replied, "I prayed to Hashem for whatever I wanted. This brought me to a constant awareness of Hashem." He then quoted a passage from Duties of Our Hearts (Chovos HaLevavos; The Gate of Introspection #10) that describes what high levels a person can achieve through remaining aware of Hashem constantly: "He can see without using his eyes, hear without using his ears, speak without using his tongue, and feel things that cannot otherwise be felt ...." (This is a level of Divine Inspiration.) "And," he continued, "I know that it's true." At that moment he realized what he had said about himself, caught himself, and changed the subject immediately. Nevertheless, his "slip of the tongue" gave us a glimpse of how close one can come to Hashem, even in our times.

Teaching children to pray for everything they want is an excellent method of instilling in them awareness of Hashem's guidance; through it they can learn that Hashem controls every aspect of one's life. When you are doing or planning something together with your children and you are hoping for success — if you are going on a family outing and you want it to succeed; if you are hoping that it will not rain; if you are waiting for a train that is delayed — pray together with your children. The more you do this, the more they (and you) will become aware of Divine Providence in your lives (and you might experience a great deal more success in your life as well).

Show Them the Benefits

Do not try to lecture your children about the more significant benefits of praying; pray together with them, and let them arrive at their own conclusions. Do not tell them, "This is a wonderful way for you to become aware of Hashem!" Do not introduce praying for personal matters as a form of ethical practice; approach it as practical advice. Tell your children, "In this way you can achieve what you want."

In general, lecturing children in spiritual matters will not be as successful as showing them how they themselves benefit from performing the mitzvah. I refer to a quote from R' Shach, which I cited in a previous chapter. He said that the way to educate students nowadays is to teach them and show them how fortunate a *Torah loyal Jew* is here in this world. (Of course, we do the mitzvos because we must; nevertheless, cultivating the attitudes mentioned above will help develop in one's children a *love* for mitzvos, greatly strengthening their tie to the Torah, and diminishing thoughts of rebellion.)

Cultivating the Desire for Torah and Mitzvos

R' Moshe Feinstein said that when it comes to *chinuch*, if one fosters in himself the attitude that he *wants* to do a mitzvah, as opposed to the pressured feeling that he *must* do it, he can achieve true greatness is the service of Hashem. This, R' Moshe explained, is why the Torah states, "*velo sasuru acharei levavchem* — and you will not stray after your hearts," in connection with the mitzvah of *tzitzis*. *Tzitzis* have the power to protect you from temptations, because one is not obligated to keep this mitzvah unless he wears a four-cornered garment. Precisely for this reason — because it is an "optional" mitzvah, one can reach even higher levels of closeness to Hashem through *tzitzis* than one can through many other mitzvos.

R' Moshe exhorts us to apply this attitude in every area of our service to Hashem. Through doing things with an attitude that we *want* to, as opposed to feeling that we *must*, we can reach ever higher levels. Cultivating the desire to do mitzvos, as opposed to forcing and pressuring, will certainly lead to more success in one's service of Hashem. Yet it will lead to even more success in the *chinuch* of one's children.

What to Do When Hashem Answers No

Question: "When we encourage a child to ask Hashem for everything he wants, what do we say to that child when he does not get what he wants?"

A parent might tell his child the following: "If we hope to receive what we want, Hashem is the only address to turn to. Still, it is

Praying for What You Want — a Powerful Tool / 167

only Hashem Who makes the decision about whether or not we will actually receive what we want.

"Praying to Hashem it is not like pressing a button on a vending machine; nor are we telling Hashem what to do. When we pray we are asking Hashem for an unearned gift — a present that is not necessarily coming to us. Yet Hashem in His boundless love for us allows us to ask Him for it!

"But can we be upset if He decides not to give us a gift — one that we didn't deserve in the first place?"

After allowing this to sink in, one should then turn to the child and tell him with a wink, "... but it's still worthwhile to pray — because there are many times that Hashem answers 'Yes'!"

16

Taking an Active Interest

Extraordinary People

An individual who lives in Canada made the longest chewing-gum wrapper chain in the world. His now-famous chain measures 5 miles and 1,458 yards long. It may also interest you to know that the world record for crawling consecutively while maintaining constant, unbroken contact with the ground with either knee is shared by two people, both of whom crawled a distance of 31 miles and 778 yards.

People are willing to go to great lengths just to have their names listed as "record holders." They are even willing to do silly, purposeless things for the sake of having their names recorded for posterity. One fellow decided to set the record for having eaten the most watches. He ate five stainless steel watches, each of which measured one inch in diameter, including the watches' glass faces, but not their straps.

Some people will even risk their lives in order to become record-holders, such as the fellow who holds the world record for kissing cobras on the head. He locked himself in a cage that contained twenty-one cobras, bringing with him two assistants to keep the snakes at bay, and he placed a number of the snakes on separate tables. One by one, he then worked at calming them down until he was able to kiss each of them on the head. When he had succeeded in kissing ten snakes, he began to sweat. At that point he decided that it would be dangerous to continue, for snakes are extremely sensitive to body heat, and he knew that his sweating might cause these snakes to attack. (Until then, he did not consider himself to be in such danger as to warrant his discontinuing this activity of kissing poisonous snakes on the head. I cannot help but recall a T-shirt I once saw a fellow wearing, which displayed in big, bold letters the phrase: "Why be normal?")

What is it that pushes people to engage in such activities? Why is it that people are willing to endanger their very lives just to set or break a record? The Guinness Book of World Records challenges its readers, "Many people have accomplished extraordinary feats. Do you have what it takes to become one of these extraordinary people?"

People want to be extraordinary; they need to feel that they are special. And in our competition-filled, achievement-oriented world, it is too often the case that the only way they can feel this "specialness" is if in some way they can be "better" than everyone else.

The Chazon Ish states:

> Working to perfect one's character traits should not detract from one's love of self. The desire for glory is in fact a necessary cog in this living machine that we refer to as the human being. If, in pursuit of character improvement, a person attempts to eliminate his natural tendency to try to attain honor, it does nothing to build him up; on the contrary — it destroys his very essence. Far from telling us not to love ourselves, the Torah and its ethical teachings instruct us to love ourselves and to obtain honor. However, we must come to know the meaning of true honor. True honor is Torah; true honor is humility; true honor is fleeing from (imaginary) honor.
>
> *(Emunah U'Bitachon 4:14)*

It is this natural desire for honor that makes us want to be special. "*Baruch Elokeinu she'beranu lichvodo, vehivdilanu min hato'im venasan lanu Toras Emes* — Blessed is He, our God, Who created us for His glory, separated us from those who stray, and gave us the Torah of truth." Fortunate are we that we need not engage in empty pursuits in order to prove our specialness. The Torah and our Torah giants open our eyes to see how special and unique we *already are.*

Alei Shur (Vol. II, p. 414) states:

> Anyone who stops to consider his own uniqueness will be astonished. Of all those who lived from the time of Adam through today, there has never been anyone else like you; and of all those who will live from now until the end of time, there will never be another person like you, with that unique combination of abilities, characteristics, particular traits, strengths and weaknesses that you possess. Every individual is so special and unique in all of creation that he is required to say, "The world was created for my sake."

It is crucial that we understand and internalize this Torah attitude. Every person has a mission, a Divine calling to which each of us must hearken. If we fail to recognize our individuality, if we are not fully aware of our uniqueness and the unique life situation in which Divine Providence has placed us, we will not be able to determine our unique calling. We will not fulfill that purpose for which Hashem created us.

Naturally, everyone is obligated to keep the 613 mitzvos, yet each of us, with his individual abilities and in his specific life situation, has different tasks that he alone must fulfill, and different tests which he *alone* must pass. This attitude is the basis of our service to Hashem, as stated in the *Path of the Just* (*Mesillas Yesharim*): The foundation and root of perfect service of Hashem is for the person to clarify and realize *his* obligations in *his* world.

Chinuch Defies Standardization

This attitude is likewise the basis of the *chinuch* of our children: to realize that each child is a unique individual, and needs to be dealt with accordingly. "*Chanoch lana'ar al pi darko* — Raise the child according to *his* own path." In a frightening explanation, R' S. R. Hirsch tells us that the reason Esav developed his complex, sinful personality is that he studied in the same yeshivah as Yaakov!

> *R' Wolbe describes a "tzaddik" who brought his son in for a consultation. "My son is unreasonably shy," he said. At first the son's behavior seemed to confirm this, because he would not answer when the rabbi addressed him. Unfortunately, it subsequently became apparent that the*

child was refraining from speaking not out of shyness, but out of anger. His father, because of his exceptional "piety," never allowed the boy to leave the house. He would not let him play. "One must learn," he felt. Playing is in the category of purposeless speech and actions. The child hated his father with such a passion that even R' Wolbe could not lessen his hatred. The child's shyness soon gave way to adverse consequences that were far worse, and eventually he was lost to his father completely.

No one can find success in his educational techniques if he does not take into account the individual needs and characteristics of those he wishes to educate.

Chinuch by definition defies standardization. Its very essence is individualized. Because of the vast number of children in our schools, giving students individual attention in a classroom setting may be difficult to accomplish (although not impossible). (Just yesterday I met a rebbi who described to me how one of his students, even years after leaving his class, was willing to open up and talk about his problems with no one but this rebbi. "You're the only one who showed me that you loved me," the boy told him.) If we wish to have our child's individual needs met, it is *we as parents* who must accept that responsibility.

It Is Our Obligation as Parents

It is our obligation to get to know our own children, to come to know their specific abilities, their talents and their needs. There was a yeshivah student who learned in the Lomza Yeshivah in Petach Tikvah. He was accustomed to learning very quickly, and he had covered an impressive number of tractates. The standard in this particular yeshivah, however, was to learn slowly, and the yeshivah's staff wanted this student to change his approach to learning. Yet his father, who knew his son quite well, explained to the staff that the faster style of learning was the *only* method that could fit his son's character. This student grew up to become a great sage; his name is R' Chaim Kanievsky (one of the leading sages of our generation).

Of course we are not in a position to follow the example of this father. As a general rule we cannot change the system to fit our child's specific needs, but if we are aware of those needs, we *can* make small, significant changes *within the system* that can make a tremendous difference for our child. Just this week, a parent consulted with me about his child, who was not succeeding in his studies. It became clear to me during the course of the conversation that the child did not catch on quickly to the material that was being taught in class. I recommended that the father take time out at the beginning of the week to help his son prepare for the material his class would be covering in the upcoming week. In this specific case, preparing him ahead of time could enable him to succeed in class.

In fact, if we put forth the effort necessary to get to know our children, we might realize that we are not giving them what they actually need. One child who transferred into our school lacked any desire to learn, and was being given a good deal of extra-curricular remedial help. When he had spent just a few months in our school, we realized that he is a very smart boy. I contacted his father and asked him, "Do you know how smart your son is?"

I was shocked to hear the father's response: "What — do you mean to tell me he has brains?" This father had not the slightest inkling that his son was extremely bright, and so he had his son placed in all kinds of special-education programs.

Another child in our school had gained a reputation as a dreamer. He had been looked down upon at the school he had attended previously because of his daydreaming. He had motor difficulties and walked a little strangely, which contributed significantly to the way he was viewed by his former teachers and fellow students. When he came to our school, we placed a great deal of emphasis on encouraging him. In time he began to open up and reveal his true talents. This boy was a genius! When he graduated our school he was accepted in one of the best yeshivah high schools in the city. At that school, I was told, boys would wait in line to ask him questions.

Getting to know our children is a vital element in our responsibility to raise our children. If we are to properly fulfill the verse, "*Chanoch lana'ar al pi darko* — Raise the child according to his own path," then we must know what the child's "path" is. We must determine what are his specific characteristics and his specific needs.

Indeed, we give our children over to rebbis and teachers to assist us in educating them, but these teachers are only our messengers. Ultimately our children's *chinuch* is only *our* obligation, and as our Sages say, "*Mitzvah bo yoser mibishelucho* — The commandment lies in one's own hands more than in the hands of one's emissary."

Of course we cannot be expected to curtail all our other activities and dedicate every moment of our time to working with our children. This is why we have rebbis and teachers. Nevertheless, the obligation of *chinuch* remains *our own*. It is we who must get to know our children and to know what is good for each and every one of them specifically.

I like to think of myself as a dedicated educator. I love and care about the children with whom I work. Yet with all my dedication, I alone cannot provide the ideal environment for my students. I cannot give them the best I have to offer if their parents do not participate actively. I cannot remember *even one time* when a parent came to speak with me about his child and his child did not benefit in some way. My meeting with the parents brought the child's needs to my attention and resulted in the extra focus needed.

The Benefits of a Close Bond

A parent should keep in touch with his child's teachers (calling each about once every two weeks). More importantly, he *must* be in touch with his *child*. He must get to know his child, and this is possible only if he takes an *active interest* in the child. By this I do not mean simply an interest in whether his child in doing well in his studies; I mean rather a general interest in his child, and in everything about his child. One must work at developing a relationship with his child.

R' Wolbe once told me, "If parents have a close bond with their child, and they stand behind him and are there for him, then they can help him make it through the most difficult situations (even if, for example, he must endure years with difficult teachers) with success."

Who doesn't experience difficulties? Life is full of them! Yet it is the parents' love and encouragement, and it is the child's knowing that he has their emotional support and that they believe in him, that can see the child through.

Following are excerpts from a letter written by a teenager who was nearly lost to his family and his faith. This child encountered uncommon difficulties and underwent countless struggles in his religious observance, and he had no father to help him through this difficult period; yet he made a great comeback. It was his bond with his rebbi that saw him through, and he wrote this letter to his rebbi at the end of the year:

> *I really want to thank you for helping me get rid of all the garbage that I was surrounded by, and of all the emptiness that I thought was "the life." For helping me get my act together — for putting my very life back into line and for getting me back on the right path, the true and only path [emphasis his].*
>
> *Thanks to you my future will now consist of genuine Judaism, Torah, mitzvos and, with the help of Hashem, a house full of happiness and nachas. Without you I cannot imagine which lifestyle I would have chosen. What I do know is that it would have been full of falsity and emptiness.*

What magical method did this rebbi use to save this boy? What tool was able to bring about such a major change of attitude? The boy describes it himself:

> *I can only thank Hashem for guiding me to the right person at the right time ….*
>
> *This is without mentioning all the time and money you spent on me. You have shown me how much you loved and cared for me. I don't think any father would be able to match that.*
>
> *I would like to conclude, thanking you once again for everything, for changing my life, for always being there whenever I needed you, even for the smallest things.*

Although this boy did not have a father who could be there for him, his rebbi's *acting as a father*, caring for him and being there for him, was what saved him.

How much more can a child benefit if his real father (or mother) is there for him!

If the parent-child relationship is strong and close, it can carry the child through the many trials and tribulations that life brings to everyone. This bond can keep the child strong and bolster his courage so that he can succeed under all circumstances.

17

A Close Connection — a Must in Our Turbulent Times

The Tallest Building in the World

What building is the tallest in the world?

This simple question has given rise to major disputes among several countries. Being the country to house the tallest building seems to be a source of great pride, for this accomplishment "proves" that the country is in some way more powerful, or perhaps more deserving of honor than other countries.

It is interesting to note that our holy Sages teach us just the opposite, as the Midrash tells us that each of the mountains that participated in the quest to be the one on which the Torah would be given were considered undeserving due to their haughtiness. As the prophet states (*Yeshayah* 57:15), "Hashem dwells with those of humble spirit." Yet for the nations of the world, seeking honor resulting from oversized dimensions is a favorite pastime, as well as cause for controversy.

Housing the world's tallest building is so great an honor in fact, that countries are eager to make the claim even if it is undeserved. The people of Korea claimed that their Seoul Tower was the tallest in the world. Their claims were credited for some time, until someone realized that they had included in the measure of its height the mountain on which the tower stands.

For over twenty years the Sears Tower in Chicago was considered the tallest building in the world, but the race to build ever higher skyscrapers continued. A tower built in Kuala

Lumpur, Malaysia, completed in 1996, is, according to some claims, the tallest yet.

How Does One Measure?

The main issue here is how to measure these buildings. Are spires and antennas to be taken into account, for example? In order to settle questions such as this, the Council on Tall Buildings and Urban Habitat (yes, a council was actually set up to ponder this nonsensical issue of "major importance") defined four categories for measuring tall buildings:

(1) Height to the structural or architectural top
(2) Height to the highest occupied floor
(3) Height to the top of the roof
(4) Height to the top of the antenna

According to these criteria, a Chicago Public Library report ranked Sears Tower in the lead in the second and third categories, the Petronas Tower in Malaysia in the first category, and at the time the report was issued the Twin Towers in New York City in the last category (together with its antennas they measure at least 1,758 feet).

This data offended many Canadians, for why was the famous CN Tower in Toronto overlooked? It measures 1,816 feet, making it taller than any of the three buildings mentioned above.

The Council on Tall Buildings and Urban Habitat's stand in the matter is that the CN Tower is not considered a "building." It contains few occupied floors; most of the structure is merely a concrete shaft that houses elevators. The other buildings, such as the tower in Malaysia, have a hundred or more occupied floors that include shopping malls, swimming pools, hotels and offices used by thousands of people. And lest you think that the CN Tower is the tallest *tower* in the world, there is a petroleum tower standing in the Gulf of Mexico that measures 1,900 feet.

The Higher the Building, the Stronger the Foundation Necessary

But let us move on to more important matters: How much time does it take to build such a structure?

A report on the tower in Kuala Lumpur states that the construction began in October of 1991 and continued until 1996. The first phase was widening the ground area and excavating the soil from the construction site. This phase took six months.

The next phase began with the construction of the foundation and basement of the tower. Approximately 50,000 cubic meters of concrete were poured continuously for 31 hours. The foundation work was completed by April 15, 1993.

The work on the foundation took eighteen months — nearly one-third of the total time spent on the building of the tower. In fact, the main structure was completed in September of 1994, when the antenna mast was installed. It was only the installation of facilities and amenities (executed to ensure comfort and safety) that took another two years.

It is amazing that the work on the foundation actually took more time than the work on the building itself. Such is the law of architecture. The higher the building, the more work must be put into the foundation. Only in this way will the building remain standing safe and strong, having been built on solid foundations.

Laying Foundations for Our Child's Growth

As Jews, we are not interested in tall edifices. Our principal interest is our children. We want to make sure that they will be "tall" on the spiritual plane; that they will be great of *stature*; that they will be truly great people.

If we hope to turn these aspirations into reality, we must invest a great deal in laying the foundations for their growth, for as we have indicated, the "taller" we wish them to become, the stronger their foundation must be — and the more time we must put into developing that foundation.

What is the foundation for our child's growth, and how do we build it?

The foundation is the bond — the close connection between us and our child. The more time and effort we dedicate to the laying of this foundation, the higher can be our expectations for our child's growth, for *if the foundation is solid, the building will remain standing.*

We must also understand that if we do *not* invest time and effort into laying the foundations, we cannot expect much to result from our children's *chinuch*; for how can a building stand without a foundation?

Why is a close, warm relationship with one's child the foundation of our successful building of his chinuch?

In *Chovas HaTalmidim* the following is stated:

> Commands and routine are not *chinuch*. They are nothing more than tools that can be used to educate. True *chinuch* involves bringing out the child's potential to the greatest extent possible, and doing so in a way that "even when he grows old he will not stray from it," in a way that will remain with him even after he leaves the sphere of our influence.
>
> In previous generations, even if one would only give commands and demand routines, without giving particular attention to either *chinuch* or "according to his path," it could succeed. Even if parents or teachers disciplined harshly it helped, for children then accepted both the discipline and the blame. A child would feel that it was he who was at fault, and would thus come to correct his ways.
>
> Not so in our times!
>
> Today's youth consider themselves to be mature adults. They feel their own independence. This attitude has so pervaded our times that, shockingly enough, we see even small children showing this spirit of chutzpah and independence.
>
> [R' Wolbe mentioned on numerous occasions how we can observe this behavior even in 3-year-olds. Nowadays, when parents hit a young child, it is not uncommon for the child to raise his hand and try to hit back. Even if his parents do not allow him to actually strike them, we can recognize the child's attitude of unwillingness to accept authority.]
>
> One of the evils that results from this attitude is that the child looks at everyone who comes to educate him as a foreign tyrant, someone who is robbing him of his independence and free will.

These words were written in the year 5692 — seventy years ago. How much more do they apply today, in our turbulent times, when respect for authority is all but nonexistent, and when the main motivating force in the world is *doing what I want*. This force has become the ideal of our times; *what I want* is now the primary value of modern-day life. It follows automatically that a child who sees himself as an adult will desire to do only *what he wants*.

But the foundation of Judaism is to do what Hashem wants!

Nevertheless, if the spirit of the world is moving in the opposite direction, if children see themselves as independent and are unwilling to accept our authority, what are we to do?

The answer is that if we create a strong bond with our children — one in which love and closeness are the dominant feelings, then they will feel that we are out for their benefit and they will be willing to accept our authority. If our relationship is close, then even when we discipline them they will know that we are on their side. In fact, even when we make mistakes, such as when we overreact to something they have done, it will not have adverse effects because a strong connection bonds us and our children. The foundation is strong!

Discipline — Not a Contradiction

I am often asked about discipline. Of course we must discipline. In fact, it is a crime not to discipline (as has been stated in earlier chapters). Yet disciplining children does not contradict forming a bond with them any more than building a skyscraper is a contradiction to laying its foundation. *Both are necessities.*

Gaining Their Trust

When there is a healthy relationship with our children, we can have high aspirations for them, because we have laid the foundations properly. Yet if our relationship with them is lacking, they will not accept our authority nor will they see how much we care for them — they will see us only as being out for our own best interests (even though this may not be the case).

R' Y.Y. Yaakovson quotes a wayward teenager:

> *I don't believe what my father wrote — that he loves me. It can't be that all these years he didn't love me and now suddenly he loves me.*

Now he says he loves me because I ran away and he wants me to come back home. He doesn't want to suffer the embarrassment, and he has other, personal reasons to want me back. But he doesn't care about me! When I was home, he would smile to me only when I would bring him honor or good grades, or when I would help a lot. Once or maybe even twice he hugged me and gave me a kiss, but most of the time he treated me as if I were somebody else's kid, not his own son.

He used to get angry and hit me when I went to visit my aunt, because her family is not so religious. But I went anyway — particularly so, because my aunt always used to smile to me. As soon as I would open the door she would already be smiling and happy that I came. She treated me as her son, without my having to do anything good to deserve it.

Afterwards we moved far away and I couldn't visit my aunt anymore. I cried a lot. Even before that I used to cry a lot, but only at night — when they wouldn't see. My father gets angry if I cry for no reason. But when we moved, I couldn't hold myself back and sometimes I cried even during the day.

Once I told my mother that I was crying because no one cared about me. I said I wish I would die; then they would feel bad and would cry and care about me. My mother told my father what I had said, so my father called me over and said that if I want him to love me, then I should be a good boy and behave properly. But I think that even if I would behave, and he would hug me and give me things, I wouldn't believe that he really loves me.

If no bond exists between our children and us, our children will *not* turn to us with their problems.

A secular therapist quoted a girl with whom he dealt:

It got to the point where I just couldn't confide in my mother at all, even about the littlest things, like school-work. I'd be afraid I flunked a test and I'd tell her I didn't do well and she'd say, "Well, why not?" and then get mad at me. I started lying. It was like two different peo-

ple talking to each other. Neither of us would show our feelings — what we really thought.

One wayward boy I know told me how the process began: He used to have very long payos (sidecurls). When he went to a more Lithuanian style yeshivah where most boys did not have such payos, the boys would make fun of him and pull his payos. This continued for a number of months, and when he felt that he could no longer withstand the tormenting, the boy decided on the spot that he was going to cut off his payos. This was the beginning of the end.

When I spoke with this boy I asked him why he did not simply tell his parents about what was going on. He answered that his parents are terribly religious and would have taken no interest in hearing about boys teasing him and pulling his payos.

The fact is that children have never needed their parents' help and support more than in our times. It is therefore essential that we make sure our connection with them is strong, so that they will *want* to turn to us.

You Are Doing It Anyway

Several questions present themselves at this point. In a practical sense, how do we go about forging a bond? If we have been blessed with a large family, is it feasible to form a relationship with each child? And how can we find the time to create such a connection when we are constantly grappling with hectic schedules that leave us so little time?

The rule of thumb here is that we must focus on the *quality* of every minute we spend with our children.

There are many occasions when we are together with our children. If we make these times enjoyable by taking an active interest in them as opposed to ignoring them, we can make a great difference in our relationship with them.

One busy mother was driving home one day with her daughter in the car. The mother had her mind on the various activities in which she was involved. "Look at that pretty bird," the daughter commented to her mother. The mother glanced in the direction indicated, but really did not have the time to pay attention. Her heart was on "bigger and better things." As the daughter went on to talk about the bird, the mother nodded absently in reply, but wasn't really "there."

When they arrived at their home, the daughter ran upstairs and returned after a few minutes. "Mommy, I have an important note for you!"

"I'm sorry, sweetie — I don't have time now," her mother answered.

"But Mommy, it's important," the girl insisted.

"Sorry, some other time. Right now you have to go to sleep." The girl made her way up to her room and went to sleep.

Later on that evening, with some feelings of remorse, the mother went up to check on her daughter. She found her sleeping, some ripped pieces of paper on her bed next to her. Realizing that this must have been the note her daughter had tried to give her earlier, she picked up the pieces and fitted them together. The note read:

"Mommy, I love you so much, and I know that even though you are very busy, I'm very special to you. I know that even though you don't have so much time, you care so much about me. I wanted to thank you and let you know that."

During those times when we find ourselves with our children, let us give them our attention. If they ask us questions, let us answer them, focusing on the conversation and partaking *happily* of the exchange. We are with them anyway — we might as well utilize the opportunity to our mutual advantage. (As one great scholar said about praying, "Since you are praying anyway, you might as well put your heart into it.")

You can also arrange such opportunities to "be with your child anyway" by taking a child along to places where you need to go. This is a wonderful opportunity to spend time together without having to set aside extra time.

More Practical Techniques

Another time that can be used effectively to forge a close bond is bedtime. Sitting with the children for a few moments before they go to sleep, talking with them and expressing love and warmth, can work wonders.

One wonderful father recently told me about how he "rests" with his children while putting them to sleep. He spends that time talking with them about themselves and about all kinds of silly things. He has a number of children and tries to spend private "bedtime-time" with each of them once a week. He spends only about five minutes with each child, but the children enjoy this time immensely and ask him, "Tatty, can you spend time with us again?" These five minutes once a week are precious to his children.

In general, any time spent with a child in a neutral setting, talking about general topics, can contribute greatly to building a close relationship.

Another thing that can be of tremendous benefit to your relationship with your children is to laugh or play with them. *Chovas HaTalmidim* states:

> In our generation, in order to heal the wound of alienation between teacher and student — the teacher has to try to win the hearts of his students and draw them near to him. Cheerfulness and joy is the way to do this. As a teacher [or parent] increases the cheerfulness in his relationship with the child, the child will show increased love and an increased will to be close with him or her.

Just have a good time with your child for short periods now and again — but do it consistently.

> *The late R' Yisrael Mendel Kaplan, rebbi in the Yeshivah of Philadelphia, was most astute in his knowledge of students. A number of years ago, he spoke words which seem prophetic and quite apropos for our times. Once when he passed a group of students having a snowball fight, he mentioned that "nowadays [this was perhaps twenty-five years ago], in order to have a proper connection with students, a rebbi must show his approval of his students' pleasure and enjoy their snowball fight.*

In years to come, in order to have a close connection with his students, a rebbi will have to join the snowball fight himself."

Another important part of building a close bond is to express love to your children. When children hear phrases such as "I love you"; "I enjoy your company so much"; "You are so precious to me"; "I am so happy that you are my child," the closeness they feel toward their parents only grows. These are not words of praise or encouragement, but rather words of unconditional love, expressed when the child has done nothing to "deserve" them. We feel and say such things just because these are our children! Love that is expressed can have a very powerful effect.

A set of twins was born prematurely and each was placed in her respective incubator, but only one of them was expected to live. Against hospital rules, a nurse placed both babies in one incubator. When they were placed together, the healthier of the two threw an arm over her sister in an endearing embrace. The smaller baby's heart rate then stabilized and her temperature rose to within normal range.

The power of love cannot be overstated!

18

Tipping the Scales in Your Favor

The Chafetz Chaim on the Moon?

"**O**ne small step for man, one giant leap for mankind."

These famous words were uttered over thirty years ago, at 10:56 p.m. (EDT) on July 20, 1969, when Neil Armstrong became the first man to step onto the moon's surface.

R' Shlomo Wolbe once asked, "What would have happened had the Chafetz Chaim been the first man on the moon? What would he have said?"

R' Wolbe is quite sure of what would have happened: "He would have achieved the level of prophecy!" The planet Earth, R' Wolbe went on to explain, is full of people, and since there are so many people here, there are also many sins, for invariably, people commit sins. These sins become barriers between us and G-d, distancing us from Him. On the moon, where there are no people, there are no sins, and so there are no barriers between us and The Holy One, Blessed is He. It is therefore obvious that if someone like the Chafetz Chaim would have been the first man on the moon, he would certainly have achieved prophecy!

When the first man landed on the moon, R' Yechezkel Abramsky commented, "Man may have reached the moon, but he has yet to reach himself!"

Hidden Talents

Getting to know oneself takes effort; without effort it will not happen.

Getting to know others also takes effort, and without effort that will not happen either. For a surface view of things tends to make them seem far different from what they actually are.

Consider the child who did not speak until he was 4 years old, and did not read until the age of 7. His teachers described him as slow mentally, and adrift forever in foolish dreams. He was expelled from school and later was refused admittance to the Zurich Polytechnic School.

This child's name was Albert Einstein.

One gentleman you may have heard of failed in business at the age of 25 and suffered a nervous breakdown when he was 27. He was defeated in his bid for a congressional nomination at age 34, and was defeated in a race for the U.S. Senate at 46. He ran for Vice President when he was 47 — and lost.

His name was Abraham Lincoln.

In a totally different context, a young yeshivah boy who had a quick mind was failing all his tests in school. Even the questions he answered correctly were marked wrong because he had a severe writing disability. At one point, this boy found a typewriter and learned how to use it. From then on he brought it to class whenever he had a test. He went on to become a great *talmid chacham* and a prolific writer. He was the late R' Aryeh Kaplan.

These people had hidden talents, yet those who did not know them well would have thought otherwise. Eventually, through sheer determination, they succeeded, but these cases are the exceptions, not the rule. Many people, both children and adults, have great hidden talents. Not everyone merits to bring out the talents that lay dormant within.

Getting to know our own children also takes effort, and without effort it will not happen.

> *A couple came to discuss their son with R' N. Einfeld of Beer Sheva. The boy would soon graduate high school, and his rabbis in yeshivah were saying that he was very slow and did not understand the lessons. They felt that his chances of getting into a good post high school yeshivah were very slim. The distressed parents turned to R' Einfeld for help.*

After speaking with the boy for some time, R' Einfeld
realized that he possessed a sharp mind, but since he was
very quiet and reserved, he gave people the impression
that he was not very bright. R' Einfeld himself learned with
him in order to prepare him for an entrance exam, and he
was accepted into one of the most prestigious yeshivos in
Israel. Eventually, he became one of that yeshivah's choice
students. Yet this student might not have attended post
high school yeshivah at all had the proper effort not been
made to get to know who he really was.

It is imperative that we do all we can to get to know our children — their strong points, their talents, their needs, and the various problems and challenges they may be facing. If we are *aware*, then we can help them through all that they encounter in life. If we are *unaware*, they will have to try to manage on their own — quite a dangerous task in our difficult times.

The Merit That Can Cause a Favorable Judgment

The thought crossed my mind that perhaps in the days preceding the High Holy Days, *chinuch* should not be the foremost topic on our minds. Perhaps we should focus our attention on more urgent matters, such as doing *teshuvah*, repentance. When all the inhabitants of the world are being judged, dare we "waste time" on issues related to *chinuch*?

Our great rabbis, however, saw the matter in a different light. R' Yitzchak Zilberstein of Bnei Brak relates the following incident about R' Yehoshua Leib Diskin's father, who was the rabbi of Brisk:

One year the community was waiting for the rav to arrive
for Kol Nidrei. When he did not show up, the people were
extremely concerned, for the rav was known for his punc-
tuality. He never kept the community waiting and never
caused the public unnecessary discomfort.

One of the officers of the shul went to the rav's house
and found him sitting with his son learning a chapter of
Mishnayos. The officer was in shock, and called out, "The

whole community is waiting for our great teacher. How is it that he is sitting and learning with his son?!"

"I did some introspection," the great sage answered, *"and concluded that I need many more merits in order to come out with a favorable judgment. I was looking for a big mitzvah that could add many merits to my account at once. I couldn't find a bigger mitzvah than teaching Torah to my young child."*

Indeed, concludes R' Zilberstein, the proper *chinuch* of our children can be the deciding factor that may tip the scales in our favor. It can be the great merit through which we will be judged favorably on Rosh Hashanah and Yom Kippur!

The Entrance Exam at Grodno

R' N. Einfeld tells of the student who described the entrance exam R' Shimon Shkop gave him before accepting him into the Yeshivah of Grodno:

My parents were very poor and could not afford to send me to Grodno by train. And so I walked. It was a three-day journey by foot. They gave me what little food they had, with instructions that when the food was finished I was to ask people for more. I set out on my way and did as I was told.

I was very young and very much afraid. Would I find my way? Would I be able to get enough food, and get it often enough? Would I pass the entrance exam? If not, I would have to return the same way I came. I was able to relax only by focusing my thoughts intensely on the page of Gemara that I was to be tested on. I reviewed the page time and time again until I knew it thoroughly, word by word.

I got a little food here and a little there, and I slept on benches in shuls. I spent one night outside, sleeping in a corner on the ground. Tired and hungry, I finally reached the yeshivah, but I was ready for the exam. The entire page was crystal clear in my mind. I went to the office of the head of the yeshivah (R' Shimon Shkop) to be tested. (The office, incidentally, was the kitchen of his home.) R' Shimon greeted me warmly and invited me to sit down.

He then inquired as to my name and hometown. Having dispensed with the initial formalities he said, "I have only two questions to ask you."

I was tense with anticipation. "Number one," he said. "When was the last time you had a hot meal?"

Much taken aback, I answered him truthfully that it had been three weeks ago. R' Shimon stood up and said, "I'm sorry that I'm not as good a cook as my wife, but since she is out of town, my cooking will have to suffice." He then proceeded to cook a meal for me. Before long he placed a plate full of food in front of me, and when I finished it he refilled the plate. When I finished that I was so full that I could not have eaten another bite.

After I said Grace After Meals the Rosh Yeshivah said, "And now for question number two." I waited for him to question me on the Gemara.

"When is the last time you slept in a bed?"

"I don't remember," I answered.

R' Shimon went to his room and prepared the bed for me. He returned and asked me to lie down in it. He covered me well. I was so tired that I was asleep within moments and did not wake up until the next morning. Later I fount out that the bed I had slept in belonged to R' Shimon himself.

That was my entrance exam!

This student, who is today a great G-d-fearing individual, went on to emphasize that he was beset by a great many tragedies over the course of his life, including witnessing his entire family wiped out in the Holocaust. Yet through it all, what kept him steadfast in his observance were those two questions that he was asked as his entrance exam for the Yeshivah of Grodno.

The great rabbis showed their students such dedication because they viewed them as their own children, in fulfillment of the words of our Sages, "You shall teach your children — these are the students": one must consider one's student to be one's child. We can learn from our great rabbis how we must relate to our true children.

How was R' Shimon Shkop able to discern the student's needs without the student having asked for anything? The answer is that he was searching for the boys' needs, and someone who is searching for something will recognize it.

Kindness Begins at Home

For us this may be no easy task. We live in the 21st century! With so many technological developments, life moves at a highly accelerated pace, faster, it seems, than ever before. One secular author expressed the thought that life moves so fast nowadays that one has to run faster and faster on the daily treadmill just to stay in place. The unfortunate consequence is that we hardly have time to think about anything other than ourselves.

Yet we are duty-bound as Jews — and as parents — to think of others. "One who wishes to be saved from difficulties which will transpire before the coming of Mashiach must immerse himself in Torah and kindliness" (*Sanhedrin* 98b). Without a doubt, we are living in the days preceding the coming of Mashiach. The painful tribulations of our turbulent times are part of the birth pangs of his coming. Torah alone — learning and supporting Torah — is not enough. We must also turn our attention to others, and kindliness begins at home! We must think of our spouses and our children.

Consider this sobering thought expressed by R' Chaim Vital:

> When a person faces his judgment in the World to Come, they do not evaluate him according to how much he helped other people. He may be a tremendous activist, may be constantly running from one affair to another, may be constantly involved in one project after another, but his worth is measured according to how he behaved with his (or her) spouse and children. The way a person acts with his family members reflects who he really is.

Listening and Understanding
— the Greatest Kindness

The greatest kindness we can do for our children or for our spouses is to understand them and learn their needs, and the only way we can accomplish this is by developing within ourselves the art of listening.

> *Recently, I heard two horrifying stories. The first occurred several years ago, when a rebbi noticed that a boy in his class who had become a bar mitzvah a few*

weeks earlier still did not own a pair of tefillin. When the rebbi approached the boy's parents to discuss the matter, the father responded, "He's not a good boy. He's not behaving himself. [This boy was a weak learner, and could not tow the line in standard yeshivos; he had already been in and out of a number of yeshivos.] Tefillin cost money! I'm not going to waste my money on such a boy. When he shapes up — then I'll get him a pair of tefillin!"

How differently would this father have spoken about his son if his focus had been on listening and kindliness.

Another boy was learning in a top-notch school, but was failing due to a lack of motivation in his learning. The boy was obviously troubled, yet no one had ever tried to understand him until recently. His rebbi befriended him and forged a close relationship with him, and the boy confided in the rebbi that his parents were separated and he could not tolerate the atmosphere in his home. He was not learning because he just did not have the stamina to deal with all that was happening in his life.

If we learn to listen to our children, they will open up to us and confide in us. They will turn to us for help with the many problems they themselves do not know how to deal with, and we *will* be able to help them, with the help of Hashem. But if we do not listen, they will not turn to us at all, and then who will help them out of their difficulties? How will they succeed?

I recently came across a letter written by a student to his former principal:

I have no doubt that a tremendous amount of the credit for my success goes to you. I always felt that I had a fair and understanding ear in the highest office of the yeshivah. I would literally go there on my own for what I now realize was lifesaving help. I remember the time my mother was hospitalized with colitis and the laundry piled up. One day I came to yeshivah with pants that were much too short, and sure enough, the comments started coming. I ran in tears to the only place I felt loved — your office.

Today I am a successful teacher, and I recently started my own school for boys who need a second chance. People say that I help boys develop their strengths and reach their potential. You have a big portion in that. I certainly count you among the special kindnesses Hashem has done for me.

Hashem Will Judge Us With Understanding

There is no question in my mind that listening to and understanding our spouses and children can be a great merit for us for the days of judgment. For the formula of judgment is "measure for measure," and if we listen to and understand our spouses and our children, then Hashem will surely listen to and understand us and our difficulties, and He will judge us with understanding.

Even though this book is about *chinuch,* I include spouses in this calling by direction of one of the leaders of our generation, who told me that the principle regarding children and spouses is one and the same: *"Ve'ahavta lere'acha kamocha* — love your friend as yourself."* Just as we wish to be understood by others, so too must we try to understand others — especially our children and our spouses.

> *One Shabbos a few weeks ago, one of my younger children was crying, and did not want to come to the Shabbos table. I tried, with gentleness and warmth, to determine the problem, but despite all my efforts, he was not willing to open up. Rather than allowing myself to become upset, I simply left him alone. Later, he came to join us at the Shabbos table, but still would not tell me what was wrong. Much later, he opened up to me about a matter that, to him, was very serious.*

Just Listen

The first rule in listening is to listen; just listen without saying anything, and try to put yourself in the other person's shoes. And, as has been noted: you cannot put on the other's shoes until you take off your own.

We must understand that even if something is not the least bit important to us — even if we consider something insignificant, it may be of major importance to someone else. R' Yisrael of Salant made an amazing statement: If a child's toy ship breaks, the child experiences the same anguish as an adult merchant whose ship just sank at sea.

Listening With the Heart

The second rule in listening is that listening with one's ears is not enough. One must also listen with one's heart. We must listen with the intent to understand. This means that before we criticize, even before we give advice, we must *listen*. Many times we are so anxious to give advice or to reprimand (or perhaps we are so upset), that we do not take the time to listen first. We just express our feelings immediately.

(I am reminded of the doctor who gave his patient a set of crutches, telling him, "These will help you in your recovery." The patient protested, "But doctor, I have a stomachache!")

Listen First, Then React

Of course as parents we have to give our children proper guidance, but there will always be time for us to express our feelings afterwards. First we *must* listen and understand! It is impossible to both express our feelings and listen at the same time. And if we have listened, but have not understood, then we have not listened properly. Listen and understand *first*! Then give yourself a little time to think things through. Only then can you decide on an appropriate response. Many times, once you have understood your child, you may feel differently, but even more important, your child will feel differently. Even if you disagree with him and decide on some action that is not in accordance with his desires, he will still feel that he was understood. This can make all the difference.

Consider this true practical example.

> A boy had been taking money from his parents' drawer without permission. If we would discover that our child

was doing such a thing, we might naturally be quick to react with anger. We must educate him, we say.

However, his parents decided to discuss it with him first. They sat him down to talk in a non-threatening atmosphere, and asked him what happened. Because he felt confident that his parents were truly interested in understanding him, he began to explain to them that he is not popular in class, and feels like an outcast.

In order to win the favor of the other boys in his class, he came upon the idea of buying a lot of nosh and handing it out. In that way, he hoped that everyone would begin to like him.

Once we understand what is motivating our child, we may decide to react differently. In the case cited here, we may consider him a unintentional and not a willful transgressor. We may feel that a discussion and a warning are sufficient this time, or we may have him pay back the money out of his allowance, taking off some of it each week until the debt is paid off. However we decide to handle the situation, one thing is certain — we will understand him and feel for him.

Knowing that he does not feel good about himself, we may also decide to work at building up his self-esteem. We can embark on a program of complimenting him and pointing out his successes, of telling him how proud we are of him and how pleased we are with him, of expressing to him how much we love him and how important he is to us.

Accepting Our Children for Who *They* Are

Perhaps one of the most difficult things about parenting is being able to accept our children for who *they* are. Maybe our children are not living up to *our* expectations. Maybe they do not fit the mold that we have cast for them. Maybe they have disappointed us. Nevertheless, if we listen to them and try to understand them, we might just learn who *they* are. And we might begin to see *their* strengths, *their* hopes and dreams, *their* personality. We might begin to see the difficulties *they* are experiencing, the fears *they* have. In this way we might be able to help *them* according to who *they* are — *chanoch lana'ar al pi darko,* raise the child according to **his** path, not *al pi darki* — my path.

You Are on the Right Path

Being a parent is not easy. (I know; I'm a parent too.) The ideas expressed in these chapters are aspirations; they represent a yearning for improvement. We all struggle. We may even be far from fulfilling the concepts discussed in these pages, but if the ambition is in our hearts and in our minds, *we are headed in the right direction.* And the right direction is what counts.

I once approached the known *tzaddik* and Kabbalist, R' Yaakov Hillel, a few days before Rosh Hashanah, and asked him: "In the few days that are left, what can one do to improve oneself?"

He answered that the most important thing is one's direction. If a person can change his direction to move toward the proper way, then he will prevail in his judgment.

If you are reading this book, then you are interested in improving. You have already changed your direction, and are on your way to success.

19

There Is a Better Way

Mr. G. and His ...

Please fill in the blanks (use the same word for all the blanks):

Mr. G. was taught that unending patience is the secret of success with any _____. Rather than striking, he was told to repeat instructions constantly, using rewards for accomplishments and mild rebuke for failure. Mr. G. also learned the value of consistency: presenting yourself every day to the _____ in the same way.

As to the secret of his success, Mr. G. answered, "I am the boss; but they know that I am also their friend. I feel very close to my _____. If I miss a morning with them, I feel bad. Once you have become totally involved with your _____, they become a part of you. They are like my family."

Every session brought new problems, but nothing that Mr. G. couldn't overcome with constantly repeated instructions, rewards, soft words for success and mild scoldings for failures. His triumph was to understand the personality of each individual _____ and find the magic combination of rewards, rebukes and reassurances that would make the _____ want to learn.

This is not a story about a teacher who discovered the secret of success for controlling classes in an especially difficult school district — the missing word is not "student."

The missing word is "animal(s)," and the above is an excerpt from an article about Gunther Gebel-Williams, one of the most successful animal trainers of all time.

He was able to control eighteen tigers at one time and to direct a herd of thirty-two elephants, using his voice alone. With his unique training methods he put together an act that was unprecedented in circus history, in which tigers, horses and elephants performed together. The act's debut was reputed to be one of the great moments in circus history. Most intriguing were the atypical methods he used during the act. Instead of whip-cracking, there were lumps of sugar and a caress for the horses; instead of prodding with a bull hook, there were pats on the back and a loaf of bread for each of the elephants; and instead of pistol shots, there were affectionate cuffs for the tigers.

"Only people who understand how much horses and elephants fear beasts of prey," Mr. G. explained, "will realize how much time and effort went into the act."

As Jews, our feelings may be aroused when we hear about someone whose life revolves totally around his animals and who is so dedicated to them that they become "a part of [him] ... like [his] family." We may also be duly impressed by the innovative training methods this man employs; as our Sages taught us, *"Chochmah ba'umos ta'amin"* — we may appreciate the fact that wisdom can be found among non-Jews.

We can also learn a great deal from the unique methods Mr. Gebel-Williams used with his animals.

Harshness and Force — Ineffective

If consistency and perseverance, accompanied by encouragement, incentives and "soft rebukes" or mild scoldings were more successful than harshness in training wild animals, how much more true must this be when it comes to the *chinuch* of our children, who are the children of Hashem.

It is important that we realize that harshness and force will never inspire anyone to do willingly what we wish him to do. The most we can hope for is that he will obey us begrudgingly, for lack of choice; but his heart will not be in it. This being the case, through harshness and force we will not be able to get our children or students to perform tasks that are very difficult for them, because in order to do that which is difficult, one must want to do it.

Gebel-Williams was able to induce Royal Bengal tigers to leap-frog over one another and, balancing on their hind legs, to jump around like kangaroos. There is no doubt that harsher methods could not have accomplished this. Many times we want our children to do that which is difficult for them. (The degree of difficulty of any task is altogether subjective; something that may seem very easy to us, such as behaving as we expect them to or succeeding in school, may actually be tremendously difficult for our child.) On these occasions, consistency, accompanied by warmth, encouragement and gentle persuasion — with perhaps the addition of an incentive, will be far more effective than shouting, criticism or other harsh methods.

Rebuke — Mildly and With Loving Care

Even a rebuke or a scolding, if administered mildly and with loving care, can achieve the desired results. R' Nosson Einfeld, in his booklet "Chanoch LaNa'ar" cites the following true episodes:

> A teacher of one of the upper grades in a yeshivah elementary school arrived in class one day to find that his class record book was missing; it was clear that one of the students had taken it. This was certainly a serious infraction of school discipline. Immediately, the teacher reprimanded the class harshly for their disrespect. He also demanded that the record book be returned to him within 10 minutes.
>
> Ten minutes elapsed and the record book was not returned. In a rage, the teacher descended upon the boy whom he surmised was the culprit. He also screamed at the entire class, using the words of our Sages to humiliate them: "Ein lecha mishpachah sheyesh bah listim she'ein kulam listim — There is no family of which some are thieves, without all of them being thieves."
>
> The end result was that the record book was not returned, the class did not learn that day, and the behavior of this teacher accomplished nothing.
>
> A similar incident occurred with a different teacher of a different class in a different school. When he realized that

his record book was missing, the teacher continued teaching as if nothing had happened. During recess of that morning, he called over a student, whom he suspected of taking the record book, to speak with him privately. The boy approached the teacher nervously and with great trepidation, but the teacher turned to him with a relaxed smile and said, "Do me a favor and bring me the record book. I need to check something."

The boy, caught off his guard and somewhat confused, said, "I saw the record book in a corner. I don't know who put it there, but I'll bring it right away."

He brought it to the rebbi, who looked into it for a moment. Then, turning back to the student, the rebbi said, "Thank you for returning the record book. Now let's work things out between us, without involving the principal or your parents, and without punishments or fines. You hid the record book — correct?"

The student broke down in tears and admitted that he was guilty. He tried to explain that he had been seized by a spirit of mischief, but that he realized his mistake and how very wrong it was. He asked forgiveness, promising that he would never do it again.

The teacher forgave him, but at the same time stressed that should such an incident happen again, there would be no choice but to involve the boy's parents.

With this rebbi's response, everyone gained. The record book was retrieved, the class learned, no one was humiliated, and the student learned his lesson. In fact, the student felt deep appreciation for his teacher, who related to him with wisdom and compassion, rather than with anger and harshness.

Children Are Also People

It is important to note that the rebbi who dealt calmly with his student was also fulfilling the mishnah in Ethics of Our Fathers: "Make the honor of your student as precious to you as your own honor." There is no mitzvah of honoring one's fellow man that applies to dealing with animals, but the mitzvah of honoring one's fellow man certainly applies to our relationships with our children.

A group of 13-year-olds in the Etz Chaim Yeshivah once came to R' Isser Zalman Meltzer to be tested. R' Isser Zalman asked them about a certain Tosafos, and one of the students was quick to respond — with the wrong answer. With a smile R' Isser Zalman answered, "Wonderful! You surely meant such and such ..." and he began to explain the Tosafos properly.

The young boy countered, "No, Rebbi, that's not what I meant," and he reiterated his incorrect response.

Unruffled, R' Isser Zalman said, "I understand. Come, let's see." He then proceeded to explain the Gemara in detail, returning eventually to the question of Tosafos. Afterwards he explained Tosafos' answer in such an erudite fashion that its meaning was beyond doubt.

Yet the boy stood his ground. "Why doesn't the Rebbi understand — I explained it differently!"

By now the other boys in the class were grinning, and their rebbi was becoming increasingly upset. Yet for the next 10 minutes, R' Isser Zalman tried again and again to explain it to the boy, and again and again he would ask, "You probably meant this — right?"

Yet the boy would not relent — "No, no ...."

Finally, when the situation had gone beyond all reasonable limits, R' Isser Zalman excused himself and left the room. Curious to see where R' Isser Zalman had gone, the rebbi opened the door quietly and peeked into the hallway. He saw the great scholar pacing the hallway, repeating to himself over and over, "When the Torah commanded us to have honor for other people, it was referring to children also; honoring one's fellow man includes children!"

Shortly thereafter R' Isser Zalman reentered the room, returned to his place once again and turned to the student with a shining face. Once again he asked, "Now, please tell me, how do you explain the words of the Tosafos?"

Helping to Get the Message Across

The "fringe benefit" (which is actually the main advantage) in this type of response (remaining calm) is that it actually does get the message across. When one deals with children harshly and with impulsive anger, the lesson one hopes to convey is lost. The child (or adult) will erect a defensive barrier that will prevent his hearing and internalizing any message at all. The teacher or parent might feel that he is teaching the child a lesson, but in fact the student is not absorbing the lesson. On the contrary, he is resisting it!

When the educator or parent deals with firmness yet with care, with mild rebuke or scolding yet with warmth, as in the second case of the "stolen" record book, the child will be able to absorb the seeds of the *chinuch* that we wish to plant in his heart. Moreover, the child might come away with feelings of appreciation, respect and love for the teacher or parent, whom he can see is truly interested in his benefit.

It is doubtful that those who discipline out of anger and impulsiveness are really aiming for the benefit of their students or children. They may insist that they wish to teach the child a lesson, or they may challenge us with the question: If we do not get angry, how is the child supposed to learn to do what is right?

But the real question is: If we do discipline out of anger and impulsiveness, how is the child supposed to learn to do what is right? When he is "taught" with harshness and anger, he will not learn anything at all!

What Harshness Truly Teaches

However, says the Chazon Ish, he will learn a major lesson from this type of "teaching" — he will learn how to develop negative character traits (although in this instance the Chazon Ish was referring to teachers, the same holds true for parents):

"When a teacher rebukes his student with harsh expressions and shouts of anger over the unacceptable things the child has done [even if it will make the student stop his problematic behavior], it is a very detrimental approach." The student will begin to consider impatience and anger as acceptable responses, since he sees his rebbi employing them every time he rebukes him. As our Sages taught, "Learning through example is greater than learning by teaching." Therefore, the lessons the student picks up from the rebbi's actions are stronger than the lessons he picks up from his words.

The Chazon Ish stresses that the more a student is under the influence of such an educator, the more he will inherit bad character traits. (Refer to his work, *Emunah U'Bitachon* 4:16.)

Several points must be stressed here:

(1) Our times are stressful, the pressures with which we live are intense, and we all lose ourselves at times. This is only natural, and no harm will be done to the child as a result of the parent losing him-/herself occasionally.

   It is when the parent or teacher deals harshly with his children consistently, or as an intended approach, that it can be very detrimental.

(2) I am not professing that anyone spoil his child, or give in to all the child's whims. As Mr. Gebel-Williams said, "I am the boss and they know it." We are not advocating a permissive approach to discipline. We are saying that one not discipline harshly, that one not discipline impulsively or out of frustration and anger.

Had the rebbi in the second episode not reacted at all, he would have neglected his obligation to be *mechanech*. The point is not to abstain from disciplining — it is to discipline more effectively; it is to discipline in a fashion that the child will want to do what we want him to do. Most important, it is to discipline in a way that will have no adverse side effects in the long run.

Rabbi Wolbe (in his *Zeriah U'Binyan BeChinuch*) describes a typical scene of parents coming to him for advice about their teenagers. "I don't know what's going on with him," say the parents. "He doesn't tell me anything. In fact he hardly speaks to me at all!" Then, says R' Wolbe, he asks the parents if they disciplined him harshly when he was younger. Generally their answer is, "Yes, of course — we had to be '*mechanech*' him."

"What is happening now," R' Wolbe explains to them, "is that you are paying for the harsh discipline you gave him years ago."

Long-Term *Chinuch*

What R' Wolbe tells parents is that everything we do in relating to our children has a residual effect. This brings us to one of the most important considerations in *chinuch*:

Our *chinuch* must take into account the larger picture of our child's life. We must not aim merely for *chinuch* for the moment, *chinuch* that will bring only on-the-spot results, for this is not real *chinuch* at all. Our *chinuch* must also lead to desired results in years to come. It must bring out our child's potential in a way that will provide him with the tools and the will to continue on the path of success even after he leaves the sphere of our influence.

There is in fact a very valuable technique we can employ to help ourselves remain focused on such an approach to *chinuch*, one that will last in the long run. This technique is having a goal.

If we have a goal for our children's *chinuch*, then we have a clear destination. We know in which direction we are heading, and when we are sure of our course, we will be able to overcome the temptation to turn off the road when we encounter road signs that point to other destinations.

Imagine that you are trying to find a lift to upstate New York for Shabbos. "Where are you going?" you ask your friend who is traveling in that general direction.

"Somewhere in upstate New York," he responds.

"But where?" you ask.

When he answers, "I don't know," you look elsewhere for a ride. We could guarantee that you will not travel with this fellow, when he does not even know himself where he will end up.

I strongly recommend that you decide on a specific goal in raising your children, and put that goal into words — preferably into a single sentence. Writing it down and referring to it can help greatly in your day-to-day reactions and responses to your children.

By referring to our goal from time to time we will be reminded of our destination, and we might adjust our reactions accordingly, deciding not to turn off the road and head for other, closer (and, in the short term, easier) destinations.

One father described how this strategy saved the day in a very challenging situation that presented itself in his home.

> He came home one day to be greeted at the door by his son who exclaimed, "Daddy, I'm really a big helper for Mommy."
>
> Later on the father heard the full story behind those words. While his mother was occupied downstairs, the little boy had emptied a half-gallon jug of water from the refrigerator onto the kitchen floor. As soon as the mother

came up she saw the mess, and her first instinct was to yell at her son and spank him. But before she reacted, her goal — "I want my son to feel loved and appreciated" — came to mind. This caused her to stop for a moment and reevaluate what her reaction ought to be. Instead of showing her anger, she decided to ask the little boy, "What were you trying to do?"

"I was trying to be your helper," he responded with confidence and pride.

"What do you mean?"

"I washed the dishes." Sure enough, right there on the kitchen table were all the dishes he had washed with the water he had taken from the refrigerator.

"Why didn't you use the water from the sink?"

"Because I can't reach the sink."

"Oh," said his mother. "And what do you suppose you can do next time so that there won't be such a mess?"

"I'll wash them in the bathroom!" he said ecstatically.

"That might not be a good idea, because they could break there — but I have a better idea. How about if you call me, and I'll move a chair over to the kitchen sink for you, so you'll be able to reach the sink?"

"That's a great idea!" he said.

Because this mother had a goal, she decided to redirect her initial course, reacting in a way that would help her achieve this goal. And her son, instead of feeling guilty and humiliated, felt loved and encouraged. (He was also asked to clean up the mess, of course.)

During one of the staff meetings in our school, we decided upon the following goal:

To help each child develop his full potential, according to his unique abilities.

We put this in writing and we refer to it from time to time. It has helped us to reevaluate our instinctive reactions, and at times to adjust them accordingly in order to do what is best for the child.

Whatever goal you choose, it must be for the child's benefit, as opposed to goals that may fit "my needs," but that may not necessarily be in the child's best interests.

An Invaluable Tool for Turbulent Times

There is another technique that we can employ, which is an outgrowth of the *chinuch* approach that is focused on long-term results.

We live hectic lives, and most of the time we find ourselves under pressure, and are unable to find the emotional wherewithal to react to our children as we would like to. I once saw excerpts of an average mother's communication to her child during a typical day. It went something like this:

> *Put your plate in the sink, please.*
> *Don't hit your sister.*
> *I'm talking now.*
> *Just a minute; can't you see I'm talking?*
> *What do you mean, "There's nothing to do"?*
> *Read a book.*
> *Clean your room.*
> *Hurry up.*
> *Hurry up, everyone's waiting.*
> *I'll count to five, and then we're going without you.*
> *Did you go to the bathroom? If you don't then you can't go with us. I really mean it.*
> *Why didn't you go before we left?*
> *Stop it.*
> *I said stop it.*
> *I don't want to hear about it.*
> *Stop it or I'm taking everyone home right now.*
> *Is your homework done?*
> *Stop yelling — if you want to tell me something, come here.*
> *STOP YELLING! IF YOU WANT TO TELL ME SOMETHING, COME HERE!*

In view of the myriad small issues that crowd out real communication with our children, I would like to offer another suggestion that can make a great difference in the long run:

Set aside one hour a month for each child, and spend that hour in open listening time with your child.

During this hour only listen, and do not advise. Our purpose should be only to be there for our child, to let him express his feelings and air out whatever is bothering him.

If we are approaching *chinuch* with a view toward the future, then this hour of listening each month could be our most effective tool, keeping the lines of communication between us and our children open. If we give our children an opportunity to tell us anything they have on their minds in a safe environment, they will continue to turn to us with their problems in later years, when their problems might be more complex and of great significance in their lives.

I know of a girl whose parents kept to this method, spending an hour with her in safe, comfortable communication once a month, and eventually this is what put her life back on track. No matter what came up in their busy schedules, her parents would always try to keep this once-a-month "appointment" with their daughter, so that she could air her grievances and feel understood. During this hour they kept to a strict policy not to offer advice, become upset, or go on the defensive. This hour belonged totally to their daughter.

At one point, their daughter began to act out at home. They knew that something serious was bothering her, but they did not know what it was. The daughter simply would not discuss it. Strangely enough, however, during one of their monthly appointment hours, the daughter finally did open up.

She told them that she had been cheating in school, and that no one realized it. She had found out where the teacher kept her personal test notebook, and so she was able to find out all the answers before a test. The teacher had begun complimenting her in front of all the other students, and she was getting the highest marks in the class. Their daughter was now feeling trapped in a downward spiral and she did not know how to get out. During one of these sessions she felt that she could finally open up to her parents and seek the help she so desperately needed to get herself out of this complicated predicament.

Her parents were very supportive and together with their daughter they came up with a plan that succeeded in reversing a dangerous trend. Through their monthly hour of listening to their daughter, they were able to stop this child from falling into what may have been the beginning of a long, complex path of deceit and misery.

Look toward the future. Discipline your children, yet keep the lines of communication open, so that your child will always remain close to you, and close to Hashem, all his days.

20

Teaching
Responsibility (Part 1)

The Taxi, the Administrator and the Preschool Teacher

What do the following three incidents have in common?
(1) I was riding to school in a taxi today, when the driver suddenly stepped on the gas and moved into the left turning lane. "Aren't you going straight?" I asked the driver in surprise.

"Apparently you didn't realize," he explained, "that you're in a *taxi*. We [taxi drivers] own the streets — they belong to us, and we can do as we please on them." (This brazen attitude is not universal among taxi drivers. I know many who would be appalled at such a statement.)

As soon as the light changed and the flow of traffic resumed, our friend the taxi driver continued on *straight*, passed up a few other cars (all illegally, against traffic rules, of course) and eventually moved back into the correct lane.

(2) A close friend of mine described his recent bout with bureaucracy. He heads a yeshivah here in Jerusalem and was surprised one morning to be awakened by a call informing him that there was no water in the building. Someone had seen municipality workers come and shut off the water. Although he had received warnings at one point that the water might be shut down, these warnings were few and far between. Moreover, the yeshivah had not received many of the water bills as they had been sent to a

wrong address. My friend had felt, therefore, that he was safe in ignoring cutoff warnings, until that fateful morning.

He had his secretary contact the municipality to explain, but these efforts accomplished nothing. "You must come down and pay," they said. (The bill was a mere 11,000 shekels.)

My friend quickly made his way to the Safra Plaza, where City Hall is located, arriving just five minutes before it closed for the day. He parked illegally next to a sign that said "*k'nas megudal*," which indicated that violators would have to pay an inflated fine, ran into the main building, barely making it before its 1 p.m. closing time, and went directly to the clerk who handles the accounts of institutions. When this clerk heard his story, he had a bill printed up immediately and handed it to my friend with a cheerful, "Now all you have to do is pay. After you pay, just bring me the receipt and I'll issue orders to reconnect the water."

No problem, thought my friend, as he rushed his way down the hall to the cashier. Just then, however, he realized that he had not brought along any of the yeshivah's checks. How would he pay?

Fortunately he had a credit card in his pocket so, approaching the desk with more confidence, he requested that he be allowed to pay by credit card. He hoped that he would be able to arrange to divide the bill into several payments, to mitigate somewhat the shock of having to pay such a large sum of money in one lump sum when he was so unprepared. The cashier answered in the affirmative, "As long as we get an okay from the credit card company." My friend stood patiently as the cashier swiped his card through the machine and waited for an answer.

"I'm sorry, but the credit-card company will not approve this payment," said the clerk after a short wait.

"What do you mean they won't approve it?" exclaimed my friend. "I'm calling my bank right now!" When he finally got through, the bank official explained that he had a credit limit of only 5,000 shekels.

"Listen, couldn't you please make an exception this time? This is a school full of kids, and they have *no water*!" After careful deliberation and consulting with the bank manager, the official agreed! "We will allow it to go through — just this one time."

My friend turned in triumph to the cashier with the good news, but his happiness was, unfortunately, premature. "You still need the credit card company's approval," she said.

"But the bank said it's okay."

"It makes no difference," the cashier countered. "I'll call them for you." She did, and the company representative told her that they would call the bank. The cashier explained that nothing could be done until they called back.

It was now 1:45. The first clerk, who had sent my friend to the cashier, came over to him to hand him a small paper with a phone number, telling him, "I'm sorry, but we closed officially at 1 o'clock. I waited for you till now, but I must leave. In case you work it out and pay, just call this number and they'll reconnect your water.

And so they continued to wait, less patiently now, for the credit card company to get back to them after contacting the bank. When 2 o'clock came and went with no reply, my friend urged the cashier to call back the credit card company. The clerk agreed reluctantly, and when she called she found out that they hadn't even called the bank yet.

The bank closed at 2 o'clock.

To make a long story short(er), somehow the bill was finally paid, but by that time everyone had left and there was no one who could authorize a reconnection. My friend tried the phone number the clerk had given him, but it was too late for them as well to authorize a reconnection.

When my friend saw that all his efforts to get the water service restored on that same day had failed, he left City Hall dejectedly and made his way toward his car, only to find a ticket in the windshield, with, of course, the exorbitant fine — the *k'nas megudal.*

(The yeshivah managed to make it through the crisis somehow, and the water was reconnected the next day.)

(3) A truly righteous woman in Bnei Brak passed away recently, when she was about 70 years of age. She had been a preschool teacher for forty years, and no doubt she already knew each weekly portion of the Torah reading quite well. Still each week, week after week, year after year, she would sit and prepare what she would tell her preschoolers about the weekly *parashah.* One might think that forty years of repetition would have been enough to prepare her to speak to groups of 3-year-olds, without needing to prepare afresh each week. Nevertheless, she never dispensed with her weekly sessions which she spent planning how she would present the weekly portion to her young students.

What these three incidents have in common is that the protagonist in each had something to do with the trait of *responsibility.*

In the first case, the taxi driver was devoid of responsibility. Whether or not he believes that he owns the streets, nothing gives him the right to drive recklessly.

In the second case, my friend was blessed with a lack of responsibility (on that particular occasion — generally he is a most responsible fellow). He should have paid the water bills on time, whether he received two warnings or ten. (He should have brought checks with him, and left earlier for City Hall so that he could have parked with more care.)

In the third case, the righteous teacher had an unusually strong sense of responsibility. As befits a grandchild of our forefather Yaakov (who worked day and night to meet his obligations to Lavan in the best way possible), she felt it necessary to prepare her preschool classes *every week,* even though she was only speaking to very young children. If one is responsible, what difference does it make to whom you are speaking?

Actually, someone who is truly responsible might prepare *even more* for teaching young students, because they are especially impressionable, and whatever they are taught leaves an indelible impression on them.

The Atheism of Our Times

Responsibility is the very reason we were placed in this world. Because we have free will and can choose what we will do, we are held responsible for our actions and can be rewarded and punished accordingly. It is for this that we were created (see *Da'as Tevunos* by R' Moshe Chaim Luzzatto).

Indeed R' Wolbe cites R' Yitzchak Hutner, who said that the atheism of our generation is in the realm of free will. Thus, rather than focusing on denying the existence of Hashem as people did in the past, people today are choosing to stress denying that human beings possess free will. This is a form of evading responsibility, for one who admits to having free will must also admit that he is responsible for his own actions.

There is a general trend in the secular world today to avoid responsibility (except when it will lead to monetary profit, prestige or some other personal gain). We find that secular courts acquit people who have committed the worst of crimes, as long as they can cite a valid psychological reason for their deeds (*Alei Shur* II, *Sha'ar* 1, Ch. 5).

Such is the world in which we live, and we are not immune to its influences. Who has never had his hands full getting his children to help around the house? How many parents complain that their children do not clean up after themselves, or that they do not keep their rooms neat, or that they are not interested in doing well in school?

How are we to teach children responsibility in our turbulent times, and do it in a way that will make them willing to accept — and appreciate — responsibility?

A Crucial Question

There are a number of approaches that can be helpful in this area, but we must first understand *why* our children must approach responsibility willingly. Why should we not just force them to accept responsibility, whether they like it or not, until eventually they grow accustomed to it? Don't our Sages say that "a person is formed according to his actions"? (see *Sefer HaChinuch*, *Duties of the Heart,* and others). If this is the case, can we not assume that the more tasks and chores children perform that demand responsibility, the more responsible they will become?

The renowned educator R' Y.Y. Yaakovson in his book *Al Techetu Ba Yeled*, refers to the Chafetz Chaim who also asked this question, and he couched his answer in terms to which people living in his generation could relate.

> At the turn of the century, the term "Cossack" was used to symbolize the paradigm of tirelessness, quickness and industriousness. The Cossack troops were characterized by their lightening-fast speed, along with the strong determination with which they carried out their tasks, and with the energy with which they handled that which stood in their way.
>
> Yet these same Cossacks, once they retired from the army and were supported by the Czar for the rest of their

lives, became prime examples of extreme laziness, lethargy, boredom, idleness and waste. They would live out the remainder of their lives just lolling about near heated ovens, doing nothing.

Why didn't their multitude of army-related activities, into which they invested tremendous diligence, influence their personalities and tendencies, making them industrious human beings even when they could manage on their pensions?

The Chafetz Chaim answers that all their intense efforts and all their running was done only with the intent of bringing themselves closer to the heated oven. Their sole purpose in everything they did was to be able eventually to sit next to a warm oven and do nothing!

Indeed it is true that a person is formed according to his actions — but in which direction will these actions take him? Invariably, they will lead him in the direction he holds in his heart! And if in his heart he wishes only to lie next to the oven, then it is in this direction that his actions will take him.

This is an amazing insight, and it can open many new vistas for us.

Simply forcing responsibility on someone will not make him a responsible person. It all depends on the direction in which his heart is moving. If his heart accepts and wants the responsibility, he will become responsible. If his heart rejects responsibility that was placed upon him against his will, then he will move away from responsibility in general, and all attempts to train him to be responsible might have the opposite effect, as in the case of the Cossacks.

(Of course, all parents must make demands of their children, even when the children are not pleased with those demands. It is very healthy for children to learn that their parents will not indulge their every whim; it is healthy for children to be taught to do even the things they do not want to do, so that they will not become spoiled.

Yes, by doing so parents will train their children not to be spoiled, however, this will not teach children responsibility. In order to be *mechanech* them to be responsible, we have to do it in a way that will draw their hearts to accept our *chinuch*, as we have stated earlier. Only in this way will our children become responsible in the true sense of the word.)

Responsibility for an Entire Nation

Our great rabbis in all generations were and are truly responsible individuals. They have always borne the burden of our holy Nation on their shoulders.

Many people wanted to meet with R' Shach, and it was not always easy to find a moment when he was free to speak with them. One visitor from London, however, who was very close with R' Shach, was generally admitted immediately whenever he came. Yet one time he was made to wait; the rabbi's assistant told him that R' Shach had asked not to be disturbed.

The visitor noticed a middle-aged couple sitting in the room with R' Shach, both of them obviously nonreligious. The visitor's curiosity was aroused as to the identity of this couple whom the rav deemed so important that they were cause for him to delay his receiving this esteemed guest. He was even more baffled when one of the great tzaddikim of the generation came in, and R' Shach likewise did not permit him to enter. Again, the assistant said that he could not be disturbed.

The gentleman from England finally approached the assistant for an explanation, and he recounted this couple's story:

The husband had made his millions at a relatively young age, and decided to retire early and move to Kenya, Africa. In order to set his plans in motion, he needed to change a large sum of Israeli currency. He was told that in Bnei Brak he would be able to find a dealer who could do this for him. While he was in Bnei Brak seeing to the task, he mentioned his story and his plans to the moneychanger. One of the people who was in the room at the time was a relative of R' Shach, and he overheard the story. When this man returned home he told the story over to other family members, and eventually R' Shach heard about the matter.

Immediately upon hearing it, R' Shach sent a messenger to request that the man come to him. When he arrived R' Shach began explaining to him that in Kenya there is no Jewish community, and if he were to move there, there is no doubt that his children and all future generations would become totally assimilated. "Even though you are not religious yourself," R' Shach told him, "you are still Jewish, and you want your descendents to be Jewish."

The man accepted R' Shach's reasoning and agreed to cancel all his plans and remain in Israel, but when he went home, he found that his wife would not accept his decision. When R' Shach heard this, he asked him to return together with his wife, and this was the couple with whom R' Shach was speaking when the man from England walked in. This single concern was uppermost in R' Shach's ladder of priorities.

In addition to the great love that our leaders have, and always had, for each and every Jew, they have and always had a powerful feeling of responsibility toward our People. Fortunate is the Nation that has such leaders!

21

Teaching Responsibility (Part 2)

Why Be Normal?

"**A**re you normal?!

You could be saving yourself 10,000 shekels on mortgage insurance and you haven't called us yet?!"

Just the other day this ad was staring me in the face as I sat in my car behind an Egged bus, stuck in a traffic jam. According to this ad, anyone who fails to call that company to buy their insurance might not be normal. No need to worry, however; a T-shirt I once saw worn by someone jogging in the street declared to the world, "Why be normal?"

Kidding aside, it is a fact that society all around us is deteriorating at a very rapid pace, and we must be aware of this. Nowadays, the very value of normalcy is considered debatable.

Yet Hashem has placed us in just this society, and given us a most important role here: to bring up children who will be loyal and responsible servants of Hashem. No one has the right to shirk the responsibility of consistently working toward this goal; those who will accept this task with appreciation and optimism will meet with the utmost success. In the previous chapter, we discussed at length the question of raising children to be responsible and caring. In this chapter, with the help of Hashem, we will explore some aspects of the answer.

The Five-Step Formula

We can employ any or all of the following five methods to help us achieve this goal:

1. Expressing love
2. Encouraging more and criticizing less
3. Making our children our partners
4. Putting children in charge
5. Planning in advance

Let us examine each method individually to see how it can help us in our efforts toward teaching our children the trait of being responsible.

The First Method: Expressing Love

The prerequisite for teaching children responsibility is to give them the emotional strength to be able to handle responsibility. If we want to teach a child to be able to lift heavy objects, for example, we must first help him develop the muscles he will need to lift the appropriate amount of weight. Similarly, if we want to teach a child to be able to bear the yoke of responsibility, we must work to strengthen his emotional muscles. If we show him love, he will feel good about himself and will develop the attitude that he is important and capable.

One young adult I know has never been able to handle responsibility. Whenever he is given "too much" responsibility, he begins to feel overwhelmed and at such times he tends to get sick. It did not surprise me to learn that his parents did not show him much affection when he was young.

(Do not make the mistake of thinking that helping a child feel good about himself is training him in conceit. The Chazon Ish, in his book *Emunah U'Bitachon* [4:14], insists that love of oneself is vital to the proper functioning of this living "machine" called man. There are many things one can deny oneself without suffering adverse affects, but any attempt to deny oneself this love of self not only will not build the person, it will actually destroy his very being.)

A great "fringe benefit" of expressing to our children our love for them on a consistent basis is that a child who feels his parents' love will tend to be less belligerent and more cooperative. The desire to please his parents and not cause them anguish will become ever stronger.

"The foundation of success in every form of *chinuch*," R' Wolbe wrote recently in a letter, "is for the *mechanech* [either parent or teacher] to love the *mechunach* [child or *talmid*] with a true love that the *mechunach* CAN FEEL. Failing to do so can lead to most undesirable results."

A child who had been orphaned at a very young age was placed under the guidance of the Rav of Ponevezh and lived in a dormitory in Bnei Brak. Years later the child described how sometimes in the middle of the night, when he was fast asleep, he would feel the Ponevezher Rav bending over him and giving him a warm kiss on the forehead.

In a previous chapter we cited a psychologist (whom leading rabbis recommended) who told me personally that he has witnessed teenaged children healed from serious emotional problems through a simple method: their mothers began the practice of giving them a kiss on the forehead before they would go to sleep each night.

R' Wolbe described how at a wedding once he was approached by a 90-year-old man, who took his hand and asked him his name. When R' Wolbe introduced himself, the elderly man repeated his name emphatically and exclaimed, "It used to be that when one Jew would meet another Jew he had never seen before, he would offer praise and thanks to the Master of the universe that he now had someone new to love!"

This is the love that true Jews show to other Jews. How much stronger is the love we must show to our own children.

There are many other ways to express love. It is told that the children of R' Shlomo Zalman Auerbach would be given new yarmulkes for the High Holy Days, but in a very short time these yarmulkes would be ruined. When their father would bless them on *erev* Yom Kippur, his tears that would come flowing in rivers at that time would completely soak the yarmulkes.

Parents can make sure that their children hear from them on a regular basis phrases such as, "You're very special to me"; "You make me happy"; "I have a special place for you in my heart"; "You're a joy"; and other such positive, loving comments.

One tool that is an especially effective means of expressing warmth and love is a smile. This poem I came across recently expresses it well:

A smile costs nothing but gives much.
It enriches those who receive it without
making poor those who give.
It takes but a moment, but the memory
of it sometimes lasts forever.
None is so rich or mighty that he can
get along without it, and none is so
poor that he cannot be made rich by it.
A smile creates happiness in the home, fosters good
will in business and is the countersign of friendship.
It brings rest to the weary, cheer to the discouraged, sun
shine to the sad, and it is the best antidote for trouble.
Yet it cannot be bought, begged, borrowed or stolen, for it
is something that is of no value to anyone until it is
given away.
Some people are too tired to give you a smile.
Give them one of yours, as no one needs a smile so much
as he who has no more to give.

It Is Crucial in Our Times

This valuable "tool" may always have been necessary, but it is so much more crucial in our generation.

Once when a student of the Gaon of Vilna was sailing to Israel with his young son and daughter, the ship was wrecked by a violent storm and he found himself in the middle of the sea holding his son and daughter, and grasping for dear life onto a plank of the debris. After some time passed he felt his strength ebbing away, and knew he could not support the extra weight of both his children much longer. When finally he felt he had no strength left whatsoever, he spoke lovingly to his children, explaining that he could not possibly hold both of them anymore, said Shema with them and let go of one of them first. As the father drifted away still clutching

the other child, he heard the first child scream, "Father!"
At that moment he somehow mustered some hidden
source of strength and pulled the child back to him. He
managed to hold them both until they reached the shore
safely, and then he fainted.

When a parent hears his child cry out to him, he finds the strength somehow. But need we wait until our children cry out in desperation? Can't we have the foresight to give them what they need before they call?

Children today need love more than ever before, and they need to be *shown* that love. I stress that they must be shown love not only when they are younger, but even when they are older. So many times wayward children I meet have told me, "My parents and I don't get along."

Years ago R' Wolbe told the Chazon Ish, "Nowadays young men are not made of the strong stuff they used to be made of. Nowadays they need to be encouraged and built up emotionally." The Chazon Ish nodded in approval at these words. Recently I heard the very same words spoken by another of the leaders of our generation.

Specific Times

Our lives are often terribly hectic, and we may find that in our daily interactions with our children we are not expressing much love — the opportunities simply do not seem to present themselves. The fast pace of our days coupled with our many responsibilities might not allow us to open our hearts to our children to express our love. If you find this to be the case, then picking specific times in which to express love can improve the situation in amazing ways. There are, in fact, many times that are not swallowed up by the rush hour of family traffic.

Before a child goes to sleep, for example, or immediately when he returns home from school, or when things have quieted down at home and the child is ready to begin his homework, are times that present golden opportunities for parents to express their love. These are times parents often spend with their children, and at such times children are very receptive to the emotions parents express. You can be sure that expressing love to a child will get him to do his homework — or cooperate in general — more willingly.

No matter what the situation, it is always a worthwhile investment to find the most suitable times when you can express love to your child on a consistent basis.

Giving vs. Giving In

It is important to note once again that expressing love to your children does *not* mean giving in to them. On the contrary, if you express your love to them consistently, you can be firm in your discipline without having to worry about adverse effects, because your children are secure in their awareness of your love for them.

When asked what to do when a child who does not get his way cries, "You don't love me!" Rabbi Shmuel Kamenetsky responded that, rather than giving in to his demands, give the child a kiss and tell him that you love him. The child who is confident of his parents' love can accept this type of response (even if he *acts* as though he is not accepting it).

The Second Method: Encouraging More and Criticizing Less

Once we have assigned our children a task and they have done it, we have a choice. Either we can focus on the part they accomplished successfully, or we can focus on the part they have failed to accomplish successfully. In most cases, both possibilities will apply: the child will have succeeded in part and failed in part. It is up to us to choose where we will place our focus.

A cartoon I saw depicted a cup sitting on a psychologist's couch, undergoing therapy. "Doctor, I'm constantly confused," it was complaining to the psychologist. "I never know whether I'm half full or half empty."

Unfortunately, I know of many children whose parents focus on the half-empty part of them. If the cup requires therapy when it is not sure whether it is half empty or half full, how much therapy would it need if it would be shown only that it is empty!

A child once transferred to our school. He was not particularly bright, and in his previous school he had often been told,

"You are not worth the chair that you're sitting on." At our school this boy received a great deal of encouragement, and the results were soon evident. All year he learned with much desire, and by the end of the year he had a beautiful notebook which he had filled with various commentaries and concepts that the rebbi had discussed in class throughout the year.

The rebbi offered to purchase this boy's notebook (each year, this rebbi collects a few notebooks from boys in his class, to keep as a memento), but the boy refused to sell it. He was not willing to part with his beautiful notebook.

On one of my trips to the U.S. I passed a father and son walking along the street. Apparently the father had given the son a job to do, and the son had not done it properly. "You klutz!" I heard the father scream at his son. It made no difference to this father that they were in the middle of the street, and passersby could hear and see everything that was transpiring between him and his son.

The Thief and Other Stories

One teacher employed such methods and made a dreadful error, with disastrous results. The story came out when someone came to a rabbi with a halachic question. The fellow was about to get married and did not feel at peace with himself. The following incident gave him no rest:

> When he was in elementary school, he stole a watch from one of his classmates. The teacher warned the boys that the watch had better be returned or else. This dire warning was sufficient to frighten the child into returning the watch. Instead of giving the watch back to its owner directly, he placed it in the briefcase of another classmate. After a thorough search, the watch was found in the briefcase of this innocent boy. All of the victim's efforts to vindicate himself were useless. The rebbi considered him the culprit, for he had been "caught red-handed." The teacher led him in front of the entire class and called him, "Thief, thief!" again and again.
>
> This fiasco caused the child irreparable damage. Knowing this, the boy who had actually stolen the watch

approached a rabbi and asked how he could repent, to which the rabbi replied, "You were a minor; you were under 13 years of age and weren't considered responsible. The teacher, however, will be held responsible in the heavenly court."

Someone related to me how when he was a child he could not have been considered orderly by any standards. One day his teacher, who was a stickler for order, took this child's notebook and showed it to the entire class. "This is how one should *not* be," said the teacher.

What teachers and parents such as these fail to realize is that these methods are at best totally ineffective. If one wants a child to succeed, one must point out to the child what he is already doing successfully.

The more we focus on what a child does right, the more he will do things right. If we give a child responsibility and we point out where he has succeeded in fulfilling that responsibility (even if one must search to find that modicum of success), then he will succeed even more, and he will come to accept responsibility willingly. He will grow up confident in the knowledge that he is capable and can handle responsibility successfully. If, on the other hand, we focus on what he has done incorrectly, then we are training him to focus on his own faults and we will raise a "broken vessel," one who will be incapable of doing anything and who will certainly not be able to handle responsibility.

One person related that when he was younger he was made fun of and criticized when he served as *shaliach tzibbur*. To this day, he told me, he shudders whenever he has to do anything in public. He shakes when he is called up to the Torah and must recite the blessing aloud.

A parent or teacher who sincerely has his child's or student's best interests in mind must know that harsh or consistent criticism can lead to devastating results. One who is truly interested in the child's benefit must focus on what the child is doing correctly, and encourage him in this way.

If we want our children to learn to be responsible, then when we give them responsibility we should focus on the half-full results of their efforts, pointing out to them what they have done correctly, and encouraging them for it.

The Third Method:
Making Our Children Our Partners

Responsibility is a burden. Yet if we give our children the feeling that they are partners with us in bearing that burden, they will feel honored to do it, and will not look at it as a burden, but rather as a privilege.

R' Wolbe learns this basic principle from Yaakov Avinu and his children. The verse states that Yaakov told his "brothers" to gather stones. Rashi explains that in fact they were his children, yet in this case, because they helped him, they were considered his brothers. Involve your child in something *you* are doing; ask him to help you.

The point here is that being your partner makes your child feel important, and this makes him feel good about the responsibility placed upon him. You can provide your child with opportunities to share in your responsibilities in a number of ways:

First, through special projects: A parent might pick a special project that he and his child can undertake together.

> *One father had a hobby of gardening, and one day he suggested that his son help him in the garden. His son did not at first realize that this would mean spending hours in the hot sun, shovel in hand, digging and getting blisters and simply working hard.*
>
> *But his father worked alongside him and took the time to explain everything to him. They worked together.*
>
> *Later, when they picked the various vegetables that had grown, the boy found great satisfaction in the outcome of his undertaking. Thereafter, he himself took a special interest in making sure that the garden was kept weed-free and in good order.*
>
> *As the child himself remarked years later, "... and now I found that this experience was a help for me in just about everything I do. I learned to define the task at hand, to clearly see what needs to be accomplished, and to create a goal — what end result do I have in mind."*

There are many projects you can undertake with your child to make him a partner in your work and do it together with you.

A mother can try out a new recipe together with her daughter, or a father can involve his son in a kindness project in which he is involved.

Another way you can provide your child opportunities to share in your responsibilities is to ask him to do something in a way that makes him feel like he is truly contributing something to ease your burden.

If you make your request in a way that makes your child feel that he is your partner, then he will more readily accept the responsibility. Asking children to help you do things that you normally do on your own makes them feel capable and needed. Offering younger children the opportunity to do adult chores can open up new worlds for them. One of my children was a very rambunctious 5-year-old. A renowned educator told me to let him do "sponja" (the Israeli method of washing the floor; we could always go over the floor again after he had finished his task, as long as he was not aware that we were doing it).

Even an older child can be made to feel like your partner when you express to him your sincere appreciation and tell him how much his work has helped you. "If not for your help I couldn't have had the house cleaned in time for Shabbos!" "Because of you I was able to finish the work in half the time." (Even in asking the child to do the chore, if you express to him how much of a help it will be for you if he does it, he will do it more readily.)

Many adults would much prefer to do things by themselves, and involve their children in household chores only when they are desperate. Perhaps they are hesitant to let their children do more because they feel that the children will not get the job done properly.

This reminds me of the wise farmer who bought several cows, so that he could teach his children about farming. One individual who observed how the farmer's children were bungling through their work with the cows exclaimed to the farmer, "Why do you let them do this work?"

"I'm raising children, not cows!" replied the farmer.

If raising children is our priority, this may at times be even more important than getting the job done right (and besides, you can always go over the floor again).

The Value of a Life

Just how important do Arabs consider their children's lives to be?

Before I relate the following true, hair-raising incident, allow me to ask a different question. Just how much value do Arabs place on life altogether?

Perhaps you are familiar with the Arab custom to take random rifle shots at their weddings. My friend, who lives in a neighborhood on the outskirts of Jerusalem, is intimately familiar with this custom. One day his 12-year-old daughter was sitting on the back porch reading a book when she decided to enter the house for a moment. Upon returning to the porch, she noticed a hole in the plastic chair on which she had been sitting. Looking under the chair she found a bullet shell.

She called her father to see what had happened, and they realized immediately that there had been a wedding in the Arab village nearby, and since their mood was so festive, they shot several rounds with their guns. Only Hashem's lovingkindness spared the girl from a dire fate when she left the porch just in time.

Obviously then, Arabs do not consider human life to be of great importance. Perhaps you will think, however, that this attitude of theirs applies only to Jewish lives. The following true story, which was told by the soldier who was there at the time, may change your impression.

An Arab living in northern Israel had been serving the Israeli cause, helping the Israeli army from his unique position. One day a soldier brought him a message from the Israeli intelligence services warning him that other Arabs had found out his secret, and in an act of vengeance, his Arab friends had booby-trapped his truck.

As the soldier watched, the Arab turned to his son and told him to go and start up the truck. The soldier was aghast. Even if this fellow did not believe him, how could he risk his son's life by gambling on even the slightest chance that the soldier's words were true? Noticing the soldier's perplexed expression, he explained himself. "A child is replaceable; but if I start the truck and it blows up, who will be there to make money for my family?" And with that explanation he stood back and watched as his son started the truck and was blown up in front of his very eyes.

It is of Yishmael (the father of the Arab nations) that our father Avraham was told, "*Garesh es ha'amah hazos ve'es b'nah* — Send away this maidservant and her son," so that the Patriarch Yitzchak would not be exposed to such a negative influence; and it is with Yishmael and his influence that we are confronted in our times. May the *Ribbono Shel Olam* show us, His children, mercy, and redeem us quickly from their midst.

Keeping the Chain Unbroken

To Jews, our children are priceless, and it is only by safeguarding them that we can perpetuate the nation of Israel, the holiest nation on earth. It is imperative, therefore, that we place the *chinuch* of our children at the very top of our list of priorities.

To perpetuate our people, however, making *chinuch* a top priority is not enough. We must at the same time make educating our children in such a way that *they will perpetuate our people* a top priority. *Many* of our children are, tragically, being lost to negative influences. They are becoming severed links in the unbroken chain which stretches from Mount Sinai down to us. It is therefore incumbent upon us to examine carefully our methods of *chinuch*, and to make sure that we are reacting to our children not only in a way that is convenient for us, but rather in a way that is best for the child, in a way that reflects the tremendous value that we place on our children as perpetuators of our holy tradition. And as two top psychologists in the field of children in crisis said, this attitude is at the heart of prevention.

The Missing Tabernacle

The book, "The Coat of Shmuel," the biography of the late great tzaddik R' Shmuel Aharon Yudilevich, relates that in his youth R' Shmuel Aharon studied under a teacher who had "golden hands." The teacher had fashioned a model of the Tabernacle out of paper and cardboard. During recess everyone went out to play, except for Shmuel Aharon, who remained in the classroom to learn. When the boys returned from recess, the Tabernacle was missing. Shmuel Aharon had been so engrossed in his learning that he had not even noticed anything that transpired in the classroom.

The teacher led the young boy into an office and read to him the chapter from Prophets that describes how Achan stole from the booty that the people of Israel had taken. He read the whole chapter, verse by verse, including the punishment Achan received, and the boy began to cry hysterically. Just at that moment the office door opened. The real culprit stood in the doorway holding the model of the Tabernacle. He had been hoping to hide it in an empty room.

When the teacher returned to class he poured out his wrath on poor Shmuel Aharon. "You should be ashamed of yourself!" he screamed. "How did you let me think you were guilty of a crime that you didn't commit? Why did you cry? Who were you trying to fool anyway? Enough time has been wasted! Bring the Tabernacle and we will carry on with the lesson."

The teacher then picked up the Tabernacle gently and spoke of it lovingly. "This is the Aron HaBris," and he demonstrated the miniature facsimile of the Aron he had made. "And these are the Keruvim. The Aron represents the Torah, and the Keruvim represent a teacher and his student. Their faces are turned toward each other to demonstrate the great love between them."

R' Nosson Einfeld cites this story, asking: What permisssion did the teacher have to embarrass this student in public? Is it then permissible to do whatever one feels like just because one has to discipline?

R' Einfeld then brings out yet a stronger point. It is a teacher's responsibility to know his students. This teacher should have known that Shmuel Aharon was a *tzaddik*, and that he was incapable of such behavior.

He then cites R' Yaakov Kamenetsky, who said that there was one teacher whom he had never forgiven. He related that one day, on his way to yeshivah, an old woman asked him for help. Since he helped her, he came late to school. When he arrived at school he explained that he was late because he had helped an elderly woman. It happened that there was a church parade in progress at the same time, and the teacher accused Reb Yaakov of delaying to watch the parade on his way to school. Then he slapped Reb Yaakov.

Reb Yaakov explained that he never forgave this teacher because it is a melamed's responsibility to know his students. "He should have known that I don't lie," said Reb Yaakov.

If this is true for teachers, how much truer is it for parents. Parents have the responsibility to know their children and to guide them in a way that is good for them. R' Pam said that parents are certainly included in the prohibition against shaming another person. Even a small child is sensitive to shame, and a teenager is even more sensitive. If a child is embarrassed by his mother or father, it can do irreparable damage to his developing personality.

The Fourth Method: Putting Children in Charge

This means, at times, trusting our child with total responsibility for certain situations. Many times we may feel hesitant about giving our children responsibility, and even when we do assign them a specific task, we are often the ones ultimately to bear the responsibility. Hence, if our child is unable to complete his homework, we may end up doing it for him; if he does not straighten his room, we may end up doing it for him.

(In exceptional circumstances, this practice may even be recommended. I know a wonderful father whose son came home from school one day with a worksheet that he did not know how to do. He went to sleep that night feeling very frustrated, and awoke the next morning depressed, apprehensive about what awaited him in school. How pleasantly surprised he was to find the answers all written out in his father's handwriting on a separate piece of paper that lay next to his homework worksheet, with a note saying "I love you." The boy quickly copied over the answers and happily dashed off to school. Incidentally, when he returned home from school, the child informed his father that some of the answers had been marked wrong; the father had made a few mistakes.)

As a general rule, however, if we take responsibility for our children on a consistent basis, we are depriving them of the opportunity to take responsibility for themselves.

It is understandable that the practice of allowing children to take responsibility can be a very difficult one for parents. We may not have the patience to wait for them to do what has to be done, or it may be easier to do it ourselves than to invest the time and the emotional energy it takes to fight with them about doing some task we have assigned them (especially, for example, on *erev* Shabbos when you have not yet begun to cook).

Yet if it is *chinuch* for responsibility that we intend to give our child — that the child will develop a positive attitude toward accepting responsibility — then we must take the time to find a task our child will enjoy, or a way to approach the task so that our child will accept responsibility *willingly.*

22

Teaching Responsibility (Part 3)

The Car Accident

If there would be a functional Sanhedrin today, what would its judges have ruled regarding driving a car?

The Steipler Rav was known to have said that if the Sanhedrin were functioning today, they would have prohibited driving a car. Because of the amount of casualties incurred through car accidents, the Sanhedrin could not have permitted its use, despite the tremendous benefits we gain from cars; the ends do not justify the means. The Torah places such high value on human life that even a small number of fatal car accidents would be adequate reason to prohibit the use of cars.

> *I myself was involved in a serious car accident many years ago. I was driving my parents' car home from yeshivah when I decided to race my friend, who was driving in the lane next to me, to the next traffic light. As I was picking up speed the car skidded into the left lane. Not realizing what had just occurred, I stepped down hard on the gas, my only thought being to get to the intersection before my friend. All I remember after that is the harsh, clanking sound of metal against metal.*
>
> *A taxi driver who was driving a short distance behind me witnessed the entire incident and later described what actually took place. As I pressed down on the gas pedal,*

the back of my car began to skid towards the left, while moving simultaneously across the avenue toward the curb. As the car was moving and skidding, I jumped out. (I was the only one in the car.) The moving car knocked me down and under it. My car stopped when it wedged itself under another car that was parked along the curb, and I lay under those two cars, my hand locked under the tire of the bottom car. Since the gas tank of the car I had been driving was punctured, I was lying in a pool of gasoline. Those who had come rushing to the scene were unable to free my hand. It was necessary to call a tow truck to lift the cars off me; only then was I able to get up.

What happened to me?

Nothing.

Miraculously, the A-mighty brought me out of that "valley of death" with only a few bruises and some minor chemical burns from the gasoline.

My family doctor, who was not religious, recommended that I give a few coins to charity. Even he realized that this was no ordinary occurrence. Someone who knew me commented, "It seems the Ribbono Shel Olam wants you to accomplish some kind of task in your life, and that's why He's keeping you around."

At that time my parents made a thanksgiving meal, and every year since then I have tried to give thanks publicly to the Ribbono Shel Olam. I guess I was quite fortunate. Even without guessing, I know I was totally irresponsible. I could have killed myself. I could have killed someone's parent or child. It was only Hashem's kindness that had limited the damage. I recognized this — and my parents knew that I had learned my lesson.

I am forever grateful to my parents for having retained their trust in me and allowing me to continue driving after that (although for a number of weeks after the accident I would shake every time I got into a car — not unlike someone to whom I once gave a lift here in Israel. He had been on a bus that was bombed a few years ago, and ever since, has not been able emotionally to handle the fear of traveling on a bus; he will travel only by car or taxi.)

I learned the hard way to drive responsibly. Indeed, this method of *chinuch* was very effective in teaching me responsibility, although obviously it is not a method that can be recommended.

The Fourth Method:
Putting Children in Charge (Cont.)

There are a number of means by which to encourage a child to agree to accept a task willingly. The key tool is *discussion*. If we discuss things with our children we will also hear their point of view, and we will come to understand which tasks they enjoy or how to best work things out in a way that is acceptable not only to us, but to them as well. I stress that we are not proposing a democratic approach to parenthood; a child must listen to his parents even if he does not want to. Nevertheless, the relationship between parents and children must be a close one, and one will never lose any authority or discipline by discussing matters with and trying to understand one's children. Especially when being *mechanech* children for responsibility, discussion can be very effective in inspiring them to do tasks willingly.

Once we have determined which tasks our child has chosen to do willingly, or once we have arranged with him through mutual agreement that he will do specific tasks willingly, we should place upon him the entire responsibility for those tasks. He will be totally responsible and we should not interfere and take over the responsibility for him.

> One father allowed his children to choose which jobs they wished to be in charge of. One child stated emphatically that he wanted to be in charge of keeping the backyard clean. This was no small task, since the backyard had gotten rather messy over the summer. And so father and son made an official agreement. First the father pointed out to his son what results he expected to see. "Keeping the yard clean means that there will be no garbage or food wrappers lying around, no string, papers, sticks, or anything else for that matter." To illustrate his point, the father cleaned up half the yard and then told his son, "This is the way it should be."

The father then turned to his son (who was all of 7 years old) and asked if he understood clearly what needed to be done. Then he asked his son if he was ready to take on the job. "I want you to understand," said the father, "that if you're ready, it means that you're taking the job. I will no longer clean the yard. You're the one in charge. Of course, if you need my help I'll be glad to be of assistance, but it's your job. You're in charge."

The father then scheduled regular "accountability sessions," times when the father and son would walk through the yard together, and the son himself would assess what kind of job he had done. It would not be the father's job to hold the son accountable; he would be there only to help the son hold himself accountable. Since the son had taken total responsibility, the goal was that the son would be his own overseer. "Twice a week we will walk around the yard and see how things are going," the father told his son. The father discussed it with him a number of times until the son understood fully that he was the one in charge, and that his father would be there only to help him judge himself.

A few days passed and, surprisingly enough, the yard became quite dirty. The father was upset and he felt a strong inclination to berate his son, but he stuck to the agreement. "Lets go out to the yard," he told his son when the scheduled day for the accountability session arrived, "and you can show me how you're doing."

The son broke down in tears and said, "It's so hard!"

"I'm your helper," said the father, "as we agreed. What can I do to help?"

"Please help me. There's so much garbage, I don't know where to begin." And so the father helped his son, but all along it was the boy who felt responsible. The father was merely helping him. After that first experience the boy took total responsibility and kept the yard clean on his own through most of the summer. He even reprimanded his siblings when they left things out in the yard.

What ensured the success of this father's plan is that there was an agreement. The son agreed *willingly* to clean the yard. The second point is that after this was accomplished, the father gave the son *total* responsibility. Whatever the father would do to assist his son's efforts would not be *doing* it for the son; he was only the son's helper; it was the son's job.

The father demonstrated his dedication to this principle by not berating the child for his negligence. Had the father become overly critical of the son, it would have proven that the father was in charge and that he considered the yard to be his worry. Instead, the father wisely waited for the accountability session, when the son himself examined his own progress and only enlisted the father's services in the role of helper. It was the son's job, and he alone was responsible.

Discussion is successful not only as a means for teaching our children responsibility. It is also a powerful tool for establishing communication with our child, and when we communicate with our children, they react altogether differently to our requests.

Discussion, Communication, Understanding — a Winning Formula

We mentioned that communication is another benefit that is a direct result of discussion. When we communicate with our children, we said, they react altogether differently to our requests.

When a child in our school was sent out of class for misbehaving, he complained to me that the teacher picked on him unfairly. I listened, and then asked him if there was anything that he himself had done that he should not have done — regardless of how he felt the teacher had treated him. He admitted that there was. "I shouldn't have called out in class, even if the teacher did not treat me the way he should have."

I then told the child that I would speak with the teacher (to make the teacher aware of the child's grievances), but only on condition that the child would agree to accept responsibility for his own behavior, and would no longer behave in ways that were unacceptable. The child agreed immediately, and he kept to his word.

There is an interesting sequence that discussion sets into motion:

Discussion leads to *communication*, which leads to *understanding*, which leads to a *solution* that is amenable to both parent and child.

This sequence can serve us very well in working with our children in general. If it is the child who suggests the solution, then it will be even more successful, for if the child himself *comes up* with the solution (not only agrees to it), then he will be even more interested in carrying it through.

One mother I know had been experiencing great difficulty in getting her son to return home on time after playing. She tried just about everything she could think of, but nothing worked.

I suggested to the mother that she discuss the problem with her son and have him come up with a solution that could work for him. In fact, the son came up with a fantastic solution — a specific system for having himself reminded, and a consequence that would follow if he would not come home after the reminder. What is more important, he took the initiative to implement the solution, because it was his own idea. This is a wonderful example of *placing our children in charge.*

Homework

Another practical area in which children can accept responsibility is in the area of homework. At the recent Agudah Convention this topic was discussed in a round-table forum. Many pros and cons of the principle of giving homework were brought up. One of the panelists handed out a list of comments, some made by experts, others by students or parents. Some of these are:

"Children need homework to practice their reading and math problems."

"My brother doesn't have enough to do at night and being that he's the youngest he doesn't have to help much. Homework keeps him busy for a while, and for him that's important."

A high-school student was actually quoted as saying, "I think it's important; in order to retain what you have learned you have to study."

On the other hand, there were those who opposed the concept of homework:

"When doing homework with my son, I am half-teaching. I'm not sure if he's picking it up in school."

A medical student said, "It causes children to think of it as an obligation as opposed to a learning tool."

One mother said, "I'm very opposed to a lot of homework, especially because I end up doing it myself."

Many parents (and teachers) present at the discussion expressed their views, and there was general discussion regarding what changes can be made in the system to minimize any adverse effects homework may have.

I personally do not consider myself qualified to voice my opinion on a matter that should certainly be decided by our leading authorities. Yet throughout these discussions I was thinking, why wait until they change the system? You, together with your child, can develop *your own system*, which is suited for your child's individual needs. This can be accomplished through the sequence mentioned above: discussion, communication, understanding, and arriving at a solution that works for both of you. In almost every instance, when parents and children discuss openly problems that are related to homework, the parent will discover that the child who is unwilling to do his homework is not an "intentional transgressor" but rather an unintentional one.

Few children fail to do their homework for no reason at all, and once you engage in open discussion with them, the reasons will come to light. You might find that the child takes the work seriously, yet he feels that the workload is beyond his capabilities. Maybe he cannot deal with the pressure. Perhaps the child is going through a difficult period, whether with friends, with a specific teacher, or in general. Perhaps he feels choked, and just needs a little more free time.

Show Understanding

After discussing and listening to him, you should show him understanding (read: let him see that you understand what is bothering him and that you truly care). Sometimes it is helpful just to mirror the child's feelings, repeating to him what he has told you in different words. Thus, if the child says something like, "I can't take this any more," you might respond with, "You're very tense because of the homework." Then the child will probably say something like, "That's right, the load drives me crazy," and he might continue expressing his feelings.

Conversations such as this will often open the door for the child to air his pent-up feelings, and in some cases this alone may be enough. At this point, do not try to reprimand your child. Try only to understand him; understanding can work wonders in building up a child and giving him emotional strength — and is that not more important than the homework? You may be surprised to know that understanding alone will be much more effective than rebuke or force, which do not take the child's feelings into account when it comes to helping your children do what you want them to do.

Illustrating this point, R' Pam related an experience his mother had when she was a young girl of 8 or 9:

> She wanted to fast on the tenth day of Teves, just as the adults did. She knew her parents would not allow this, so she spent the day at the homes of friends and did not come home until nightfall, when it was time to eat. My grandfather (her father) was well aware of what had happened. In the room with him at the time was an influential member of the community who became very angry at the child. He insisted that she be punished; she must be taught a lesson, he said. My grandfather, who was the rav of the city, remained silent. The child was given supper and went off to bed.
>
> My grandfather followed her to her room, where he embraced her lovingly and said, "My child, you wanted to do a mitzvah. If one is commanded to fast and he fasts, it is indeed a mitzvah. But when one is not commanded to fast, it is not a mitzvah. One should not punish one's body unnecessarily. G-d willing, when you will be a bas mitzvah, then you will fast and it will be a real mitzvah. Now you must be very tired; go to sleep and sleep tight. Good night."

To quote R' Pam, these words warmed her heart as long as she lived; and she lived past the age of 90.

R' Pam ends his account with the recommendation that, "We should always bear in mind that the primary purpose of the family is to bring up a Torah-loyal generation. Everything else is of minor importance [including homework]."

This principle applies ever so much more when it comes to raising children who are rebellious.

Recently I came across a beautiful letter that a student wrote to a wonderful educator, whom I know personally. The student (a girl) said, "Rabbi C., you have single-handedly changed the way I look at Judaism forever." What techniques did this educator use to bring about such a revolution in this girl's life? She writes:

> Rabbi C. is unique not only because he is an excellent teacher, but because he is an excellent friend to hundreds of his students. At first I thought, here comes another boring teacher, but my opinion changed within the minute. From the very beginning it was clear that he cared about us.
>
> This reason for admiring a teacher may seem trivial to many, but definitely not to me. For years prior to meeting Rabbi C. I was going through an internal religious rebellion. This did not mean that I didn't keep Shabbos or eat kosher. It meant that I was slowly dying inside. Just like a flower needs water and nutrients, it equally needs sunshine and warmth. I received adequate scholastic nutrients, but I desperately clung to the atmosphere for sunshine.
>
> I recall with awe the last month of my senior year. All the teachers pressured the girls to go to seminary; I had other plans. After an extensive session with one teacher who failed to understand me, Rabbi C. approached me and said that he wanted to speak with me. I took a deep breath and waited for the usual speech. To my shock, Rabbi C. asked me what I was planning to do after graduation. He seemed genuinely interested in my concerns, not so that he could find fault with them, but so that he could appreciate them.
>
> Rabbi C., you regenerated in me the respect for religion that was seriously being depleted. With an unimaginable amount of gratitude I thank you for changing the way I look at Judaism and for changing the way I will teach Judaism to my children.

Notice that Rabbi C., who has many students and who is an extremely busy person, did not spend that much individual time with this particular student. It was his sincere caring and understanding that his student sensed, which made a lasting impression.

How much more sensitive are children to the caring and understanding that *parents* show them. What is most necessary is not that you spend hours and hours with your child, but rather that you show him that you care. Show him that you are his friend and ally, that you are on his side. This does *not* mean that you will shoulder his responsibility for him; it means that he is not alone, and that he has a friend who understands him. You are that friend, and that can make all the difference.

Now, having followed the sequence set forth above, which begins with discussion, communication and understanding, we are ready for the next stages: (1) Finding a solution (2) that works for both parent and child.

Finding a Solution

Sometimes, the discussion and understanding of the child is itself the solution. However, in many cases this will not be enough to resolve the difficulties. It is usually not hard to tell from the child's reactions if there is need for further discussion. In the case at hand, in a problem-solving discussion regarding homework, at this point the parent should discuss with the child how much of the homework he feels he can do on his own, how much he needs help with, and how much is beyond the scope of his abilities. (If the child is having extreme difficulties it is suggested that parents seek outside advice from a recommended professional. It is possible that some undetected learning disabilities may be complicating the situation.)

Then the parent should call the teacher and discuss the situation. Teachers can often be strong allies when they are approached respectfully. If you explain that you feel X amount is just the right balance of homework for your child, they will usually comply; after all, you both have the child's best interests in mind. (It might be effective to make this plan contingent on the child's not telling anyone about it. If other students are not aware of it, the adjusted homework load will not have any adverse effect on the teacher's or the school's authority.)

This general approach has many advantages. Once you have communicated with and understood your child, and together you have determined the load that he can carry, you can feel comfortable *giving him the entire responsibility*. Schedule accountability sessions, when you will meet with him and discuss his progress (perhaps once a week). It is not harmful to sometimes offer an incentive for when he progresses nicely. There is also nothing wrong with offering your help; let your child know from the beginning that you are available to help him, but he must initiate it by asking you for help when he needs it. Homework is now his responsibility.

At the aforementioned Agudah Convention one expert rebbi offered his opinion that parents should not do homework for their children. I am in general agreement, although sometimes the situation is too difficult for the child to handle. However, once you have already worked things out with your child, it is fair to let *him alone* shoulder the responsibility for his homework. Of course you can help him if he requests your help, but do not do it for him. Even when helping him, try to guide him in such a way that he will come up with the answers himself. Thus he is certainly learning to bear responsibility for himself, and you are teaching him this in a way that has built him up rather than knocked him down.

Many children have problems getting up on time in the morning. Caring parents often bring their children to school by car, or write a note asking the teacher to excuse the child's lateness, explaining that it was really not his fault. But will this teach the child responsibility? On the other hand, allowing a child to suffer the consequences all alone seems cruel. How should a parent deal with this problem?

The solution is the very sequence we have discussed. First, *discuss* with the child the reasons for his tardiness and what he can do about it. Do not do the thinking for him. Ask him questions and let him come up with his own answers. No matter what the child tells you, there is no question that he is not happy about walking into class after the morning routine has begun and most of the children are already there. No one wants to stand out for being different from others, especially when standing out does not necessarily present him in the best light.

If the child has some specific difficulty that exacerbates the problem, be understanding. Then think of a solution that works for both of you, or, better yet, ask your child to come up with solutions. You may offer some suggestions to help his thinking processes get started, but the ultimate solution should be one your child has suggested.

Once the child has suggested a reasonable solution to his problem of tardiness, put him in charge. Give *him* the *total* responsibility for being on time, and let him suffer the consequences if he is late. After you finish your discussion with him, make it clear that from now on it is his sole responsibility. Do not shelter him from the consequences, especially after you have discussed them with him and worked out the solution. You should certainly make it clear to him that you are there to help him if he has difficulty, and if you see that the child is not managing to be more punctual you can even initiate a discussion with him as to what is happening. Under no circumstances, however, should you take responsibility for his schedule. Like the father who guided his son to help him learn to keep the backyard clean, you must give your child the responsibility for being on time. At most, you can help him fulfill *his* responsibility, but do not do him the disservice of taking responsibility for him.

A word of caution is in order here. This method can be very helpful regarding issues that you have already discussed and worked out with your child. However, it would be very unfair of a parent just to make a blanket statement to the effect that, "This is his problem; let him (or her) take responsibility for it." Such an attitude could be most detrimental to a child, especially when the problem at hand might in truth be far beyond the child's capabilities to deal with.

One child I know of was being regularly berated and criticized for not participating in school and for constantly daydreaming. It was not until someone examined the child more closely that it was discovered that he was partially blind. We can never know all the challenges with which our children must contend. It is crucial that we be supportive of them in all circumstances.

The Final Method: Planning in Advance

The final method for teaching responsibility is *planning in advance*. This method may be used in conjunction with the previous methods. Few of the ideas we have mentioned above will work when attempted in a spontaneous fashion; life's daily routine is too pressured for that. As one famous individual expressed it, "There's more to life than increasing its speed." It is necessary, therefore, that we take out the time and plan with our children *in advance* the various things we expect of them. Rather than wait until the moment when the need arises, speak with your children several days earlier and plan out with them what errands they are expected to run over the course of the week, what chores and tasks they are expected to do, and so on.

Much friction can be avoided by advance planning, especially since advanced planning leaves room for discussion and thus communication. It bears repeating that children react altogether differently when they have taken part in the planning. Moreover, if you decide on the various responsibilities in advance, it will give the child a chance to voice his objections, and you will be able to work out an amenable solution with him. In this way the child will fulfill willingly whatever responsibilities he accepts, as opposed to doing his jobs grudgingly, and in this way he will accustom himself to *approaching responsibility willingly*.

I stress that no one should make the mistake of thinking that children should only do things they agree to do. Children must listen to their parents whether or not they enjoy doing what they are told to do. Nevertheless, there is no special mitzvah for parents to make children do things by force, without taking into consideration the child and his feelings. More importantly, the more you take your child into consideration, the more he will cooperate *willingly* in the long run. And is this not what *chinuch* is all about — getting them to *want to do* what you want them to do.

Those who lack time must realize that in reality they are saving time. If they take out the time to organize their child's responsibilities properly when the children are younger, they will not have to extend much more time later on, when the problems will have escalated, and the solutions will not be so readily forthcoming. To quote R' Shmuel Kamenetsky, "The earlier responsibility is ingrained in a child, the more effective the training will be, and the more responsible the child will become."

May we be merit to raise children who will appreciate responsibility, and who will remain loyal to their ultimate responsibility, to fulfill their mission in this world.

23

The Real Goal at the Seder

How the Intifada Began

Rabbi Amnon Yitzhak retells the following story:

Salah had already given up. He was convinced that the Palestinians would never meet with success in their struggle against the Jews. He despaired of the Palestinians getting even a small piece of land in Israel that they could call their own. Salah walked around with this mindset for years. One Pesach, his mindset was changed.

There is not a Palestinian child who has not heard of Salah, who does not know what he looks like and who does not want to be just like him when he grows up.

A Palestinian hero, Salah al-Tamari earned his claim to fame by staging numerous PLO terrorist attacks against Israel in the years leading up to Operation Peace for Galilee in 1982.

After capture and trial, al-Tamari was sentenced to a lengthy prison term. There, he quickly rose to become undisputed leader of the Arab inmates. Prison authorities had no choice but to work through him when it came to dealing with Arab prisoners.

Tall and strong, al-Tamari looks more British than Arab. In addition to his native language, he is fluent in English, French and Hebrew. Considered one of the better-educated members of the PLO, al-Tamari has even had a book written about him by a well-known Israeli journalist.

What happened that Pesach to so abruptly change al-Tamari's worldview? He describes the incident in detail:

"I remember the scene well," al-Tamari says. "I was in my jail cell, closed in and cut off from the rest of the world. Only the steel bars of the cell door separated me from the long hall where the Israeli warder paced back and forth with his gun, 24 hours a day. I called him to come. I noticed that he was eating a pita sandwich.

"'You are a Jew,' I said to him. The fellow nodded yes. 'Why are you eating chametz on Pesach? You know a Jew is not permitted to eat chametz on Pesach.'"

"The prison guard, taken aback by the words of the Palestinian prisoner, thought for a few moments before answering.

" 'I am not obligated by things that happened over 2,000 years ago. Whatever went on at the redemption from Egypt has no connection to me.' "

Al-Tamari continues his description of that fateful evening. "I sat on the mattress in my cell and said to myself, 'A nation whose people have no connection to their past and who are capable of desecrating the laws of their faith in public is a nation that has severed its roots to its land. We will be able to achieve our goals!'

"That night, I had a significant change of attitude. I couldn't fall asleep. Throughout those dark hours, I sat on my bed thinking. I found it hard to comprehend what had happened to me in that short encounter with the Jewish warder who ate chametz in public, right in front of Arabs.

"The next morning I called a meeting of the Palestinian leadership in the prison. I spoke to those who have been aware of my opinion for many years. I addressed those who were aware of how discouraged I was from getting even a small percent of the land from the Israelis. I then told them about the trauma I had undergone, the feelings I had experienced and the conclusions I came to.

"I made it clear to all that beginning from that very morning we were taking a new approach. 'We are at war for the entire land — not just for a small percentage of land or for the few crumbs they throw us!

> *" 'Facing us is a nation devoid of any connection to its roots, a people that no longer has any interest in its past. It is clear that this nation will be devoid of any desire to fight for its cause, for it has no cause for which to fight.' That's how I ended my speech.*
>
> *"Since then, I have told my story to tens of thousands," says al-Tamari. "I have succeeded in convincing them to change their attitudes and fight without compromise."*
>
> *Al-Tamari is a minister-without-portfolio in the Palestinian Legislative Council. He was offered a position as a member of Arafat's cabinet, but declined. He holds a unique position among the people and continues to win Palestinians over to his new approach — the one he formulated that very evening after his encounter with the prison guard.*

Rabbi Amnon Yitzhak added the following words of insight and explanation:

> *"The damage caused to the Jewish people by that one Jewish warder, through his words and actions that evening several years ago," says Rabbi Yitzchak, "cannot be fixed today by thousands. Who knows how many Jews have been killed in this most recent intifada because of the chametz sandwich that warder ate on Pesach."*

In other words, a few refugees standing against us with super-human effort and total dedication to their cause, without an army of their own, feel themselves stronger than we are. They have decided to fight for it all and without compromise!

What gives them the nerve to do so?

They are emboldened by the fact that those they face are root-less. Their opponents lack tradition and values — and a nation without values is a nation without strength, without the dedication to fight for its cause.

The Essence and Purpose of the Jewish Family

But we *have* values. We *have* a tradition, unbroken for thousands of years. Breaking away from the traditions of our parents is only a recent phenomenon, emerging within the past 200 years.

How unfortunate that those who have strayed know not the beauty and benefit of that which they have forsaken, even in this world. As one great rabbi said, "The plague of our generation is ignorance more than it is rebellion."

Now more than ever, we have a responsibility to strengthen our children's ties to Judaism so that our children remain steadfast and loyal to our heritage their entire lives. Now more than ever, it is incumbent upon us to teach them the beauty and benefit of Judaism so that they never entertain the thought of parting with that which is their very lifeline.

To quote R' Pam, "This is the essence and purpose of the Jewish family: to raise Torah-loyal children. This is the main goal. Everything else is of minor importance and pales in significance compared to this goal."

Pesach, especially the night of the Seder, is the time when we can plant the deepest and most powerful influence in our children's hearts, one that will remain with them for the rest of their lives. I have been told by those who are active in the field of outreach that even those who are alienated from Judaism still keep some semblance of a Seder. The Jewish feelings instilled in a child at the Seder remain deeply ingrained. Therefore, if he has left the Seder, then you know he has severed all ties to Judaism.

Let us also draw inspiration from Salah. If blatant desecration of Pesach can bring such destruction, certainly observing Pesach can bring tremendous strength to help us all in these turbulent times.

I recently had a conversation with an elderly sage, someone who was close to the Chazon Ish for forty years. This person is by all standards a *tzaddik* (the Steipler Rav would stand up for him when he entered the room) and a master educator (he was a principal for forty years). When I mentioned this chapter to him, he discussed the following points that he felt were worthwhile to contemplate when Pesach is approaching.

As Important as a Bar Mitzvah or Wedding

Pesach gives our children faith for the entire year and possibly for their entire life. It is a must, therefore, that we plan ahead. Just as one prepares for a bar mitzvah or a wedding, so too must one prepare for Pesach.

[In case you are thinking, "My spouse and I are busy cleaning and shopping until we drop. What more preparation is necessary?" let us remember to keep focused on our goal, which is to raise a Torah-loyal family. If this is our goal, then we must see to it that Pesach is planned in a way to help us succeed in carrying out this goal.]

Work Together With Your Children

The physical work for Pesach, all the cleaning and other preparations, is demanding. It creates pressure, and in every normal house, it creates a lot of tension. Yet let us not lose focus of our *chinuch* goal to bring children up as Torah-loyal Jews. This does not mean we will not feel pressured. Expecting that of ourselves would be unrealistic and unfair.

The point is to try to work together with our children instead of just making this a time when we are only interested in getting the cleaning and other chores done properly. If cleaning is our main goal then anyone who gets in our way and does not willingly cooperate will be screamed at and dealt with harshly. When cleaning is the most important thing, relating to our children and dealing with disturbances only stands in the way of reaching the goal. Those who are unwilling to cooperate in reaching the goal will be coerced into helping. In this scenario, there is simply no time (or patience) to deal with family members who are fooling around.

However, if raising noble children is our goal, the picture changes. We may decide it worthwhile to take out time (it need not be that much time) to elicit our children's willingness in cooperating. We might decide to discuss chores with them with the goal of finding which suit them better than others. We might decide to make sure they join us in whatever we are doing (instead of us doing it all by ourselves) so that they feel part of what is going on.

True, the children may not clean as well as their parents and besides, who has time for such things right before Pesach? But then again, it depends on what your priorities are. When we say there is no time for something, that means we have chosen other, more important things which take precedence. But if our main goal is *chinuch*, then we will settle on having the house a drop less clean but our children a little more involved in a pleasant and cooperative way.

In the long run, you yourself stand to gain by taking a little bit of time to work *with* your children (as opposed to working against them or feeling that the children are in your way). You will soon find yourself with an army of allies instead of enemies.

The Seder Also Requires Preparation

Offer incentives or small prizes for children who prepare questions ahead of time to ask during the Seder itself.

And make sure the children rest on *erev* Yom Tov for at least an hour and a half.

It is also a good idea to make sure the children, especially the older ones, eat lunch on *erev* Yom Tov. Naturally, the food should comply with halachah, such as potatoes and cream, eggs, fruit, and so on. It is preferable that children not be too hungry coming into the Seder because this can be a major source of impatience and frustration. A child's hunger will make him constantly try to rush things instead of enjoying the Seder.

It is worthwhile to offer a prize for any child able to stay up until the *afikoman* is eaten. Some parents purchase a number of small prizes beforehand and have them handy to give out right after the *afikoman*.

Q *Is this chinuch — to be giving out prizes on such a holy evening?*

&A The sage told me that on the night of Pesach we are not supposed to be *mechanech*. We can save the *chinuch* for other times of the year. At the Seder, our goal should be to give the children a love of their faith and an experience they will cherish and enjoy. This will provide them with deep faith for the rest of their lives.

The Focus Must Be on the Children

There is another major point to be brought out with regard to the Seder: The focus must be on the children. Even if there are adult guests (or relatives), this time is for the children. The adult guests can wait until after the *afikoman* to receive their attention.

The sage stressed this to me very strongly and told me that R' Elchanan Wasserman was once sitting with a number of important rabbis on a Friday night. He got up in the middle, excused himself and said that Friday night belongs to the children.

There are those who give their attention to the children until *Mah Nishtanah* (the Four Questions) and then they like to let the adults take over. But this is not the proper way to run the Seder. The night of the Seder is for the children, and one must give them his entire attention throughout the entire time, at least until after the Grace After Meals is recited.

To do this takes a little (*not* a lot of) preparation. One should go over the Haggadah beforehand and pick out those parts he feels will be most beneficial in making the redemption real to his children and the parts he feels will be most useful for teaching them the foundations of belief.

Making the Exodus Real to Our Children

It is not a time for intellectual exercises and the like. It is a time to make the Exodus real to our children.

You do not have to make any big productions to accomplish this.

My esteemed friend told me that to this day he remembers how, at the Seder, his grandfather would take the matzah, wrap it up and put it on his shoulder. He would then say, "This is how our ancestors went out of Egypt."

The sage told me that his son once came into the room of R' Yechezkel Levenstein on Pesach. R' Yechezkel had set up two benches and was walking between them reciting the Song at the Sea. He wanted to make the splitting of the Red Sea real and tangible for himself.

In our school, we give out a small booklet with questions and points geared to this goal.

Some points are:

(1) How many people (including women and children) actually went out of Egypt?

Rav Shlomo Bloch of Mattersdorf (a student of the Chafetz Chaim) used to say in the name of the Chafetz Chaim that 5 million went out.

(2) If so, then how many were in Egypt?

We know that only a fifth went out. This means that there were 25 million Jews in Egypt.

(3) Since they started only with 70, during the period of the 210 years in Egypt how many descendants did each Jew have on the average?

357,142 descendants (5 million divided by 70).

(4) What did the Egyptians feel like during the plague of blood?

A papyrus has been discovered with these words of an Egyptian: "The river is blood. The plague is in all of the land. There is blood everywhere. People can't stand the taste. They are thirsty. This is our water! This is our wealth! What can we do? Destruction is everywhere."

There are Haggadahs, such as the *Me'am Loez*, that emphasize the Midrashim and what actually happened. Still, it is incumbent on the father to take time out before Pesach to prepare from the Haggadah of his choice those things he feels will be the best for his children to hear.

During the actual Seder, there are also various ways to keep the kids awake and interested. One father I know gives out interesting pictures relating to topics in the Seder. He does not show his children the pictures until the Seder. Then, when they see a picture for first time, it arouses their curiosity.

Another idea is to purchase trivia cards with questions and answers about Pesach for the children to look at. Another idea is to take them to the store before Pesach and let them choose a Haggadah they like, preferably one with interesting pictures at which to look. The point is that the Haggadah be interesting for the child at his level. Then, put the Haggadah away until the seder so that it will keep the child interested and busy during the Seder.

Another point is that one should make sure to sing various parts of the Haggadah, especially if there are tunes the children specifically enjoy in the Haggadah. While singing with the children, one can do harmony or let one child sing a stanza and another child another; then everyone can join together as a choir for the chorus.

Another challenge is coping with very small children who cannot sit still for more than *Mah Nishtanah*. One father I know buys his very small children a game. After *Mah Nishtanah*, they go to the side and play.

Q & A What should a parent do if his children disturbs during the Seder?

The sage told me that whatever the parent does, he should be sweet no matter what. The Seder should be a sweet experience — without shouting, criticism or hitting. Parents should give prizes and be sweet.

The Chazon Ish held that throughout the year making Judaism appealing and attractive for the child is better than using force, but certainly so at the Seder. As previously mentioned, Seder night is not a time to be *mechanech* your children. It is the time to implant in them love for their faith, and this takes precedence over all other goals, which pale in insignificance.

Q & A What if this does not work? Is a parent never supposed to tell his children to behave during the Seder?

A parent can be firm and strong. First, let him try with sweetness. If a child is getting rowdy, let the parent walk over to him, hold his hand and say the Haggadah together with him. He can even sing with him. If this does not work, a parent can say firmly but softly to the child that he wants him to behave. Being sweet does not preclude preventing the children from acting wild.

Q & A What if you tell the children, and they still do not behave?

I posed this question to the sage and here is his answer: "Parents cannot fix everything in one night. Parents who do not have any connection to their children and do not show an interest in their children the whole year round cannot come to the Seder expecting everything to automatically fit into place.

"One must work throughout the entire coming year by showing interest in the children and developing a relationship with them so that he will be able to have an enjoyable Seder at least for the coming Pesach next year."

The sage told me that a father should spend 45 minutes a day doing *something* for the *chinuch* of his children (besides working to pay for the tuition). Then he can be assured that he will have *nachas* from his children and that things will turn out well.

R' Yitzchak Zilberstein brings in the name of the Chafetz Chaim that just as one has to set aside set times for Torah study, and just as he must set aside time for saying *Shema* and *dav-ening*, *even more so* is his obligation to set aside time for the *chinuch* of his children.

Q&A *Should parents also refrain from disciplining harshly during the rest of the holiday and Chol HaMoed?*

With regard to the rest of the holiday, including Chol HaMoed, the intermediate days, the previous rules of the Seder apply. A person should try to refrain from screaming, criticizing and hitting throughout the entire eight days. If necessary, a parent must discipline and be firm, as mentioned before, but not in a harsh way.

The sage also told me that throughout Pesach a person should tell his family inspirational stories from his own life that show how Hashem saved him personally. He should also encourage his children to do so.

In general, it should be a sweet time for everyone.

The sage told me a beautiful parable. If a person wants his tea to be sweet, he must put in either one or two cubes of sugar. Yet if the person holds the sugar in his mouth, then he can drink a whole cup of tea and more with about half a cube. The point is this: if a person tries to make others happy his chances of succeeding are slight. If he makes sure that he himself is sweet, then the entire family will become sweetened with much less effort.

Remember that even the great rabbis were sweet with their children. R' Reuven Feinstein relates that his father, R' Moshe, used to give the children piggyback rides all year long.

If we find it hard to be sweet all year long, at least let us do so for the duration of the holiday.

Q&A *What if I find it difficult to be sweet?*

In 1897 Mark Twain wrote:

If the statistics are right the Jews constitute but one percent of the human race. It suggests a nebulous dim puff of stardust lost in the blaze of the Milky Way. Properly the Jew ought hardly to be heard of; but he is heard of, has always been heard of. He is as prominent on the planet as any other people ... He has made a marvelous fight in this world, in all the ages; and he has done it with his hands tied behind him ... The Egyptian, the Babylonian and the Persian rose, filled the planet with sound and splendor, then faded to dream stuff and passed away; the Greek and the Roman followed and made a vast noise and they are gone; other peoples have sprung up and held their torch high for a time, but it burned out, and they sit in twilight now, or have vanished. The Jew saw them all, beat them all, and is now what he always was, exhibiting no decadence, no infirmities of age, no weakening of his parts, no slowing of his energies, no dulling of his alert and aggressive mind. All things are mortal but the Jew; all other forces pass, but he remains. What is the secret of his immortality?

We are an immortal people with a cause. Let us stand up and fight for our cause. Let us be sweet and kind of heart to all those close to us, throughout the entire Pesach, so that the Name of Hashem be sanctified and so that we raise children, loyal and devoted to Hashem all of their days.

This is our purpose; this is our goal.

24

The Shabbos
Table Revisited (Part 1)

I Surrender

A recent visit to a New York bank found me with several hundred checks to deposit. We had just completed a fund-raising campaign for our school, and, in addition to the larger donations, we received numerous smaller donations as well. Before my return to Israel, I went to deposit the checks.

As I waited on line, I suddenly remembered that I had not endorsed the checks. I had no choice but to go to a side counter and to begin the tedious task of signing hundreds of checks with the name of our school and the account number.

To alleviate some of the monotony of this time-consuming task, I occasionally glanced around the bank. I noticed a strange fellow standing at the same counter as I was. He seemed to be observing me rather closely. I guess it was all the checks I was signing that caught his interest.

I immediately let my bank companion know the truth of the matter. The money was not my own, I explained. It consisted of contributions to a nonprofit organization, a school in Israel, and it did not amount to that much. Most of the checks, I told him, were for minimal amounts.

"I thought you owned a sweater store," the man exclaimed.

We continued talking, and the man shared with me his frustration with one of the bank tellers.

"I was at the front of the line, and the woman said I was next. Then she changed her mind and began talking with some other customers who came after me. She told me I have to wait. I am really frustrated with her," he said.

Half-joking, he said, "I wish I could resort to sixth grade level. That way, I could throw some spitballs at her like we did to some of our teachers back then."

Leaning closer and lowering his voice, he added in mock seriousness, "I would like to bring this bank teller to a new low of emotional pain." At that, he laughed.

I laughed along with him, hoping he was not serious.

With a polite apology, I returned to my check-signing task. Soon enough, though, my curiosity got the best of me, and I asked the man the question that was on my mind.

"Do you have children?"

"I have two children," he said.

"How do you deal with your children when they are upset with you and wish to bring you to a new low of emotional pain?" I asked.

Half laughing, he held up his hands and said, "Hey! I just surrender."

Yes, no matter how strong a parent may feel himself to be, children can be formidable opponents. There are times when a child can make matters very difficult for his parent.

Take the Shabbos table for example. Listen to what one parent wrote:

At the Shabbos table, he is particularly difficult. I am not talking about sitting through a lengthy meal. I am talking about making it through the first course!

He may rip the plastic tablecloth with his fork during Shalom Aleichem, make silly faces during Kiddush, or shpritz water all over the kitchen when it's time to wash. I have tried various incentives such as distributing pickles (which he loves) as a reward for good behavior. This worked for a few weeks, but the novelty soon wore off.

The Shabbos meal often turns into a string of confiscations. First we take away the grape juice, then the pickles, soda and maybe even the dessert.

One time, he even flung mashed sweet potatoes across the room. Of course, I was very upset, and I'm grateful he did not do this again. However, his lunchroom supervisor at school told me he did something similar there.

Another parent states:

I find the Shabbos table to be a very unpleasant experience. If I don't discipline my children, they get out of hand fairly quickly. Sometimes they will just push me too far, and I lose it. Then everyone behaves because they're afraid. This usually lasts until the next meal.

Either way, I do not enjoy the Shabbos table, and I am sure that they do not either. There must be a better way. Perhaps you can offer some advice.

In the previous chapter, I referred to a conversation I recently had with an elderly sage regarding the Yom Tov of Pesach.

Wanting to hear his opinions and views as to how to deal with the Shabbos table, I approached him again. Here are a number of insights he shared with me about how to make the Shabbos table a better place.

Q *Why is the Shabbos table so difficult? It seems that all kids get wild and rowdy.*

&A "The holy books say that Shabbos is the main time for *chinuch*," the sage said. "The evil inclination apparently knows the extent to which a positive Shabbos experience can help mold our children for the good and so makes it his business to disrupt this time.

"There is nothing new here. This has been a problem throughout the generations. Our parents and grandparents also sought ways to enhance Shabbos and make it a rewarding experience for our children. When I was a child, we had an oral quiz every Shabbos not only to test the children, but to give us an exciting event to look forward to.

"I also remember being at various relatives' Shabbos tables, some of them prominent rabbis today, where the children were out of hand, and it was necessary to think of ideas to keep them in order."

Still, the sage told me, even those children grew up to become *tzaddikim*. The Steipler Rav used to say that the street took care of at least 50 percent of the *chinuch*.

In our times, we cannot be so bold as to leave our Shabbos table a mess and hope that the street will accomplish the rest of the *chinuch*.

Q *Should one discipline at the Shabbos table?*

A "Absolutely not."

Q *You said, though, that this is one of the main times to be mechanech.*

A "The *chinuch* referred to with regard to the Shabbos table means to make the Shabbos table a pleasurable and enriching experience for our children."

(I am reminded of the words of the *Chovas HaTalmidim*, written by the Piaseczner Rebbe in prewar Europe: "Commands and routine are not *chinuch*. They are nothing more than *tools* that can be used to educate. True *chinuch* involves bringing out the child's potential to the greatest extent possible, and doing so in a way that 'even when he grows old he will not stray from it' — in a way that will remain with him even after he leaves the sphere of our influence.")

Chinuch means seeing that the children's experience at the Shabbos table is a positive one that will foster the child's desire and love for Shabbos.

There are some families where the Shabbos table becomes the day of reckoning. A father who does not see his children during the week may see the Shabbos table as an opportunity to educate his children. To this purpose, he takes pains to show them all what they are not doing right, offering as much criticism as he can to make up for lost time. In this, he feels, he is fulfilling his parental duty to educate his children.

To these parents I offer the words I heard directly from one of the leading rabbis of our generation: "The Shabbos table is not a courtroom."

We must remind this father (or mother) and all those who follow in their footsteps, that *chinuch* is not just instant problem solving. *Chinuch* is educating with a look to the future. Parental action that gains the desired effect momentarily but which has devastating effects in the long term is not *chinuch*.

Just this morning a father came over to me to ask advice about his son who does not get up for *minyan* on Shabbos. In fact, the boy sometimes sleeps until late afternoon.

During our discussion, the father confessed to me that he used to be especially tough on his son when it came to Torah and mitzvah observance. The Shabbos table was part of this.

Given this background, the boy's current situation came as no surprise to me.

"I think I have to change my tactics and back off," the father told me at the end of our conversation.

Despite all that has been said and written about the detrimental effects of discipline at the Shabbos table, some parents will just not give it up. They may even wind up screaming, punishing, hitting — or all of the above.

The power of association can create lasting impressions, and it is important to remember that the Shabbos table is no exception to the rule. If the Shabbos table becomes an arena for discipline, the children will walk away with a bitter taste for the Shabbos table and for Shabbos in general.

One boy who left the ways of his parents once confessed to me about the first time he desecrated Shabbos.

> *My parents never made Shabbos a pleasant experience for me. All they were concerned with was what would the neighbors and other people think. This was the guiding force in their lives. "What will everyone say?"*
>
> *So when I went to be mechallel Shabbos, I went into the room and closed all the windows and shades. I even put pillows in the windows to make sure no one would see me. My thinking was, if no one sees me, there's no problem.*

Eventually, this boy returned to a Torah-loyal life.

The Shabbos table is not a time to be *mechanech*. Or to put it more accurately, the Shabbos table *is* a time for *chinuch* — genuine *chinuch*. It is a time for the type of parenting that will make an indelible *positive* impression on the child and will stay with him for years to come.

Q&A *If we do not discipline our children, how can we keep some semblance of order at the Shabbos table?*

Believe it or not, having a wonderful Shabbos table that the whole family enjoys is possible even without discipline — even in our turbulent times, and even with many children. In fact, I have a friend whose children enjoy Shabbos so much they cannot wait for Shabbos to come.

The first step is for the parent to make it his or her responsibility to prepare and put in the effort needed to make the Shabbos table experience a successful one.

Even parents who put in a full, pressured week should take responsibility for making the Shabbos table a pleasant experience. This is one of those mitzvos that cannot be done by others. Our children have no other parent who will be able to do this for them.

Q&A *It can sometimes be very hard for a parent not to be tired at the Shabbos table. How is he expected to have a nice Shabbos table when he is so tired?*

I posed this question to the sage and this is what he told me. If one has an offer for a big business investment, one that could bring him many dividends and financial security for the rest of his life, won't he take time to look into the matter? Won't he spend time preparing properly?

He certainly will. His future depends on it!

Why should the Shabbos table be any different? If a parent knows that the main *chinuch* is accomplished at the Shabbos table, then he will put in the time and effort necessary to make it a success.

The sage told me that a parent should begin his preparations for the Shabbos table on Monday!

The Shabbos Table Revisited (Part 2)

25

Protect Your Health

TWC = .081 x (3.71 x sq. rt. (V) + 5.81 − 0.25 x V) x T (T-91.4) + 91.4

This is the old formula, which is actually outdated. The new formula is:

$$TWC = 35.74 + 0.6215T - 35.75 (V\,0.16) + 0.4275T (V\,0.16).$$

Despite the formula's practicality, one expert predicts that the public may not embrace the new formula. "Everyone hates change, and some people are not going to like it," he said.

Before I reveal the identity of these formulas, allow me to explain how I became interested in this subject altogether.

Many years ago, when I had just taken a job as principal, I went to R' Wolbe to seek his advice.

"What is my foremost responsibility as principal?" I asked. I was not expecting the answer I received.

"You must be careful to take proper care of your health," R' Wolbe said.

I cannot say that I have properly heeded his words, but, in retrospect, I can say that he was right on the mark. Everyone, especially those in tension-filled situations or those overburdened with major responsibilities, has a special obligation to protect his health. Those in public positions have an even greater responsibility to do so for they must remain healthy to continue their public service.

It is this obligation that has forced many of our *great sages* to involve themselves in physical exercise, in various forms and fashions.

I cannot forget the time many years ago when I saw R' Shach at the beach in Netanya. He was helped into the water by two young men, one on each side, and remained there for a while. If you are ever in Israel in the summer, it is certainly worthwhile to go to the beach at Netanya. You will come across many distinguished rabbis, gathering strength at the sea for the coming year.

This phenomenon is not unique to Israel. A friend once went swimming in the States only to meet up with a renowned rabbi and halachic authority who was also swimming there for health reasons.

At this stage in my life, and with the rigorous schedule I keep, my doctor told me I must engage in some sort of physical exercise on an ongoing basis. I decided upon swimming as my form of exercise, feeling myself in good company as I think of the rabbis mentioned above.

On one of my trips to the pool, I noticed a vent blowing hot air in the changing room. "That's appropriate," I thought to myself. "People who feel chilled coming out of the pool can warm up."

When I came out of the pool, I went over to stand near the vent, expecting to be warmed by the hot air flowing out.

Much to my dismay (and surprise), the vent was now emitting cold air. How strange. Before people entered the pool, it blew hot air, and when people left the pool, it blew cold air. Wouldn't the opposite be more appropriate?

I remained surprised and puzzled by the pool administrators' strange choice.

One of my next visits to the pool left me even more in the dark. Once again, upon entering the changing room I noticed that the vent was blowing hot air. Yet as I was standing there feeling the flow of hot air, another person who had just finished swimming came over and began to complain about the cold air blowing from the vent.

"How is this possible?" I wondered. Both hot and cold air was blowing out of the same vent at the same time. How did the vent know who got the hot air and who the cold?

I expressed my amazement to one of the other people in the locker room.

He smiled. "It's the wind chill factor."

This fellow was a physics major, and he began to explain the workings of this strange phenomenon. Although he seemed to understand what he was saying, I cannot say I came away with the same clarity.

His explanation went something like this: When a person is wet, the heat blown by the vent works to evaporate the water. Because the heat is used up in this activity, only cold air remains. On the other hand, the person entering the pool is dry, so no heat gets used up. Therefore, the air coming from the vent feels hot.

What this has to do with the wind chill factor still was not clear to me, and so I did some research. What I came up with was that when wind blows on a person, it dissipates his body heat, making his body feel colder.

Most people think that the wind chill factor is a figment of the person's imagination. He feels cold because the wind is blowing. But in reality, the wind actually causes body heat to dissipate and his body does actually become colder, though the air temperature remains constant. Thus, when the wind blows strongly it can even cause water in a glass to feel colder than the actual temperature.

The formulas given at the beginning of this article are two separate ways to calculate wind chill factor, the old way and the new way. "TWC" refers to the wind chill in degrees, V is the wind speed in MPH, and T is the temperature in degrees Fahrenheit.

Focus on the Recipient

You may find this lesson in physics to be rather lacking, and I agree except that there is a very powerful *chinuch* lesson to be learned here.

We see that though *hot* air is being blown out of the vent, the recipient may actually experience it as *cold* air, depending on other environmental factors.

We may feel we are being a good parent because of the effort we put forth. Yet the message of the pool vent is that it is not enough to look at what we are doing; we must focus on the person on the receiving end — in this case our child. We must look at the results our efforts are producing and at the impressions formed on the recipient's heart as a result of what we are doing.

This rings especially true with regard to the Shabbos table.

> I feel that the Shabbos table is a pressure. My husband wants us to speak words of Torah the entire time, and if anyone starts talking about anything else, he gets upset. What do I do?

Although we may be full of words of Torah and on a higher level than others, we must realize that what others might be receiving from us is "cold air."

If we want to develop in others a love for Torah and the Shabbos table, then we must make sure that the Shabbos table is not a scene of pressure but of pleasure, pleasure not only for us but for those on the receiving end as well.

The sage mentioned in the previous chapter told me that the words of Torah should be given in small bits rather than in an overbearing way. Allow for regular conversation at the table and insert the Torah thoughts in a way and at a time that your family will be receptive to them.

Active Involvement as Opposed to Passive Acceptance

Still, if we wish the Shabbos table to be an *experience* for our children, their passive acceptance of our Torah thoughts and world outlook is not sufficient. It is their active involvement that we are looking for. Rather than using the Shabbos table for lectures to our children, let us involve them in our discussions. Their participation is net profit, and it is exactly what will help them enjoy the Shabbos table more.

The following suggestions, by no means a complete list, are geared to help involve children in what is going on at the Shabbos table.

(1) Discuss halachos or *hashkafah* topics that give the children a chance to voice their own opinions and tell over their own personal experiences.

One father uses *Cases in Monetary Halachah* by R' Tzvi Spitz. This book relates cases brought before the rabbinical court, including what the litigants claimed and what the court decided. The father gives his children all the information, but does not tell them the final ruling. A lively discussion then ensues as each child offers his or her opinion as to what the verdict should be. After they finish, the father reads his children the correct decision.

In our boys' afternoon group on Shabbos, we learn R' Tobalsky's book, *Hizaharu BeMamon Chavreichem*. We cover the chapter where he brings real life situations and their halachic implications. We discuss this with the children, and we ask them to bring examples they have seen or give their opinion on how they think a particular halachah applies in everyday situations. The examples are many and include common events such as going in front of someone else on line (with or without permission, or when your friend signals you to stand with him), throwing trash in private or public places (apartment buildings, stairwells, the street,) using someone's book without permission, and so on.

Any halachah book can be used for this type of discussion. Pick examples from real situations that are in front of the children's eyes. One father I know learned from *The Halachos of Muktzeh* by R' Yisrael Pinchas Bodner. Rather then just reading from the text he uses items that are in the room as examples. This brings the subject alive for children. The Shabbos table is the time to bring things to life.

(2) As we have previously mentioned, quizzes on the weekly portion are also a way to get children involved and interested. One may even add some good questions from *Sifsei Chachamim*. If the quiz is made interesting, the children have even more of a desire to listen. One father I know would prepare questions that were aimed at catching the children's interest, such as "Where do we find the color brown in this week's reading? Which verse contains advice on how to become wealthy?" Nevertheless, even simple questions can bring the children to participate. Children love challenges, and it helps make things exciting.

Fun Exercises

Baseball based on the weekly *parashah* is a variation of this.

A friend (a foremost scholar) who lives in the States told me that on Shabbos, he plays baseball with his family. The children are divided into two teams. One parent acts as the pitcher and asks the questions. Each child is asked if he wants a hard question (home run), easier question (triple), even easier question (double), and so on. The kids love it.

This same friend told me that in his community non-religious parents bring their children to learn *Mishnayos* every Sunday. After the learning session, they play *Mishnayos* football. My friend said that children have actually become religious due to these games.

Singing is also an idea. But again, sing with the children what *they* enjoy. Allow them to suggest some of the songs, and sing along with them. The sage mentioned in the previous chapter told me that one should set aside a time during the week to teach his children a special song to be sung at the coming Shabbos table.

Fun exercises that encourage good character are also a possible Shabbos table activity. Each person can mention two good traits about someone else at the table. At first, the children may laugh. But experience has shown that they can really get into it. Variations are possible, such as asking everyone to give an example of a praiseworthy deed they saw someone, perhaps even a family member, do.

Imagine what this can do for your children! It can help develop in them the habit of speaking positively about others. Just think what such a Shabbos table does for a child, being a place where he can come to build up others and be built up at the same time. How different is this from the type of Shabbos table where children come away with negative feelings about themselves and the Shabbos as well.

> In his new book, "Lulei Torascha," R' Asher Bergman brings the following story. R' Shach was told about a man who lost his wife and slipped into a deep depression. He personally went to visit the man at his home. After knocking on the door and not receiving a reply he decided to try the door himself. The door was unlocked and R' Shach walked right in. He sat down next to the man, who was lying on the couch, put his arm around the man's shoulder and said with great emotion, "I understand you so well. I am also a widower. My world has also become darkened. Listen, you need to be cheered up and so do I." The man lifted his head. It seemed that a spark of life had just entered his seemingly lifeless soul.

R' Shach continued, "I have an idea. I know how to pre-pare a wonderful cholent for Shabbos. I will cook the cholent on Friday and send it to you. On Shabbos I will come over. We will sit together, eat together, sing together, and take encouragement from each other."

Needless to say the man declined the offer. "Rabbi! I will not hear of such a thing"

"Then you think of a different idea," said R' Shach. "In any case I am coming to you tomorrow. Being near you cheers me up."

Indeed, the true Shabbos table is a source of encouragement, bringing everyone together in harmony and good will.

> **Q & A** What if I have guests at the Shabbos table?
> What should we do if we have important people at the Shabbos table, such as grandparents, etc. Isn't it disre-spectful not to give them their proper attention?

We have already mentioned R' Elchanan Wasserman who was sitting with a number of distinguished rabbis around the Friday night table. He excused himself to give his full attention to the children. "Friday night belongs to the children," he said.

R' Elchanan did not feel this was disrespectful to the rabbis, and we need not feel that way either. In truth, there is no disre-spect here. To the contrary, the "important people" will enjoy the meal much more if they see the children participating and enjoy-ing Shabbos. They will also appreciate and admire that the chil-dren are being taken care of.

Our family once played " baseball" at the table with the chil-dren when a neighbor was eating the meal together with us. She wished to play along with everyone else, and she became part of the action.

In the previous chapter we asked:

What is meant by preparing for the Shabbos table and what methods can be used to make it successful?

Using the methods mentioned above can certainly help make your Shabbos table a success, with the help of Hashem. It is also obvious that putting into practice any of the above ideas involves preparation.

26

The Shabbos Table Revisited (Part 3)

Why I Won't Talk to the BBC

Someone gave me a copy of an article written by Douglas David, London correspondent of *The Jerusalem Post*. He described a recent phone conversation.

"Would you be available to appear on the Nicky Campbell program tomorrow morning? It should be very interesting. We want to discuss whether Israel is a morally repugnant society."

"Thanks, but no thanks," came the reply.

The author, frequently interviewed on the BBC and not shy about voicing his opinions — sometimes critical ones — on the Middle East, explained what brought about his change of attitude. It began on September 11.

> *Even as the Twin Towers came crashing down (writes Davis), the BBC was interviewing Arab studio analysts who solemnly intoned that it was racist to assume that Arabs or even Muslims were responsible. More likely, they said, it was the Mossad, because such an event "played into Israeli hands."*
>
> *But, even if Arabs or Muslims had flown these planes, they said, was it not obvious that the United States itself was the real culprit? After all, it was the United States that was pursuing a pro-Israel foreign policy, dictated by the Jewish lobby; it was the United States that was ignoring the occupation and turning a blind eye to the settlements; it was the United States that was contemptuous of Arab*

sensibilities. Could anyone blame the Arabs for wanting to vent their humiliation, frustration and rage at this one-sided American policy?

Apparently not. At least not at the BBC, which could not get enough of it.

As I followed events I felt increasingly as though the rest of the world — or at least that part of it, which was inhabited by the BBC — had gone stark raving mad. Disbelief, it seemed, was suspended at Television Center as logic was turned on its head and victim became perpetrator.

But far more shocking than the repeated ventilation of these bizarre views was the fact that they went virtually unchallenged by the BBC's usually robust interviewers.

Did the BBC, which reaches into virtually every British living room, make a conscious policy decision to allow this arrant nonsense to become an established fact on its airwaves? I doubt it. Rather, I believe that the profound anti-Israel bias — and now I am convinced that it does exist — has, over the years, become ingrained in the BBC's corporate culture.

Since September 11, however, I have refused all invitations to appear on BBC radio or television. The reason is not that I wish to avoid a debate, but rather that I believe that the BBC has crossed a dangerous threshold.

In my judgment, the volume and intensity of this unchallenged diatribe has now transcended mere criticism of Israel. Hatred is in the air. Wittingly or not, I am convinced that the BBC has become the principal agent for reinfecting British society with the virus of anti-Semitism.

But it was not just the lamentable standards of journalism. I parted company with the BBC over its hysterical advocacy of the most extreme Palestinian positions — an advocacy that has now transmogrified into a distorting hatred of a criminal Israel, and by extension, into a burgeoning hatred of Jews closer to home.

It is astonishing that a little more than half a century after the Holocaust, the BBC, guardian of liberalism and political correctness, should provide the fertile seedbed for the return of "respectable anti-Semitism" that finds expression not only in the smart salons of London, but also *according to the experts who monitor such phenomena, across the entire political spectrum, uniting the far-Left with the Center and far-Right.*

I still receive a couple of calls a week from producers and researchers at the BBC, but they should know by now that I am no longer a candidate to make up the numbers in order to allow them to justify the injection of yet more poison in the national bloodstream.

Nor, as Nicky Campbell's researcher so sweetly asked, am I prepared to defend the legitimacy of Israel's existence — and, effectively, the legitimacy of my own existence as an Israeli and as a Jew. To that I say, "Get stuffed."

⚜

A neighbor here in Neve Yaakov had an encounter with the BBC which served to prove just how true these words really are.

Several weeks ago (after a series of terrorist attacks, including the one in the Beis Yisrael neighborhood in Jerusalem in which nine were killed), the BBC decided to film various sections of Jerusalem. They wanted to catch both Jews and Arabs on film to show how people were reacting to the recent chain of events. They were looking specifically for areas where Jews and Arabs lived in close proximity to one another.

One day, a few people with television cameras came to our block and began filming the children playing and riding their bicycles outside.

"What are you doing?" asked my friend.

"We're from the BBC, and we're interested in filming certain sections of Jerusalem so that we can see how Israelis are going about their daily lives, in view of the recent attacks."

My friend had been told by a neighbor that the BBC reported only one or two people killed in the Beis Yisrael bombing. He felt that this was a golden opportunity to voice his objection to this blatant lie.

"Why did the BBC report that only one person was killed in the bombing in Beis Yisrael?" he asked the reporters.

They seemed not to know about the inaccurate report-
ing of the news, but they did ask my friend if he would
like to be interviewed. That way, they said, he could voice
his opinion on distortions in the news and say what he
thought was really going on.

My friend felt it was an opportunity to create a kiddush
Hashem, and so he consented. After a few moments of
preparation, the interview began.

"Are you afraid?" came the first question.

"Yes. To be honest, I am afraid, but I carry on with my
daily routine in spite of the fear. As religious Jews, we are
aware of Divine Providence. We know that each and every
bullet has its address, and that G-d is with us at all times,
looking after us and protecting us.

"Do you hate the Arabs?"

"We Jewish people do not hate anyone. We are not inter-
ested in hurting anyone or causing anyone harm. The way
we are being treated by the Arabs is totally one-sided, as
we would never do anything even remotely similar. We
wish to be left alone so that we can continue to live in
peace. It is a pity that the world distorts the truth and paints
a picture as if we are the evil ones, full with hatred and
venom toward our Arab neighbors. We are a kind people."

"You said that you originally came from the States. Do
you plan on moving back in view of all the goings on?"

"This is our land, and I am privileged to live here. It is
the holy land, and we are here to stay."

The entire interview lasted for about 10 minutes.

The interviewers commented on how different this inter-
view was compared with that of the Arabs they inter-
viewed. The Arabs, they said, were full of hatred and
want to wreak havoc and destruction upon the Jews.

My friend (along with the small crowd of neighbors that
had gathered) felt that he had made a true kiddush
Hashem. He was rather excited at the fact that millions of
people around the world would witness the interview. The
reporter told him the interview would be broadcast on
BBC World News that very evening.

We began trying to help our friend find someone with a
relative or acquaintance who would be watching the

news broadcast. It was not until the next day that we received feedback from numerous sources, some in Israel, some in England, and some in the United States.

On air, the interview lasted about 30 seconds. The film clip showed the interviewer asking my neighbor if he was afraid and his reply that he was. They also showed the part about him saying "this is our land and we are here to stay."

They cut out anything that had to do with *kiddush Hashem*.

In fact, they only left in that which would further their views. His attempt at bringing out the truth only resulted in further distortion of the truth. And so, we too witnessed firsthand the BBC's bias and its ability to distort the truth to suit its agenda.

A Bias to Pursue the Truth

It would be naïve to think that only the BBC distorts the truth. Without the Torah as one's guide, one can report as he wishes and bend the facts as he sees fit.

A friend of mine told me about his cousin who is a top doctor. CNN wanted to interview him about a treatment he had pioneered to battle a certain major illness.

Before the interview, the reporters told him, "This is what we want you to say."

"But I do not agree with that approach," the doctor replied.

"It doesn't matter," said the reporter. "This is what we want you to say."

The doctor refused to be interviewed because he did not want to be party to an open distortion of the truth. His refusal, though, did not stop CNN from getting the interview from someone else.

I am reminded of the verse, "*v'lo sasuru acharei levavchem veacharei eineichem* — do not stray after your heart and after your eyes" (*Bamidbar* 15:39). With good reason, the holy Torah places the heart before the eyes. This teaches us that one sees only that which he wishes to see. The desires of our heart are so powerful that they can distort even the truth we see with our own two eyes.

If the heart has such a powerful influence and can serve the proponents of falsity and evil with such success, why not use it to further our own cause? Imagine how much we stand to gain if we have a bias to pursue the truth!

This can be an especially powerful piece of information regarding our children. Imagine how much stronger our influence will be if we create a bias for them with regard to Torah and mitzvos. If we get them not only to be at the Shabbos table but to *want* to be at the Shabbos table, how much stronger will be their commitment to Judaism!

Using Incentives — Is It *Chinuch?*

Before we continue our discussion on enhancing the Shabbos table and this chapter's focus on using incentives, a word of caution. There are those who may feel that using incentives is not the proper way to teach. However, I once asked R' Wolbe about using incentives and the benefits involved. He told me that those who understand how to educate nowadays realize that this is *the* way to do so. Those who disagree do not understand *chinuch* in our time.

This past Shavuos, we had a group of between 130 and 150 boys aged 8 to 12 who stayed to learn the entire night. We provided light refreshments and offered points, with the promise of a prize after Shavuos for those who earned enough points. The learning session began at 11:30 p.m. At 12:30 there was a story break and the leader told the boys an exciting story related to the giving of the Torah. At 1:15 a.m. ices were given out. Learning resumed at about 1:30. The boys were learning with tremendous energy until 4:19 a.m., the time to prepare for the morning prayers. Many people came to take a look, and they later told me it seemed the boys were learning with even greater fervor than the adults.

But keep in mind that using incentives at the Shabbos table is not just a matter of training a child to behave properly for a reward until he behaves properly on his own. Incentives can enhance the entire Shabbos table experience by helping to create an enjoyable atmosphere. This will nurture a built-in pro-Shabbos attitude that can strengthen our children to a phenomenal degree.

Incentives also get the child to cooperate willingly, thus opening his heart to the many messages we want to convey to him at the Shabbos table. Once his heart is open, the words from our heart can enter directly into his.

One mother complained to me about her 9-year-old daughter, who was causing her tremendous problems. They had gotten into a negative spiral of kvetching and rebuking. The child would constantly try to get her mother upset, and the mother would become upset. The more upset the mother became, the more the child would act out. It reached a point where the mother blew up at the child out of sheer desperation. By then, the child was being plain obnoxious and got what she rightfully deserved.

The problem was that this only gave symptomatic relief without treating the source of the problem. A short time later, the problem surfaced again and became just as difficult as ever.

When the mother asked me for advice, I suggested she try an incentive program. I explained that she and her daughter were caught up in a vicious cycle. The incentive program would be just the thing to break the momentum.

The mother first discussed the program with her daughter. Each day, the child would get a mark from 0 to 10 based on her behavior the entire day. When she received a certain amount of points, she would get something she really wanted.

The change was dramatic and almost immediate. The girl was a changed person.

Interestingly enough, the mother did not continue this program. In fact, it petered out almost immediately. However, for the few days she used it, it helped the child make a total 180-degree turn and even now, more than a month later, the daughter has been behaving rather well.

Incentives have the power to cause children to make an about-face and change their direction altogether.

On a practical note, there are a number of ways that incentives can be used at the Shabbos table. They can be given out at the end of the meal, or after the main course for no other reason than it being Shabbos. In this way, the incentives are used solely to sweeten the Shabbos table for the children, much as we would add a sweetener to our tea and coffee or add spices to make food tasty.

The sage mentioned in the previous chapters told me that it is best to choose a special treat that is reserved only for Shabbos, and to give that treat at the Shabbos table.

For those who are health conscious and unwilling to give sugary treats, look for treats without sugar (potato chips etc.) or other *special* food or drink of which the child is fond. One parent I know would go to the toy store and pick out items for a dollar or so, such as a little magnifying glass, a small pouch to keep things in, a tiny lock with a key, intriguing key chains, marbles, *kugelach* (an Israeli game using five small stones), etc. Interestingly enough these objects were well accepted by the children and served successfully as incentives. There are other inexpensive items that children collect such as napkins with designs for girls, or stickers for boys. (A well-known halachic authority in America told me these items are not *mukzeh.*) This may involve a little shopping time, but, as we noted in previous articles, the Shabbos table does take preparation, and it is certainly worth the investment.

Another way to use incentives at the Shabbos table is with a specific program in mind connected to the children's behavior. One can give points throughout the meal and give a special treat to whoever gets a certain number of points by the end of the meal. It is a good idea to have two prizes or two treats on hand, a bigger one and a lesser one. (There need not be that much difference between the two.)

Everyone participating in the program should receive at least one prize, the smaller one. However, only those earning a certain number of points should get the bigger prize.

The advantage of this type of plan is that rather than the children competing against each other, they are competing with themselves.

The point of having two prizes is that the child always comes away a winner, and the Shabbos table is always enjoyable for him, yet he still has the incentive to participate even more and gain the bigger nosh or prize.

Q *What am I going to do when the prizes become bigger and bigger?*

&A The prizes we are talking about giving at the Shabbos table are not big ones but rather *small* treats of nosh or *little* toys. You can stay within a certain price range and do not need to make the prizes bigger each week. Smaller prizes or nosh will enhance the Shabbos table much more than bigger ones, which are unnecessary. Bigger prizes also run the risk of making a child forget the Shabbos table altogether and just focus on the prize.

Q & A *I feel like the Shabbos table has turned into a sports stadium where I am the referee/scorekeeper having to keep constant track of what is going on, how many points each one has, plus make peace between kids who are complaining that the other one has more points than he does, and so on.*

As mentioned before, it is better for each child to be in competition with himself, not with others. In addition, a parent does not need to keep track of the points with the same accuracy as if he were a referee. If a child complains that he deserves more points, give him more.

The point is that the atmosphere should be pleasant, relaxed and enjoyable. The incentives are only there to enhance the atmosphere, not to make it even more tense. Therefore, adjust the program to keep the atmosphere calm and relaxed by giving the children extra points if necessary and by not being so rigid and structured in your incentive plan. It might also help for each child to keep track of his own points or be given jellybeans that he can count as points.

However, you must stick to your guns about a child only getting the bigger incentive if he puts in some work and tries to cooperate. He should not get it for nothing, because that will make your incentives lose their effectiveness. All we said was that you do not have to be rigid and precise in your plan. The atmosphere should remain relaxed and not become intense, but you should nonetheless stick to the plan.

There are certain basic rules that should be a part of everyone's incentive plan at the Shabbos table, such as no fighting or name-calling between siblings. One can give extra points for those who do kindness for others at the table and who keep the peace throughout the meal.

Q & A *Will we always have to work with incentives?*

As mentioned above, incentives should be used in two ways. To begin with, one should give incentive prizes for no other reason then it being Shabbos. In this way, the incentives are used solely to sweeten the Shabbos table for the children. This type of incentive should be used consistently, just as one spices the Shabbos food every week.

The other approach is through using a specific program connected to the children's behavior. In this way incentives are a crutch. They are the means, not the goal. They are meant to help the child overcome any obstacles on his or her way to enjoying the Shabbos table.

Used in conjunction with the techniques mentioned in the previous chapters, eventually, and with the help of Hashem, the goal of our children enjoying the Shabbos table will be achieved. (Exercise patience as this could take several months.) Once this is accomplished, incentive programs may be reduced to once in two weeks, eventually decreasing to once a month. At this point the enjoyment of the Shabbos table itself can serve as the incentive for the children to actively participate.

Q *How long should one require the children to stay at the Shabbos table?*

&A In many homes, children are expected to sit through the entire Shabbos meal.

R' Wolbe writes:

> At the Shabbos table parents require their children to sit through the entire meal even if the meal lasts for an hour and a half or more. For a young child this is impossible. He cannot sit so quietly the entire time. He must be able to move around. Sitting the entire time at the Shabbos table is way beyond his capability. It is not necessary to explain how damaging such a thing could be for a child. The results could later on be serious.

Many years ago, I joined a family that spent a very long time at the Shabbos table. The father was like a drill sergeant, and I was amazed to see the little 7-year-old sitting practically at attention the entire time. Even though the meal took *several hours*, the boy did not move from his seat and sat ramrod straight in his chair almost the entire time.

I was impressed, yet I wondered. Perhaps this was one of those cases where the methods work momentarily and everything looks great on the outside, but in the long run, much damage is done to the child's personality.

My fears were based in reality as I had a personal connection to this boy's older brother. The older son, who had not been there for Shabbos was full of anxiety and could not sit still for any given length of time. At the Shabbos table he would act wildly, sometimes even throwing things or putting his hands in the soup.

In his case, the pressure did not even work for the moment, let alone in the long run.

At the same time we are making use of an incentive plan, it is a good idea to make our children's stay at the Shabbos table easier by shortening the amount of time they are require to stay. After that, they should be allowed to leave and play until you are ready to say Grace After Meals.

Q & A *What about letting older children (over bar/bas mitzvah age) leave the table?*

The most important thing to keep in mind is to avoid forcing a child to participate. Make the Shabbos table a pleasant experience. As the Chazon Ish said, "Use appeal not force."

It would be worthwhile to ask the older ones privately beforehand to stay for a certain length of time (half an hour to 45 minutes). Events at the Shabbos table should interest them and make them want to be there.

If they leave, let them leave. They will probably wind up enjoying the Shabbos table after they have left by watching all the goings-on, rather than being forced to remain there.

Q & A *How can we get children to help at the Shabbos table? I want them to clear the table or help serve. What am I supposed to do if they refuse? Should I just leave them alone and let them get away with it?*

(This will be answered in the next chapter.)

27

The Shabbos Table Revisited (Part 4)

Shabbos in Outer Space?

We have a problem.

As if weightlessness, cramped conditions and the enormity of the galaxy were not worrying enough, a crew member of the next space shuttle mission is facing an additional problem: How do you observe the Sabbath when it occurs once every 10 1/2 hours in orbit?

Colonel Ilan Ramon, who was scheduled to become the first Israeli to leave Earth as part of the crew of Columbia, has caused consternation among rabbis by asking how — or more precisely, when — to mark Judaism's day of rest.

The problem stems from the fact that Jews are required to observe the Sabbath "every seventh day," starting at sunset on Friday evening and ending the following day "when three stars are seen."

They must refrain from any creative work on the Sabbath and say three sets of prayers, ideally in a synagogue. Observant Jews mark the beginning of Sabbath by reciting a prayer over wine — the Kiddush — sanctifying the holy day.

Aboard the space shuttle, however, Col. Ramon will orbit the earth every 90 minutes, with each orbit counting technically as a day because from his perspective the sun has risen and set. The stars will be visible to him at all times.

While Col. Ramon is not the first Jew to become an astronaut, the 47-year-old pilot is the first to want to practice his faith in orbit, to the extent that NASA has already agreed to provide him with kosher space meals.

To settle the question of Sabbath observance, however, Col. Ramon has asked his local rabbi in Florida, Rabbi K., for guidance. Rabbi K. has in turn consulted rabbinical scholars across the world.

"The rabbis I have written to are amazed the question has been asked," Rabbi K. said. "It has been a theoretical question for some time, but now, incredibly, we have to apply it to a real-life situation.

"We are told to observe Shabbat every seventh day, but if you are orbiting the Earth every 90 minutes, do you do it every seventh orbit?"

One of the scholars consulted, R' Levi Yitzchak Halperin, has already ruled that Col. Ramon should be relieved of his obligations because he will not be experiencing Earth time.

A British rabbi who has researched the subject disagrees. "Some rabbis say that because he will be in space, Earth rules don't apply," said Rabbi R. "But my view is that, as you can't exist in space without recreating Earth-like conditions — using oxygen, for example — you should observe the same routine as you would on Earth."

Rabbi R. did, however, offer a different way out of Col. Ramon's difficulty. "His fellow crew members are unlikely to appreciate him taking time off during what is likely to be a very intense mission, as it might endanger their lives. There is a Jewish principle which states that saving life takes precedence over all religious rituals, so on those grounds he could be relieved of his obligations."

Col. Ramon admits he is not particularly religious, but believes that as Israel's first astronaut he has a higher duty to consider. "I feel I am representing all Jews and all Israelis," he said.

The issue of the kosher food, which has to conform to strict Jewish dietary and religious laws, has been more easily resolved because a company in Illinois already produces it in self-heating, sealed pouches for the army.

This article appeared recently in the British newspaper "Telegraph" and concludes with the words of one prominent individual: "This is one small step for Col. Ramon, but a large step for Jews worldwide."

Though keeping Shabbos down here on planet Earth may not be as complicated, we may still find the task of creating a pleasant Shabbos atmosphere rather difficult, especially at the Shabbos table.

Yet let us make the effort, if not for ourselves, then for our children. Let us stick to our goal, for we have a "higher duty" to consider: our children's future.

The *Zohar* says that the main *chinuch* of a child is accomplished on Shabbos. Since the main part of Shabbos is the meals, it follows that the Shabbos table plays a major role in the successful *chinuch* of our children.

One mother was having a great deal of trouble with her children. She consulted a rabbi who is a master educator as well. In the course of the conversation, the Shabbos table was introduced. The mother mentioned the fact that she makes her children wear pajamas at the Shabbos table so as not to dirty their Shabbos clothes.

The rabbi suggested that the children wear their Shabbos clothes throughout the meal.

The mother followed his advice and witnessed dramatic changes in her children's behavior. There was a big improvement in the way they acted even during the week. Apparently, the more effective Shabbos table had its effect.

The Shabbos table is a major *chinuch* tool. As such, care must be taken that it is not misused.

A friend of mine who is a high school principal recently told me a shocking but true example of parental misuse of the Shabbos table. To keep the children behaving properly at the Shabbos table, a father had potential troublemakers sit next to him. If a child got out of line, he received a painful pinch on the leg.

The children were warned ahead of time not to show any reaction — or else. Other people at the table, including guests, had no idea what was really going on.

This father had absolute *control* over his children at the Shabbos table. But is this *chinuch*?

My friend described to me the not-too-surprising results of this method. The oldest child developed severe emotional problems; the second child left religion altogether. My friend was able to save the third child, who was the only sibling enrolled in his school, by keeping him away from home on Shabbos for three consecutive years.

Storytelling — an Essential Ingredient

Before we address the questions raised in the previous article of how to get children to help at the Shabbos table and how we can instill greater parental respect at the Shabbos table, it is important for us to note another essential ingredient for success at the Shabbos table: storytelling.

We are all moved by a good story, no matter what our age, but children are especially open to absorbing the message a story contains. Take, for example, the following true story, which certainly had an impact on many people, myself included.

> A certain father learned with his son every day.
>
> One night, the boy was walking home after having finished his study session with his father. As he crossed the street, he failed to see a minivan coming toward him. The van hit the boy and screeched to a halt.
>
> The impact was so strong that the van was dented in the place where it hit the boy. The boy was found lying between the front and back wheels of the minivan.
>
> Witnesses to the accident felt there was nothing to be done for the boy. They called an ambulance with not much hope in their hearts. How amazed they were to see the boy get up and walk away!
>
> Concerned despite the boy's appearance of well-being, the boy's father took his son to the hospital. There, he was checked and given a clean bill of health.
>
> It was an obvious miracle, especially considering how hard the boy was hit.
>
> In the hospital, the father of the boy met with a friend who said that in his humble opinion, the father should undertake a special mitzvah to express his gratitude to Hashem for the miracle. He said that he would be seeing R' Chaim Kanievsky in the near future and offered to ask his advice.
>
> When the friend posed the question, R' Kanievsky said the father should pay the tuition of a needy student who

could not afford to pay his tuition. The boy might be an orphan or a child from a broken home. The father should pay the tuition for this child for an entire year as a sign of gratitude to Hashem for saving his child's life.

The friend went back and told the father R' Chaim's advice. The father said, with obvious excitement in his voice, that a meeting had recently been held in his neighborhood regarding a broken family. The parents had separated, and the children were suffering. This father stood up at the meeting and said, "I am willing to donate an entire year's tuition for one of the children." He put his verbal commitment into immediate action by giving postdated checks to cover the year's tuition.

The day before his son had the accident was the day the first check cleared his bank account.

I saw this story hanging on the wall in a shul where I recently went to pray, and I found it hard to believe. I called someone I know to verify the story, which he did, directly from the father of the boy himself.

Stories can be a powerful source of inspiration. Because children (and many adults as well) love stories so much, stories have been a tradition throughout the generations to influence them.

In our times, we are blessed with a wealth of written material. Among the more recent books published are *Tuvcha Yabiu*, a collection of new and interesting true stories arranged according to the *parashah* by the renowned R' Yitzchak Zilberstein of Bnei Brak (son-in-law of R' Shalom Yosef Elyashiv), and *Lulei Toras'cha*, by R' Asher Bergman (grandson of R' Shach), which contains amazing stories about R' Shach. These two books alone contain enough fascinating stories and material for at least an entire year!

For those who prefer English, I recommend a trip to your nearest Judaica bookstore where you can choose from a practically endless source of story material.

The stories you tell at the Shabbos table may be on any uplifting topic. This will include tales of *tzaddikim*, stories of Divine Providence, noble character, kindliness and the like.

Storytelling vs. Lecturing

Before you start, a word of caution: There is a huge difference between storytelling and lecturing.

At a lecture, there is one person doing the talking and an audience. The people in the audience are supposed to sit quietly, pay attention and not interrupt. It is a great approach for conveying information in an orderly fashion. It can also create a stiff, formal atmosphere where the only one listening is the speaker himself.

Storytelling is different. It is alive and real. When a parent tells a story at the Shabbos table, listeners can participate. They can add interesting comments or share stories they themselves have heard. Participation is not only allowed, it is encouraged. The story serves as a springboard for a pleasurable group activity that gives everyone a chance to express himself.

One of our major goals at the Shabbos table is to give our children an extra-special dose of loving attention. When they contribute to a family discussion, it builds them up in a way few other experiences can and makes the Shabbos table a pleasant experience for them.

Although lecturing may be pleasant or fulfilling for us, it does not necessarily mean that our children in the role of captive audience feel the same way about it.

We ended the previous chapter with this question:

Q. How can we get children to help at the Shabbos table? I want them to clear the table or help serve. What am I supposed to do if they refuse? Should I just leave them alone and let them get away with it?

I posed this question to the sage quoted previously.

To the first question, he replied that of course the children should be asked to help at the Shabbos table. The mother is not a maid, and she need not wait on everyone hand and foot. The children must certainly contribute, in this way lending their mother a hand and sharing the burden.

Even younger children should be expected to participate. In fact, the younger a child begins, the more he will successfully develop the habit of lending a hand.

I myself witnessed the results of this sage's *chinuch* when I once had the privilege of being at his home for Shabbos many years ago. At that time, there was one son as yet unmarried. He studied nearby in Ponevezh Yeshivah and came home to eat the Friday night meal with his parents before returning to the yeshivah to resume learning.

I was rather surprised to see a 20-year-old serving the various courses throughout the meal and then washing all the dishes, making sure his mother sat and did not have to do anything. The most surprising part of it all was that his parents did not have to say a word. The boy did everything of his own accord, willingly.

Q *What if the children are not willing to participate?*

A This is not something that should be left to deal with at the Shabbos table. A parent should spend time during the week planning in advance.

First, the technical details should be covered. The children should know what their job is on *erev* Shabbos and also what their chore is at the Shabbos meal. If desired, shifts can be rotated and turns taken.

Second, and more important, is that a parent should try to foster an attitude that it is an honor and privilege to help prepare for Shabbos and an equal honor and privilege to help out at the Shabbos table.

A parent should tell his children incidents related by our Sages that illustrate the way many *Amoraim* and *Tannaim* prepared for Shabbos.

The more enthusiastic a parent is about Shabbos, the more their children will feel the same way.

> *Once R' Elchanan Wasserman came to the house of a man named R' Henoch Bengis. R' Bengis lived in Russia and was well-known for his wealth and his charity. It was raining heavily. R' Elchanan did not want to ruin R' Henoch's carpet by coming in through the front door, so he went around to the back. When R' Henoch saw R' Elchanan, who was one of the leading rabbis of the generation, coming in through the back door, he cried, "Rabbi! What are you doing? Why are you coming in through the back door?"*
>
> *"Well," R' Elchanan explained, "I don't want to spoil your beautiful carpets with my mud."*

"But you're spoiling the education of my children," R' Henoch answered. "I want my children to know that your mud is worth more than my carpets."

It was more important for R' Henoch to teach his children this lesson — that the mud a Torah scholar brings in is priceless compared to a carpet, and that a carpet is worthless if it prevents a great person like that from coming into your house — than it was for him to protect his possessions.

In the same way, if a parent truly feels the importance of Shabbos preparations, the children will absorb the message that they are privileged to help out.

Children should also be encouraged to view helping out as a way of showing their appreciation to their parent(s) who works so hard to take care of them and prepare Shabbos meals.

Not only the son of this sage impressed me. After Shabbos, a married daughter came by with her children and had one of the grandaughters wash the floors. As the rabbi confirmed, not one Saturday night passes by where the married children do not stop by and either they or a grandchild wash the floor so the mother will not have to do this task.

I was very interested in this sage's answer. Why did he stress the importance of Shabbos as opposed to the commandment to honor one's parents? His answer contained a very valuable *chinuch* lesson.

Honoring parents as it should be practiced is practically non-existent today, even in the best of homes. Although it is of the utmost value, trying to build on it alone will not be enough, and a parent will be faced with an ongoing struggle. However, the previous approach will automatically bring children to honor their parents, as illustrated to me by the children of the sage himself.

If we wish to succeed in the *chinuch* of our children, why not follow the advice of those who have already been proven successful?

28

Hashem
Is Our Best Friend

Man's Best Friend

"**W**ho is always there for you through thick and thin? To whom can you tell all your feelings, knowing he or she will never say a word? Who will be your best friend no matter what happens?

"The answer to these questions is probably sitting at your feet right now."

I recently came across these lines, written on the back of an insurance magazine that I received in the mail. To be honest, I was curious to see what the answer would be, and so I read on.

"It's your pet!" said the magazine. The magazine was urging people to send photos of their pets, or of the pet of their dreams. It promised to feature photos of these "loyal darlings" in the spring issue. The winning photograph would receive $100.

Nowadays, pets are being given a more prestigious position in society than ever before. I myself witnessed what I considered to be an amazing sight in Manhattan on a recent visit there. On the corner of Fifth Avenue, a dog was lying next to a man who was holding a sign. At first glance, I assumed that this man was another of those homeless unfortunates who was collecting money to alleviate his difficult situation.

It was only when I took a closer look that I realized what was actually taking place. The sign the man was holding read, "Abused Puppy." It went on to explain that the puppy (which was a rather large German shepherd) had been forced to participate in dog fights. As a result of this fighting, the dog developed serious sores in its mouth. The signs were beseeching the public to contribute the funds needed for laser surgery to help this "puppy."

A Substitute for the Real Thing

In fact, more people everywhere are turning to pets as sources of warmth and emotional support. One nonreligious person I know has seventeen cats and dogs. She has been through difficult times and turns to her animals for emotional support and encouragement.

People are so desperate nowadays that they turn to animals to fill their emotional needs. It may be compared to a drowning person who grasps onto a straw in order to save himself — not because the straw will save him, but rather because he is so desperate, and in his desperation he is willing to grab hold of anything.

R' Shlomo Brevda once cited the Gemara that describes how King Hurdus (Herod — a slave who rebelled against his masters and eventually became king) would walk every day between two long rows of birds. The birds had been trained to repeat again and again the words, "kiri, kiri" ("the king, the king"). When Hurdus was taking one of these walks, one of the birds made a most unfortunate error. Intead of "kiri kiri," the hapless bird said "kiri biri" ("the king, the slave"). The enraged king had the "rebellious bird" executed immediately.

R' Brevda explained that Hurdus suffered terribly from an inferiority complex. He knew that he was not the true king; in fact, he was nothing other than a rebel slave. He was therefore in desperate need of some means to quiet the voice of truth that emanated from inside himself.

And thus it was that he was willing to consider even the voices of trained birds as a source of emotional support. This is why he was enraged when the bird called him a slave.

In the same way, people today turn to their animals for comfort. Their animals are their best friends. Isn't it a pity that they do not have a true source to which to turn?

We Jews have a totally different answer to the question posed at the opening of this article. "Who is always there for you through thick and thin? To whom can you tell all your feelings, knowing he or she will never say a word? Who will be your best friend no matter what happens?"

Hashem the One and Only! He is my best friend, and He is always there for me through thick and thin! "*Gam ki eileich begei tzalmaves lo ira ra ki Atah imadi!* — Even as I walk through the valley of the shadow of death, I shall not fear, for You are with me!"

On occasion I have heard R' Shach note that in *Shir HaShirim* we refer to Hashem as *Dodi*, for He is our best friend. Many times he told the story of the group of some fifty Jews who were about to enter the gas chambers in Auschwitz, when one of them suddenly realized that it was Simchas Torah. "We may not have the Torah," they exclaimed, "but we have the *Ribbono Shel Olam* with us. Come, let's dance with the *Ribbono Shel Olam!*"

After telling this story, R' Shach added, "I would give *kol chayai* — all my life — to be able to dance those few minutes with that group of Jews, and to experience those few moments of Paradise in this world. This is the theme of a Jew in every generation, '... but we have the *Ribbono Shel Olam.*' "

We may not always be consciously aware of this truth, yet at times we will be confronted with situations that can rouse us to open our eyes.

"He That Heals All Flesh"

Recently I spent time with a close relative who was hospitalized. An operation he had undergone turned out to be somewhat more complicated than had been expected, and we were all deeply concerned. With Hashem's help, about two hours after surgery began, the doctor came in to the waiting room to let us know that everything was okay.

Eventually, when my relative was ready to leave the hospital, I was there to accompany him home. I helped him with his clothes and then waited while he recited the asher yatzar blessing. He said the whole blessing slowly and with much devotion, but when he reached the end of the blessing he repeated the last few words numerous times: "Rofei chol basar umafli la'asos; rofei chol basar umafli la'asos .... Healer of all flesh and performer of wonders."

His life had just been saved. He had been through an operation that was by no means simple, and he had come out alive. What is most significant is that he recognized and appreciated Hashem's kindness in his recovery. Yes, Rofei chol basar umafli la'asos!

Parents are always asking, "How can we develop in our children the strength to overcome obstacles? How can we provide them with the tools that will help them through difficult situations that they will encounter later on in life? How can we make sure that they will always remain loyal to Hashem, and never stray from the ways of the Torah?

Cultivating within our children the realization that the *Ribbono Shel Olam* is truly their best Friend will help them through every situation that confronts them in life. Through this realization they will also gain the countless other benefits that accompany those who have developed such an awareness (among them, never needing to turn to animals for emotional support).

How can we help our children develop this attitude?

Some very effective ways are:

• Being your child's closest friend
• Praying for what you want, and afterwards thanking Hashem
• Teaching children gratitude
• Being a role model for your child

Being Your Child's Closest Friend

R' Shimon Schwab said that the Torah requires that each parent be his/her child's best friend, closest confidant and strongest advocate.

R' S. R. Hirsch states that the relationship we have with our parents is the foundation of our relationship with Hashem. Faith means establishing the same kind of relationship toward Hashem that we had as little children toward our fathers and mothers — one of total and absolute trust, confidence and security.

Through building such a relationship with their child, parents are in effect strengthening the child's faith, because the relationship they have established will enable the child automatically to develop a positive relationship with the *Ribbono Shel Olam*.

A man I know has trouble *davening*. His father was very authoritarian, and he feels strongly that this is why to this day he finds it difficult to relate to Hashem with anything other than fear and trepidation; he has a very hard time developing a love for Hashem and for *davening*.

Being your child's best friend, however, does not mean giving in to his every whim, nor does it mean abstaining from disciplining the child when necessary. It does mean constantly and consistently doing what is truly in the child's best interests (as opposed to taking out one's own frustrations on the child), and making the child's best interests the measuring rod by which you gauge all your interactions with him.

It also means making your child a high priority in your life. A father recently shared an interchange he had with his teenaged son, who had approached him to discuss a matter that the son considered to be of extreme importance. Only a few minutes earlier the father had begun a learning session, and so he told his son that he did not have the time. The son responded that his father *never* has time to discuss things with him.

I know this father quite well, and I am aware that he loves his son very much, but I am not sure that his son is aware of that. After all, how important can someone think he is to you if you do not have time for him?

It also means caring about your child in a way that *he* can perceive. Many matters that are very important to our children are not at all important to us. We may tend to belittle these matters in the way we approach them; we may not even pay much attention to them altogether. If we will but show our child that what is important to him is important to us, then we have shown him that we are on his side and that we are his friend, *in a way that he can perceive it.*

There are various practical ways of achieving this. One of the ways is to give your child something that he likes or wants (not necessarily something expensive) without waiting for him to ask for it.

In my neighborhood we have a children's group on Shabbos afternoons, where many boys come to learn. As prizes for attending, we give "Torah cards" that the children collect and later paste into special albums. Those who fill the albums are given a bigger prize at a special event once a year.

There is a standard amount of cards that we usually give — generally six cards per child. This past Shabbos, however, I asked the children if they would mind if I gave them each ten or more cards, just this once. Of course no one minded, and my message came across to them loud and clear: I am their friend and I am on their side, and they know it.

I am not the only principal who gets involved personally in planning class trips together with the students, discussing with each class what activities they would enjoy most. I make it a point to participate in these trips often, and try to add to their fun, through telling them stories or introducing interesting competitions, quizzes and races. Relating to students in this way makes children appreciate their principal; they know that he is out for their good and is on their side.

Of course one cannot do this at all times, but it is a good idea to look for opportunities when you can give your child that which is important to him or her.

We have mentioned often in these pages that there is a tremendous fringe benefit that you can gain from this approach: if your child sees that you are interested in what he considers good for him, then he will realize that you are truly out for his benefit. A sequence will then have been set in motion: *Kamayim hapanim el hapanim* — he will respond in kind. He will accept your authority willingly and will cooperate with you eagerly to do the things you ask of him. He might not even wait to be asked. (Note that this will not happen as a result of your showing a one-time interest in your child, but rather from your maintaining a consistent position of being out for your child's good in a way that *he perceives as such*.)

The principle here is to *initiate* giving your child that which is important *to him*, and it does not necessarily have to be possessions. It can be privileges or attention or even just understanding his point of view, even if you do not necessarily agree with him. If you listen to your child and he feels understood, you have given him something very important, regardless of whether or not you have done what the child wanted. The understanding itself is the gift.

The very act of taking out time to be with your child is a great gift. It makes him feel that he is truly worthwhile. A scholar I know called me for advice regarding one of his children. When I suggested that he spend more time with his child, he seemed reluctant to accept my advice. It seems that spending time with his children did not fit into his tight schedule of learning. How unfortunate that he does not realize that being a parent to his child is a mitzvah that no one else can do; no one else can be this child's parent. Therefore, this mitzvah supersedes learning

Torah, just as any other mitzvah that no one else can do for you (such as eating matzah, donning *tefillin*, *lulav* and *esrog*, or sitting in the *succah*).

A parent who spends time with his child (not just at the Shabbos table, when the child is doing his homework, or at other pressured times) is showing the child that he is there for him, and that he enjoys his company. This parent is indeed his child's friend.

Praying for What You Want, and Afterwards Thanking Hashem

When a person develops a habit of *davening* for whatever he wants (in his own language, and at times other than the standard times designated for *davening*), he begins to realize that the *Ribbono Shel Olam* is truly his best Friend, the One to Whom he can turn, and Who is with him at all times. If he trains himself to thank Hashem when his prayers have been answered, this awareness will be heightened.

As we have mentioned previously, teaching our children to *daven* for everything they want is therefore an excellent method of instilling in them the awareness that Hashem is their best Friend. When it comes to instilling this attitude in your children, however, do not lecture them about it; do not tell them, "Pray to Hashem and then you will realize that He is your best Friend." Rather, approach the matter as a practical piece of advice.

When your child is in a predicament, or when there is something that he wants, point out to him that praying to Hashem will increase his chances of achieving the desired results. (This will be even more effective at times when you have the same desires or needs as your child, and he sees *you* praying for help.) By developing the habit of praying for anything he wants and needs, the child will automatically absorb the feeling and the recognition that Hashem is always there for him, even in the most trying of times.

Hashem is truly our best Friend, and is with us always. Hashem takes great pride in our efforts. It is not easy to be a parent (or an educator), as you will know if you have been reading this book. Yet we must remember that it is not *perfection* that Hashem asks of us; it is *improvement*. And as long as we are putting forth the effort to improve (slowly but surely), the *Ribbono Shel Olam* is happy with us!

29

Teaching Gratitude

Appreciating Our Hands

A friend described to me an evening in a kosher Japanese restaurant. As he sat with some relatives waiting for his order to be filled, a Japanese man appeared dressed in chef's garb, complete with high hat and white coat, and began to perform.

First he took a large knife and fork from the tray next to him and banged them on the table. He then proceeded to throw the knife and fork high into the air and to catch them on their way down. What followed was an expert juggling act in which the chef twirled and threw a variety of utensils, occasionally banging them on the table or against each other as he juggled them.

His theatrics did not end there. When the juggling act was over, the chef took a container of oil, poured the oil onto the table and lit the oil, transforming the table into a large fire tray. My friend realized then that part of the table was a stovetop. To finish his act, the Japanese chef spread the food on the "table" (stove) in front of the clients, then cooked, fried and prepared it on the spot.

Having hands can be lots of fun. With hands we can do many interesting things. However, hands can do much more than merely entertain others. They also serve us as marvelous tools to take care of our myriad needs each day.

Once, to demonstrate this truism, I asked for a volunteer among my students to spend the ensuing five minutes without using his hands. I made my request just before Minchah, when they were about to put on their hats and jackets. As it happened, the boy who volunteered was the class "smart aleck," and he was determined to best me.

Quite sure of himself, he raced to the rack and tried to get the hat on his head. He even tried taking his hat with his teeth in order somehow to throw it onto his head. The hat fell out of his mouth. The boy had the entire class laughing as he tried one tactic after another to get his hat onto his head, but all his efforts failed. Even he learned how useful hands really are.

On a recent visit to the hospital, I had a personal reminder of how much pleasure hands give us. While sitting in the waiting room, I happened to notice that one of the hospital personnel was not moving his right arm and hand. Finding this to be rather unusual, I looked a bit closer and realized then that this man's arm was constructed of plastic. In place of his own arm and hand, he wore an artificial limb. Seeing this gave me a new appreciation for the hands Hashem gave me.

We have been discussing the concept of teaching children to be aware of how much they have in life. "Cultivating within our children the realization that the *Ribbono Shel Olam* is truly their best Friend will help them through every situation that confronts them in life," we wrote. "Through this realization they will also gain the countless other benefits that accompany those who have developed such an awareness (among them, that they will never need to turn to animals for emotional support.)" Teaching our children gratitude can be a very effective means of infusing them with this awareness.

Not spoiling — a Prerequisite

One father asked my advice regarding his 12-year-old son. His son has only one task to perform for Shabbos, which is to set up the candles. In Israel, some people use what we call neronim. These are short candles that fit into small glass containers. This boy's job was to remove the small metal piece that remained from the previous week's candle and to place the new candle into the glass.

On this particular day, Shabbos was approaching and the atmosphere in the house was becoming a little more hectic. The boy went about his job of cleaning out the little glass containers when he noticed that one candle from the previous week had been somehow extinguished prematurely, and there was a clump of wax in one of the glass containers.

"I'm not taking out the wax," he said. "My job is to put in the candle, not to take out the wax." The father (who, miraculously, was able to remain calm) told his son gently that he was busy with other things and that the boy himself would have to take care of it. The child was adamant; under no circumstances would he give in. "That's not part of my job," he said. The father responded that if the boy would not do his job, he would not be allowed outside to play with his friends before Shabbos; but the boy would not budge. He stayed in the house all afternoon, and later, when Shabbos began, he refused to go to shul for prayers.

It was at this point that the father came to discuss the matter with me. As the situation stood, his son was still upset over the fact that he had not been allowed to go out to play, and it was questionable whether he would come to the Shabbos table. He might even begin to use praying as a tool for taking revenge against his father (especially since he knows how important religious matters are to his father). The father wanted my opinion as to whether he had reacted correctly and how he should proceed.

I advised this father to ignore his child's protests; under no circumstances should he give in to the child. He should not be fazed by the child's attempts to "get back at him" by using religion as a weapon. As the father, he too should remain steadfast in his principles, but he need not act out of anger or even out of a desire to be in charge and control the situation. Any action he takes should be done because it is the best thing for his child.

It is not good for any child to be spoiled. If we allow a child to get by without fulfilling even the minimal amount of responsibility placed on him, then we are spoiling him. (In truth, we also spoil a child when we give him so little *responsibility; but that was not this father's question.) If we then allow him to get the best of us through his protests and threats, we are spoiling him even more. We must not refrain from doing that which is in our child's best interests, out of fear that he might not like it. And it is certainly in our child's best interests that we not allow him to be spoiled.*

I told the father to be strong and ignore his child's crying and protests. He should remain calm and loving, yet he should stand by his principles.

The next morning, the father reported to me what happened. When he returned from shul he went over to his son, kissed him gently and wished him a good Shabbos. He did not run after his son begging him to come to the Shabbos table. He sang the Shalom Aleichem, and when it was time to make Kiddush he simply told his son that if he wanted to come to the table he would be a most-welcome participant. By remaining calm and unmoved by the boy's tactics, the father was in effect refusing to allow the boy to get his way. Sure enough, the son came to the Shabbos table on his own, and went to davening on Shabbos morning.

(Once, when a rebbi in our school was having discipline problems in the classroom, I advised him to work on remaining calm. If the students can get the rebbi excited, I explained, then *they* have succeeded, but if the rebbi remains calm, then the rebbi has been successful. Their attempts to get the rebbi's goat will not succeed. A calm rebbi is a successful rebbi, I told him.)

How can we succeed in teaching our children gratitude?

A prerequisite for teaching our children gratitude is that we not spoil them. Someone who is spoiled feels that he has the whole world coming to him, and that whatever he receives is rightfully his. With this attitude, how will he be able to develop gratitude? For gratitude is based on the realization that he has been *given* something, that everything he receives is a gift.

At this point a word of caution is in order. There is a fine line between spoiling your children and raising them with warmth, love and encouragement. Spoiling means giving in to your children and doing what they want because *they want it*, regardless of whether it is truly in their best interests.

An 8-year-old child I know goes to school only when he wants to. He could be absent for two weeks at a time. His parents do not have the heart (or, more accurately, the emotional strength) to be firm with him and insist that he attend school. This is obviously not in the child's best interests, yet his parents continue to give in to him, much to his detriment.

Note that insisting that your children do what is right is no contradiction to showing them love and encouragement. Show them love; give them encouragement. *Give* to them! But don't *give in* to them! If we want to succeed in teaching our children gratitude, we must not spoil them.

There are many effective ways of instilling gratitude in our children. First and foremost, *tell them the importance of being grateful, and how it can be a merit that can protect the people of Israel.*

A Merit to Protect Our People

I made an overseas call from Israel to the U.S. The person who answered the phone asked how things are in Israel. I answered with the standard, "*Baruch* Hashem, okay."

He became very upset with me. "How can you say things are okay with all that's going on? You people have to do something. Get together and start praying," he said. "Do whatever you can!"

He is certainly right. But is praying alone the answer, if we do not make an effort to improve our deeds? A rabbi told me recently what R' Shach would say about times such as these. "One must strengthen themselves in the area of doing good deeds discreetly, without others knowing about it. This can be a great merit that can protect us in difficult times."

The same rabbi related a story which he had heard about the late R' Kreisworth of Antwerp.

R' Kreisworth and the Nazi

When R' Kreisworth was a young bachur, he came to learn in a yeshivah in Vilna. In those days there were no dormitories, and students rented sleeping space in the homes of various people in the city. R' Kreisworth was in a predicament, as he had very little money to offer. Finally he found one woman who had something to offer that he could afford. She showed him the broom closet. "This may not be a room," she said, "but it's big enough to sleep in." Having no other choice, he accepted the offer. She cleaned out the area and this closet became his living quarters.

Some time later, the dean of the yeshivah approached him. Assuming he was wealthy and was living in a spacious apartment, the Rosh Yeshivah mentioned that an elderly rabbi, who is blind, would be coming to Vilna soon to undergo medical treatments. Since R' Kreisworth has such a spacious apartment, he said, he would like to place the visitor there to stay with him. Embarrassed to reveal what kind of "apartment" he really had, R' Kreisworth agreed.

For the next eighteen months, this rabbi slept in the broom closet while R' Kreisworth slept outside in the hallway, with a string tied to his foot for the tzaddik to yank on if he was in need of help. Afterwards, when the sage finished his treatments and left Vilna, no one was the wiser as to the enormous sacrifice R' Kreisworth had made for the honor of the Torah.

Around that time, the Nazis, yemach shemam, took over Vilna. They did not appreciate the sight of Jews walking the streets. One day when R' Kreisworth was walking to the yeshivah, a Nazi patrol seized him. The commander ordered one of his men to kill him immediately. Then he had a sudden change of mind. "Why dirty the streets with Jewish blood?" he remarked, and he told his assistant to take him into a nearby building and kill him there.

On the way to the building R' Kreisworth davened to Hashem, "Ribbono Shel Olam! You know that I suffered many months for the honor of the Torah and that no one knows about it. I did it sincerely, and solely for the honor of the Torah. May this be a merit before You, so that I may live."

When they entered the building, the officer turned to R' Kreisworth and said, "I don't really know why I'm in this war. I don't hate you. But if I don't kill you, then they'll kill me .... Wait! I have an idea. I'll shoot three times into the air and you'll run away. This way they will think that I killed you."

R' Kreisworth agreed and was about to run away, when he felt the German pulling at his collar. "Just a minute," he said. "You're a Jew. I'm afraid that I won't make it out of this war alive. I want you to promise me that I and my mother and sister will survive the war."

"How can I promise you?" R' Kreisworth asked. "Life and death are not in my hands. However, I can pray for you." This answer satisfied the Nazi, and he wrote his name and address on a small piece of paper, which he handed to R' Kreisworth. Then he let him go free.

Soon after the war was over, R' Kreisworth, who had been spared the dire fate of many of his brethren, was very interested in finding out what had happened to this German. He had kept the slip of paper, and when he was incidentally passing through the man's town decided to look him up. Upon reaching the village he found that all but a few houses there had been destroyed.

After much searching he found the house he was seeking. He knocked on the door and an elderly woman answered. When he told her he was looking for the German man, referring to him by name, she slammed the door in his face. Apparently she suspected that he was a Nazi hunter, out to take revenge.

He walked over to the window and, while banging, held the piece of paper up against the window. Soon after, the front door was opened again and the soldier came out. The two embraced, and then the German told R' Kreisworth his story. He had been saved miraculously, unlike many of his countrymen, and his mother and sister were likewise spared.

Such is the power of an act done secretly and without others knowing about it. Such an act is pure, for it is done neither for honor nor for other ulterior motives, and it carries great weight in Heaven.

Gratitude is a mitzvah that is fulfilled mainly through one's heart. Although there are many ways to *express* gratitude, the gratitude is taking place within one's heart. It is therefore a mitzvah that is done secretly, and so has great power to protect.

Tell your child that *his* having gratitude can be a great merit to protect *Klal Yisrael*, especially in our turbulent times.

Being a Role Model for Your Child

Another very effective method of instilling gratitude in our children is *to be a role model.*

R' Yitzchak Zilberstein of Bnei Brak once spoke of one of the famous "Prisoners of Zion" who was incarcerated in a Russian prison under impossible circumstances. At a press conference that was held after the prisoner's release, he was asked how he had been able to retain his sanity under such conditions, when so many others had not.

He answered with the following, amazing statement. "It was due to the fact that my parents never became angry with each other. All their life they related to one another with a special feeling of closeness. They always helped each other, and so they were able together to overcome all of the difficulties and tribulations of the complicated life we led. *It was their harmony and unity that gave me the emotional strength to endure.*"

Parents' harmony can play a major role in building their children emotionally and giving them the strength to endure and overcome. It can also be instrumental in helping ingrain the trait of gratitude in our children. If a child sees his parents expressing gratitude sincerely to each other on a consistent basis, then he will learn to have gratitude. We can strengthen this lesson at times by having our children participate in our show of gratitude to our spouse.

On special occasions, such as when our spouse has a birthday, we may have our children compose cards of appreciation, all the while telling them how much we owe father or mother for all they do for us. Or, on a Friday night, the father can call the children together and secretly plan with them that everyone will express thanks and appreciation to Mother, who worked so hard on *erev* Shabbos to prepare the house and make us such a delicious meal.

This principle is applicable to single-parent homes as well. The parent can initiate expressions of gratitude by the children toward members of their extended family and close acquaintances.

In truth, parents need not wait for a special occasion to tell their children of the various kindnesses that their spouse does for them (that is, for both parent and children), and how much they owe him or her. With just a bit of thought, anyone can come to realize how much gratitude he owes his spouse. In a recent class that I gave on the laws of honoring one's parents, we calculated that an average mother spends between 600 and 1,000 hours preparing meals for her family over the course of one year.

Teaching our children to express gratitude to our spouse will be effective only if *we* feel the gratitude and *we* express it. Having our children join us in expressing gratitude is effective only as a means of strengthening *our* show of gratitude, because the point here is that *we are being role models.*

Interacting with our children can present golden opportunities to be role models, for then we can express our gratitude for the things *they* do. Of course our children are not doing "volunteer work" when they do what we tell them to; they are required to listen to us. But that should not prevent us from expressing gratitude for their efforts. By *showing* them gratitude, we are *teaching* them gratitude firsthand. What a powerful lesson this can be!

There are many other ways parents can act as wonderful role models to teach their children gratitude. For instance, a parent can make it a habit to say a few words that express how much they enjoy or appreciate various things in life. Hearing his parent talk about how much he enjoys the various things life has to offer can make a very strong impression on a child. If the parent adds some words that express his thanks to Hashem, it can make an even stronger impression.

It is important to note that this kind of talk will be effective when the parent speaks of himself and his own feelings, describing his own personal experience, not if the parent uses it as a form of lecturing. Thus if the parent tells the child, for example, "You're so lucky that you have a nice nose," or "You are so fortunate to have both eyes," it will not be as effective.

The point is for the parent to share his experience with the child, and to include himself in his observation. In this way the child will learn from example rather than from the lecture. "We are so fortunate to be healthy and to have food on our table." "I just love Shabbos." "Isn't this fun?" It is a good idea to comment even on things that do not necessarily have a spiritual connection, for example, "I really enjoyed that cup of coffee. *Baruch* Hashem for coffee!" After all, if this is your feeling, then it's the truth!

Even if you feel uncomfortable and hypocritical speaking to your children in this way; even if you feel that you are not "holding on the level" to speak this way, do it anyway. Eventually, your words will become sincere. And more importantly, they will make their impression on our children.

A scholar I know, who is today the leader of an entire community, told me how he developed his joy for life. When he was in elementary school, he often heard his principal say things like, "It's so wonderful to be a Jew." Such expressions made a lasting impression on him, and he has managed to transmit this attitude to his children through the same methods. He told me that one night at bedtime, as he was playing and talking with his 5-year-old son, he asked his son why he has such a nice nose. "Because Hashem loves me," his son replied.

Obviously the fact that his father repeated constantly such phrases as, "Hashem loves us so much," and "We have such a wonderful life," had left its mark.

Working on Gratitude Together With Your Children

Some parents keep a notebook together with their children, where each day they write down one or two things that happened for which they are grateful. (This is best done not as an assignment placed on the child, but as an activity in which the parent also participates.) The conscientious parent might say to his child, "I feel I need to work on gratitude. Would you like to help me and work together with me?" Then, every day, parent and child can tell each other one or two things they enjoyed and feel grateful for.

The Steipler Rav recommended this approach of working together with one's child. Rather than telling the child that he must learn with you, say something like, "I would like to learn this particular work, and I need a study partner. Perhaps you would be interested."

It is not beneath parents' dignity to work together with their children. On the contrary, the fact that the parents are open and willing to work together with their children to improve their own character only builds up the parents' esteem in their children's eyes. Working together with them will make the activity all the more enjoyable for the children! Eventually, you will both end up with volumes of things to be grateful for.

We have so much to enjoy, so much for which to be thankful. Let us allow ourselves to enjoy. Enjoying what the world has to offer is a great mitzvah. But more important, let us allow ourselves to *express* our appreciation. In this way we will give our children (and ourselves, too) an opportunity to live happy lives, filled with appreciation and gratitude to Hashem, Who is truly our best Friend.

30

In Pursuit of Perfection

A *Tzaddik* Asleep

Have you ever seen a *tzaddik* sleeping? I once brought a group of children from our school to see R' Chaim Kanievsky. As we arrived, we were told by the rebbitzen that the rav was sleeping but was expected to wake shortly. On my way out of the house to tell the children that we would have to wait, I noticed that the rav's door was slightly ajar and I caught a glimpse of him asleep.

What I saw was puzzling. R' Kanievsky was sleeping on his side, in accordance with halachah, yet he was holding his arm in a very awkward position. It was pressed against his side bent upward. The position made a vivid impression on me, especially since I had no idea why he had slept in that position.

It was not until I went to visit R' Avraham Horowitz, brother-in-law of R' Shlomo Zalman Auerbach, and study partner of the Steipler Rav — who told me the following story — that I understood the meaning of what I had seen.

About a half hour after the Steipler Rav passed away, R' Horowitz noticed that the Steipler's hands were folded together on his chest. This seemed strange given that at the time of his passing his arms had been straight at his sides. He pointed this out to the members of burial society and to R' Chaim (who was also present). They said that when they placed the deceased on the floor, his arms were straight, but they later *moved up by themselves.*

In his lifetime, the Steipler never let his arms fall below his waist. (The Gemara relates that R' Yehudah HaNasi was called our *holy* teacher because of the same practice.) Apparently, the Steipler remained holy even after passing away.

R' Chaim Kanievsky adopted his father's practice. He too does not let his arms fall beneath his waist. It was for this reason that his arm was bent upward when I saw him sleeping. Even during sleep, he is careful.

Such practices are not for mere mortals. They are external evidence of a lifetime of spiritual toil. Yet who upon hearing of such holiness and purity is not moved to want to emulate these spiritual giants in some way? Although attaining their level may be beyond our capability, the goal is certainly worthwhile. As one sage said, "If you reach for the stars, at least you won't wind up in the mud."

Striving High vs. Unrealistic Expectations

Striving high is praiseworthy. *Living with unrealistic expectations*, though, can be very detrimental.

A youth came to R' Pam, complaining that he has not yet reached the level of the Chafetz Chaim. R' Pam later said about the meeting, "I spoke to him for quite a while until he became a normal boy again."

Unrealistic expectations of oneself, including the demand for perfection, can cause serious psychological disorders. A top social worker recently expressed dismay at the unprecedented number of teenagers seeking help for severe emotional disorders such as clinical depression, panic attacks and anorexia. Much of it, he stated, is due to the child's unrealistic expectations of himself. In the child's eyes, anything less than super achievement just is not good enough.

The Key to Success

It might come as a surprise to some, but the key to successful pursuit of one's dreams lies in a person's ability to be happy with who he already is. Being *same'ach bechelko,* happy with one's lot, does not only mean being happy with what we have materially. It includes the spiritual dimension of life as well. We can realize our aspirations by *being happy with what we are already doing correctly* and *feeling good about even the small steps we are taking in the right direction.*

Our Sages say that Hashem Himself is, so to speak, happy with his lot. R' Chaim of Volozhin explained that although with each passing generation the Jewish people decline in spirituality, Hashem always finds something about us to be happy with. We are His lot, His portion, so to speak, and so, no matter what our situation, because we are His, He rejoices over the good in us and takes pride in us.

R' Dessler says that the service of Hashem may be compared to a ladder firmly planted on the ground with its top reaching the heavens. You cannot get to the top by taking one giant leap. It takes a step-by-step climb to get there.

Let us find joy in every little step — those we have already taken and those we will yet take — for it is these little steps that will bring us to success.

I recently came across the following anonymous poem, which eloquently expresses this thought.

> One song can spark a moment.
> One flower can wake the dream.
> One tree can start a forest.
> One dream can herald spring.
> One smile begins a friendship.
> One handclasp lifts a soul.
> One star can guide a ship at sea.
> One word can frame the goal.
> One vote can change a nation.
> One sunbeam lights a room.
> One candle wipes out darkness.
> One laugh will conquer gloom.
> One step must start each journey.
> One word must start each prayer.
> One hope will raise our spirits.
> One touch can show you care.
> One life can make the difference.
> You see, it's up to you!

Cultivating this attitude within ourselves can be of great benefit to the *chinuch* of our children.

Being Happy With Ourselves

We must learn to be happy with ourselves and our gradual improvement. How many parents (or teachers) feel guilty for not living up to the high standards of *chinuch* we wish for ourselves. Articles and books by experts in the field may even serve to feed this guilt. A reader of my weekly column said, "It would seem that according to your standards, no parent is doing his job properly." This misses the point. The guidelines set forth in public talks and in print set goals worth striving for, destinations toward which to head. We are not there yet. We may even have a long way to go. Nevertheless, the determining factor is the *way* or *method* we use to pursue these goals. If we make unrealistic demands on ourselves and settle for nothing less than perfection, we will be fighting a losing battle. We will constantly feel guilty for not living up to our own unrealistic expectations. But if we take joy in what we are already doing properly as parents, and if we pride ourselves in our achievements, no matter how small they seem, we will slowly but surely come closer to the lofty *chinuch* goals we have for our children.

If you were not interested in being a good parent, you would not be reading this right now. You have already demonstrated your willingness to listen to new ideas and to change your approach or techniques, where necessary. This is something to be proud of, especially since there are, unfortunately, parents who are *not* willing to change.

I once spent hours with a parent whose child was on the brink of a nervous breakdown, yet the parent wasn't willing to make the first step. This parent was set in his ways. "If my daughter wants a relationship with me, she will have to change," he said.

Parents are the most unselfish people in the world. They receive no salary, are on call 24 hours a day, and are constantly making sacrifices for their children. In most cases, your children will hardly be aware of all you have done for them (at least until they have children of their own). Yet this does not prevent you, as a parent, from continuing to work hard, sacrifice and do what is best for your children. Take joy in this great success you have already achieved and pursue the goals mentioned in these pages, enjoying each small step of improvement.

Catch yourself doing things right, and you will succeed in doing more things right!

Being Happy With Our Children

For our children, who judge themselves according to our approval, an approving attitude can be crucial. The opposite — having unrealistic expectations and demanding nothing less than perfection — can be devastating.

Since I began writing a column for the weekly paper *Yated Ne'eman*, I have received a considerable number of faxes and e-mails. A few of them were from children brought up in homes where anything less than perfection was unacceptable. The letters were invariably filled with deep emotional pain.

One person wrote:

> *I always tried pleasing my parents, but when I would get a 99 they would ask why I didn't get 100. All I heard from my parents was what a terrible child I was. Never did I hear that I did something right. If I wanted encouragement, it wasn't forthcoming. Even so, I would try to elicit some positive response from my parents. "Aren't you proud of me?" I would ask. How many times did I want to please my parents but fail to get approval.*

Another reader wrote.

> *Before we start, let me tell you that I used to read your column in the Yated every week, but it started to drive me crazy because you spoke about different things parents should do while bringing up their children. The things you said seemed logical, but you never told the children of parents who did everything wrong how to deal with it. My father expected us to be perfect. When I was a boy, I studied a lot. During the long Shabbos afternoons, I would learn straight through from 11 a.m. to 6:30 p.m. — but have no fear, even that wasn't good enough.*

The demand for perfection or that a child attain standards impossible for him almost guarantees that the child will feel incompetent and guilty about everything he does.

Here is yet another letter:

> It hurts me to read articles like yours about how to raise my children. Every time you tell parents to do something, I think about how my parents didn't do it, and every time you say not to do something, I think how my parents did it. My parents would make me feel guilty for enjoying life or just for being happy. I find it hard to accept myself and my mistakes. I recently realized that I am motivated mostly by guilt and that I suffer from low self-esteem. Why can't my parents ever ever ever praise me?!

If we want to raise successful children, children who have a positive self-image and are highly motivated to succeed, we must adjust our demands. We must rejoice in their *gradual* progress. We must praise them for what they are **already doing right.**

There are many areas where these principles can be applied on a practical level. Let us approach a few:

(1) Spiritual development
(2) Performance at school
(3) At the Shabbos table
(4) Accepting children for who they are

Spiritual Development

We must evaluate our demands on our children in spiritual areas and see if they are in sync with the child's age and abilities.

I have mentioned a father who wanted to train his children in exercising self-control. One of his practices was to wait until the child was deeply engrossed in an adventure story and then suddenly take the book from him. After a while, the father returned the book.

His efforts certainly bore fruit. His children developed serious anxieties. However, no self-control was forthcoming.

A top psychiatrist said that one of his former clients was a young boy who excelled in yeshivah, but whose parents constantly complained about his never opening a holy book to study. Investigation showed that the boy worked hard in his learning at the yeshivah and needed to rest when he came home. His parents, though, had unrealistic demands and found it impossible to accept his need for rest. Instead, they constantly complained that the boy never opened up a book.

Performance at School

R' Pam once said that if a boy who is less capable scholastically makes a valiant effort and winds up with a grade of 60, it is an untruth to say this boy received a 60. This boy's 60 is equal to a 90, and he deserves to be placed on the honor roll for it, at least as much as the naturally talented boy who put forth less effort.

In our present school system, this may not be readily feasible. (See, however, a possible solution which is in use at the Bais Yaakov of Montreal — Ch. 37). But the boy's parents should certainly be aware of their son's efforts and should praise him for them. If parents get upset at such a child when he brings home a low grade, judging him not according to his capabilities but instead according to their expectations, they are guilty of having unrealistic demands. With this approach, they will not succeed in spurring their child toward success.

At the Shabbos Table

R' Wolbe, in his book *Zeriah U'Binyan BeChinuch,* writes that putting pressure on children to do things beyond their age level or their capabilities can be very detrimental. He cites the Shabbos table in particular as an example. Forcing children to sit quietly for long hours is something beyond the normal capacity of a child. A child must be allowed to run around and cannot be expected to sit quietly for long. Compelling a child to sit in his seat will not serve to build the child — and most certainly will not cultivate in him a love for Shabbos (or for Judaism as a whole).

I know of a family that does not allow one of their children to eat the evening Shabbos meal together with them. (The girl eats in the kitchen.) This poor child is not able to sit for such a long time and so her parents have decided that her presence at the Shabbos table would interfere with the high standard of decorum they demand. Needless to say such behaviors will not serve to benefit the child in any way. In truth I am doubtful if the parents have the child's benefit in mind at all.

Accepting Children for Who They Are

R' Wolbe (ibid.) cites the Gaon of Vilna who explains that each person has his unique personality that cannot be changed. A person's free will cannot change his personality, but enables him to utilize it for the good. Any attempt at changing a child's personality will only be futile and will certainly cause much damage. R' Wolbe illustrates the point with the following example: A child who needs to move about constantly cannot be asked to sit still for many hours of the day. Forcing such a child to sit for long hours may work temporarily, but in the long term, it will not succeed. "This is a major principle in *chinuch*," he says.

I know of one wayward teenager whose parents never accepted her for who she was. She was more lively and creative than the averge child. Instead of searching for ways to help bring out her personality within the parameters of halachah — such as giving her art lessons, encouraging her to be a group leader or counselor in camp, and other activities of this sort — they tried to change her into someone she was not by stifling her personality completely. The girl ultimately abandoned her parents' ways.

One of the most difficult things about parenting is learning to accept our children for who *they* are, although this may, at times, seem to be in conflict with our own needs. For us, it might be important that our children make a positive impression on others. If a child does not fit the standard mold, this makes it difficult and frustrating for us. We may feel disappointed with the child. Nevertheless, if we accept our children and try to understand them, we might just learn who *they* are. We might begin to see *their* strengths, *their* hopes and dreams, *their* personality. We might begin to see the difficulties *they* are experiencing, the fears *they* have. In this way, we might be able to help *them* — according to who *they* are. As the wisest of all men, King Solomon (*Mishlei* 22:6), told us, "*Chanoch lana'ar al pi darko* — Raise the child according to **his** path" — not *al pi darki*, according to **my** path.

When we follow this important guideline, we take joy in our children and their efforts. When we praise them and encourage them for what they already do well, we are in effect developing in them the most important tool necessary for success (aside from Divine assistance): their ability to rejoice in their accomplishments.

"I Will Always Be There for You"

About thirteen years ago, an earthquake in Armenia killed over 30,000 people in less than four minutes. One father raced to the elementary school his son attended only to discover that the building no longer existed; it was a heap of rubble. Recovering from his initial shock, he remembered the promise he made to his son: "No matter what, I'll always be there for you."

Although the situation seemed hopeless, the distraught father was determined not to give up. What kept him going was his promise to his son.

He mentally retraced the steps he took each morning when he brought his son to school and figured out where his son's classroom was located under the rubble. Racing over to the spot of the no longer existing classroom, he began to dig through the rubble.

Other well-meaning parents tried to pull him off the debris, saying, "It's too late. There's nothing you can do." But he just kept digging, responding to the skeptics with one sentence, "Are you going to help me or not?" They did not help him, and so he continued on his own.

Firefighters arrived at the scene of the tragedy and also tried to dissuade him. "We'll take care of it. Go home."

The father remained undaunted and just asked, "Are you going to help me or not?" No help was forthcoming because the rescue teams felt they could better use their resources where there was still hope of saving lives. At this site, it didn't seem there was anything they could do.

The father proceeded on his own, committed to the promise he had made his son. "No matter what, I'll always be there for you."

He dug for 12 hours, 24 hours — 36 hours. In the 38th hour, he pulled back a boulder and heard his son's voice. He screamed his son's name and heard a voice reply, "It's me, Dad! I told the other kids not to worry. I told them that if you were alive, you would come to save me, because I knew you would keep your promise, 'No matter what, I'll always be there for you.' You did it!"

When the building collapsed, the beams fell in a triangular wedge that protected this boy and thirteen of his classmates.

In these turbulent times, our children need us more than ever. One of the most effective ways that we can "be there for them" is by enjoying each small step *they* take toward improving, and by taking pride in what they already doing right. This is the way to cultivate in them the attitudes that will make them successful and a source of *nachas* for us all.

31

"Do as I Say, Not as I Do"

The Amazing Feat

One Shabbos I witnessed the following strange scene. A father took his son up to the bimah, the table on which the Torah is opened and read, and placed the boy's head against it. The boy's head barely reached the surface of the bimah.

I found it difficult if not impossible to imagine what this father was doing, let alone doing it during the prayers. I told myself he was probably playing with his son, showing him affection — although I was not convinced that it was the most appropriate thing to do in shul.

With a mental shrug, I turned my attention to the Torah reading. Immediately after it ended, several people began pulling a table over to the bimah. Then I understood. The boy I had seen earlier was reading the haftarah that week, and his father had been making sure his son would be able to read properly. Since the boy could not reach the bimah, they had moved a short table next to it so that he would be tall enough to reach the place from which he was reading.

But that was only the beginning. In that particular shul they read the haftarah from a parchment (which has no vowels, let alone the special cantillation notes which indicate how to read the haftarah). This short little boy who could not even reach the bimah was expected to read the entire haftarah and from a parchment yet! To complicate matters even more, the haftarah that week, Shabbos Shirah, is one of the longest in the entire Torah.

I was expecting a major catastrophe. Instead, I listened in utter amazement as the boy read the entire haftarah almost flawlessly.

After the prayers, I asked the boy how old he was. "I'm 9 years old," he told me. I marveled that such a young child could accomplish such a feat.

I expressed my surprise to the boy's father. "It must have taken him weeks to prepare."

"In all honesty," the father replied, "my son asked me last night [Friday night] if he could read today's haftarah. When I told him it was a long one, he said, 'Don't worry. I know it. You can even test me on it.' "

It seems that this boy learns in a yeshivah where they learn Prophets, cover a lot of ground and review what they have learned a number of times. The child knew the haftarah from school and only had to brush up on it before being able to read it in public.

"He must be a brilliant boy," I said.

"Actually, he's got average intelligence," the father replied. He then turned to his son and said fondly, "You gave us a wonderful surprise."

This child is certainly special and so is the school he attends, but the major factor in his success is his father (who, by the way, does not speak anything but words of Torah in shul; the questions and answers all took place elsewhere) and his attitude. He believed in his son's capabilities and willingly gave him the chance to prove them, without a moment's hesitation.

From Our Actions With Him and With Regard to Him

One of the most important facts to remember in *chinuch* is that although a child will learn many lessons from his parents the most powerful lessons will be those he learns from our actions — especially from our actions with him and with regard to him. And make no mistake about it: children have very sensitive antennas and will accurately pick up on these actions, even when we would rather have it otherwise.

This explains how children can fail to pick up on the values stressed in their very own home.

> R' Y.Y. Yaakovson illustrates this point with the story of a rabbinical student who was worried that his 10-year-old son lacked love for the Torah.
>
> After hearing the father's concerns, the boy's rebbi took his student aside for a talk. "What do you think is the most important thing in the world?" he asked.
>
> "Money," said the boy.
>
> "Really? Do you really think so?" asked the rebbi in surprise.
>
> "I sure do," said the boy.
>
> "What about learning Torah, being a Torah scholar? Isn't that also important?"
>
> "Sure," said the boy, with slightly less enthusiasm.
>
> "Why is it important to be a Torah scholar?" the rebbi probed.
>
> "Because that's what everyone says. Maybe for the reward in the World to Come."
>
> "Why do you think money is so important? Is it also because of the World to Come or because everyone says so?"
>
> The boy smiled. "That I learned on my own."
>
> "Could you explain where you learned this from?"
>
> The boy's expression immediately changed to one of bitterness and anger. "All our problems come because we don't have enough money. Every time I ask for something my father says, 'We can't afford it.' All day long father and mother talk about how they don't have any money and how they have to come up with some way to pay back all their debts. They're always worried about where they will get the money to pay for everything. Obviously," ended the boy, "if we had enough money, all our problems would be solved!"

This boy's parents sacrificed so much for Torah, yet they kept their feelings of joy and happiness with their lot to themselves. To their children, they expressed only the difficulties and frustrations.

Expressing Joy

It is imperative that parents share with their children their *joy* in Judaism by openly expressing it. They must let their children know how fortunate they feel to be of the chosen few the Creator has handpicked to fulfill His mission in this world — especially nowadays, when there are millions of Jews who, through no fault of their own, do not even know the *aleph-beis*.

This can seem a daunting task. Bearing in mind our original thought can make it easier: "Although a child will learn many lessons from his parents the most powerful lessons will be those he learns from our actions — *especially from our actions with him and with regard to him.*"

If we make sure to express feelings of joy *in our actions with him*, it can bring about the desired effect. Even in areas not related to religion, if we joke with our child and just have fun with him or her every so often, we pass on the message that we are happy and enjoy our lives. And in our times this may be one of the most important lessons we teach our children.

I have merited to be around many great rabbis and, as anyone who has been around *tzaddikim* will attest, they are happy people with a sense of humor. They may be serious, with an awesome sense of responsibility, yet this does not prevent them from joking lightly at times to make the atmosphere pleasant for all.

An elderly sage who was close to the Chazon Ish told me that all the pictures he has seen of the Chazon Ish had failed to capture the inner joy always evident in his facial expression.

By keeping the mood in our homes happy, we are teaching our child a most powerful lesson: that we are happy with our lives as religious Jews. Yet even if we are not able to portray such a positive picture on a consistent basis, by interacting with our children every so often through positivity and with joy, we will be able to get the message across.

This point is tried and proven and cannot be underestimated.

> *The true story is told of two boys who were neighbors, one the son of a great Torah scholar and the other the son of a simple, yet G-d-fearing laborer. Tragically, the son of the Torah scholar left religion while the laborer's son grew up to head an esteemed religious family. When a leading con-*

temporary Torah giant who knew both families was asked how such a thing could happen, he said, "At the scholar's Shabbos table, there were many discussions of Torah topics in great depth, far beyond the children's grasp. At the laborer's Shabbos table, there was much joyous singing."

Teaching Children to Be Truthful

Actions speak louder than words in *chinuch* when it comes to teaching good character. Take, for instance, parents who consistently preach the values of telling the truth. They are constantly telling stories about righteous people who were dedicated to telling the truth under all circumstances. In fact, just to make sure their children are telling the truth, they repeatedly question and cross-examine them, especially when they have reason to suspect the child might not be telling the truth. In their house, lying will not be tolerated!

Without realizing it, these parents are actually educating their child in the opposite direction. For when parents constantly doubt a child and question him, their actions are teaching him a powerful lesson: his word cannot be trusted! These parents are in effect teaching their child that he is a liar.

Chaim Walder, popular author and educator, supports this point by citing a study that found that parents who are naive and believe everything their children tell them (even if the children lie once in a while) will succeed in raising children who always tell the truth. This happens because the message such parents sent their child by always taking him at his word was that he was a person who always told the truth, a person whose word could be trusted. And the way we treat our child is the way he will turn out. *Chinuch* is a self-fulfilling prophecy.

The Suspicion Should Be Verified With Respect

But what should we do if we have valid reasons to be suspicious of a child? Should we ignore our suspicions altogether?

R' Pam, in a lecture to educators, answered this question. "In our generation, the way to deal with children is to treat them with respect [rather than harshly or condescendingly]. The more we treat them with respect, the more they will want to live up to our expectations and work hard not to disappoint us.

"And even if we suspect them of being up to no good, the way we express our suspicions should be in a respectful manner. This is what is meant by the teaching of our Sages, '*kabdeihu v'chashdeihu* — honor him and suspect him.' The *chashad*, the suspicion, should be done with *kavod*, respect."

R' Pam cited two incidents that illustrate this point. Once, a boy did not show up for class. The next day, R' Pam, who was the boy's rebbi, called him over and asked him where he had been. The boy gave him an answer and then added, "I can bring a note," to which R' Pam replied, "What do I need a note for? Your telling me is good enough."

Although in his heart he may have felt otherwise, he did not let the student know. Instead, he gave him a reputation to live up to. "And he lived up to his reputation," said R' Pam.

The second incident occurred when R' Pam was his class' proctor during a regents exam. At one point, he noticed a boy leaning over and talking to his friend. He could have confiscated the test paper and given him a zero. Instead, he walked over to the boy and said, "If you have any questions, you can come up to my desk and ask me."

Years later he met the boy, who told him, "Rebbi, what we learned together I've long forgotten, but that incident I will never forget."

I had a student who was headed in the wrong direction. The other students caught him taking money from the pockets of jackets belonging to students at a nearby kollel. I did not let on that I knew and instead took this boy as my study partner during class review.

At the boy's bar mitzvah, I asked him to do me a personal favor: that when he will publish his first work, he would write a small note of thanks to his old rebbi who predicted that he would one day write a book.

This boy did not disappoint me, and although he has not yet written a book, he went on to become a diligent student and one of the top boys in his yeshivah.

With Regard to Showing Them Love

Actions speak louder than words in *chinuch* when it comes to showing love to our children. No matter how many times we tell our children we love them, if through our actions we show they are in our way and that we really do not have any interest in them or any time for them, or if most of our interactions are of a disciplinary nature, accompanied by our disapproval, this is the message the child will absorb. He will learn, and in a very powerful way, that we are uninterested in him and constantly disapprove of what he does.

R' Wolbe spoke about the obligation of *chinuch*. The Rokeach comments on the verse (*Yeshayah* 59:21), "My spirit that is upon you and My words that I have placed in your mouth, shall not be withdrawn from your mouth, nor from the mouth of your offspring, nor from the mouth of your offspring's offspring, said Hashem," that the obligation of *chinuch* extends only to one's grandchildren, offspring's offspring, but no further because one's love extends only as far as his son and grandson; after that, the love is not as strong. Since the love is not as strong, he is therefore absolved of the responsibility to be *mechanech*.

"From here we see," said R' Wolbe, "that the obligation of *chinuch* is an outgrowth of our love for someone. Because we love, we therefore have an obligation to be *mechanech*, and where there is no love, there is no requirement to be *mechanech*. This is a novel thought. We normally think that one has to be *mechanech* with love. *Chinuch* comes first and then the love. But it begins the other way around: Because of love, we have to be *mechanech*."

Although the need for love in *chinuch* may be well known, said R' Wolbe, it may not be equally well practiced — especially when a child does something wrong or something of which the parent or teacher does not approve. It is especially then that the parent (or teacher) should awaken within his heart love for the child. He should say to the child, "I love you so much. That is why it hurts me even more to see you doing such a thing, because it's not good for you."

Such *chinuch* will succeed, said R' Wolbe, while a teacher who does not love his students will have no influence over them.

Love in *chinuch* must be unconditional and unceasing, R' Wolbe concluded, no matter what the circumstances, even when the child does something wrong and must be disciplined.

After the speech, one of the participants, a rebbi, told R' Wolbe the following incident:

> There was a boy in yeshivah who was constantly making trouble. One day in the middle of class, the boy got up and caused a big disturbance. All the other boys fell silent. They figured the day had come. This was the straw that would break the camel's back.
>
> I walked over to the boy and whispered something in his ear. From that day on, the boy was transformed.

What was it the rebbi had told him? He said, "It won't help you! No matter what you do I will still love you."

What the rebbi said saved the boy's life! This rebbi told me that he mentioned what he had done to another rebbi in a different class who was dealing with a similar situation and that rebbi did the same thing, achieving the same results.

With Regard to
Believing in Your Children

Actions speak louder than words in *chinuch* when it comes to believing in our child. If we only tell him we believe in him but our actions indicate otherwise, then he will learn otherwise — even with all the encouragement in the world.

> A well-known author described a startling insight he had about one of his sons. The boy was doing poorly academically. He did not even know how to follow test instructions, let alone do well on the test itself. Socially, he was immature, often bringing embarrassment to others close to him. Athletically, he was uncoordinated. He would swing the baseball bat before the ball even reached him.
>
> The father was desperate to help his son and so applied various positive mental attitude techniques. "You can do it!" he would tell the boy. "We know you

can." *Any improvement, no matter how small, was showered with words of encouragement, such as, "Keep up the good work, son." If others laughed or made fun of the boy, his father would come to his rescue, saying, "Leave him alone. He's still learning." The boy's mother also participated in this campaign of encouragement.*

Both parents felt they were doing everything possible to build their son's self-esteem, yet nothing seemed to work. If anything, things seemed to get worse. What was going wrong?

After careful introspection, the parents realized that their actions were not a true reflection of how they really felt about their son. Deep inside, both parents felt that their son actually was not capable, that he really could not make it on his own and that it was up to them to help him. And this feeling was being communicated in their every action with him. They had thought they were being encouraging but now realized that they were being discouraging.

It was at this point that they took a different approach. They began to work on changing their own perception of their son. Instead of viewing him as a charity case, they began to look for his strengths and talents. They uncovered his true potential in their minds and decided that their actions would communicate this new attitude. They began to let him handle situations on his own instead of rushing to help him. This sent a sincere message of "We know you can do it."

After several months (and some strong withdrawal symptoms; after all, he had gotten used to being babied), the boy began to blossom. He developed a strong sense of self-confidence. Eventually he went on to become a straight-A student, an all-state champion and was elected to several student body leader-ship positions.

A Few Words of Encouragement

Allow me to express a few words of encouragement.

There is special Divine assistance parents have when they put forth the effort to help their children. And it is a special gift which only parents are given.

R' Moshe Aharon Stern, the late beloved dean of students at Kamenitz Yeshivah in Jerusalem, developed two serious illnesses at the age of 7. There seemed to be no cure for either of the illnesses. From the day she found out, his mother would pray for her son's well-being every single day. R' Moshe Aharon lived a long, productive life — and passed away about thirty days after his mother's death. It seems that his mother's prayers kept him alive!

There is no one who can do as much for their child as a parent. And there is no one who is given as much Divine assistance with regard to their children as is a parent.

32

Harmony Between Parents and Children

Miracle in Meah Shearim

The miracle of the car bomb in Meah Shearim that didn't explode is one that touched all of us.

Only yards away from Kikar Shabbos, the busy intersection that links Meah Shearim with the Geulah section of Jerusalem, a car parked at an angle in front of the Eisenbach car service stand drew a complaint. The traffic enforcement agent passing the scene dutifully entered the license plate number in a hand-held device linked to a central computer at police headquarters. Within seconds, he knew the car was stolen.

When he noticed a wire extending from the car's cellular phone, he became suspicious and notified the police. Sappers quickly discovered an undisclosed amount of dynamite hidden in the car ready to blow up at any moment.

What followed was pandemonium. The police closed off both Meah Shearim and Geulah to all traffic. Residents were urged by a helicopter loudspeaker overhead to stay indoors. Shoppers and schoolchildren on their way home were among the many who were delayed for as long as five hours.

Eventually, the bomb squad successfully dismantled the explosive devices (four in all) and moved the car out *of Meah Shearim to a place where the bombs could be safely detonated. The sight of the police convoy, including ambulances and army vehicles, accompanying the car was frightening.*

Word spread rapidly of the great miracle that had taken place. There had been enough explosives in the car to cause damage within a one-hundred-yard radius. In this congested area, through which just about everyone passes, who knows how many lives were saved?

I myself happened to have been in the area just about 45 minutes before the car was found. And in what a wondrous way was it found. A friend who is in the area almost daily said that he does not remember seeing a traffic agent in the area for the last few months. It seems the agent showed up just to save hundreds, perhaps thousands, of people from being hurt. When interviewed, he confirmed this view. "Hashem sent me to save lives," he said.

The streets of the neighborhood were filled with celebrations and dancing until 2 o'clock in the morning. People were ecstatic, filled with thankfulness and gratitude.

In What Merit?

Many wonder in what merit we were saved from this terrible tragedy. There were those who pointed out that the events took place one day before the scheduled worldwide Day of Prayer. They saw in this a fulfillment of the verse, *"Terem yikra'u vaAni e'eneh* — Even before you cry out to Me I shall answer you" — a clear sign that Hashem wants our prayers.

Others saw the near miss as a warning to motivate us to properly utilize the special day of prayer, bearing in mind the extent to which our enemies are out to hurt us.

The above reasons make sense, yet only our greatest tzaddikim are qualified to draw the accurate meaning from such events. A visitor to R' Aharon Leib Steinman merited to be told the following insight: "My heart tells me," said R' Steinman, "that the reason we were saved from terrible tragedy is because of the Fathers and Sons groups that were held on Purim day."

On Friday, 14 Adar, Purim day in Israel, and on Sunday, 16 Adar, Purim day in Jerusalem, almost 25,000 boys and their fathers took time from their hectic schedules to sit down to learn together for one hour. It was this merit that R' Steinman felt saved us from impending danger.

The Fathers and Sons study sessions on Purim were truly a sight to behold. The inspiration gained just from seeing so many fathers learning with their sons is hard to describe. The atmosphere was charged with the lively learning of those who filled the study halls and shuls until there were no vacant places, at least in the shul in our neighborhood.

Yet there was an added dimension to the special feeling of those moments. It was the intense harmony felt in the air as both father and son enjoyed learning together. This feeling warmed my heart, as I am sure it did the hearts of so many others present.

The feeling of harmony between parents and children is a wonderful thing. Yet it may not always exist — especially during vacation time when our children are out of school and constantly around. In fact, a father once complained to me after vacation, "It's like Gehinnom for me when the kids are home."

Some Key Questions

We can gain insight into solving many of the difficulties we experience during vacation time by asking — and answering — several key questions:

(1) What are parents supposed to do when their children constantly refuse to cooperate? How should a parent react when even if he tells his child something a hundred times he still does not listen?

(2) How does a parent get off the merry-go-round of frustration that comes with having to constantly discipline, rebuke and criticize?

(3) What should parents do if they are not happy with their children's behavior during vacation, especially with regard to spiritual areas? How should they respond when the child is simply not living up to parental expectations? Are parents expected to give up on their expectations? (!)

Differentiate Between
Older and Younger Children

Before we answer these questions, we must differentiate between younger children and older children. Children 10 years of age and younger have a greater need for discipline. At this stage, their capacity to understand is not fully developed, and they are unable to control themselves properly of their own accord. Therefore, the need for discipline, along with clearly defined parameters and boundaries, is that much greater.

The less developed a child's understanding, the more he relies on others, especially his parents — and he needs those others to be firm and strong. Knowing that those he relies upon are strong and steadfast provides the child with emotional security.

However, make no mistake about it: Being firm is *not* being mean or cruel to a child, making fun of him or embarrassing him. Being firm means standing behind your demands consistently and seeing to it that they are carried out. If necessary, this may entail enforcing them with the appropriate consequences. Sometimes it means not giving in to the child's requests or complaints. All this is done solely because it is what is truly best for the child, as opposed to cruel measures which are never in the child's best interests, no matter what his age.

> *Several years ago, I was called upon to advise parents who could not control their 8-year-old son. The boy would simply stay home from school for weeks at a time, and the parents felt powerless to do anything about it. Once, I said to them, "Why don't you just take your son to school by force whether he likes it or not? Why don't you give him a spanking? If he stays home, why don't you just lock him out until he agrees to go to school?"*
>
> *No matter what suggestion I made, the parents felt helpless and unable to act. I recommended that they go for therapy. Later, the therapist told me that these parents were afraid of their child. In their home, it was the children who ruled, not the parents.*

Once a child approaches the teenage years, though, things are different. As a child's mind begins to develop, so does his independence. He becomes a miniature adult, and treating him as you would treat a small child can be very detrimental.

During this phase of a child's development, it is important for parents to treat him in a way that preserves his self-respect and lets him know how highly they think of him. In short, they should treat him in a way that builds him up as opposed to knocking him down.

The Teenage Years

Especially during the teenage years, parents need to focus on discussing more and disciplining less.

My rebbi, the late R' Chaim Segal, principal of Mesivta Rabbeinu Chaim Berlin and one of the foremost *mechanchim* of our generation, once told a group of high school rebbis that a child in high school, a teenager, is a *gadol* (a grown person), and we dare not shame him. He may still act childishly, yet this is natural, for he was a child for 13 years and is just breaking away from his youth.

R' Segal said that the respect we have for the child and the love we show him should be *gevaldig*. The way to interact with children of this age, he said, is with a settled mind; acting out of anger and frustration will only prove detrimental and ineffective. He then said that there was never a time he dealt with a student out of anger that he did not later regret.

Everyone who was privileged to learn from R' Segal knows that he was by no means a pushover. He showed his students tons of respect and love — but we all knew that he meant business, and, in fact, we were afraid of him. One is not a contradiction to the other.

The Arm-Wrestling Contest

One vital but little-known rule of good *chinuch*, whose principle is drawn from the following story, can completely change attitudes within the family:

> When on the lecture circuit, a well-known author often carries out the following demonstration. He picks someone in the audience who looks strong and physically fit and challenges him to an arm-wrestling contest.
>
> As the volunteer walks to the stage, the author launches a verbal campaign to rile his opponent. "I have never lost

a match," he says, "and I don't intend to now. You're going to lose, and you might as well prepare yourself for losing."

When the "victim" reaches the stage, the author sticks his face in his face and repeats the same things all over again. He lets his volunteer opponent know — in a rather obnoxious way — that in a few seconds he will be lying flat on the ground. The speaker even boasts that he has a black belt in karate.

Almost inevitably, all these provocations just steel the volunteer's resolve to win the match.

The author then asks someone from the audience to count to 30 and signal the start of the arm-wrestling match. Before they begin, he suggests to the audience that each time one of them triumphs by pushing the other's arm down, the winner get paid a dime from the audience.

Meanwhile, the author has grasped his opponent's hand and given him an intimidating stare.

As the signal is given, the author suddenly lets his arm go limp. The volunteer immediately pushes down the author's hand.

Confused at this easy win, the volunteer begins to let up the pressure a little. The author then begins to struggle and offer resistance, and the other fellow fights back. Again the author lets his hand go limp.

Eventually, the author turns to his opponent and says, "Why don't we both win?"

The other person usually allows the author to push his hand down once, but is still a little uneasy.

Then the author lets his hand go limp again, and the fellow puts him down again. Within minutes, the two are working together — almost effortlessly — moving back and forth, rapidly pushing each other's arms down, getting as many dimes as possible from the audience.

If we study the sequence of events, we see that in the beginning the volunteer was raring to go, fired up into competing to the best of his ability. When the author let his hand go limp, though, he realized that this was no competition. There was no resistance on the part of the author because he was not out to compete.

Once the volunteer realized this, he did not feel threatened and was willing to cooperate, working together with his newfound team-mate in getting as much money as they could from the audience.

We Are Not in Competition With Them

This point was brought out strongly to me once when I was teaching Gemara to a seventh-grade class. One boy began arguing against my explanation of the subject matter. As he was arguing, he began to raise his voice.

Wanting to put a halt to the disrespect, I began to raise my voice even more, but my efforts to stop this boy's insolence were to no avail.

An expert *mechanech* with whom I later consulted told me that the proper solution would have been for me to lower my voice. Each time the student raised his voice, I should have lowered mine even more. In this way, the student would have desisted, seeing that no one was in competition with him.

Parents are not in competition with their children. Yet when parents try to force issues with their older children, it can easily turn into conflict. The child, wishing to retain his independence, will resist. Even if he eventually does comply, the battle to elicit his cooperation may become never-ending. What, then, is the answer?

The **first step** is to work *together* with the child. Rather than just issuing commands, communicate with him, discuss with him, explain to him — and make sure to acknowledge his feelings.

This does not mean that you forgo your demands as a parent. It just means that you approach your child in a different way.

The Research Scientist

A famous research scientist who made several important medical breakthroughs attributed his success to an incident that happened when he was about 2 years old. He was trying to take an opened container of milk out of the refrigerator when he lost his grip and the container fell. The milk spilled all over the floor.

Instead of yelling at him or punishing him, his mother said, "What a great and wonderful mess you have made!

I have rarely seen such a huge puddle of milk. Well, since the damage is already done, would you like to play with the milk before we clean it up?"

To be sure, the child eagerly played with the milk. After some time, his mother said, "Whenever a person makes a mess like this, he has to clean it up. What would you like to clean it with — a sponge, a paper towel or a mop?" He chose the sponge, and together with his mother he cleaned up the milk.

His mother then said, "Do you know what we have here? It's a failed experiment in how to carry a big milk container with two little hands. Let's go out to the back yard. We'll fill the container with water and see if you can find a way to carry it without dropping it."

The little boy learned that if he grasped the container near the top, he would be able to hold it without dropping it.

The scientist ended his true story by saying that this incident taught him that there is no need to fear making a mistake. Mistakes, he discovered, were actually opportunities to learn something new. This, he said, was the secret of his success.

Control Is Not *Chinuch*

We may not always have the time to interact with our children in a similar way, especially if other children are in need of attention at the moment. What is important, though, is to develop this attitude, the attitude that *we are not in competition with our children, nor are we out to control them. We are out to be mechanech them, to guide them in the right path so that they will follow it of their own accord.*

Sadly, there are parents who are not willing to forgo the control they gain through discipline and punishment.

To quote R' Shlomo Wolbe in his *sefer, Zeriah U'Binyan BeChinuch*, "There is a widespread misconception that *chinuch* means punishment and discipline. The reason for this is that if parents are able to discipline and punish properly, they then feel in control. Yet being in control is not *chinuch*, and just because one is able to control does not mean that he is a proper *mechanech*."

R' Wolbe relates the story of someone who applied for the job of dean at a high school. One of his first questions was, "How much authority will I have?" He wanted to know if he would be able to kick a boy out of the school.

R' Wolbe immediately understood that this applicant was not made of the proper material. He was not a *mechanech*.

> *Similarly, R' Y. Y. Yaakovson tells of the parents who came to an educator complaining about their son. They said the boy was bitter and had given up. The parents were angry with him. "We tell him dozens of times a day that we're unhappy with the way he is acting," they said, "but he hasn't changed. He's as bitter and discouraged as ever."*
>
> *"But what have you done to help him change?" asked the educator.*
>
> *"What do you mean?" they asked. "We constantly point out to him the behavior we're unhappy with."*
>
> *"That is not going to help," said the educator. "It only makes things worse. Your son knows which behavior is wrong. What he doesn't know is how to help himself change."*
>
> *"So what are we supposed to do?" asked the parents.*
>
> *"First," said the educator, "drop all criticism."*
>
> *"Nothing doing," said the father. "We came for advice on how to be mechanech our son, not to hear someone tell us to stop being mechanech our son."*

These parents felt that if they did not try to control the situation by voicing their criticisms, they were being derelict in their duty as parents. Without the criticism, they just were not being *mechanech* their son.

What a pity they had no understanding of what *chinuch* is all about. More, how could these parents be oblivious to the negative effect their so-called *chinuch* was having on their child?

Of course, parents must discipline and even punish at times. But it must be done with the right goal in mind. Parents must say to themselves: "We love our child so much. We want so much that everything should be for his benefit. Because of this, we must discipline. Because of this, we must punish. But the discipline is not the goal. It is not even the dominant feeling we wish to have. The main feeling we want to maintain is one of warmth and love. The discipline is only a temporary measure to help the recipient return to the right path so that we can show him our love again."

Short-Term Rebuke

R' Yitzchak Hutner once wrote to a student, "I want to give you rebuke. But I don't want to write it in a letter, because a letter lasts a long time, and I don't want the rebuke to last. I want to be able to tell it to you face to face so that afterward we can hug and be close together again."

Working With Your Children

In light of the above, let us once again approach the first two questions we listed earlier, this time on a practical level.

(1) What are parents supposed to do when their children constantly refuse to cooperate? How should a parent react when even if he tells his child something a hundred times he still does not listen?

(2) How does a parent get off the merry-go-round of frustration that comes with having to constantly discipline, rebuke and criticize?

The way out is for parents to interact with their children in a way that *shows* (as mentioned above) that there is no competition. They must convey to the child that there is no struggle, that it is not a battle of "us against you." Rather, parents and child are a team together. When a child realizes that his parents have only his own good in mind, he will cooperate more readily and comply more willingly.

The Emotional Bank Account

In addition to discussion, communication and planning, there is another very powerful tool that works wonders in letting a child know how deeply his parents care for him and have only his best interests in mind. Building this feeling in a child is essential to *chinuch* because once a child is assured of the parent's true motivation, he becomes receptive and cooperative. One author refers to this feeling as the *emotional bank account.*

We can build the bond with our children by making deposits in their emotional bank account. This can be done through a variety of small actions done on a consistent basis. Each action done sincerely adds to the account until we accumulate substantial assets in our "relationship bank" with the other person.

Small actions may be:

(1) doing an unexpected favor for your child
(2) showing him appreciation
(3) complimenting him often
(4) listening to him
(5) smiling at him
(6) spending time only with him
(7) expressing love to him
(8) believing in him

One advantage of using this metaphor to look at the relationship is that if your bank account with even one child is in the red, you need not despair. For it can be put back into the black through consistent small deposits or a few large deposits.

When the Child Is Not Living Up to Our Expectations

The third question we listed earlier was:

What should parents do if they are not happy with their children's behavior during vacation, especially with regard to spiritual areas? How should they respond when the child is simply not living up to parental expectations? Are parents expected to give up on their expectations? (!)

We are to realize that a child's behavior during vacation is not necessarily indicative of his or her performance during the semester. It is vacation time and children are often inclined to be laid back and idle. The fact that there are exceptions and the neighbor's child might be learning the entire day in the *beis hamidrash* does not mean that my child is delinquent or slacking off. Everyone is different and for some, the fact that they can take it easy during vacation gives them the emotional stamina to do well during the learning period.

Are parents expected to give up on their expectations? Not necessarily, but it is important to remember that in order to influence another to change we must first understand them. And we can truly say that we understand our children only if they agree that it is so.

33

Dealing With Fighting (Part 1)

Some Interesting Statistics

These statistics appeared just a few days ago on the front page of a leading secular Israeli newspaper. It is easy to see that Israel is way ahead of the entire civilized world, topping even the United States by 14 percent.

I know. I did not tell you to what the statistics refer. Are these business statistics showing Israel's export prowess or perhaps a ranking of countries by cellular phone use?

Country	Percent
Israel	24
Australia	14
America	10
Italy	9
Belgium	8
Turkey	7
Finland	7
Canada	6
Holland	2
Japan	1

The above statistics have nothing to do with business. The countries are ranked according to the percentage of students age 12 to 13 who were assaulted by their fellow students in the year 1999.

It is heartbreaking to see that Israel leads the so-called civilized world in physical violence in the schools. (We must remember, though, that secular Israel now includes many non-Jews and many Jews who through no fault of their own were raised without Jewish values. These statistics certainly reflect both these facts.)

Although the report is several years old, it is by no means outdated. Two youths in Beersheba decided to meet to settle accounts. Their dispute began one week earlier. The two friends quarreled after one cursed the other. Later, they talked on the phone and decided to meet to set things straight.

They met at a local park and began arguing. Before long, the argument turned into a fistfight. The stronger one delivered blows to his former friend's head and face until the boy fell to the ground. When he tried to get up, the stronger boy kicked him until he lost consciousness.

On the way home, the ruthless victor passed two friends of his victim and told them to go get their friend. They hurried to the park and tried to rouse their beaten friend, but were unable to do so. They then called an ambulance, which took the boy to the hospital.

At first, the two friends lied and said the boy had fallen from a second-story window. After being questioned by the police, though, they broke down and told the truth, including naming the assailant. Doctors treating the assaulted boy said his condition was stable but that he had suffered irreversible damage.

Upon being detained and questioned, the attacker explained the reason for his actions. According to him, the other boy had put him down.

In other words, for a perceived blow to his self-esteem, the attacker was willing to extract a vicious revenge almost without limit.

The age of the fighters was 14.

Why Are They Fighting?

A 13-year-old girl underwent a four-hour operation on her foot. The reason? As she left class, another student started hitting her. She protested, and another student who came over began kicking her in the foot. She called for help, but the boy continued to kick. He finally let up and she was able to make her way home in terrible pain. Her parents immediately rushed her to the hospital, where she was operated on.

In Lod, a 16-year-old girl stabbed her 12-year-old neighbor with a kitchen knife because he disturbed her while she was cutting the salad.

Twelve thousand criminal files were opened in Israel this year concerning youths apprehended for violence against other youths. Of these, 2,500 incidents took place within the school confines.

A secular expert on education at the university in Beersheba commented regarding these events that "they pick it up from the adults." He went on to say that a society that looks up to power and believes that only through power can it ensure its existence is a society that trains its children to see brute force and violence as the only solution to problems. Parents, he said, hope violence will be used solely against the enemy. However, it is inevitable that in a society that breeds violence, violence will ultimately be directed toward members of that society.

Therefore, it is wrong to expect the schools to handle the problem. "They will not be the source of our salvation," the professor said. "One cannot expect teachers and educators to heal the maladies of an ailing society. Only a society with empathy and patience will succeed in producing schools free of violence."

These shocking statistics reinforce our knowledge that when children are brought up without a code of values, their base instincts will take over and there is no telling where those instincts will lead them. When self-gratification is glorified and self-control is disdained, there is every reason to act as one feels and no reason to reign in one's anger.

This problem is not confined to secular Israel. It is universal and a growing menace to society at large.

A car on a New Jersey highway repeatedly stalled, causing traffic to back up. Everyone knows how frustrating this can be, but for one waiting motorist the delay was more than she was willing to put up with. As she drove past the unfortunate driver of the stalled vehicle, she got out of her car, walked over to him and poured a bottle of ammonia all over his face. Not satisfied with that, she crashed her car into his several times.

Dealing With Fighting (Part 1) / 339

Fortunate are we who were created to bring honor to our Creator, Who separated us from the misguided!

Why Are WE Fighting?

Unfortunately, we are not immune to the influence of secular society and the force of our own flawed character traits. Having the Torah does not automatically make us immune to these and other abominations when we do not follow in the Torah's ways.

> *R' Elyah Lopian told of two sisters who were bitter enemies. They had not spoken to each other for years. Time passed, and one of the sisters was on her deathbed. She called for her sister, who arrived hoping for reconciliation and a chance to ask forgiveness before her sister passed away. As she entered the room, the dying sister motioned her to come closer. She obeyed and bent over the bed. At that moment, the dying sister reached forward, pulled her sister's nose to her mouth and bit it. "Now I can die in peace," she said.*

Even we, as Torah Jews, suffer to this very day from the effects of dispute. How much do we suffer from internal arguments and strife!

In a letter he wrote several years ago, R' Steinman pointed to strife as the cause of all the tragic accidents, illness and misfortunes among us.

Must Children Fight?

As much as strife is a problem for adults, it is equally — if not more so — a problem for our children. Ask any principal or teacher and he will tell you how much of the day is spent dealing with fights between students. Ask any mother and she will tell you how her children's fighting is driving her crazy.

A mother writes:

> *The following scene is repeated many times in my house. The 7-year-old (an easy and fun-loving child) will say something or do something that will get on the nerves of the 9-year-old. He's very easily angered and responds by physically hurting the 7-year-old.*

How should I respond? Do I punish the older one, the younger one or both? Or should I just overlook the whole thing, which is very hard?

Another mother says:

How do I deal with the sibling rivalry between my two boys, aged 8 and 11? I am mainly concerned about the younger one. He uses his temper in a very strong way. When he hits, it's not just hitting — you see that he means it. How can I help him?

What can we do to minimize strife among our children? What tools can we employ to stop the never-ending fighting and arguments among them?

We once had a boy in our school who was very short. This boy was extremely sensitive and would take everything to heart. He became angry easily and fought back viciously. Things got worse and worse until the boy became so insulted that he was no longer willing to continue coming to school.

We realized that because of his shortness, he was wrestling with a very serious self-esteem problem. Because he felt so low about himself, each emotional insult chipped away at whatever remaining self-esteem he did have.

The Alter of Slobodka once said that if we could conceivably take away every bit of self-respect from a person, the person would die. One cannot exist without some form of honor.

It was no wonder then that this boy was so sensitive. He was fighting for his life.

We may also understand, in part, the hurt of the non-religious boy in the opening story of this article (although we can't fathom the terrifying results of those feelings nor do we seek to justify them in any way). When a person has no self-esteem, every insult — real or imagined — is felt as an attack on his very existence. He must then fight back with all he has because he is fighting for his very survival.

In secular Israel, self-esteem is practically nonexistent.

R' Y. Y. Yaakovson was teaching a high school class of non-religious students. Wishing to bolster their self-esteem, he asked the students to participate in the following exercise. Everyone was to take out a piece of paper and write his or her name at the top. They were then to think of one positive trait they possessed. This too was to be written down. The task proved to be beyond them as not one of the students was able to come up with something positive. Finally one boy found something he felt worth mentioning. "My father is rich," he said.

(The story did have a happy ending though, as the exercise continued. Each student was told to pass the paper to the adjacent student. They were then asked to write one positive trait about their classmate. This proved to be easier and more successful. At the end of the day the students went home with long lists of positive traits that others had written about them. A number of students retained these lists for many years afterwards claiming that their lives had been deeply affected by the exercise.)

Self-Esteem Reduces Fighting

A number of years ago, there was a U.S. school district in the South whose scholastic level was one of the lowest in the state. Truancy was rampant, and school vandalism reached the point where repairing broken windows cost the school $30,000 a year. The overall morale in the school was so low that even its athletic teams consistently lost their games.

Then a new superintendent was appointed. This man had seen how improving his own self-image was a springboard to success. He immediately set up a plan for teaching self-esteem in the school district. This freed the students from the emotional limits they had placed upon themselves and their ability.

In the course of just two years, the school district had the highest state attendance record, suspensions dropped by 80 percent, its teams began to win and vandalism dropped to zero!

The first step in preventing strife is to build self-esteem. The better a person (of any age) feels about himself, the less he feels threatened by insults and slights, which begin to pale in significance.

Nowhere are the results of improving self-esteem more dramatic than in children. When a child's self-esteem goes up, his desire for strife goes down.

It Begins With Pride in Who We Are

As Jews, building our children's sense of self-esteem should be easier, for we know our heritage. We are the children of royalty. We are the descendants of Avraham Avinu, the prince of the land. Wouldn't we feel important if someone told us we were descended from the Chafetz Chaim or the Chazon Ish? Well, we come from the family of Avraham, Yitzchak and Yaakov, who were even greater than the Chafetz Chaim and Chazon Ish.

Someone once told me about an ignorant person who came over to him and said, "I don't want to be anything special. All I want is to be a plain *Jew* like Avraham Avinu."

> *I have an acquaintance whose parents moved down south when he was but 3. Although there was very little to be said about Judaism in that part of the United States, the boy's parents remained religious and exhibited a strong pride in being observant. Their attitude carried over to their son.*
>
> *One day, as they were shopping in a store during the Xmas season, a person dressed up in a seasonal costume came over to the 3-year-old. "What would you like for Xmas?" he asked. The boy raised his voice and proudly said, "I don't have Xmas. I have Chanukah."*

It is up to the parents. By developing this attitude among themselves, they can develop it in their children.

Are we seeing enough pride in being a Jew nowadays? We see a lot of Torah and acts of kindness, and a great deal of scrupulous mitzvah observance and spiritual aspirations, but the pride of being a Jew is something of which we may not be seeing as much. Perhaps it is time to renew our pride in our heritage. Perhaps it is time to remind ourselves that we are the chosen people.

Someone once came to R' Hutner and asked him what to do about despair. R' Hutner replied, "Even when a Jew transgresses he is still a Jew." Realize that within you burns a soul so holy that no matter what you do, you can never extinguish its holiness.

One way to instill these feelings in our children is to tell them stories of *tzaddikim*. However, a word of caution is in order. The point is not to use the stories to show the children what they could be; it is to show the children *what they already are*, to show the children how holy a Jew is and to remind them of their connection, as Jews, to the great people about whom the stories are told.

Tell Them About R' Moshe

Take, for example, the story I heard recently about R' Moshe Feinstein.

> *A rabbi who vehemently disagreed with R' Feinstein about one of his halachic rulings, took every opportunity to bring shame and disgrace to R' Moshe. He even had posters printed besmirching R' Moshe's name.*
>
> *Around Rosh Hashanah, one of R' Moshe's closest students was walking up the steps to R' Moshe's apartment when he saw this rabbi leaving. "He probably went to R' Moshe to ask forgiveness," the student thought to himself.*
>
> *Upon entering R' Moshe's apartment, the student went over to the sage and asked, "Rebbi! That rabbi was just here. He probably came to ask forgiveness."*
>
> *When R' Moshe made no reply, the student repeated his question. "He did ask forgiveness, didn't he?"*
>
> *R' Moshe, seeing his student's anxiety, said, "No, he didn't come for forgiveness. He came to ask a favor."*
>
> *What was the favor? The rabbi's contract had expired, and his shul was not interested in renewing it. A prestigious shul was willing to sign a contact with him provided he brought a letter of recommendation from R' Moshe. That was the reason for his visit.*
>
> *The student was furious. "Rebbi, how could you give him such a letter? Not only did he have the nerve not to ask for forgiveness, but he asked for a letter of recommendation?"*
>
> *R' Moshe told his student, "It says, 'There are those who acquire their portion in the World to Come in an instant.' I felt that this moment with that rabbi was my instant."*

Acting this way was hard even for R' Moshe — but he did it.

Tell your child this story. Then say, "Do you see how holy you are to belong to a nation that has such people in its midst?"

George Washington and the Chanukah Lights

There is a well-known folktale about a Jewish youth who came to America in his teens, fleeing the anti-Semitism and persecution in his native Poland.

The young man arrived in America, and eventually was drafted into the army. At that time the colonies were fighting for independence. George Washington was the commander of the revolutionary forces, and the tide was turning against him and his men. Heavy losses along with bitter cold and waning supplies threatened to defeat the struggling soldiers.

Then came the first night of Chanukah. Although afraid to practice his religion so openly, the youth was determined to light his menorah. He waited until the other men were asleep and carefully lit the candle. As he sat there watching the Chanukah lights, his thoughts turned to his family and the tiny menorah his parents had given him before leaving. "Take this with you, it will be a source of blessing," they said. He began to cry.

Suddenly, he felt a hand on his shoulder. "Why are you crying, soldier. Are you cold?"

It was his commander — George Washington himself!

"No, Sir," he respectfully replied. "I have come here to escape the persecution and oppression of my homeland." He explained that he had kindled the Chanukah lights as Jews had done for centuries, a symbol of their faith in G-d and their trust in Him to fight their battles.

"You are also fighting for the cause of truth and justice," the young soldier said to his commander. "You are fighting for freedom from oppression, and I am certain G-d will help you win."

"You are a descendant of a nation of prophets. If you say I will win, it must be true," the general said.

The rest is history. George Washington won the Revolutionary War and went on to become the first president of the United States. The Jewish soldier survived the war and settled in New York.

One year later on the first night of Chanukah, the young man heard a knock on his door. He opened it to find non other than General Washington himself standing there.

The general handed him a small medallion showing a menorah with one burning candle. Inscribed were the words, "As a sign of thanks for your candle."

"Like all those who were at Valley Forge, you will be receiving a hero's medal, but I wanted to give this to you as a special sign of gratitude for your encouragement on that dark night."

The peoples of the world look up to us, for they know we are the descendants of the prophets, Avraham, Yitzchak and Yaakov. Should we not look up to ourselves?

34

Dealing With Fighting (Part 2)

Who Am I?

I am your closest companion. I am your greatest helper or heaviest burden. I will help you to go forward or drag you down to failure. I am totally at your command. Half of the things you do, you might just as well turn over to me, for I will be able to do them quickly and correctly.

You need only be firm with me, for I am easily managed. Show me how you want something done, and after a few lessons I will do it automatically. I am the servant of all great individuals, and, alas, of all failures as well. Those who are great, I have made great. Those who are failures, I have made failures.

I am not a machine, though I work with all the precision of a machine plus the intelligence of a human. You may run me for gain or run me for loss — it makes no difference to me. Take me, train me, be firm with me, and I will place the world at your feet. Go easy with me, and I will destroy you.

Who am I?

(No, the answer to the question is not "your child," despite that last paragraph!)

Before we give the answer, let us consider a question asked by several parents: Why should we make such an issue of our children fighting. Will the fights not disappear along with all the other immature behavior our children eventually outgrow? Why not just let time take its course?

Now we can give the answer to our first question. Who am I? I am Habit! And habit is the reason we cannot ignore our children fighting.

They Stick With Us

Habits are very powerful, and the negative ones will stay with us unless we replace them with positive ones. The verse, "*Gam ki yazkin lo yasur mimenu* — Even when he grows old he will not stray from it," refers to habit — for better or for worse.

> In Cambridge, Mass., Mr. J. was sentenced to a six to ten year prison term. The reason? At a hockey game he was involved in an argument with Mr. C. He felt that the team on which Mr. C.'s three sons were playing was using overly aggressive tactics against the team on which his son was playing. The two men ended up on the floor with Mr. J. beating Mr. C. (while Mr. C.'s children were standing and watching) until he severed an artery in Mr. C.'s neck, which led to his death.
>
> It is interesting to note (besides the light prison sentence) that the reason Mr. J. was upset in the first place was because he objected to overly aggressive behavior. Unfortunately, the only way Mr. J. knew to deal with overly aggressive behavior was by being overly aggressive. The fact that he is a human being and not an animal, and an adult to boot — which should have afforded him many more civilized ways of dealing with whatever problem he felt he had — made no difference. Obviously, Mr. J. had a bad habit deeply ingrained in him because no one had ever taught him otherwise.

Is Hitting Back Okay?

> About twenty-one years ago, shortly after moving to Israel, I spent some time visiting the various schools, try-

ing to decide on a suitable one for my eldest son. During my search, I had the opportunity to sit in on a class in which I saw the teacher do something very strange. He called two children up to his desk and told one of them to take off his glasses. He then turned to the other student and told him to hit the first boy in the face.

Needless to say, I was puzzled by this strange command (which the student did not obey), and after class I asked the teacher what was behind his request. He readily explained. "The first boy was bullying the second boy throughout the entire class. The second boy has a meek personality and so did not respond or strike back. I wanted to teach him to stick up for himself. I therefore called them both to my desk and told them what you heard."

I have heard R' Wolbe answer in a similar vein, on occasion, when asked what to tell a child when other children are hitting him. He answered that you can tell them to hit back, and he cited the *Sefer HaChinuch* regarding the prohibition of *ona'as devarim (hurting one's feelings)*, which says that a person is permitted to react to another's insults, for he is not required to be like a stone.

However, when I recently discussed the incident with one of the leading sages in America, he told me that he has no doubt in his mind that the teacher described above is unfit to be a *mechanech*.

I then went back to R' Wolbe and asked about the advice he had given. He told me that it is only a last resort where there is no other choice. If there is a different way to react that can successfully deal with the problem, then that way is certainly the recommended approach.

I then understood the words of the sage. Of course there are times when a child has to resort to physical means to protect himself — but this is only when he has no other choice.

A teacher is someone who should be showing the child the *best* way to act. He should be showing him the preferred choice, the proper way to react. If the teacher in the above incident saw physical retaliation as *the* way to react, then he is indeed unfit to be a teacher.

Much of our children's fighting and arguing is a matter of habit. Fighting is their initial reaction to solving a problem. It is an instinctive reaction that comes from feeling there is no other option. It is therefore our duty to teach them better ways to react, thus giving them positive habits that will stay with them into adulthood. This will enable them to find solutions without becoming involved in disputes.

If we teach them, they will learn; if we do not teach them, they will be stuck with only their base instincts to go by — and, "even when he grows old he will not stray from it." I know of a shul where two congregants got into a fistfight on Yom Kippur, during Ne'ilah. Indeed, "even when he grows old he will not stray from it."

(When we talk about fighting, this includes not only physical fights. How many times have we heard of adults embroiled in family disputes for years, not getting along with each other sometimes to the point of not even talking with one another. It is therefore incumbent on us to help our children develop **solution-oriented** habits that will avoid strife altogether.)

How Should We Handle Fighting?

The first question to be addressed is: What should we do when the actual fighting takes place? As the mother quoted in the previous chapter asked, *"How should I respond? Do I punish the older one, the younger one or both? Or should I just overlook the whole thing, which is very hard?"*

Overlooking "the whole thing," as she puts it, is a recommended approach when possible. Yet it is not always practical. We are all too familiar with the scenario where one child picks up a metal toy truck with which to hit the other one, while the other child has his baseball bat in hand, ready for action. In many cases, ignoring the whole thing is asking for a quick trip to the emergency room.

The most successful approach seems to be not to allow any fighting whatsoever (at least in the house, between siblings, which is somewhat within our control). Anyone who fights will be punished with a consequence (such as staying in his or her room for a while, losing half an hour of playing time or forfeiting other privileges).

When two or more children are caught fighting, each one will receive a punishment — regardless of who started the fight. The punishment need not be harsh, but it must be strong enough to serve as a deterrent.

This approach has its disadvantages. When one child starts a fight, what should the other one do? Shouldn't he defend himself? Punishing both seems unfair.

In reality, it is not.

We are offering our child other options to fighting. We want to teach him other more successful ways of reacting. Punishing all those who choose fighting in place of the other available options will help teach this lesson.

On the other hand, trying to find out who started the fight is problematic. If you decide to apply for the job of referee, I highly recommend that you find someone else to take your job as mother or father, because being a referee is a full-time job. Besides, 99 percent of the time you will not be able to determine exactly what happened anyway.

Despite the drawbacks, punishing *both* children may be the only way to break a child's habit of constantly resorting to fighting to resolve problems. To break this habit, we must go to the other extreme of not allowing fighting altogether.

An elderly scholar once demonstrated how to break a habit. He took a piece of paper and bent it in one direction. He then asked me what needed to be done to straighten it. The only solution was to bend the paper in the opposite direction. Similarly, to break the habit, we must first stop our children from fighting altogether. Only then can we move on to the next step of teaching them more effective problem-solving techniques.

Teaching Alternative Solutions

As a rule, you should have a discussion with the children some time after they have stopped fighting, when they have calmed down. This can even be a day or two later. At that time, you can rehash the events with your children and give them basic guidelines for different solutions. You can then ask the children themselves to come up with other options that would have been more effective than fighting.

Some examples of other options to fighting are: answering an insult with humor (thereby showing that the remark does not bother you); communicating by telling the other person exactly what you want and repeating this several times.

Note that it is not enough to leave the child with a general statement such as, "The next time he makes fun of you just answer with humor," or, "The next time he takes your ball just tell him exactly what you want." Be specific in your instruction. Give the children examples of sentences they can use and rehearse those sentences with them. For example, when a child's possession is taken away teach him to say, "I would like you to give that back to me please," in a gentle but firm way. If this is not effective the first time, teach the child to have patience and repeat the sentence several times. He will be surprised at the degree of success that his efforts will achieve.

But by far, the most important guideline to be used in solution finding is called the *win-win principle*. Train your children to find solutions that end with a gain for both parties involved. In this way, the children will begin to realize that it is not a competition. Both of them can win. Slowly but surely, this method can help the children work together. In time, they will learn that there is nothing to lose by working together, but everything to gain.

> *As the legal counsel for a large business firm, an expert lawyer was involved in negotiations to purchase a company owned by the widow of the founder. There were teams of lawyers on both sides but the negotiations reached an impasse. The widow who was the sole shareholder wanted $1 million more than the purchaser was willing to pay.*
>
> *A personal meeting was set up between the lawyer and the widow. He approached the situation looking for a third alternative, one that would work for both parties. In order to do this he first listened to the widow's concerns. Why was the final million dollars so important to her that she was not willing to compromise?*
>
> *She explained that she wanted to make sure her children and grandchildren were provided for. She wanted to set up trust funds so that her children and grandchildren would be financially secure, even after her passing. Due to previous commitments and responsibilities, without the extra million she would not be able to achieve this goal.*
>
> *After fully understanding the widow's concerns, the lawyer came up with this suggestion. His company will buy an insurance policy on the woman's life for one million dollars. They will pay the premiums on the policy until her death. In this way after she passes away her children and grandchildren will have the financial security that she wished for them.*

> *The deal went through, as the solution was one which worked for both parties. (The cost of the policy was about $50,000, considerably less expensive than one million.)*

This principle, widely applied in the business world, has met with much success. It can certainly bring us success in an area more important than finances — the daily interactions of our children and ourselves between man and man.

The key is to *set aside the time* to discuss and help our children implement these methods (not only while the fights are taking place). The added influence of our personal example, working together with them to find solutions, will certainly help make our efforts of getting them to work together with each other more effective.

Another way to get children to work *with* as opposed to *against* each other is *positive discipline*, which we have spoken about often in this column. Incentive programs have the power to motivate children in ways that other methods do not.

A father asked how to deal with the constant bickering between his two oldest children, a boy and a girl, especially at the Shabbos table. I told him to use the jelly bean method: each time they work together and help each other, a jelly bean is put into a cup. Eventually, when the cup is full, they receive a major prize.

At our school we dealt with a boy, let's call him Shimon, who was picking on another boy, let's call him Reuven. The problem was compounded due to the fact that Shimon was a leader and generated a great deal of influence in the class. Anyone who was Shimon's enemy, was inevitably the enemy of the entire class. We called in Shimon and told him that we are hiring him to be Reuven's bodyguard. Beginning immediately he will receive a salary for his work. Needless to say the problem was taken care of.

There is an important point to bring out. Our suggestions of other problem-solving methods will be most effective if we make them *after* we have listened to our child and understood his side. This does not mean that we are taking sides. It does mean, though, that we understand his side. It is important for a child to feel that his parent or teacher has heard him out. A child who feels understood will cooperate more readily with any suggestions offered.

Take the case of the 7- and 9-year-old mentioned in the previous chapter:

The following scene is repeated many times in my house. The 7-year-old (an easy and fun-loving child) will say something or do something that will get on the nerves of the 9-year-old. He's very easily angered and responds by physically hurting the 7-year-old.

Even though the mother may feel the 9-year-old should not react in such a strong way to such a small thing, it is important to realize that the 9-year-old does not see it that way. To him, what the 7-year-old did might be very hurtful. Because he feels so hurt, it is hard for him to realize he is overreacting.

The right thing would be to take the 9-year-old aside and hear him out. Just listen to him and understand him — and *show him* that you understand him. Afterward, and only afterward, tell him that although you understand how he feels, you want him to use a different method of reacting instead of using physical force. Which method? Work one out together with him. Use the methods mentioned above to find a solution: one that does not involve physical force but at the same time keeps him from being hurt.

Go to the Source

Sometimes attacking the problem at its source will eliminate the entire problem.

For example, if a child is repeatedly falling and hurting himself, we must tend to his bruises and bandage them. But if that is all we do, we are only addressing part of the problem. At the same time we are bandaging his bruises, we must ask ourselves why he is falling. We may find out his falls are caused by poor eyesight. He may need special exercises or glasses. By treating only the results of the falls, we fail to look for ways to prevent them from happening in the first place.

A father complained about his 7-year-old who seemed to instigate most of the fights with his siblings and was getting under everyone's skin.

I made two suggestions: (1) that the father spend some special, private time with his son; and (2) that he catch his son three times during each day doing something right and compliment him for it.

The father told me that the night after hearing this advice, a golden opportunity arose, and he made good use of it. He planned to drop his wife off at the entrance to the subway and leave the car parked nearby so that when she returned, she would have it. He would walk back home.

The father decided to take his son along with him on the ride and the walk home. It was no big deal for the father, but his son was ecstatic. The fact that it had begun to snow and that father and son were walking through the snow together at night only added to the boy's excitement.

The father told me that he has already seen improvement with regard to his son picking fights with others. Ending on an emotional note, he added, "I think this is one of those special times my son will remember for the rest of his life."

35

Dealing With
Fighting (Part 3)

Have You Ever Been at the Site of a
Terrorist Attack?

Ilive in Neve Yaakov, one of the newer sections of
Jerusalem. Although it is a 15-minute drive from the
center of town, we celebrate Purim on the 15th of
Adar along with the rest of Jerusalem. (This ruling
was made a number of years ago by R' Elyashiv, based
on the fact that there is an unbroken connection to the
Old City.)

On the night of 14 Adar (Purim in most of the world), as
we were bringing the groceries from the car to our house,
we heard loud noises. At first, I thought it was pranksters
playing with dynamite — despite the many public
announcements by rabbinical authorities calling on the
public to refrain from using any explosives, such as fire-
crackers or cap guns, on Purim. (Unfortunately, many
children and even adults have been seriously injured over
the years by these and similar dangerous items.)

When I heard the bangs coming in rapid-fire succession,
I realized it was a machine gun. There had been a shooting!

I knew it must be nearby, but I had no idea where.
Moments later, I heard ambulance sirens and realized — as
would any resident of the holy city — that a terrorist
attack must have taken place.

Sure enough, within minutes we heard a neighbor shout, "An Arab opened fire in Neve Yaakov."

A friend quickly made his way to the scene of the attack, which is only a short drive from our street. He later described to us what he witnessed, in vivid detail.

When he got there, police were still in the process of searching for a second terrorist. Clothes and shoes (along with empty bullet shells) lay scattered in the street. Teams of soldiers were running in and out of the adjacent buildings. Dogs had been brought to the scene to help with the search.

My friend spoke with some of the people who live in the apartment buildings directly fronting the scene of the shooting. One woman told him that she was looking out her window when she saw the Arab open fire. Frightened and confused, she ran to the bathroom and locked herself in, hoping she would be safe. Another woman told him she was actually standing outside when the terrorist attacked. She said a woman police officer was there at the time, and the Arab grabbed her gun. She begged him not to shoot, but he ignored her pleas. She succumbed to her wounds a short while later.

To the right there were large numbers of flashing lights from the many ambulances and police cars waiting nearby. Across the street, a noisy crowd gathered. Ehud Olmert, mayor of Jerusalem, was there and many residents took the opportunity to voice their protests and their fears. By now, the media had arrived and photojournalists were busy taking pictures and asking questions.

The mayor crossed the street to where others were standing, including some children.

"Children, what do you think we should do?" asked Olmert.

"We've gotta kick them [the Arabs] out of here," said one teenager.

"Why would the mayor ask children for advice?" wondered my friend. "He probably just wanted to make them feel good. Maybe it was easier for him to deal with the children than with the bitter adults surrounding him on all sides."

Mayor Olmert's "interest" in the children's answer was evident from the speed with which he departed the area.

My friend remained preoccupied with the question. What should we do? Is there anything to do?

This attack was considered a minor attack because only one person was hurt and only about nine were injured.

The attack that took place two weeks later on Saturday night was considered by the media a serious one. In a suicide bombing in the Beis Yisrael neighborhood in Jerusalem, nine people were killed and over fifty injured. Those killed had been attending a family bar mitzvah at the guest house of Yeshivas Machane Yisrael, accommodations generously provided for those wishing to experience Shabbos in religious surroundings. Among those killed were an infant and several small children.

As if this was not enough to satisfy the bloodthirsty terrorists, the next morning another shooting took place north of Ofra. Ten people were killed and others injured.

Upon hearing about the attack in Beis Yisrael the streets of Ramallah were crowded with Arabs dancing and celebrating, ecstatic that innocent Jewish blood had been spilled.

Is There Anything to Do?

This is a question everyone is asking. How heartbreaking that more than half a century of Zionism has left secular Israelis with nothing to grab onto except soccer.

Friday, March 1, the IDF launched a major assault on the Balata refugee camp near Nablus. The purpose was to destroy the terrorist infrastructure in the camps, considered hotbeds of terrorist activities. Although the scope of this move was unprecedented since the Oslo talks, secular Israeli newspapers did not give it top coverage. Instead, their headlines trumpeted the Israeli soccer team's victory over Italy's team.

Not that the average Israeli man in the street ranks the sports win as more newsworthy than a major military operation. It is only that he has reached the pit of despair and is looking for something to distract him. As one sports fan said, "At least today we don't have to hear about bombs and unemployment. Let me tell you, this game fortified me for an entire year."

This phenomenon grew to new proportion on that *motza'ei* Shabbos. At the moment the terrorist blew himself up in Beis Yisrael, an Israeli soccer game was being broadcast on TV. Unwilling to interrupt the live coverage, the station managers decided to compromise.

They split the screen.

Two-thirds of the screen was given to the terrorist attack, while the remaining third continued to carry the soccer game. Live coverage of those killed and maimed by the explosion competed with kicks of the ball. Scenes of the injured being carried away amid fire and smoke, and reports of babies dying, ran alongside players racing against time to score a goal.

The station's poor taste drew a barrage of criticism even from secular Israeli newspapers. Yet it is obvious: terrorist attacks are occurring too often. People want to forget about it. It disturbs daily routine and prevents people from enjoying their regular recreational activities. So, the philosophy goes, if there is nothing you can do about it, you might as well ignore it.

Yet we who are closer to Torah must truly ask ourselves: *Is* there anything to do?

A Powerful Tool for These Turbulent Times

The words of R' Yissocher Frand, spoken at a Tishah B'Av event (sponsored by the Chofetz Chaim Heritage Foundation), still echo in my mind: "In order to have *shalom*, one must make *shalom*." **If we want peace, we must first make sure that we have peace among ourselves.**

These words, originally expressed a few hundred years ago by R' Yehudah HaChassid in his *Sefer Chassidim*, provide us with a powerful tool for these turbulent times.

If it is peace we want, we must put forth our efforts to stop discord and strife. And the first place to begin is at home, among our close family and among our children.

In the previous chapters, we discussed fighting among our children. We mentioned various methods to help prevent fights and suggested ways to come up with more effective solutions.

Yet underlying all the methods mentioned must be the basic realization that *shalom* is more important than fighting and even more important than winning. Only then can we motivate our children — and ourselves — to *want* to find alternative solutions such as those mentioned in previous articles.

Impress Upon Them
the Significance of Their Actions

We can achieve this by impressing upon our children the significance our actions have for the entire Jewish nation in its present situation. Tell them that if *they* refrain from discord and fighting, they can help protect the Jews in Israel (and America, too). You can say something like, "Through your making *shalom*, Hashem will make *shalom* and lives may be saved. Maybe even one less Jew will be killed. Your actions are so precious to Hashem that your efforts to refrain from fighting may be able to prevent a terrorist attack from taking place altogether."

Note that it is not enough to expect the child to make *shalom* on his own. We can, though, expect the child to give his full cooperation when we help him find other solutions to conflict, such as those mentioned in the previous chapter. (A brief summary appears at the end of this chapter.)

The ideal time for discussion of these thoughts is in a neutral setting when the atmosphere is calm. R' Y.Y. Yaakovson says that the best time to transmit a value or to ingrain an important lesson is soon after the child performed that mitzvah successfully. Such times are golden teaching opportunities because the child is happy about what he did and is interested in hearing the significance of his positive action. Discussing these concepts after a child has been fighting will hardly be as effective, for then he will be defensive and find it hard to absorb the intended lesson.

Remember that words that come from the heart will penetrate the heart. If what you say to your child stems from a true concern for the current plight of our people, then your words will hit home and have a profound effect upon your children.

Every year before the High Holy Days we tell our students that it is their *tefillos* that can help us, the adults. We have transgressions, and they (as minors) do not. Their *tefillos* are accepted immediately. We ask them to *daven* specifically for their parents and family, for their relatives and neighbors, and for the entire Jewish people.

We have received many notes from parents telling us how their children prayed intently, with great devotion, some even standing for hours and others actually crying during the prayers (an accomplishment to which many adults are not able to lay claim).

Children are very cooperative when they become aware that their *tefillos* and other deeds as well are significant and can be of major help to others.

I recently spoke in a number of schools in the greater Toronto area. In one school (whose students numbered in the hundreds), I asked the children to take upon themselves not to hurt anyone else's feelings for the next few hours. At first, not all the students were willing to accept my proposition, because the request was not such an easy one to fulfill. Then I asked if any of them knew of a sick person who was in need of a complete recovery. A name was mentioned. I suggested that we all take it upon ourselves not to hurt anyone's feelings for the next several hours as a merit for that person to have a complete recovery. At that point, the entire student body volunteered to participate and other students mentioned names of ill people they wanted the resolution to benefit as well.

Easy + Consistent = Habit

Be very specific when telling children to make peace. A vague reference that you want them to make *shalom* is too abstract — and it is also too difficult to keep. Notice that the resolution we made in the school was only for a few hours. It was (1) a specific task (2) for a set period of time and (3) within the children's ability to keep.

> When R' Shalom Shwadron was a student in the Chevron Yeshivah, he asked his teacher, R' Leib Chasman, what resolution he should make for Yom Kippur. The rebbi told him to go home and come up with something he would be able to keep and stick to without a doubt. R' Shalom gave the matter some thought and returned to R' Chasman with what he thought was a good resolution, one he would certainly be able to keep. The rabbi told him,

"Okay, now take that resolution and cut it in half. That is what you should take upon yourself."

Our great rabbis know the secret. It is not the big resolutions that will make the difference; it is the *small* actions done *consistently* that truly bring about major change. The secret formula goes like this: Easy + Consistent = Habit. It is the development of proper habits that eventually brings to change for the better.

Make your *shalom* campaign with your children easy and specific. Be sure that whatever program you suggest is for a period the children will definitely be able to keep. Then, at the end of that time period, you can renew the campaign or else take a break and begin anew at a later time.

For example, you can tell your children that you want them to take it upon themselves not to hit anyone on the following day. If there is a disagreement, for the sake of *shalom* they will agree to wait until one of the parents can help arbitrate and come to an agreement. If this works, you can extend the campaign for another few days.

Catch Them Doing It Right

Make sure to catch the children when they are successful in sticking to the resolution and praise them highly for it. (As mentioned above this is also an opportune time to talk to them about the value of *shalom* and what a merit they have in helping protect the Jewish people. The lessons you teach at this time will certainly be absorbed with tremendous desire!)

About-Face

You may wonder what value there is in keeping *shalom* for only one day. First, you have enabled your child to change direction. This is an achievement of major significance. You enabled him to make an about-face, even if only for a short time. You can now continue to help him proceed in this new direction. The point is to help the child develop a *habit* of not fighting. Creating momentum in this direction, even if only for a short while, is the beginning. Continuing the campaign will eventually bring the child (with the help of Hashem) to replace his habit of fighting with the habit of *shalom* instead.

Follow up on the one-day period with another day the following week. After three successful weeks, move up to two days. This will build a healthy momentum that will last.

One may decide to designate a specific hour or two each day during which every family member will be especially careful not to hurt the feelings of others.

[Imagine the merit that could be generated for our people if the persons reading these words (parents and their families, teachers and their classes, principals and their schools) accept upon themselves (*bli neder*) one specific hour during which they are careful not to hurt the feelings of another.]

The possibilities are endless and they vary according to your specific situation, and the age of the children involved. The main thing to keep in mind is to work in conjunction with the principles mentioned above. Make sure the ideas you wish to implement are easy to carry out and that they can be kept up consistently.

The One Ingredient Vital for Success

However, there is one vital ingredient upon which the success of the above formula depends. If it is there, the formula can work; if it is not, any effort to get a child to pursue peace will prove futile. The ingredient is you, the parent! A parent's words to his children regarding making peace for the sake of protecting the Jewish people will hold weight only if the parent himself puts this message into practice in his or her own relationships with others, especially one's spouse.

If parents preach *shalom* but do not practice it, the message will have no impact. As the Chazon Ish says in *Emunah U'Bitachon* (4:16): "Even if the lesson is good and proper, it will not enter the heart of the student when the teacher is not sincere. The child will learn more from what the teacher *does* than from what the teacher *says*."

The same applies to a parent who wishes to teach his child the value of *shalom*. If parents preach *shalom* but do not have it between themselves, their children will learn more from their fighting than from their preaching.

I am reminded of the father who was called to come down to the school because of his son's use of improper language. Upon entering the principal's office, the father began screaming at his son. "You #&*#! How many times have I told you to watch your language!"

If it is *shalom* we want for our children and for the Jewish people, the first place to begin is at home, with the people closest to us, especially our spouse.

Allow me to offer a word of hope. Even if your *shalom* record has not been that good in the past, you can start now. You can even say something to the children to the effect that because *shalom* is so vital right now, you are also going to put forth a strong effort to make peace and avoid fighting. The fact that you are working on this at the same time as your children will strengthen them in their quest for peace.

> We have mentioned the story of a man who came to the Steipler to discuss problems he was having with his child. The Steipler told him to learn an ethical work with his child daily, using an easy text like "Orchos Tzaddikim." After some time, the father returned to the Steipler and expressed his frustration that his son was not responsive to his attempts at learning with him. "I told my son that the rav said he has to learn about character improvement," the father lamented.
>
> "That's not the way to do it," explained the Steipler. "The way to approach your son is to tell him that you would like to learn about character improvement — for yourself — and that you need a study partner. Then ask him if he would be willing to learn it with you."

Do not get discouraged. Begin a *shalom* campaign now, together with your children. Together become a source of merit to protect us, so that the Master of the world will see our plight and bring us redemption from our enemies, speedily and in our days, Amen.

Does *Shalom* Mean Always Giving In?

"By teaching my child to seek shalom, aren't I teaching him to be a dishrag? Won't this teach him that people can just walk all over him because he won't react in return? Is this healthy for a child?"

This is not what is meant by *shalom*. Seeking peace means that maintaining peace is our top priority. This need not mean that a person or child should not express himself or try to get what he wants. It does mean that he expresses himself in a communicative way as opposed to a hostile or physically aggressive way. *Shalom* does not mean that a person has to forgo obtaining his or her needs. It does mean that the way to go about obtaining one's needs should be consistent with maintaining *shalom.*

Again, it is important to stress that *shalom* does not preclude speaking up for oneself. It does not rule out working through your differences with the other party. It does mean that things should be worked out in such a way that *shalom* will be maintained. The option of forgoing one's desired goal always exists, but this is not the message of making *shalom.* Pursuing peace is not about being a "dishrag" and "letting people walk all over you." Actually, seeking peace means respecting yourself enough to act in a dignified manner and working things out with other people instead of striking back in a hostile manner.

How to Keep Your Children From Fighting

A summary, based on the previous chapters on this topic:

(1) The first step in preventing fighting is to build self-esteem. The better a person (of any age) feels about himself, the less he feels threatened by insults and slights, which begin to pale in significance.

(2) Begin by teaching your child to take pride in his Judaism.

(3) With regard to physical fighting, the most successful approach is not to allow any fighting whatsoever (at least in the house, between siblings, which is somewhat within our control). Children know that anyone who fights is punished with a consequence (such as staying in his or her room for a while, losing half an hour of playing time or forfeiting other privileges).

When two or more children are caught fighting, each one will receive a punishment — regardless of who started the fight. The punishment need not be harsh, but it must be strong enough to serve as a deterrent.

Despite the drawbacks, punishing *both* children may be the only way to break a child's habit of constantly resorting to fighting to resolve problems. To break this habit, we must go to the other extreme of not allowing fighting altogether.

(4) As a rule, you should have a discussion with the children some time after they have stopped fighting, when they have calmed down. This can even be a day or two later. At that time, you can rehash the events with your children and give them basic guidelines for alternative solutions. You can then ask the children themselves to come up with different solutions, ones that would have been more effective than fighting.

Some examples of other options to fighting are: answering an insult with humor (and in this way showing that the remark does not bother you); communicating by telling the other person exactly what you want and repeating this several times.

(5) By far, the most important guideline to be used in solution finding is called the *win-win principle*. Train your children to find solutions that end with a gain for both parties involved. In this way, the children will begin to realize that it is not a competition. Both of them can win. Slowly but surely, this method can help the children work together. In time, they will learn that there is nothing to lose by working together, but everything to gain.

(6) Another way to get children to work *with* as opposed to *against* each other is positive discipline (i.e. offering an incentive for working together). Once again, be careful to ask for a specific action or actions that you want from the child such as helping set the table for Shabbos together or not fighting at the Shabbos table, and do not demand too much to soon. Incentive programs have the power to motivate children in ways that other methods do not.

(7) There is an important point to bring out. Our suggestions of other problem-solving methods will be most effective if we make them *after* we have listened to our child and understood his side. This does not mean that we are *taking* sides. It does mean, though, that we understand his side. It is important for a child to feel that his parent or teacher has heard him out. A child who feels understood will cooperate more readily with any suggestions offered.

(8) Sometimes attacking the problem at its source will eliminate the entire problem.

36

Working With Incentives

The Power of Motivation

A few months ago, a boy was chosen winner of a *Mishnayos* contest in Haifa. Although he attended a non-religious school, he put in many hours of study to memorize full volumes of *Mishnayos*. Rather a remarkable feat for someone from a non-religious family, wouldn't you say?

Even more remarkable in this case were the number of obstacles the boy had to overcome to reach this plateau of accomplishment. The biggest among them being that his name was Jamal, and he was not even Jewish. (He was an Arab.)

A man looking to break the world record recently held seventeen scorpions in his mouth for a period of about 1 minute. (Upon being interviewed he said that this was not dangerous and the only thing he really was concerned about was that no scorpion try to crawl down his throat.)

A man wishing to become a "saint" according to the guidelines of his particular religion tied himself to a tree and did not move from there for seven years! (Even for purposes of personal hygiene.) Throughout that entire period, his diet consisted of nothing but grass.

This same man, feeling that he was not yet "holy" enough, decided to roll on the ground for a distance of over 2,000 miles to reach a certain temple. Dressed only in shorts and bare from the waist up, he made his journey by rolling on the ground daily from sunrise to sunset. After several gruelling months, he finally reached his destination.

Motivation is a powerful force. Not only does it serve the insane and mentally ill (like the people mentioned above), but it can serve us as well — especially when it comes to doing mitzvos.

Last week, I went to visit a student of mine who was born without the ability to walk. He has always been confined to a wheelchair since his legs do not function at all. His brain was also slightly injured at birth. (When I brought this boy to R' Shmuel Auerbach for a blessing, R' Shmuel stood up for him.)

Recently, this boy underwent an operation. His doctors hoped that a new method would enable him to walk. The doctors performed surgery to broaden the bones of his feet so they could support his body.

The boy was told that the post-operative pain would be considerable. Still, this young hero of the spirit was willing to go through the operation.

The operation was a failure. The pain was excruciating.

When the doctors told the boy they thought they could succeed if they operated one more time, the boy said he needed some time to think it over. His decision was to go through with it.

My visit to him just a few weeks ago came a short while after his second operation. I asked him what it was that pushed him to go through such pain a second time. He told me he felt the operation would give him his only chance to walk and that the *Ribbono Shel Olam* wanted him to be able to walk. This is what gave him the strength and motivation to agree to the second operation.

A person can accomplish great things when he is motivated. With motivation, we can accomplish that which otherwise might have been considered unattainable.

If we can motivate our children, they too can achieve success.

Positive Discipline

Positive discipline is training a child to behave properly by offering him a positive consequence if he does so (as opposed to a negative consequence if he does not).

First, clearly state the specific behavior expected of the child. Then, choose a specific consequence. The consequence can be

a reward, a certain privilege, or even a consequence that is a natural outgrowth of the child's actions (i.e. if the child gets ready
for bed quickly, there will be enough time for Mommy to sit and
read a story).

After clarifying the consequence and the specific behavior necessary to earn it, it is crucial for a parent to stand firm and not give the
child the positive consequence unless the child actually did what
was expected of him. It is at this point that the positive approach
becomes discipline. If the child behaves, he will receive the consequence. If he does not behave, he will not. It is that simple

The main value of positive discipline is that it harnesses a
child's willpower and motivates him to *want* to do what we want
him to do. It is therefore an invaluable tool for the *chinuch* of our
children, especially nowadays.

Yet many questions remain. *Is positive discipline the best
approach in all situations? Can rewarding a child for specific
behavior be considered chinuch?* And, as many parents ask, *"Will
we always have to work with incentives? Aren't we teaching the
child to always expect a prize for what he does?"* Let us take a
look at these areas of parental concern.

Is positive discipline the best approach in all situations?

Not necessarily. In extreme situations — and they certainly exist
— stronger measures may be necessary. Also, when a child is being
disrespectful and taking advantage, he need not be given incentives
to stop. Saying "If you behave and act respectfully for a while we will
give you a present" is the wrong approach. It is not the right time to
apply positive discipline; it is the right time for a punishment.

However, even as a punishment, positive discipline, with a
slight variation, has its place. When a child deserves a punishment and is punished by *taking away a privilege*, this will in effect
force the child to cooperate and behave properly because he
wants to get back his privilege.

Let's look at an extreme example.

> *A girl of 14 liked spending time in her room to the extent
> that her parents rarely saw her because of all the time she
> spent there. She would come out only reluctantly for fam-
> ily meals, which she would sit through resentfully.
> Immediately afterward, she would retire to her room and
> close the door.*

If her parents wished to speak with her, they would have to knock on the door and wait for her to respond. They would sometimes have to knock several times before being answered.

Even after all of the above, the daughter would not open the door (that was the parents' job). She would just unlock the door and "allow" the parents to come into her room. The parents would find her sitting on the bed reading a book or something like that. If the parents asked that she change her attitude, the situation only became worse.

Interestingly enough, this girl was the delight of her teachers in school. It was only at home that she would be rude and obnoxious.

One day, as they were eating a meal together, the father made a joke and his wife laughed. Their 14-year-old daughter obviously did not like the joke and made a nasty comment calling both her parents by a derogatory name.

The parents were totally shocked and finished the meal in silence. That night, the parents talked. The next day, the girl came home from school to discover that her room — her very own private room — had no door!

The girl came running down the stairs to the living room and began to rant and rave about wanting her door back.

"We gave your door away," her father told her.

He then went on to explain that she would be without a door for a whole month. At the end of the month, a family conference would be held to review her behavior. If her behavior was sufficiently proper, they would allow her to buy a new door — from her own money. But if she acted disrespectfully even once, they would have to begin counting the month all over again.

"By the way," her father added. "The month begins in exactly one hour."

Needless to say, the daughter stepped back in line and quickly turned over a new leaf.

This is certainly an extreme case, and this method should not be used without proper guidance because sometimes the damage done offsets any gain. Yet the principle applied here may be useful: When a child is a *meizid*, that is, when he is deliberately act-

ing disrespectful and deserves a punishment, taking away a privilege can be very effective. (This should be discussed with the
child beforehand. If he knows what he will be getting himself into
if he misbehaves, it is even more effective.)

Can Rewarding a Child for Specific Behavior be Considered *Chinuch?*

A great rabbi once told me an important principle of *chinuch.*
I was having difficulty with one of the students in the *cheder,* and
I figured out a way to reach him with positivity. (I knew that negativity would not work with this particular boy.) Yet, I felt that this
boy should be taught a lesson, for the sake of his future development. My question was, should we deal with him positively at a
time when he needed to be disciplined.

The rabbi told me that the purpose of discipline is to get the
evil inclination in line. If you can get the evil inclination in line
with positivity, than you have achieved your goal: to get the evil
inclination in line.

Besides, getting the child to tap into his own desire to accomplish — in other words, motivating him — is the most effective
chinuch there is.

I recently asked R' Wolbe about positive discipline and its benefits. He told me that those who understand how to educate nowadays realize that this is *the* way to do so. Those who disagree do
not understand *chinuch* in our time.

The Friday Night Group

*Many parents ask, "Will we always have to work with
incentives?"*

Incentives are a crutch. They are the means, not the goal. They
are meant to help the child overcome any obstacles on his way to
developing proper habits.

However, once the child begins to do well, many other variables
take over, such as the child feeling good about himself for being
successful and behaving well. (In all honesty, the one who loses
out from acting belligerent is the child himself, and deep down,
every child knows it.)

There is yet another point to be stressed. When a child is offered an incentive, it creates a positive association in his mind. He then begins to enjoy the behavior for its own sake, not only because it earns him a prize.

> *In our neighborhood we have a group for children on Friday night. Toward the end of Maariv, they stand in the women's section and answer "Amen" and "Amen, Yehei Shemei Rabba." After Maariv, the children are rewarded for their efforts with a small treat.*
>
> *The boys in the group are awarded points, and, at the end, those who receive the most points get to receive an extra treat (aside from the regular treat given to everyone). Last week's special treat was a bottle of cola. When the points were totaled, three boys wound up having the exact same number. This was a serious problem since there were only two bottles of cola.*
>
> *The leader of the group decided to give a quick quiz on the weekly portion. The two boys who gave the best answers would be the winners.*
>
> *The questions were asked, and the two winners were given their cola. Yet the leader felt very badly for the third boy, especially when he saw how his face dropped and he seemed on the verge of tears.*
>
> *The leader had a brainstorm. He had a bag of small candies with him. He turned to the third boy and asked him to hold out his hands. "I'm going to pour candies into your hands," he told him. He did, until the boy was holding about fifteen candies in his hands.*
>
> *"I'm going to pour again," the group leader told the boy, "and you can keep as many candies as you can hold in your hands without dropping them on the floor."*
>
> *The leader wound up pouring three times until the boy had about fifty candies in his hands.*

Leaving the issues of health and sugar aside (not that they are to be ignored, but a different point is being brought out here), not only was this little boy's spirit not broken, he will automatically *love* coming to the group and saying "*Amen, Yehei Shemei Rabba*" because of the positive association. The impression formed may even last him a lifetime.

Absorbing the Message

There is yet another point. The positivity and prizes the child receives will open the child's heart to the various messages the learning, *davening*, etc. are providing. A child is young and can not always relate to the depth of content that spiritual activities have to offer. Nevertheless, if the experience is made positive for him *on his level*, he will absorb the message being given at that particular time, whether that message will be a love for *davening*, learning, listening to a *shiur* or whatever else is offered.

The Prayers of the High Holy Days

These ideas, apropos the entire year, may be especially helpful during the *Yamim Noraim*, when children find it difficult to remain in the shul throughout the considerably longer *davening*. Even those children who do stay in shul the entire time may do so begrudgingly. This can lead to a build-up of resentment and even dislike for the *tefillah*. Our goal, though, is the exact opposite: we seek to develop in each child a love for *tefillah* that will grow with time and last a lifetime. Positive discipline can accomplish this.

> *A father recently related that his son complained about the tefillos in shul. "They're too long," the boy said, "and I don't have the energy to stay for such long, drawn-out davening."*
>
> *When his father forced him to come to shul to daven, the boy would attend begrudgingly — all the time looking for the first opportunity to leave. At 11, the boy was fast losing his desire for davening altogether.*
>
> *With Rosh Hashanah on the horizon, the father became very concerned. He decided to use positive discipline. He took his son aside and said, "I know it's hard for you to stay for all of Shacharis and Mussaf, so I'm going to offer you an incentive. If you stay for the tefillos, you will get a prize worth five shekels after Yom Tov. If you daven nicely, you will get a prize worth 10 shekels. And if your davening is exceptional, you will get a prize worth 20 shekels." (Naturally, the amounts will vary from family to family.)*

The boy davened exceptionally well, and after Rosh Hashanah his father brought him a walkie-talkie set that cost 20 shekels. The boy was thrilled, and the father pointed out to his son how his efforts in davening were worthwhile even if done for personal gain.

When talking with the boy, the father also noted how he cried during certain parts of the davening, such as Nesaneh Tokef. The father also mentioned that the boy sneezed a number of times at the beginning of Mussaf and told his son that the Shulchan Aruch states that this is a sign that one's tefillah is being accepted.

It seems that the incentives allowed the boy to daven purely and for the sake of Heaven.

In other words, the incentive made the actual *davening* itself pleasant for the boy, who *davened* sincerely and with emotion.

This does not mean, though, that the problem is solved. This boy may have *davened* beautifully on Rosh Hashanah, but still feels that *davening* is a burden. However, this method of positive discipline can be used again and again until the boy begins to develop a desire for *davening* for its own sake.

The Power of Your Child's Prayers

If, at the same time a parent gives his child an incentive, he tells him how important his *tefillos* are, the impression made will be even stronger.

Once, a man fell from a roof and was so seriously injured that his life was in danger. In this emergency, we called all the children out of class to say *Tehillim* together for him. The boys screamed and *davened* with great intensity in a crescendo of fiery *tefillos*.

A short time later, we received word that the man died. Someone came over to me and asked to see the name of the ill person. He looked at the piece of paper on which the name was written and said there was a mistake. We had *davened* for the wrong person.

Months later, before the *Yamim Noraim*, I used this example to show the children how important their *tefillos* are. Hashem had decreed that this man should die at that specific time. Yet, the *tefillos* of children are so powerful that if the children had *davened*, the man would not have died. Since it had already been decreed that his time had come, Hashem caused a mistake in the name so that the children would actually not be *davening* for him.

Offering our children an incentive to make the *davening* more pleasant for them while at the same time explaining to them how significant their *tefillos* really are, is a winning combination. With it, we can help them develop a love for *davening*.

We once wrote about a child who entered our school a number of years ago and had been labeled hyperactive. He had a hard time in his previous school because his teachers were not equipped to deal with him. Our main approach in working with him was to give him as much encouragement as we could.

When he had been in our school for only a short time, his father exclaimed to me, "My son has started to eat again!" It seems this boy had lost his appetite as a result of all the pressure and aggravation he was experiencing. Encouragement gave him renewed hope.

Before Yom Kippur, when I spoke to all the students in our school, I discussed the following parable of the Dubner Maggid (which I have previously mentioned):

> *Once, a father and young son were traveling to a distant city. On the way, they came to a stream. Turning to his father, the son complained, "Abba, it's too deep for me. I can't cross this stream." The father answered him, "Don't worry, son. I will take care of you." Immediately, he lifted his son and carried him across the stream, and they continued on their way.*
>
> *Suddenly, they were attacked by a band of robbers. The father said, "Son, stand behind me, and you will be safe." The child obeyed, and with the stick he was holding, the father fought the robbers and warded them off.*
>
> *(When I was about 8 years old, my father did the same for me. We lived in an Italian neighborhood, and once, when I was playing with a friend, a boy approached me, called me a derogatory name and shoved me. I was no pushover, so I shoved him back. He left, but a quarter of an hour later he was back with some 20 friends, apparently to teach me a lesson. My father came running out of the house with a baseball bat, screaming at the top of his lungs, and the gang ran away, terrified.)*

The father and his son continued on their way, but soon came to a high fence. "Abba, how will I climb over this fence?" the boy asked. His father replied, "Don't worry, son," and, taking the boy on his shoulders, he climbed the fence with him.

When finally they reached their destination, they found the gates to the city locked. They searched everywhere for a way to enter. Suddenly, the father cried, "Son, look! There is a small opening. I would never be able to get through it, but you can."

Gently, he continued, "My child, I've carried you and taken care of you on this entire journey. Through all our trials and tribulations, I have helped you. Now it is your turn to help me. This opening is too small for me, but you will be able to fit through it. Once you are inside, you can open the door for me!"

In the same way, said the Dubner Maggid, at times the gates of tefillah are closed to adults. We are too big and carry too many transgressions. It is now the time for the children to enter through the small opening that remains. "Go in, children," he would say, "and open the gates for us. Daven for us, and your tefillos will be accepted."

After telling the children this *mashal*, I explained to them that many children make a mistake in assuming that the main *tefillos* are those of the adults, and that their *tefillos* are of secondary importance. In fact, just the opposite is true! The children's *tefillos* are the main ones, and their *tefillos* can help and support us, the adults. I then urged them to *daven* for their parents, for their siblings, for other family members, and even for their neighborhoods and for other people and causes.

Note that I also told the children I would give a prize to anyone who *davened* sincerely and with great *kavannah*.

After Yom Kippur, the hyperactive student in our school brought me a note from his father describing how he stood for *hours davening* with great *kavannah* on Yom Kippur. "He literally went through a *techiyas hameisim!*" his father wrote.

Realizing how important his *tefillos* were brought him to love the *tefillos* and to *daven* with all his heart, something disciplinary measures could never have achieved.

Davening shelo lishmah led the boy to *daven lishmah*. And, as we said, the incentive makes the *tefillah* itself all the more enjoyable.

After writing about this incident (I wrote this in an article about a year ago), I received a letter from a reader saying that such a change was only temporary and would not last. "I'm sure," he wrote, "this boy didn't change overnight."

He is right. From that one improved *davening* experience, the boy will not change. Nor will a person lose fifty pounds from successfully sticking to a diet for one or two days. It is the consistent use of these methods that brings about permanent change, *b'ezras Hashem*.

The follow-up? The next year, after the *Yamim Noraim*, this student brought an equally enthusiastic letter from home. His parents ended it by saying, "He is a changed boy."

Positive discipline, using incentives, is a tried-and-true method that many parents find invaluable. Why? Because it works.

And, as many parents ask, "Aren't we teaching the child to always expect a prize for what he does?"

If the discipline is tendered properly this is not an issue. A child expects prizes when he gets something for nothing. But when he has to work hard to receive what he wants, he does not develop the feeling that it is coming to him.

It is also important to make sure not to offer too many incentive prizes at the same time. If the child receives a prize for everything, he then learns that one does not do anything without getting paid for it.

Positive Discipline and Bedtime

My son Aharon didn't want to put on his pajamas and was fighting me every step of the way. I kept putting them back on while trying to make a game out of it. "See the little fish trying to wriggle away?" I'd say, but he still fought, trying hard to take off whatever I put on.

When he takes something off that I've put on, I give him a slap or remind him that he'll get a slap from me if he takes off what Mommy puts on. That is a general rule that I follow when dressing or undressing him, and it works well in stopping him from taking the clothes off.

The slap is only effective if I give it on his bare leg. Otherwise it doesn't hurt, and he doesn't care.

When a child goes to bed, we want him to do it with a good feeling. In this case, although routine discipline may seem easiest to do, it will not accomplish the desired goal. Positive discipline will.

Positive discipline means that the child works toward receiving a positive consequence, one that will give him an incentive to keep to the routine. For it to be effective, there must first be a routine.

A parent should sit down with the child and plan the bedtime ritual, and how it should proceed. What time should the child begin getting into pajamas? When should he brush his teeth? When will he actually go into bed? Is he allowed reading time? At what time should the lights be put out?

All of the above should be decided beforehand. It does not hurt to plan it together with your child. Of course, cooperation in the planning will vary with age.

After you have worked out a routine together, tell him the incentive prize toward which he will be working. One idea is to have two prizes worth different amounts of points. The child will earn the prize he can "afford," according to the points he has earned.

After both you and the child have a clear understanding of what the prize(s) will be, the child should be told how many points each activity is worth. For instance, two points can be awarded for brushing teeth without being reminded and one point if they are brushed after being told.

Points should increase according to the effort the child puts forth. For example, going into bed on his own and shutting the lights on time might deserve three points, with a reduction to two points if he does it only after being reminded.

It is helpful to keep a record of the points earned in a small notebook or on a wall chart. Adjust the point system so the child does not have to wait longer than two weeks to earn a prize. With smaller children, they should not have to wait for longer than one week.

After a number of months, the habit of the bedtime routine will be sufficiently developed to allow the parent to tone down his incentives gradually. Still, it is impractical to think that children will willingly go to bed on their own — ever. Yet we need not despair. There are many ways we can offer rewards without offering incentives.

As a rule, any positive consequence a child receives as a result of properly following bedtime routine is considered an incentive. For example, if a child gets into bed at a certain time, he can have the light on for another 10 minutes to read; or, father or mother will sit and speak with him for five to 10 minutes. Children will cooperate wondrously when they stand to get something they want, even if that something is not a prize but a privilege or a positive consequence.

One point to remember, though, is that once the agreement has been made the parent should be firm and not give the child the reward if he is not making a serious effort to keep to the routine.

One father used this method when one of his children was older and wanted to use the family car. Parent and teenager agreed that driving laws must be obeyed and that the car would be properly maintained. It was also mutually agreed that sometimes the child would have to chauffeur his parents, plus he would have to do chores around the house willingly.

If the child agreed to these conditions, the parents would pay for the gas, insurance and, of course, allow use of the car.

The agreement was that simple. As long as the child kept his part of the bargain, he could continue using the car. If he did not stick to the agreement, he would not be allowed use of the car.

This method proved highly effective, and the child stuck to it, realizing that the privilege was contingent on his keeping his part of the deal.

A Reputation to Live Up to

Giving a child a reputation to live up to is also a positive consequence.

The school year has just begun, but one of the boys in the older grades had already begun causing trouble. He would disturb in class, become belligerent on occasion and would even make fun of the rebbi behind his back.

We knew we had to take immediate action, right now, at the beginning of the year before it progressed any further.

Our assistant principal came up with an ingenious plan. The next time the boy was sent to his office for misbehaving, he asked the boy if he wanted his parents to know about it. This particular boy is very afraid of his parents and naturally answered no.

Rabbi L. then picked up the phone and asked the boy for his phone number. He dialed the number and got the voice mail. He then began to speak.

"Shimon is in my office, and we just had a nice talk," Rabbi L. said. "In fact, I am convinced that this year will be the best year Shimon has ever had in his life. I think it's worthwhile to give him a treat when he gets home as a sign of encouragement and recognition for his resolution to be very successful this year" — and he hung up the phone.

The boy was in shock, but he now had a reputation to live up to.

I cannot say that this one incident cured the problem entirely, but we continued dealing with this child along these lines. When I gave the class an oral quiz, I tried to catch him at moments when he was doing something right and compliment him on it. I would tell him he was excelling and so on.

Interestingly enough, in just a short time, the boy has improved remarkably. In fact, just yesterday I tested his class (which I do once a week), and after class I took him aside and gave him a big compliment. I then turned to him with a big smile and said, "This is going to be the best year you ever had, isn't it?" He smiled back and nodded in agreement.

When you believe in a child, let him know it, and later catch him doing things right. This is the most positive consequence you can find for dealing with children.

A rebbi I know takes pictures of his students and hangs them on the wall. Next to each picture, he hangs a saying from *Chazal* that he feels is appropriate for that particular boy's strengths and weaknesses.

For one boy, he hung the words, "*Aizehu gibbor? Hakovesh es yitzro* — Who is a hero? He who conquers his evil inclination." (This boy was known for frequently getting into fights.) Whenever the boy got into a fight, the rebbi would point to the wall and say to him, "That's you. This is who you really are."

Needless to say, the message got across.

Judging Children Favorably

Only one ingredient is needed for this to be effective. It is called *focusing on the positive*. Recognize the good points and strengths of your children (and spouse as well). There is not a Yid in existence who is not a wellspring of talents and G-dly character traits. Every Yid is a *chelek Eloka mima'al* — he has in him a piece of Hashem, so to speak. Not always is it noticeable, but it is always there, and if we look for it, we will find it.

Especially now, during these turbulent times, we want Hashem to judge us favorably. *Chazal* tell us how we can accomplish this: "*Kol hadan es chaveiro lekaf zechus, Hamakom yadineihu lekaf zechus* — He who judges his fellow favorably will be judged favorably by the One Above."

R' Chaim Shmulevitz asks how it is possible for Hashem to judge favorably if He knows exactly what happened. He answers that the judging favorably meant here is when one focuses on the good traits and noble intentions of a person. This will evoke a parallel response above: Hashem will also focus on that person's good traits and noble intentions and so come to a favorable judgment.

There is no doubt in my mind that parents who look favorably upon their children and believe in them are included in the promise that those who judge *lekaf zechus* will be judged *lekaf zechus*.

Klal Yisrael is in dire need of salvation. Focusing on the strengths and virtues of others (including our children) will certainly help to invoke the Divine favor that we are so desperately in need of, now more than ever.

May we merit to look upon others favorably, in this way hastening the redemption. And may this be the year for which we have been waiting for so long, the year that we will witness the coming of the Mashiach, *bimeheira beyameinu, Amen.*

FAQs on Chinuch

37

A word of caution:

The guidelines in this chapter are presented to provide a broad picture, to suggest ideas and to offer direction. However, just as buying a scalpel does not automatically equip us to perform major surgery, so too safe and effective use of these valuable tools requires expertise.

For serious problems or complex situations, it is best to consult a competent, experienced authority. Parents who are given clear guidelines and implement them as part of an individualized approach will see improvement in even the most difficult situations.

Much has been said about children at risk. With the increasing numbers of children at risk, should all parents worry that their children too might be at risk?

Though there is no guarantee that our children will follow the path we wish for them, a child does not become at-risk overnight. When a child moves in a direction unacceptable to us, it is a long, drawn-out process that develops over a number of years. Parents should be concerned if, even at a young age, a child falls into problematic habits or pursues, on a regular basis, interests of which they do not approve. If a child starts having problems in school — even if his grades slide for a period of only a few weeks — parents should seek the cause.

The crucial question here is not whether we should worry. The main point is that we should do something about it! The growing number of children at risk should motivate all parents to use the *chinuch* methods best suited to our unique generation. These methods, which are discussed in depth throughout the book, are the most effective way to prevent children from drifting toward or heading for the fringe.

Q & A *Can anything be done to prevent the increasing numbers of instances where those that have already left religion continue to dress and act as if they were observant? In effect, they are non-observant yet externally they appear religious, thus allowing them to deceive others along with themselves as well.*

As mentioned above these situations are not created in one day. They are the result of years of confusion and difficulty.

Fortunate are the parents who forge a close bond with their children. They will be able to discern the various difficulties and challenges the child may be facing, as they come about, thus being able to offer their assistance and guidance before the situation becomes serious.

Even in instances where the parents are unable to recognize any problems, the child will *open up to and share with* his parents that which they are unable to discern on their own.

> *As mentioned previously, I know of a girl whose parents spent an hour with her in safe, comfortable communication once a month, and eventually this is what put her life back on track. No matter what came up in their busy schedules, her parents would always try to keep this once-a-month "appointment" with their daughter, so that she could air her grievances and feel understood. During this hour they kept to a strict policy not to offer advice, become upset, or go on the defensive. This hour belonged totally to their daughter.*
>
> *At one point, their daughter began to act up at home. They knew that something serious was bothering her, but they did not know what it was. The daughter simply would not discuss it. Strangely enough, however, during one of their monthly appointment hours, the daughter finally did open up.*

She told them that she had been cheating in school, and that no one realized it. She had found out where the teacher kept her personal test notebook, and so she was able to find out all the answers before a test. The teacher had begun complimenting her in front of all the other students, and she was getting the highest grades in the class. She was now feeling trapped in a downward spiral and did not know how to get out. During one of these sessions she felt that she could finally open up to her parents and seek the help she so desperately needed to extricate herself from this complicated predicament.

Her parents were very supportive and together with their daughter they came up with a plan that succeeded in reversing a dangerous trend. Through their monthly hour of listening to their daughter, they were able to stop this child from falling into what may have been the beginning of a long, complex path of deceit and misery.

Look toward the future. Discipline your children, yet keep the lines of communication open, so that your child will always remain close to you.

It is this closeness that can bring a solution from the very onset, thus preventing difficulties from resulting in tragedies such as the ones described in the above question.

Q & A *When parents have a valid reason to be suspicious, is searching through their child's drawers or belongings a recommended practice?*

Though it is impossible to generalize, parental detective work usually does not lead to a solution. It may even complicate matters, as attested to by countless real-life interactions. More often, what brings about improvement is the parents' close connection to and trust in their child.

One father and mother who routinely searched their son's drawers felt reassured that things were under control. Unfortunately, they had no inkling of how far the child's behavior had deteriorated and what he was doing behind their backs.

On the other hand, I know of many other situations where the parents kept the relationship close. They retained their trust and belief in their child. In these cases, the child usually came around eventually.

Chinuch is not about instant solutions; *chinuch* is educating with a look to the future. Parental action that gains the desired effect momentarily but has devastating effects in the long term is not *chinuch*.

Q&A *When dealing with difficulties, at what point should parents turn to an outside source (tutor, mentor, advisor, rabbi) for help?*

In all areas, seeking advice and guidance is a sign of strength not weakness. It is also a recommended practice. This is doubly true for parenting. A parent who maintains ongoing contact with a competent authority will be attuned to problems when they are in the beginning stages. This gives ample time to prevent them from becoming serious. Such a parent will also benefit from the authority's wealth of experience. Instead of learning from mistakes made with one's own children, each of which carries a price tag, the parent will be able to tap into a reservoir of tried-and-true techniques and approaches. Also, someone outside the family circle who is not personally involved is able to offer a fresh perspective.

It might be worthwhile to select one of the child's teachers or principals as your advisor. With the right approach, teachers, principals and other school staff members can sometimes be a parent's greatest ally.

Choosing a teacher from previous years, one who was particularly successful with your child, is certainly an option.

Still a word of caution is in order. Any mentor or advisor you select must fulfill two basic requirements. (1) They are interested only in the benefit of your child and his parents. (2) They have a keen understanding of children, providing them with a long track record of success, thus qualifying them to guide you in finding the best path for your child. (If they are also blessed with a bit of humility you can be even more secure with their advice, as they will direct you toward the proper outside sources in situations beyond their capabilities.)

To put your trust for the guidance of your child in the hands of someone who is not particularly out only for your child's welfare, and perhaps may be offering advice based on ulterior motives such as impatience or frustration, or the benefit of the school as opposed to the benefit of your child, is tantamount to consulting with a doctor who is being paid to experiment with a certain medication. One cannot be secure that his advice is unbiased and in your best interest. (Given, at times a principal or teacher must be out for the benefit of the school as opposed to the benefit of the individual child, as this is their duty, nevertheless this is not the one you wish to select in guiding you to find the best for your child.)

In situations where the parent has not found someone in the school who fits the necessary criteria, guidance should be sought elsewhere from competent authorities in the field.

As a rule, if your child's problem or difficulty continues two months or longer, do not delay. If you can help him past the rough spot, there is no need for outside expertise. If, though, your methods have not succeeded it is time to seek outside help. There is no reason for a child to suffer because his parent wants to do it all on his own.

Q *You often discuss not disciplining harshly. Doesn't the Torah encourage discipline and strictness with children?*

&A Only the Torah sages and their disciples throughout the generations are qualified to interpret the Torah and explain its practical application for changing times.

The great rabbis who, in their wisdom, can see and understand where our generation is headed, have told us repeatedly to adjust our methods to meet the emotional and spiritual needs of *this* generation. Today's children are less tough and have less stamina — both physical and emotional — than children in previous generations.

It is worth noting the words of *Chovas HaTalmidim* by the Piaseczner Rebbe written some 68 years ago and quoted numerous times in this book:

> In previous generations, even if parents or teachers disciplined harshly, it helped, for children then accepted both the discipline and the blame. A child would feel that he was at fault and would thus come to correct his ways.
>
> *Not so in our times!*
>
> Today's youth consider themselves mature adults. They feel their own independence. One of the evils that results from this attitude is that the child looks at every-

one who comes to educate him as a foreign tyrant, someone who is robbing him of his independence and free will.

Our spiritual leaders have taught us how careful we must be with our children's precious souls. Contemporary giants no longer with us, including the Chafetz Chaim, the Chazon Ish, R' Elyah Lopian, R' Yaakov Kamenetsky, R' Shlomo Zalman Auerbach, R' Eliezer Menachem Man Shach, R' Avraham Pam and R' Avraham Chaim Brim, and those still with us, including R' Shlomo Wolbe and R' Michel Yehudah Lefkovitz, all say we must educate our children with love, *not* with harshness.

Any parent who is shouting at his children, rebuking them harshly and instilling fear in their hearts must accept full responsibility to ensure that his methods do not cause any adverse effects, which may emerge only years later. Experience in the field has proven repeatedly that harshness is *not* the key to raising children who will continue in the ways of their parents.

The Torah tells every Jew — in all eras, and no matter what the surrounding cultural values — not to be angry or impatient. The Torah never suggests as *chinuch* methods parental discipline based on venting one's anger, letting out one's frustrations or other ulterior motives. The only discipline the Torah recommends is that which is in the best interest of the child.

Q & A *Why aren't teachers and rebbis being told these things?*

They are.

There are so many conscientious teachers and rebbis who care about and are genuinely interested in each and every child. We must be careful not to attack the whole system even if we encounter a teacher or rebbi who is not doing his job in the most effective manner possible. Also, we should keep in mind that the vast majority of educators are constantly seeking new ways to build children in a positive way.

Remember too that it is always easy to blame the establishment, but there is so much the parents themselves are able to do. R' Wolbe once told me that if a child feels a close connection with his parents, they will be able to see him successfully through any difficult situation, including having a tough teacher.

Q & A *Why does Hashem punish certain people by giving them difficult children? Aren't they also entitled to true nachas? Is it wrong to want to have children who are a pride to their people and their Maker?*

It is not for us to understand the mysterious ways in which the Master of the universe, in His infinite wisdom and kindliness, gives us situations as He sees fit for our benefit. Still, there is a thought that may be somewhat reassuring: a principal will often assign his best teacher to a difficult class. It is precisely because this teacher is an expert that he will be assigned the challenging class. In this case, the problem children are indicative of the teacher's successes rather than his failures. The teacher was assigned the problem class because he is the one best equipped to help them.

The same holds true with parents and children. We do not pick our children! We are assigned them by the Master Principal. He may often assign children with difficult natures and temperaments to those parents He feels are most skilled and expert. Only in their capable hands is Hashem sure these children will receive the best upbringing they possibly can. In this case, the difficult child (who was difficult from the very onset and not due to some failure on the part of the parents) is an indication of the parent's skill and expertise. Precisely because Hashem holds these parents to be capable of success is why He gave them such tough assignments.

Q & A *How should a parent react if the teacher or rebbi responds to the child in a way the parent feels is inappropriate? Should the parent take the rebbi's side or the child's side?*

A child must always feel that his parent is on his side and wants what is best for him. Being on the child's side must be constant and unconditional.

However, at times the child is in the wrong and needs to be disciplined — *for his own good.* I have seen situations where a child was acting out and intentionally disrupting an entire class. The child was in need of a strong dose of discipline, yet the parents took the child's side and prevented him from experiencing the consequences of his actions. He lost an opportunity for improvement.

Being on the child's side does not rule out proper discipline when necessary. On the contrary, being on the child's side means giving him proper disciplinary measures when necessary

— because that is what is truly best for the child. If the parent responds to his child positively most of the time — with actions that are based on warmth and love — then even when he has to discipline, the child will know that his parent's intention is for the child's benefit.

In other instances, the teacher or rebbi may truly have done something wrong or made a mistake. If the incident is insignificant or minor, a parent should help his child to understand that mistakes are part of being human. This should not be allowed to diminish the child's respect for his teacher.

Explain to your child the *reasons* he should respect a rebbi or teacher. Do not just give it over as a dry rule such as, "You have to respect him because you have to, that's all." If you yourself understand why it is important, you will be able to explain it to your child in a way he can accept. You might say, "A rebbi is a emissary of Hashem sent to help you succeed in life. He is also a Torah scholar, and your connection to our unbroken tradition all the way back to Mt. Sinai." Concerning secular studies, you can tell your child that respecting a secular studies teacher is in effect sanctifying Hashem's Name, while doing the opposite is a desecration.

Your lessons on this theme will be far more effective if you first listened to what your child had to say. Try to understand it from his point of view, without giving any advice or rebuke. Before saying anything, just listen! After the child has finished speaking, tell him that you truly understand how he feels. (The child will know you mean it only if you really do.) Only then should you begin educating the child in the ways of proper respect for teachers.

If the incidents are ongoing or more serious, seek guidance, especially in situations where the teacher or rebbi is disciplining the child harshly, or embarrassing and insulting him in front of the other children. In these situations, the parent's emotional support (under the proper guidance) will prevent these unjust methods from leaving an indelible mark on the child's emotional psyche.

Q *When criticism of a rebbi is called for, are there specific ways in which to criticize a rebbi?*

A There are definitely effective ways to approach a rebbi when you must call attention to something he is doing that is not helpful to your child. First, express your appreciation for all the efforts the rebbi has put into his students and his teaching. (Even if you don't feel it, say it anyway. Every rebbi puts in effort; teaching — even ineffectively — is no easy task.) Then ask the rebbi a question about what is going on in his class, as if you are asking his advice. In this way, he will not feel that he is being attacked, and together you will be able to work out a successful solution to the problem.

Q & A How should one parent react when he/she feels that the other parent's methods are detrimental to their children's chinuch?

It is important to differentiate between parenting methods that you feel may cause severe damage and those you feel won't.

When one parent feels that the methods his or her spouse is using are actually doing great damage, a competent authority must be consulted. It is impossible to rectify extreme situations without clear, specific guidance.

When you feel your spouse's approach is wrong but not that detrimental, follow the rule of not arguing with your spouse in front of the children. Even though you feel your spouse's methods are wrong, by arguing in front of the children you will cause far more damage.

It is impossible to overemphasize how helpful marital harmony is for effective parenting. So much can be accomplished when parents are united. Conversely, it can be terribly traumatic for children to see their parents arguing, especially if the argument is about them. Also, the child often feels very guilty about being the cause of the argument.

Arguing will almost *never* change your spouse's feelings or methods. As a sign I came across said:

If you scream, people hear you.

If you talk, people listen to you.

If you smile, people like you.

Conducting yourself in ways that cause others to like you certainly make them more amenable to seeing your point of view.

With your spouse — with anyone, in fact — the way to deal with a difference of opinion is:

(1) Speak at a non-threatening time and in a non-threatening way and in a non-threatening tone of voice. Do not discuss any issue that is not life-threatening in the midst of a crisis. Wait until many hours — even a day or two — have passed.

(2) When you do discuss the issue, do not come to your spouse with complaints but rather with a sincere desire to understand his or her point of view. *Listen* with the intent to understand, and do not state your opinion until you have truly and sincerely understood your spouse's standpoint. (By the way, only your spouse can tell you if you have understood his or her viewpoint. Check it out.)

(3) Then tell your spouse how you feel.

If there is a right and a wrong involved in the issue, it is likely that at this point, *if the above steps have been followed properly*, your spouse will concede the point about the mistake of his/her methods. And if not, at least your spouse will have heard your message.

Often, though, the discussion will not concern questions of right and wrong, but rather two different approaches, each with its advantages and disadvantages. In these situations, if couples work together, they may come up with new methods that work for both of them. They can then coordinate their efforts as a unit. In this case, 1+1=3, for the new methods they discover can fit into the styles of both of them. To accomplish this, each must be willing to compromise. If there is a feeling of teamwork between them, their joint efforts can create a beautiful solution.

Surprisingly enough, the ones who gain the most from parents working together are their children. When there is strife between husband and wife, a child feels like his world is crumbling beneath him; when there is harmony, he feels secure. Isn't that more important?

Q *How can one instill in a child deep feelings of faith and true fear of Heaven?*

&A There are many different ways and means to achieve this goal, yet the decisive factor is undoubtedly the role model the parents or teachers present. R' Wolbe once told me that parents should recite blessings aloud. This behavior on a parent's part trains even a very young child to have faith.

When your baby sees you talking to someone he cannot see, it makes him realize that G-d is with us although He is not seen. The younger a child is when he absorbs this understanding, the deeper his faith will be.

If reciting all blessings out loud is difficult, a parent can pick one blessing to recite aloud all the time, encouraging his children to answer Amen. Choose a blessing like *shehakol*.

One father I know chose one blessing to recite aloud. When the children are around, he makes sure to recite it aloud in front of them, and they respond Amen. He always thanks them for saying Amen (because our Sages say that when one answers Amen after another person's blessing, it makes the blessing more complete). Eventually, the children began coming over to their father — of their own accord — to recite this blessing aloud so that he would answer Amen.

When parents give their children this kind of *chinuch*, the children feel they are doing the parents a favor by answering Amen. Since they too want their blessings to be complete, they also recite them aloud so others will answer Amen to their blessings. This method is its own built-in incentive and can succeed in ingraining faith and fear of Heaven very deeply in children. It's a tried-and-true method that works, with the help of Hashem!

Ultimately it is the parents' sincere interaction with the children with acts of deep faith which implants in the children deep seeds of faith and fear of Heaven.

How can we deal with chutzpah? What do you say to a 17-year-old yeshivah boy whose response is, "Why should I?" when told to do something like go to yeshivah or go to minyan on time?

(It is imperative to again stress that we are not offering guidance here for extreme situations, where relationships between parent and child have become strained, nor for situations where children have become physically violent, throwing things or engaging in some other physical acts against their parents. It is not within the scope of these pages to address situations such as these; personal guidance must be sought.)

First, we need not be surprised, nor should we despair, when we see our children acting with chutzpah. Parents are often shocked and become upset when their children speak with chutzpah. With such reactions, they will not be able to respond properly. It is important for us to realize that chutzpah is rampant nowadays, for these are the times immediately preceding Mashiach's arrival, when the world's moral code has eroded drastically and when respect for authority is practically nonexistent. Such is the world in which we live, and we are not immune to its influence.

The second important point to remember in dealing with chutzpah is that not everything that seems like chutzpah is fueled by chutzpah. Our families and communities are not immune to the influence of the world around us and not everything that we see as chutzpah is such in the eye's of the child. It is therefore important that our first step be to determine if the child is intentionally being chutzpadik or if his behavior was a thoughtless copy of what goes on in the surrounding culture. If the child was chutzpadik unintentionally or if the parent is unsure, the recommended approach is one of communication. Communicate to the child that what he did or is doing is wrong and tell him clearly what you want him to do instead. For instance, you might say, "What you just said is chutzpah. I would like you to speak with respect."

If the child repeats the infraction, or if it is clear that it was intentional, then we are ready for the next step.

The age of a child is a very important factor here. Younger children (usually around 10 and under) have less understanding of what is expected of them and are less able to control themselves. They therefore need more firmness and discipline to train them in self-control. If they persist in their disrespectful behavior, a stronger reaction is necessary. One can begin by saying calmly but firmly, "That is chutzpah, and I do not allow it." (As opposed to just communicating as mentioned before, here the parent is firmly taking a stand and stating clearly that he does not allow this behavior. This alone, if said firmly, can be considered a strong reaction.) The parent can repeat himself if necessary.

If the child persists in his behavior, he should be given an immediate consequence. For other types of misbehaviors, one might consider giving a child another chance, but not for chutzpah, since it is a serious transgression.

Appropriate consequences may be losing playtime; going to bed earlier; not being given a treat at supper; being sent to one's room for a 10-minute time-out; not being allowed to use a favorite toy (a walkie-talkie or walkman, for example). The point is to deny the child some small privilege. One can begin with small doses of punishment and increase the dosage if the infraction is repeated.

With older children as well, the initial reaction should be one of communication. Communicate to the child *what* he is doing wrong and what you would like him to do: "Shmuel, you are talking with chutzpah. Speak more respectfully please."

If the child persists in his chutzpah, discipline is not necessarily the most effective approach. Any disciplining of an older child (especially teenagers) involves a power struggle. You might be stronger than the child and therefore win the battle, but this does not mean you have won the war; even if you do win the battle, the war will rage on. Besides, you may not even win the battle.

This is not to say that a teenager should not be disciplined. Rather, as a child grows older the recommended approach is more one of communication and discussion than one of discipline.

We are not advocating that parents give up their demands. We are saying that the most successful way to have your demands met with older children is through communication of these demands and discussion as to why these demands are not being met by the child.

If the relationship between parents and child is a healthy one, most of the time the child will cooperate and comply with the parents' wishes. In such a home, the child will rarely openly and intentionally go against the wishes of his parents. He will not want to cause his parents anguish.

It would therefore be more effective to ignore the chutzpah as it takes place and instead to set up a discussion with the child at a later time (not in the heat of the moment). At that time, ask the child openly why he was speaking or acting disrespectfully. Make up your mind to listen and understand his point of view so that he really feels understood. Then express your wishes that he desist from the disrespectful behavior. If the discussion was successful, then if the child again demonstrates disrespect, a small reminder should suffice.

If an older child (especially a teenager) persists in his chutzpah, it is usually an indication that something is amiss. When the relationship between parent and child is a close one, then the child wants to please the parent and respect him. A child continuously demonstrating disrespect is usually an indication that the relationship is a strained one. Therefore, it is wise to deal not only with the behavior but with the root cause of the behavior. In such a case, a parent would do well to put in the time and effort to reestablish a close relationship between him and his child.

In the case of the 17-year-old the main issue is not the chutzpah but his not wanting to fit the framework he is in, such as going to yeshivah or going to *minyan.* This is an issue of the child not properly performing the mitzvos. (Besides, he probably answered out of defensiveness, not chuzpah.) In this case, discussion and understanding is certainly the recommended approach. Once we understand what is bothering the boy and why he does not want to go to yeshivah, then we can move on to finding a good solution to the problem. The parents would be wise to involve a third party who may be able to help the boy work out his difficulties as well as help mend the parent-child relationship.

Q & *You often mention understanding our children. Why this emphasis on understanding them? Won't we gain more control by being strict?*

A It is not control we are looking for, it's *chinuch. Chinuch* means that even when the policeman is not looking or when the child becomes an adult, he will follow in the ways we have taught him. "*Gam ki yazkin lo yassur mimenu* — Even when he is older, he will not turn away from it.*"

Q & *What do you think about hitting?*

A Any discussion about whether or not to hit usually misses the point. Even those sages who permit hitting do so only if certain conditions are met: (1) hitting is done only very rarely; (2) it is not done out of anger; (3) it is not done out of frustration or impatience. The Torah never suggests discipline based on letting out one's frustrations, venting one's anger or any other ulterior motives. (See *Orchos Yosher* by R' Chaim Kanievsky.)

Most parents who hit do not meet these requirements.

In addition, since hitting — if used at all — should be used sparingly (only once in a while) and only under extenuating circumstances, at any rate we are in need of other disciplinary measures to turn to on an ongoing basis.

These methods are discussed throughout this book.

A parent who hits his children on a regular basis must accept the full responsibility to ensure that his methods will not cause any adverse side-effects that will show up only years later. Experience in the field has proven repeatedly that harshness is not the key to raising children who will continue in the ways of their parents.

Why is it that various problems such as ADD, hyperactivity and learning disabilities didn't seem to be around in past generations? Is this a phenomenon specific to our times? Dare we say that perhaps the emphasis on these problems is exaggerated and these aren't real problems?

One who asks such a question must in turn ask why the degree of decadence that exists today did not seem to be around in previous generations.

In the 1940's, the leading disciplinary problems in the public schools were talking out of turn, chewing gum, making noise, running in the halls and littering. In the 1990's, the leading disciplinary problems in the public schools were substance abuse, suicide, robbery, assault and indecencies inappropriate to mention here.

Dare we say that these are not real problems but a figment of our imagination? Let those who suggest they are illusory not step into a public school.

In previous generations, we lived a more sheltered life, and, as mentioned in the name of the Steipler, R' Yaakov Kanievsky, the street took care of 50 percent of a child's *chinuch* (Ch. 1). Even one who was not integrated into the yeshivah system would be successful in pursuing his religious obligations. So while these problems may have existed in previous generations, the community structure allowed people with learning disabilities to function successfully and live as noble Jews.

Not so in our turbulent times "when atheists and apostates among us hold their heads high and act like non-Jews; when children are exposed to a barrage of evils at every turn. Anyone who does not give his children a proper Torah education is *almost certain* to see them drawn away entirely from the Holy Torah."

Today, a child lacking the ability to integrate into the regular yeshivah classroom is in danger of being pulled away from the

Torah altogether. It is a blessing that Hashem has opened our eyes and bestowed us with the wisdom to diagnose and treat learning disabilities.

Q&A My son doesn't want to pray or go to shul. Should I force him? I don't want to make praying distasteful to him. On the other hand, if I leave him alone, he won't go to shul at all.

With regard to praying, positive discipline as discussed in Chapter 36 can be very effective. Begin with an incentive program and keep it up for a long period. You may wish to begin with smaller incentives given after short periods, build up a positive momentum and gradually work up to bigger incentives rewarded after a longer period. In the interim, encourage the child for his successes and praise him for his efforts. After a while (possibly a number of months), his success in going to pray, together with your encouragement and praise, will serve to create a positive association that will make praying more pleasant for him. Put this together with the habit already developed, and you have a winning combination.

Q&A How do I know if my expectations of my daughter are realistic or if I am demanding too much from her?

A child faced with unrealistic demands usually shows signs of stress. If the child maintains his basic happiness and optimism, then he is probably okay. If he becomes serious and bitter, or seems constantly under pressure, adjustments must be made.

We are not referring to the normal objections or disapproval most children voice when demands are placed on them. These are normal and to be expected. We are referring to an ongoing change of mood or disposition.

Another invaluable tool in helping parents gauge the validity of their demands is to set aside one hour a month for listening to their child. During this hour, do nothing but listen. The purpose is to let the child air out whatever is bothering him and to keep the lines of communication open. If we give our child an opportunity in a non-threatening setting to tell us what's on his mind, he will turn to us with his problems. Then we will truly be able to assess just how difficult things may really be for him.

Q & A *Is there a successful method for getting children out of bed in the morning and into bed in the evening?*

Incentive programs as discussed in Chapter 36 can be very helpful.

Q & A *Is there any way to adjust the grading system in the schools so that grades reflect effort instead of just achievement — so that weaker students can also receive good marks?*

A reader of my column in the *Yated* sent a letter describing the system used in the Bais Yaakov of Montreal:

There are three possible avenues by which one can be listed on the coveted honor roll. One is that any student who has achieved a 90-percent average or above on her report card is automatically listed. The second is that any student who has achieved an average of 80 to 85 percent can be placed on the honor roll with the recommendation of at least three teachers. Last, any student who has achieved a 5 percent gain in her average, even from a 60 to a 65, automatically is listed. The girls in the last group have obviously toiled and sweated; their accomplishments are duly recognized and thus rewarded. Since the reason for a student making the honor roll is confidential, no one knows to which of these three categories the person belongs.

This is but one example of how it can feasibly be done.

Q & A *Our 9-year-old-son for the most part is well behaved and exercises a fair level of self-control. However, there are occasions when he loses his temper and becomes uncontrollable, slamming the door to his room and screaming about how unfair we are as parents. It is usually because of something trivial. While we are making progress at getting him to control his anger, what should we do when it gets to this stage?*

During the tantrum, there is not much to do provided the child is not causing damage or hurting others, in which case he should be stopped.

At times, going over to the child and expressing warmth can serve to speed up the calming-down process. Saying things like, "You must be very upset. Something must really be bothering you," accompanied by holding his hand or a warm embrace (do not be discouraged if he puts up resistance; do it anyway) can have a soothing effect on the child.

At other times, ignoring the child and just waiting until he comes out of it is the only option.

In any case, remaining calm and not allowing the child to get you upset is the recommended practice. A demonstration of anger or frustration might actually provide reinforcement for the child's misbehavior, encouraging him to persist in his undesirable behavior. Children sometimes have a vested interest in making their parents upset and may enjoy the feeling of power they gain from doing so.

After the child calms down, the first step is to see that he bears the consequences of his or her anger. If he threw things or made a mess, he is responsible for cleaning it up and should not be allowed out of the room until he does so. The same goes for any other disorder he caused while angry.

After the child finishes this task and calms down, resume the regular routine as soon as possible. Dealing with the issue that brought about the anger should be pushed off until later, the later the better.

Later, discuss the issue at length with the child. Begin by trying to see the situation through the child's eyes. What might seem trivial to an adult may loom large to a child. As R' Yisrael Salanter once put it, to a child the capsizing of his toy boat in a puddle is as distressing as the sinking of an ocean liner is to its owner. One must first access the situation through the child's eyes and only then determine if the matter is trivial. If you still are convinced that your child's anger is unjustified, follow the same steps mentioned above, utilizing the discussion with your child to teach him that he need not resort to angry behavior to express his feelings. Tell him that the lines of communication are always open and discussion with you is always available. Help him come up with alternative solutions that would have been more effective, thus teaching him that one stands to gain nothing by being angry.

Q & A *Our child throws a temper tantrum that lasts a long time whenever we say no to him. However, when we offer him a packet of stickers, he accepts the no immediately. We feel that using bribery constantly is bad chinuch. What should we do?*

Don't be fazed by a child's antics. You are the parents, and your word goes. It is healthy for your child to see that you will not give in just because of his tantrums. If your child has to receive a prize in order to accept your no, then *you* are not educating *him* — *he* is educating *you.*

Q & A   *How should a parent cope with the pressures children cause when they compare their family's standard of living with the neighbor's?*

For instance, when three or four neighbors made additions to their homes because they needed the space and were able to afford it, my children wanted an addition too. We also need it. Likewise, almost all of our neighbors have decent cars. We don't.

Even though we, as parents, can make do with what we have, our children feel they can't. They feel less than their friends and neighbors, who while not rich and spoiled, seem to have more than we do.

This is a very contentious point in our house. Matters have reached the point where my teenagers are angry with us and accuse us of not caring about what is important to them. "Why do we have to be the only ones" — either on the block or at school — "who have such an ugly house or car, etc." They are embarrassed to invite friends over or to be seen in our car. They say their friends comment about it as well.

What are we to do?

The first step is to listen to your children with the intention of understanding them. Use compassion and care while listening and try to truly put yourself in their place. This should not be too difficult because you yourself agree that the house needs an addition.

Sometimes this is enough. The very fact that the children are able to air their feelings while being listened to and understood can be sufficient.

In your case, though, I do not think it will solve the problem, although it may alleviate much of the tension between you and your children.

The next step is to *consider your children's feelings important,* thus giving them the message that what is important to them is important to you. Again, this does not mean that you have to *do* as they want. It *does* mean that how they feel is important to you. Although you may be able to live with certain compromises, they suffer great embarrassment, mainly from peer pressure, so for them the burden is a much harder one to bear.

Once you truly understand them and feel for them, then it is time for the next step: a plan of action.

Here you are in a predicament, because even if you would like to expand your house, get a new car and so on, your income does not allow for it. You might say something like this to your children: "Your feelings are very important to me, and I would do something if I could."

This alone can make your children feel better, as long as you are sincere when you say it.

It may be worthwhile to make the improvements a priority, so that your children will really see how important their feelings are to you. If you get extra money, it could be set aside for this.

Even if you make an improvement in *only one area*, it is worthwhile, for you are showing your children that **what is important to them is important to you.** You will also enjoy a fringe benefit: your children will begin to reciprocate and make what is **important to you, important to them.**

In general, if children feel that parents consider their feelings important, they will feel much more appreciated by the parents and much less bitter.

Sometimes, children will offer to get involved in helping earn the necessary funds for the job. I know of one teenager who was very bothered by the fact that the furniture in her house was old. She knew, though, that her parents did not have money and so she offered to forgo getting new clothes, in this way helping her parents toward the desired goal.

In any case, considering your children's feelings and expressing their importance to you, will certainly bring about a dramatic change for the better in your situation, *b'ezras Hashem.*

Q&A *Instead of telling parents to appreciate their children, don't you think the children should appreciate the parents?*

Yes, but children are not born perfect. They are "raw material" and cannot be expected to behave as they should entirely of their own accord. It is the parents' responsibility to educate them in methods of proper conduct.

The most important method of parental instruction is the parents' interaction with the children. When parents show how much they value their child's feelings, they are teaching him, through their own personal example, to value and respect other people's feelings — including their parents'!

Q. *Why this business about feelings altogether? Why not just tell the child that he must have respect, and he will?*

A. Are you sure? Telling him, even forcing him to respect you may work — on the surface (if you are lucky). **But the child won't respect you in his heart. And in the long run, it is the inner respect that will dominate his deeds.**

Q. *My daughter, who is 11, buys shampoo with the babysitting money she earns. Once she bought six bottles of different types of shampoo at one time!*

A. As a rule, whenever a child engages in behavior that is extreme or very out of the ordinary, the intervention of competent professionals is necessary. There are often serious reasons behind the strange behavior, and they can be taken care of only with proper guidance.

Q. *How can a mother stay calm if her children scream a lot?*

A. Does the mother also scream? If she can follow the Rambam's instructions to always talk softly (if not always, at least when she is around her children), chances are her children will copy her example and talk softly too. They will have no desire to look foolish by screaming back at her when she is talking softly to them.

The most effective method of *chinuch* is the parental role model the child sees in his interactions with the parents. Speaking softly is no exception.

Q. *What is meant by spoiling children, and what is wrong with a child being spoiled?*

A. Spoiling a child means giving him whatever he wants — just because he wants it — regardless of whether or not it will benefit him. Raising a child this way in effect develops a child with a dependency. It makes him weak, for he will not be able to function properly unless he gets everything he wants. When this child matures, it is likely that he will remain with this dependency — he will need to have everything go his way.

More problematic still is the fact that this child will not be prepared for anything that does not go as he would like — and life is full of situations that do not necessarily work out the way we would like them to. This being the case, someone who was spoiled as a child will go through life always feeling frustrated and unable to cope.

Moreover, he will be forced to go through life without ever having learned to work hard to get anything. He will have grown accustomed to receiving everything on a silver platter. One who is not prepared to work hard will not be able to succeed, for success comes only through hard work. Someone who has been spoiled is, in effect, handicapped in dealing with life's difficulties and frustrations.

Our goal is to raise children who remain strong in the face of adversity — children who know that hard work is the way to success, yet who are ready for the challenge; children who have high aspirations, and who possess the courage and the confidence to pursue them, with Hashem's help.

Q *Should we be concerned that giving praise and encouragement to our children will spoil them?*

&A If properly tendered, praise and encouragement will have precisely the opposite effect: they will give children tools that enable them to work hard toward success, even in the face of obstacles. Praise and encouragement supply a child with optimism and hope, which will stand him in good stead in the times of trials and tribulations that are part of life.

In fact, in an amazing statement, renowned educator R' Yaakovson declared that he had never seen a case where encouragement, properly given, was not effective.

Q *Why is it so necessary to encourage our children?*

&A The more we encourage our children, the more they will do things right! There are two reasons for this: (1) Success breeds success. If a child sees himself as a success already (even if only in a small way), then he will want to succeed even more. (2) Life is confusing and complex; it is like a maze. A child is not expected to know the right path to follow. When we catch him doing something right and we tell him so, we are pointing him in the right direction. It's like a road sign telling him, "Yes, you're on the right path. This is the path you should follow."

Q & A *Can praise ever be detrimental?*

Praise can be extremely detrimental when it is given without any basis in reality. One parent I know of praised his son constantly in exaggerated ways. The son did not fall for these false accolades, and eventually the boy developed an inferiority complex. Praise is like a check drawn against a bank account — there must be something to cover it. Without money in the bank, the praise will not be accepted, and it will bounce.

Q & A *Is it good to give a child rewards?*

In general, rewards are a good thing. *Chazal* have told us that "*Mitoch shelo lishmah, ba lishmah* — From doing something for unrelated reasons, one comes to do it for the right reasons." In fact, R' Chaim of Volozhin says that just as one cannot reach the second story of a building without using a staircase, neither can one reach the level of *lishmah* without using that of *lo lishmah* as a stepping stone.

Nevertheless, rewards can cause problems when they are overused. This can happen in one of two ways:

(1) Rewards can have an adverse effect if a child is offered incentives for everything or for many things. Some children are given rewards for *davening*, rewards for learning, rewards for doing their homework, rewards for going to sleep at night, rewards for waking up on time .... In fact, I saw children in one particular class at the beginning of the year who would not agree to begin learning, even after the rebbi instructed them to do so, until they were told what prize they would be given for cooperating. In this case, the rebbi who taught the class the previous year had given them prizes for just about everything.

Children should not get prizes for fulfilling basic responsibilities such as speaking and acting respectfully, or for being where they have to be at the proper time. Prizes should be offered only for those activities with which the child is having difficulty. Even when prizes are called for, rather than being given a prize on the spot, it is usually better if the child could earn points (either written on a chart, or through some other system, as jellybeans that accumulate in a cup, for example), and only after he obtains a certain amount of points be given his prize.

(2) Another way in which incentives are sometimes overused is if they are not given in proportion to the effort the child has to put in. If a child is offered a major incentive for something into which he hardly needs to invest any effort, this encourages laziness. (Note, however, that whether or not it is easy must be determined not according to our standards, but rather according to the child's standards. Some things we might consider easy might be extremely difficult for the child.)

If we take these two factors into account, we can offer incentives in effective ways, and they can often be most useful in helping our children to discover their potential.

Q & A *Will we always have to work with incentives? Aren't we teaching the child to always expect a prize for what he does?*

Incentives are a crutch. They are the means, not the goal. They are meant to help the child overcome any obstacles on his way to developing proper habits. However, once the child begins to do well, many other variables take over, such as the child feeling good about himself for being successful and behaving well.

There is yet another point to be stressed. When a child is offered incentives for something, this creates a positive association in the child's mind. He then begins to enjoy the thing for the sake of the thing itself and not only to earn a prize.

A child expects prizes when he gets something for nothing. But when he has to work hard to receive what he wants, he does not feel that everything is coming to him on a silver platter.

Q & A *How can you get your child away from friends who are not beneficial for him?*

The point to realize is that when you forbid your child to play with certain children, you cannot be sure he will listen. He may still play with or hang around these friends without your knowing about it. As with many other *chinuch* issues, this is not just a matter of control, added to the simple fact that the control might not work.

As a rule, the younger the child, the more control you have. The older the child, the more you must use other *chinuch* methods. In this case, discuss with the child the dangers and negative influence that certain friends can have and explain why it is not to his advantage to associate with such children. A wise sage once told me that from a very young age one should constantly have discussions with his children to stay away from friends that are not a good influence.

In some instances gradually minimizing the relationship may be the recommended approach. It may be too difficult for your child to immediately break up with his friend. Presenting suggestions for minimizing the time together (such as meeting only twice a week, only allowing that friend to come to your house but not allowing your child to go there, etc.) may be easier for the child and may help to elicit his or her willing cooperation.

At the same time that you discourage your child from associating with the wrong friends, encourage him to associate with the right friends. Try to help him make the right friends by encouraging him to invite a potential friend home or by setting up situations in which your child will automatically be together with the children with whom you want him to associate, such as school clubs or activity groups, going to the same camp and so on. The older the child, the more discreet you may have to be in your arrangements to avoid his resistance.

Discouraging your child from associating with the wrong friends he has already made, without providing him with a reasonable replacement in the form of a good friend, will probably not succeed in the long term. To quote R' Shlomo Wolbe, true *chinuch* can be compared to "holding a match to a candle until the candle's flame burns on its own."

Remember: our goal is to bring our children to the point where they themselves want to do what is right, even when we are not looking.

As Solomon, the wisest of men, said, "*Chanoch lana'ar al pi darko, gam ki yazkin lo yassur mimenu* — Teach him so that even when he gets older and is out of our control, he will still practice that which we taught him."

38

True Chinuch — Viewing Children as Raw Material

The Arrival of the Divine Presence Is Accompanied by Stillness

My trip to the airport this time came as a sort of relief. It was the airport in Israel, and I was not the one traveling. A close relative I had not seen for some time was flying in, and I was there with two of my young sons to pick him up.

As we were waiting, we noticed a group of about five men, each with a drum and drumsticks. Apparently, they were also waiting to greet someone and wanted to give him a reception he would not soon forget.

Curious, we approached the group and asked who they were waiting for.

"Mordechai ben David," came their reply.

It did not take us too long to realize they were pulling our leg. Still, we were curious. Who were they waiting for? Which VIP merited an official drum roll times five, in public, upon his arrival in the Holy Land?

These and other thoughts were put aside as our attention was drawn to the sudden flurry of people, just arrived, coming through the doors. We waited for our guest with heightened anticipation, my small children ready to run over and jump on him as soon as he came out.

As the minutes passed, many people came out the doors, but our relative was nowhere to be seen. We waited patiently, yet with mounting anxiety. In the interim, watching the various highly emotional encounters between friends and relatives served as a distraction.

Suddenly we heard a loud noise. "Mo-she! Boom! Boom! Boom! Mo-she! Boom! Boom! Boom!" It was the boys with the drums. Their friend had arrived, and they were banging the drums while calling his name. Moshe (not his real name) seemed extremely uncomfortable at having all eyes focused on him. Looking startled at the noisy welcome, he appeared fairly unhappy at having his name screamed out in public.

Moshe gently steered the crowd of young admirers over to the side as they continued to bang and scream, "Moshe! Boom! Boom! Boom!" Eventually, with a little guidance from Moshe himself, they quieted down.

A short time later, our relative exited. The children, although somewhat distracted by the previous spectacle, got right into it, jumping all over our esteemed guest and giving him a warm welcome. Although our welcome was not as loud as Moshe's, our guest seemed to be at least as pleased — if not more.

Before leaving the arrivals building, I glanced around and noticed R' Shmuel Birnbaum, Rosh Yeshivah of the Mirrer Yeshivah in New York, standing nearby. He was speaking with a small group of people, probably family members and close students. Presumably, he had arrived on the same plane as Moshe and our relative; nevertheless, in midst of all the goings on, I had not taken notice.

(I'm reminded of the Midrash telling of R' Sheishess standing next to another man, waiting for the king's entourage to pass. There was a loud noise, and the other man cried, "Here comes the king!" "Not yet," said R' Sheishess. Even more noisy fanfare followed, and the man again excitedly exclaimed, "Here comes the king!" "Not yet," said R' Sheishess. Then it suddenly became quiet. "Now the king is coming," said R' Sheishess. This was rather puzzling since R' Sheishess was blind. How did he know? R' Sheishess answered by quoting a verse in Navi:

"Lo bara'ash Hashem, ki im bekol demamah dakah — The arrival of the Divine Presence is accompanied by stillness.")

Putting the Blessing in Its Proper Perspective

I had my two young boys with me and, eager to seize the opportunity, we ran over to get a blessing. "Could the Rosh Yeshivah give a blessing for my children?" I asked.

"What are you doing for them?" he countered.

Caught by surprise, I became flustered and was at a loss for words. Within seconds, I regained my composure. "I am principal of a yeshivah elementary school here in Jerusalem, and I do a number of things to help my children spiritually." Desperate to receive the blessing for my children (and to save face), I tried recalling some of the things I do with my children. Happily, a few things came to mind.

"If so, then I will give you a blessing that your efforts succeed and that you should have Divine assistance in that which you are trying to do."

The Rosh Yeshivah (probably realizing that I had been put in an uncomfortable situation) spoke very warmly and explained to me that we cannot expect Hashem to do the work for us. However, if we are trying and putting forth effort, we can then hope — and request Divine assistance — that our efforts will be successful.

In truth, I had been taught this lesson once before. Many years ago, when I was with my two older sons (who were then quite young), we noticed the Amshinover Rebbe picking out willow branches for the upcoming Hoshana Rabbah. Excited at encountering such an important tzaddik, I ran over with my children and asked for a blessing.

The Rebbe did not give the blessing immediately. Instead, he began to concentrate and think for a few moments. He then gave a blessing that I will never forget: "You make sure to plant, and Hashem will help that you reap the fruits."

(Someone once came to the Chazon Ish requesting a blessing that he become fluent in the entire Babylonian

Talmud. The Chazon Ish asked, "With learning or without learning?" The Chazon Ish wanted this person to understand that no blessing can make a person instantly know the Talmud. But if he learns diligently, the blessing can serve to bring him success.)

Indeed, we must put forth *effort* to be *mechanech* our children, for only then can we hope for the Divine assistance that will make our efforts successful.

In our turbulent times, this is not that simple. Many parents are overburdened and overworked. Mothers bear the enormous responsibility of running the household, looking after the children and, in many cases, working outside the home at a part- or full-time job. Fathers are either working full time, learning full time or doing a combination of both.

Is It Fair to Ask Parents, After a Full Day's Schedule, to Give to Their Children too? Isn't That Asking a Bit Much?

R' Shmuel Kamenetsky repeated a joke that psychologists tell among themselves. A child with emotional problems was brought to a therapist. After just six visits, the child was cured. His colleagues praised the therapist highly for his success. The therapist countered, "I can take no credit for curing this child. I actually had nothing to do with it." "Then what helped the child get better?" "It was his mother. Since she had to bring him for six sessions, she spent some individual time with him along the way, bought him a treat here and there and showed him warmth. That is what cured the child."

After relating this joke, R' Kamenetsky said, "It's not a joke. It's the truth."

Parents are to realize that their children have no other parents. If the parents are too busy to be parents, then who can perform their job? If the parents do not give their children the individual attention and warmth so desperately needed for their successful growth — let alone emotional stability — then from whom will the children receive this nurturing?

This need not be left for the end of the day, when parents are exhausted and overworked. What is meant by *effort* is that parents make their children a top priority, to be fitted into their daily schedules just like (only more so) the many other priorities they manage to find the time for, such as social affairs, friends, events, good deeds, jobs, etc.

A busy father told me that he recently began reading his children a story at bedtime. Due to his busy schedule, he felt his children were being neglected. In this way, he would be utilizing quality time with them.

This father travels for business reasons yet will call his children long distance to tell them a story even while he is out of town on business. Because he does not know that many stories, he bought a storybook the children enjoy, and he reads to them from this book.

The message his children are receiving is that they are important. They are a top priority on their father's list. The degree of emotional security this can bring a child cannot be overstated.

Some Points That Require Further Discussion

"Is it fair to ask only the parents to put forth effort? What about the children? Don't they also have to make an effort?"

"We are already putting forth much effort yet we don't see any results. Actually, things seem to be getting worse!"

I received a letter suggesting that instead of lectures for parents there should be more of an emphasis placed on teaching our children how to fulfill the mitzvah of honoring one's parents. This, the writer suggested, will bring the children to do what is expected of them and so make things easier for the entire family, especially the parents.

Although I may agree in part (that the mitzvah of honoring parents should be taught to children; I myself gave classes to children on the relevant halachos for many years), this very suggestion, as well as the previous questions, is *based on a misconception.*

A Mistaken Understanding of *Chinuch*

Children are raw material. They are not finished products. They may be born with various talents and capabilities, yet these must be brought out, developed and refined. To expect our children to *already be as they should* without our giving them the tools and guidance is tantamount to expecting a newly mined raw diamond (without having been cleaned, cut and polished) to be beautiful and attractive.

This is a mistaken understanding of *chinuch*. We feel our children should already be behaving properly and doing the right things. When they do not comply or do not live up to our expectations, we become upset and frustrated and even let them know we are not happy with them. With this we feel we are being *mechanech* them.

In truth, rather than expecting our children to already behave and perform as they should, we must guide them and help them to be as they should.

We have previously mentioned the story of a second grader whose notebook was not the most orderly. One day, the teacher asked the girl to take out her notebook and come up to the front of the class. The teacher then held up the notebook and announced to the entire class, "This is an example for all of you of how *not* to keep your notebooks."

Besides this teacher's serious violations of halachah (among them the prohibition of embarrassing someone in public, hurting someone with words and failing to love your fellow as yourself), she was mistaken in her understanding of *chinuch*. Rather than becoming upset with or making fun of this little girl for not being organized, she should have taken the girl aside privately, in a loving way, and demonstrated to the child how to organize her notebook. If the child did not understand after one time, the teacher should have made it a project to teach her how to do it — each time with love and patience. This would then be considered *chinuch*.

And, as I have heard from our leading rabbis, if the teacher cannot find the patience or love to help a child who needs help, then he is exempt from the mitzvah to be *mechanech* them, and he should find a different field of work.

R' Wolbe once came to the Chazon Ish regarding a difficult child in his yeshivah. The Chazon Ish told him that a yeshivah can be compared to a hospital: those that come there are not well and need our help. It is our job to make them better.

The same is to be said about parents and *chinuch*. Our children come to us with imperfections, and it is our job to help them overcome their imperfections. Rather than becoming upset at them for having these imperfections, we must lovingly guide them and give them the tools to overcome them.

The Piaseczner Rebbe in *Chovas HaTalmidim* says,

> Wouldn't we laugh at a person who heard about the wonderful qualities of the *esrog* and grabbed one of the pits or a small non-ripe fruit to eat? He might scream, "*Oy*, the *esrog* is such a bitter and terrible fruit!" We would consider him a fool. "Wait," we would say to him, "until the fruit becomes ripe. Then you will see how truly sweet it really is."
>
> Even if we see children demonstrating bad character like anger and stubbornness, we should not say that the child has bad character or a bad nature. The Baal Shem Tov already taught us that there is no such thing as a bad character trait in a Jewish child. We must only know how to guide the trait and cultivate it properly so that it will be used for the good.
>
> For example, if the student is stubborn, the teacher should realize that when this student becomes an adult and takes upon himself the yoke of Torah and service of Hashem, his service will be with perseverance and resolve, with all the stubbornness necessary to succeed.

It is our responsibility as parents to guide and help our children to become sweet fruits, to raise them to become polished diamonds. And it is primarily through our proactive (not reactive) *chinuch* as parents and as teachers that we will successfully mold them into the very special individuals they are capable of becoming.

A Letter of Appreciation

Many teachers have shown me letters of appreciation they have received from former students regarding their teacher's love and understanding. One such letter, which I received only last week, beautifully illustrates the thoughts expressed above.

There was a time when I was all alone and just wanted to leave yeshivah. One day in October, I just didn't feel like going to school, and I remained home. I heard a knock on the door, and you walked in. You spoke to me and gave me confidence. Then I knew I had someone on my side. Someone on my side for the first time in my life. Someone who felt what I went through.

And when I failed the test, you spoke to my parents and gave them confidence, and you spoke to me and made me feel special. You taught me how to write notes in shiur. You bought me my notebooks for Bava Basra, Succah and Kiddushin.

When I wanted to go to the big baseball game in tenth grade, and I couldn't go, you spoke to me and my father, and you got me to go.

Then you started telling me I had a brain and I was able to learn. Until then, I had never learned in my life. Maybe I had ancestral merit for Hashem to send you to save me; without that, I don't know why I was worthy.

Before you came I hated — hated — yeshivah. I did not like to learn, and I did not enjoy my life. You changed my life. You changed the way I think, talk and live. I feel that you are Eliyahu Hanavi sent from heaven.

You called my parents countless times to rave about me even though I did not deserve it. You have no idea how much it did for me, how much it made my parents respect me.

All those kumzitzes in the last two years, when you gave me such warmth, such closeness. I never experienced anything like it in my whole life.

When it was time for me to move on, you spoke to my parents about 100 times and did the impossible by convincing them to let me go to Eretz Yisrael.

You were the first rebbi in my life who instead of throwing me out of class spoke to me nicely and gave me more love instead of yelling at me like the other teachers.

I remember the first day of tenth grade. I acted disrespectfully. I wanted to see how angry you would get, but you just spoke softer to me.

*I was shocked. I never saw anything like it. Later, I tried to get you angry, but you never got angry. **I can*** *bear witness that in the past two years you never yelled at me once.*

Please forgive me for the insolence, for not giving you the proper respect that you deserve.

This year you inspired me to finish Gemara Kiddushin, and you were very firm about it. That really changed me. I started to stay up late to learn, to get to every class and to watch my actions more — and I loved it!

I could and should write pages and pages more, but you know I don't like to write! The only way I can pay you back a little is by doing mitzvos and learning. Each time, the merit goes to you because without you, I would never have done it.

The only blessing I can say to such a perfect tzaddik like you is that may other students have the great merit to learn from you and be affected like I was.

Your lifelong student.

The Rebbi's Reply

From the rebbi's letter of reply, we can understand the methods he used to help this student. They included not getting upset at the student for being disrespectful and not performing, but rather trying to understand the student and his difficulties. Most of all, they included believing in the student and giving him the tools to overcome his personal roadblocks on the way to success, accompanied always with love, encouragement and unending patience. Here is the rebbi's reply to the student's letter:

The words you wrote me were a source of great pleasure. I will place them close to my heart and will always be reminded of the bond that was formed between us, a bond from heart to heart through Torah, fear of heaven and noble character.

Even though you thank me, yet know, my son (for one who teaches Torah to his friend's son is as if he had given birth to him) that all your success was due to your own perseverance and hard work. I remember days when it was so hard for you to work, whether it

came to diligence in learning or acquiring good charac-
ter. But you broke your evil inclination to go higher and
higher in the way of Hashem. For all the times when
you passed the test and came out the winner, your
reward is great. Only Hashem knows how true this is.
And the happiness that you brought me with all your
hard work! Especially the siyum you made on masech-
es Kiddushin. I will never forget it.

Know, my precious one, that every rebbi davens that
he should merit to have a wonderful student like you.
Even though today you are far away, you are close to my
heart, and I am certain the closeness between us will
remain always.

Please keep in touch, whether by phone, letters or visits.

And if you ever need me for anything, please don't
hesitate to ask. You will not be bothering me, because it
is my happiness to be busy with you.

Fortunate is the nation that has such rebbis in its midst!

Isn't it obvious? This student was not wonderful at all in the beginning. Yet this *tzaddik* of a rebbi, acting as both father and mother together, had the wisdom to see the student's potential and the heart to help him bring it out.

Only Acting as Parent

Yet this rebbi was only acting as the parent. Shouldn't the actual parents act as parents? When we see our child not living up to our expectations, rather than get angry and frustrated, let us understand him and help him with unending love and patience. Let us guide our children and show them the way to overcome the difficulties, while at the same time encouraging them by believing in them and being on their side.

This is *chinuch*!

And it works! (with the help of Hashem).

39

Never Lose Hope

The Insane Man

There was once a deranged individual who developed a strange habit. He would stand in his room at the mental hospital, hold his hand up in the air and remain in that position the entire day. None of the staff members was able to get through to him. The situation became more complicated when he refused to abandon his position even for meals.

Finally, one wise person came up with an idea. He walked over to the man, put his hand up in the air in imitation of him and then said, "I'll take over now." The man seemed relieved as he immediately left his strange position.

When asked for an explanation, the wise man replied, "That fellow thought he was holding up the world. When I came over and held up my hand the way he was, he felt released from his task and could go about his business without worrying about the entire world falling down in his absence."

The 80/20 Percent Ratio

To a certain extent, we are all like that poor man. We may not think we are holding up the entire world, but we may think we hold up our own personal world. We may labor under the mistaken perception that we determine our destiny and the destiny of everyone around us.

We often feel that our efforts — whether at home, on the job or in the community — are what determine the outcome. We certainly may feel this way when it comes to our children. "Our *chinuch* will determine the outcome," we tell ourselves.

What a mistake! As one sage said, successful *chinuch* is 20 percent effort and 80 percent prayer.

Yes, our efforts are important! They are a full 20 percent of our children's *chinuch*!

But only 20 percent. The other 80 percent depends on prayer.

Without prayer, we stand no chance of succeeding; with prayer, we can succeed even when the situation appears hopeless.

The illustrious R' Baruch Toledano was asked how he merited that many of his children were great rabbis and scholars. He replied that every night after midnight he would cry for half an hour that all his descendants be noble, G-d-fearing Jews.

It would be a worthwhile investment for every parent to pray on a regular basis for his children's success. However, we may find the thought overwhelming, especially in view of our hectic lives and busy schedules.

The Power of Brief Prayers

The answer for us is to make it a habit to say brief prayers in our own words at the time we feel the need.

A friend of mine told me that one day he was stopped for speeding even though he usually made sure to stay within the speed limit. He pulled over to the side, rolled down his window and waited for the patrolman. Imagine his consternation when he was asked for his registration and realized with a shock that he had left it home.

The patrolman said he was going to give him two tickets: one for speeding, and one for driving without his registration.

As the patrolman walked back to his car, my friend decided to say a short prayer in his own words. The speeding ticket alone would cost a few hundred dollars, not to mention other unpleasant ramifications. This, in addition to the other fine.

Surprisingly, by the time the patrolman returned to my friend's car, he had had a change of heart. He decided that a warning would suffice with regard to the speeding, and that he would only give my friend a small fine for driving without his registration.

[I again stress that my friend is a law abiding citizen. This lapse is in no way indicative of his attitude in general. Speeding endangers lives and should not be tolerated.]

If we realize that Hashem is running the show, we need never despair. No matter how bleak the situation may seem, He can bring about a total turnaround.

Many years ago, a close friend of mine was in a desperate situation. His son was almost about to be expelled from his yeshivah high school and seemed ready to join a band of hoodlums. That Purim, my friend got drunk and broke down crying uncontrollably. He was mumbling something, but it was hard to make out the words.

Later, he told me that he had been praying for his son. He prayed that his son grow to be an *erlicher Yid*, a noble Jew.

Not immediately, but as the years went by this boy had a major turnaround. He continued his education in other schools and began to succeed.

Recently, my friend told me about a conversation he just had with his son (now some seven or eight years after the above incident). As they talked, the son made this statement to his father: "Dad, I have one aspiration in life. I hope to become an *erlicher Yid*. That's all I want."

Never give up! Hashem is on your side and behind you every step of the way — especially in your efforts to parent your children. Turning to Him with sincerity of heart will surely bring about dramatic changes for the better.

In Closing

Anyone who experiences all that the average parent goes through — the work and the aggravation, the pressure and the pain — surely can recognize how unselfish he really is!

Parents are the most unselfish people on earth; they sacrifice everything for their children, receiving no remuneration in return, not even recognition. They are on duty 24 hours a day, with no vacation. Parents should never allow themselves to become discouraged, for they must realize that their efforts themselves represent success.

One teacher in the public school system would regularly teach her class inspirational sayings that she felt would one day benefit them. The students did not take these phrases seriously but, given no choice in the matter, they memorized them. One of her students, a particularly difficult boy, was eventually expelled from the school and sent to a correctional facility for juvenile delinquents.

In a state of despair, the boy saw himself as a total failure and decided to take his own life. He took actions to do so, and as he lay there waiting to die, a phrase he had learned from this teacher came to mind: "The only failure is not trying." He realized then that if he allowed himself to die, it would be a prime instance of "the only failure." At that moment, he decided to try again, and he called for help.

The very fact that you are reading this means you are willing to try; it means that you are already a success. May Hashem help you have *continued* success and true *nachas* from all your children. Continue in your *chinuch* efforts and even when the going gets rough, *don't* give up. You will surely see success with the help of Hashem.

The following poem sums it up beautifully:

✑ Don't Quit

> *When things go wrong, as they sometimes will,*
> *When the road you're trudging seems all uphill,*
> *When funds are low and the debts are high*
> *And you want to smile, but you have to sigh,*
> *When care is pressing you down a bit*
> *Rest, if you must — but don't you quit!*
>
> *Life is interesting, with its twists and turns,*
> *As every one of us sometimes learns,*
> *And many a person turns about*
> *When he might have won — had he stuck it out.*
> *Don't give up, though the pace seems slow —*
> *You may succeed with one more blow.*
>
> *Often the struggler has given up*
> *When he might have captured the victor's cup,*
> *And he learned too late, when the night came down*
> *How close he was to the golden crown.*
>
> *Success is failure turned inside out,*
> *So stick to the fight when you're hardest hit*
> *It's when things seem worst that you mustn't quit!*

With sincere wishes for your continued success and with a brief prayer that you see true *nachas* from your children/students always.